CW01401849

English G 21

D2

Differenzierende Ausgabe

Cornelsen

English G 21 • Band D 2

Im Auftrag des Verlages herausgegeben von
Prof. Hellmut Schwarz, Mannheim

Erarbeitet von
Susan Abbey, Nenagh, Irland
Barbara Derkow Disselbeck, Köln
Allen J. Woppert, Berlin
sowie Laurence Harger, Wellington, Neuseeland

unter Mitarbeit von
Wolfgang Biederstädt, Köln
Joachim Blombach, Herford
Helmut Dengler, Limbach
Martina Schroeder, Stedtlingen
Jennifer Seidl, München
Udo Wagner, Voerde
Herbert Willms, Herford

in Zusammenarbeit mit der Englischredaktion
Kirsten Bleck (Projektleitung);
Dr. Eva Grabowski (verantwortliche Redakteurin);
Susanne Bennetreu (Bildredaktion); Julie Colthorpe;
Dr. Philip Devlin; Bonnie S. Glänzer; Mara Leibowitz;
Anne Linder; Kathrin Spiegelberg; Uwe Tröger;
Klaus G. Unger *sowie* Nathalie Schwering

Beratende Mitwirkung
Walter Droste, Spenge; Manuela Feierabend-Vonhausen, Rossfeld; Birgit Heinemann, Neu Wulmstorf; Ivette Huxol, Wilkau-Haßlau; Bernd Jost, Salzbergen; Heike Jurenz, Neukirch/Lausitz; Dr. Dieter Krohn, Hannover; Heike Meisner, Bad Klosterlausnitz; Gabriele Rotter, Wiesbaden; Karl Starkebaum, Diekholzen

Illustrationen
Graham-Cameron Illustration, UK: Fliss Cary, Grafikerin
sowie Roland Beier, Berlin

Fotos
Rob Cousins, Bristol

Layoutkonzept und technische Umsetzung
Aksinia Raphael; Korinna Wilkes

Umschlaggestaltung
Klein und Halm Grafikdesign, Berlin

Für die freundliche Unterstützung danken wir der Cotham School, Bristol.

www.cornelsen.de
www.EnglishG.de

1. Auflage, 1. Druck 2007/06

Alle Drucke dieser Auflage sind inhaltlich unverändert und können im Unterricht nebeneinander verwendet werden.

Druck: Stürtz GmbH, Würzburg

ISBN 978- 3-06-031317-4 – broschiert
ISBN 978- 3-06-031367-9 – gebunden

Inhalt gedruckt auf säurefreiem Papier aus nachhaltiger Forstwirtschaft.

Dein Englischbuch enthält folgende Teile:

Welcome back	Einstieg in das Buch – hier triffst du die Lehrwerkskinder wieder
Units	die sechs Kapitel des Buches
Topics	besondere Themen – z.B. die Geschichte von Robinson Crusoe
Skills File (SF)	Beschreibung wichtiger Lern- und Arbeitstechniken
Grammar File (GF)	Zusammenfassung der Grammatik jeder Unit
Vocabulary	Wörterverzeichnis zum Lernen der neuen Wörter jeder Unit
Dictionary	alphabetische Wörterverzeichnisse zum Nachschlagen

Die Units bestehen aus diesen Teilen:

Lead-in	Einstieg in das neue Thema
A-Section	neuer Lernstoff mit vielen Aktivitäten
Practice	Übungen
Text	eine spannende oder lustige Geschichte

In den Units findest du diese Überschriften und Symbole:

Looking at language	Hier sammelst du Beispiele und entdeckst Regeln.
STUDY SKILLS	Einführung in Lern- und Arbeitstechniken
DOSSIER	Schöne und wichtige Arbeiten kannst du in einer Mappe sammeln.
Background File	Hier findest du interessante Informationen über Land und Leute.
GAME	Spiele für zwei oder für eine Gruppe – natürlich auf Englisch
GETTING BY IN ENGLISH	Alltagssituationen üben
MEDIATION	Hier vermittelst du zwischen zwei Sprachen.
LISTENING	Aufgaben zu Hörtexten auf der CD
Now you	Hier sprichst und schreibst du über dich selbst.
POEM / SONG	Gedichte/Lieder zum Anhören und Singen
PRONUNCIATION	Ausspracheübungen
REVISION	Übungen zur Wiederholung
WORDS	Übungen zu Wortfamilien, Wortfeldern und Wortverbindungen
Checkpoint	Im Workbook kannst du dein Wissen überprüfen.
Extra	Zusätzliche Aktivitäten und Übungen
👥 👥👥	Partnerarbeit/Gruppenarbeit
🎧 🎧	nur auf CD / auf CD und im Schülerbuch
>	Textaufgaben
//	parallele Übungen auf zwei Niveaus
○ ●	leichtere Übung / schwierigere Übung

Inhalt

Inhalt

Welcome back – After the holidays

1 🎧

15th August

Dear Jack

We travelled to Cornwall on Saturday. There were no holiday flats, so we're in a caravan by the sea.
On Monday it was cold and windy and rainy, but yesterday it was hot and sunny. We went swimming and met a nice girl on the beach!

Dan Jo ☺

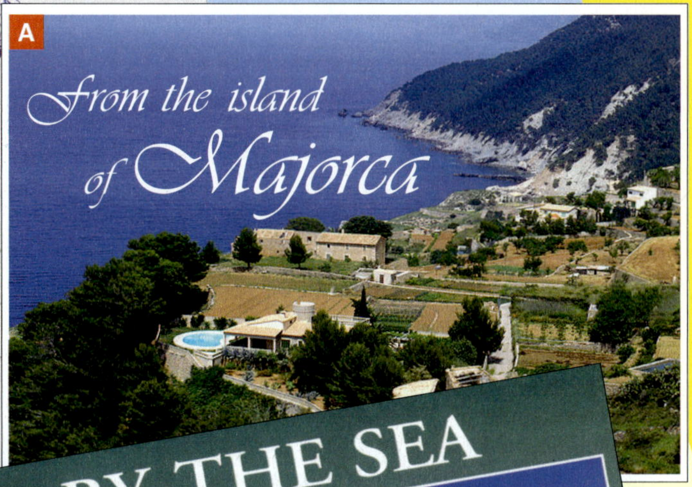

2 🎧

Dear Sophie

We're staying at home this summer, but here's a funny postcard for you anyway!
Last week it was warm and sunny, so I went into town and watched some street theatre. It was great. I took lots of photos.
There's a nice French family here this week.
Yesterday it was cool but sunny, so I went for a walk in the country with the French boy.
It was fun – really!
Call me when you get back.

Jack

3 🎧

Dear Danandjo!

FREE ECards

This city is soooo great! We flew here on Monday.
This was the view from the plane.
We went on a boat trip yesterday – all round Manhattan.
We saw a lot! It was cloudy, but that was good. It's very very hot when the sun shines!

See you soon.
Ananda

To:
From:
Sent:

4

Dear Ananda

It's great here. The weather is fantastic – blue sky and hot sun every day. And we've got a house and our own pool! On Sunday we were in the mountains. We went there by car. Yesterday we rode our bikes to the beach because Emily wanted to see 'something new'. (Boys of course!) But I think it's more fun at our pool, so that's where I am today!

Lots of love
Sophie

D

C

1 The cards

a) *Read the texts. Match the texts to the pictures.*
Text ... and picture ... go together.

b) **Extra** *Give reasons for your choice.*
In picture **B** there's a beach.
Text **1** says 'by the sea' and 'on the beach'.
I think this card is from ...

c) *Collect holiday words and phrases from the cards. Can you think of more?*

places	weather	activities
by the sea	cold	swimming

2 Your holidays – at home or away?

Make appointments with three students.
Ask each other about the summer holidays.

1 Where were you?
2 What was the weather like?
3 Who were you with?
4 Was it nice?

It was great.
It was very hot.
I was with my family.
I stayed at home.

My appointments

1 o'clock	Marek
2 o'clock	...
3 o'clock	...

► SF Learning words – Step 1 (p. 121) • WB 1–2 (p. 1)

3 What's the weather like in …?

Partner A: Ask questions about the weather in three countries.
Partner B: Look at the weather map.
Answer Partner A's questions. Swap after three questions.

A: What's the weather like in Spain?
B: It's 29 degrees. It's sunny in Spain.

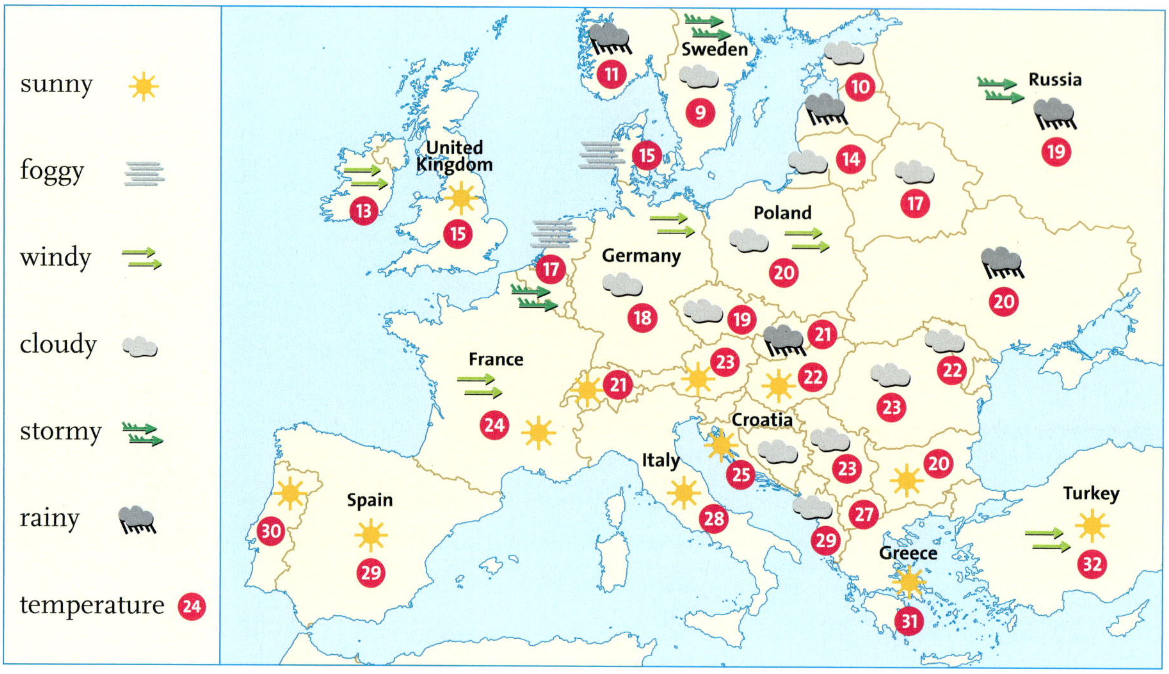

4 Holiday weather

a) *What is good and what is bad weather for …?*

swimming • riding • a walk in the country • a boat trip • shopping in town • a film • reading • the library • a day on the beach • …

Rainy/Sunny/… weather is good/OK/bad for …

b) *Listen to the weather forecast and find out: What is the best day for the beach – today or tomorrow?*

c) *Listen again. Take notes.*

	today	tomorrow
morning		
afternoon		
evening		

► *SF Taking notes (p. 127)*

d) **Extra** *Imagine you are on holiday by the sea. Look at your notes. What can you do today? What can you do tomorrow?*

5 Extra ACTIVITY

Make a weather calendar for your classroom.
You can change it every day.
Today is Monday, the 4th of …
The weather is very nice. It's …

► *WB 3–4 (p. 2)*

6 A holiday diary

Dear Diary

It's holiday time and the house is empty. I'm sad. My family went to Spain and I had to stay at home alone. It rained last night and it's cold and cloudy today. And it's very boring.

Well, it isn't boring all the time ...

On Friday I played in every room and nobody grumbled. That was fun!

And on Saturday I spoke to Uncle Henry. Then we played tennis in the afternoon! That was fun too!

Yesterday I listened to all Emily's CDs and then I threw them on the floor. Then I tried on all Emily's clothes and put them in the fridge. And then I read all Emily's magazines and put them in Toby's room.

Yesterday was great! Hee, hee, hee. ...

Who stayed at home? Where does she live? What did she do in the holidays? Find at least four things.

7 Now you

a) *Collect ideas for a diary page about your holidays.*

b) *Make a nice page about your holidays. You can add pictures or maps. Use your notes from a).*

STUDY SKILLS Mind maps

Denk daran: Mindmaps können dir helfen, Ideen zu sammeln und zu ordnen.

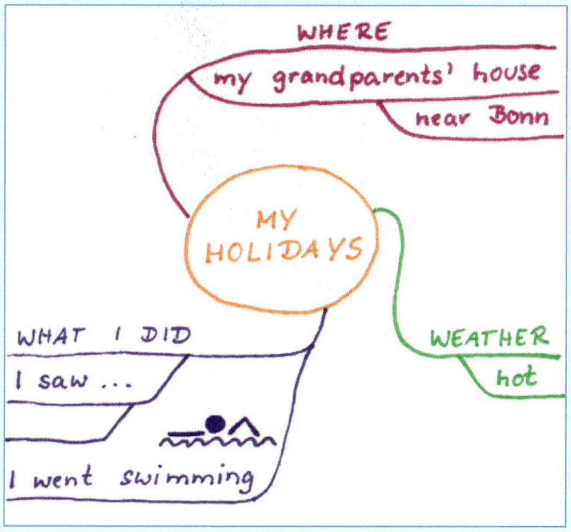

DOSSIER *My holidays*

In the holidays I stayed at home. I had a great time. The weather was hot and sunny. I went swimming a lot in a lake near my house. Here is a picture of the lake.

One weekend we visited my grandparents. They live near Bonn. We went by train. I saw all my cousins. We went ...

► SF Mind maps (p. 122) • WB 5 (p. 3)

Back to school

1 Talking about school

Look at the Cotham School website. What's the same at your school? What's different?
At Cotham School they've got a canteen.
We've got a … too. / We haven't got a …

2 Describing pictures

STUDY SKILLS Describing pictures

Um ein Bild zu beschreiben, musst du sagen können, wo sich etwas genau befindet. Am besten gehst du dabei in einer bestimmten Reihenfolge vor, z.B. von unten nach oben oder von vorne nach hinten.

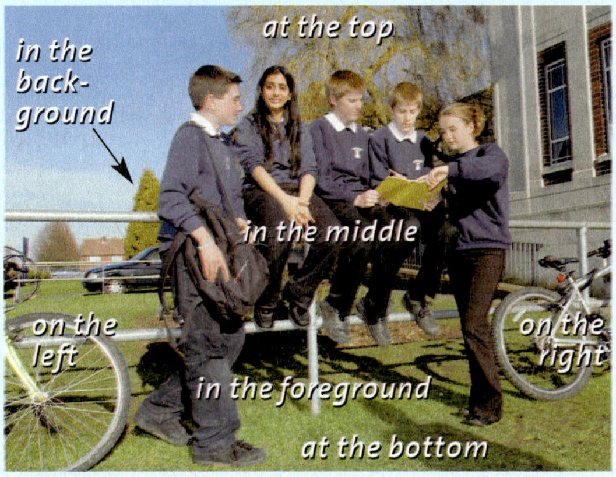

a) *Listen to the descriptions. What picture does the student talk about first? And then?*

b) *There's a mistake in three of the descriptions. Listen again and write down the numbers of the pictures.*

c) **Extra** *Say what the mistakes are.*
Picture …: The student says … But that's wrong …

3 Find the red balls

*Say where the red balls are in the pictures. You can use the words in the box and the words from **2**.*
In picture **1** there's a red ball …

behind • between • in front of • next to • under

► *SF Describing pictures (p. 123) • P 1–4 (pp. 16–17) • WB 1–4 (pp. 4–6)*

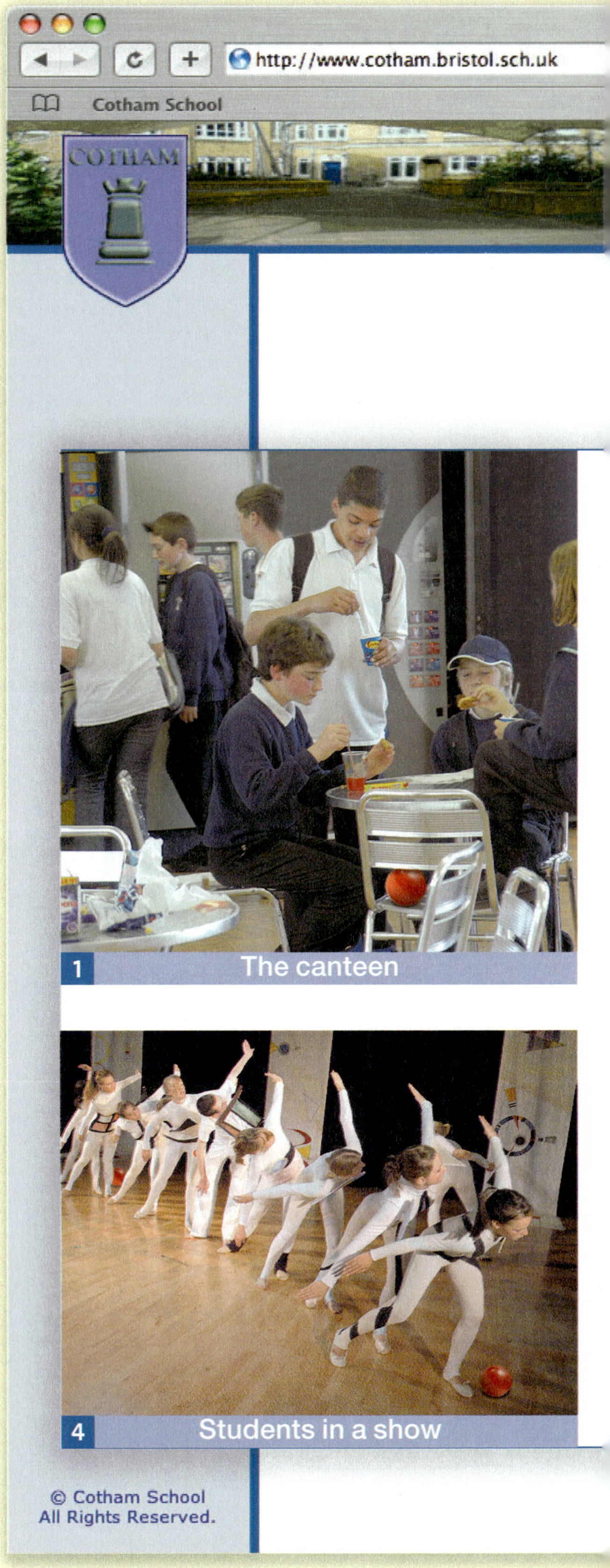

Cotham School

Welcome to Cotham School

2 In front of the school

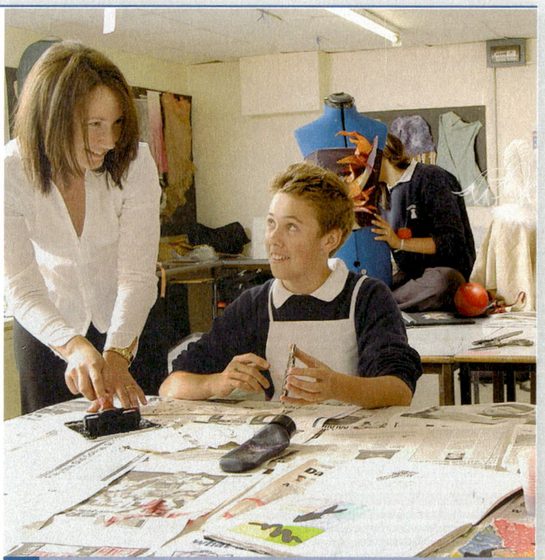

3 The Art room

5 A PE lesson

6 The library

1 Friends meet again

Jack Tell me about New York, Ananda.
Ananda Oh, Jack, it was so fantastic. We stayed with my aunt and uncle – they were really great, the weather was great, ...
Jack You were there with Dilip, right?
Ananda Well, we flew there together, but he came back a week before me.
Jack Was the flight OK?
Ananda Well, it was my first time on a plane, so I was a bit nervous. But it wasn't scary. Not like the subway – that was scary!
Jack Yeah, I heard that the underground is dangerous.
Ananda No, not dangerous – just very fast.
Jack Oh look, there's Sophie.

Sophie Hi, you two. So, what was the best thing about New York, Ananda?
Ananda The Empire State Building! We took the elevator ...
Sophie Oh, the lift.
Ananda Right, we took the lift to the top. It's amazing! You can see for miles and ...

What two American English words does Ananda use? What are the British English words?

Extra Background File

The Empire State Building
The building is 443.2 metres high and has got 102 floors, 73 lifts and 1,860 stairs and 6,500 windows.
The fastest lift in the building travels over seven metres in just one second. A fast runner can do it in ten minutes.
From the 86th floor, you can see over 120 kilometres (75 miles) on a clear day.
To find out more, visit the building's website at www.esbnyc.com.

Looking at language Revision

*Ananda talks about what happened in the past in **1**. Find the **simple past** forms of:*

be • stay • come

Which verb is regular?

► *GF 1: Simple past, positive statements (pp. 133–134) • P 5–6 (p. 18) • WB 5–9 (pp. 6–8)*

2 A new girl

When they got to their classroom, the friends saw a new girl in the room.

Sophie — Hi! I'm Sophie and this is Ananda. Are you new?
Lesley — Of course I'm new.
Ananda — What's your name?
Lesley — Lesley.
Sophie — Hi, Lesley. Where are you from?
Lesley — Mind your own business.
Sophie — But we ...
Lesley — I didn't want to come here, you know.
Ananda — Come on, Sophie. Let's go back to the others.
Dan — Well?
Ananda — She doesn't like us!
Sophie — And I don't like her!
Jo — What happened?
Ananda — She didn't say much.
Sophie — We didn't ask much. She said, 'Mind your own business!'
Jack — That was rude!
Dan — Maybe she was nervous or ...
Jo — Yeah, yeah.
Jack — Hey, here comes Mr Kingsley.

> *What can you say about the new girl?*

Looking at language

*Find all the negative sentences in **2**. Write the sentences in two lists.*

Simple present	Simple past
She doesn't like us	I didn't want ...
And I ...	She ...
	We ...

*How do you make the negative form of the **simple past**?*
Check your ideas in the Grammar File.

▸ GF 2: Negative statements (p. 134) • P 7–9 (p. 19) • WB 10–13 (pp. 9–11)

3 Now you

a) *What do you do on school days? How were your holidays different? Make sentences.*
I get up early on school days. But I didn't get up early in the holidays.

Here are some more ideas:

go to school • see my teachers • eat in the school canteen • sit in a classroom • do my homework • work in the library • learn English words • go to bed early

b) *Tell a partner.*

4 Lunch break

Who wants to be nice to Lesley – Dan or Jo?

Dan The food is better this year.
Jack Do you really think so?
Dan Yes, I do. This veggie burger is very good.
Sophie It's fish, Dan.
Dan Oh ... Hey, I can't see the new girl.
Jo Well, she's right behind you.
Dan Maybe she'd like to eat with us.
All No way!
Dan Come on. She's new. Let's talk to her.
Jo Did she talk to Sophie and Ananda? No, she didn't.
Dan Did you talk to her, Jo? No, you didn't. Did you try to be nice? No, you didn't. Of course not. You are always so ...
Jack Hey Dan, calm down.
Dan Oh ... I'm going outside.
Jack He's really angry with you, Jo.
Sophie Yeah, why did he get angry?
Jo Oh, it's nothing. Let's eat.

Looking at language

Look at the following questions:
1 Do you really think so?
2 Did she talk to Sophie and Ananda?
*Which question is in the **simple present**?*
*Which question is in the **simple past**?*
*Find more questions in the **simple past** in 4.*

5 Now you

a) *What did you do at the weekend? Write down three things. Here are some ideas:*

go to the cinema/to a party • help at home • go swimming/shopping/for a walk • listen to ... • meet friends • play ... • watch ...

I went to the cinema. And I ...

b) *Ask different partners about their weekend. Find somebody who did two of the same things as you.*

Did you go shopping?
Yes, I did.
Did you go for a walk?
No, I didn't!

► GF 3: Questions and short answers (p. 134) • P 10–14 (pp. 20–21) • WB 14–18 (pp. 11–13)

6 A role play

a) *How can you complete the dialogue? Think of ideas.*

A: Hi, my name is ... Are you new here?
B: Yes, I am. My name is ...
A: Well, welcome to ... School.
B: Thanks. What are the teachers like?
A: Most of them are OK/nice/...
What school did you go to last year?
B: I went to ... School.
A: And where do you live?
B: We've got a flat/... in ... What about you?
A: I live in a ... in ...
B: I really like football/shopping/... Have you got any hobbies?
A: Yes, I have. I like ...
B: Great. Maybe we can ... together.
A: Good idea.

b) **Extra** *Listen to the students. What do you think of their dialogues?*

	Dialogue 1	Dialogue 2
It was clear.		
It was very fast/slow.		
They had good ideas.		
They didn't forget things.		

c) *Prepare a dialogue. Act it out in class.*

► *P 15 (p. 21) • WB 19 (p. 13)*

7 Extra CHANT Friends again

I had a best friend.
We had a big fight.
I wasn't very happy.
But he thinks he's right!

CHORUS
But he thinks he's right!
But he thinks he's right!
I wasn't very happy.
But he thinks he's right!

'Mind your own business!'
'I don't like you!'
'You're so rude!'
'And I hate you too!'

CHORUS
And I hate you too!
And I hate you too!
You're so rude!
And I hate you too!

So I had no friend.
I was alone.
No one to talk to.
I just went home.

CHORUS
I just went home.
I just went home.
No one to talk to.
I just went home.

I called my friend
Later that day.
I said, 'I'm sorry!'
Now it's OK!

CHORUS
Now it's OK!
Now it's OK!
I said, 'I'm sorry!'
Now it's OK!

1 WORDS School

a) *Complete these lists with words from the box. Each person in the group writes one list. Compare your lists.*

School subjects	Things in my school bag	People or things at school	Things I do at school	Sports and activities
Art	book	classmate	answer …	…

answer questions • Art • basketball • Biology • book • CD player • chair • computer • cupboard • desk • do a project • Drama • English • exercise book • felt tip • football • French • Geography • German • History • hockey • listen to the CD • look at the board • Maths • Music • paint pictures • PE • pen • pencil • pencil case • pencil sharpener • play with my classmates • practise pronunciation • RE • read • rubber • ruler • Science • sing songs • spell • swimming • talk to my friend • talk to the teacher • tennis • timetable • volleyball • work with a partner

b) **Extra** *Write about one of these topics. Use words from your lists.*

A day in the life of my school bag

I'm Pia's school bag. In the morning, Pia puts lots of books in me. Her mother gives me a sandwich box. Then we take the bus to school. The first lesson …

or

A day at school

A: Hi Ben. How was school today?

B: Oh, we had a really easy day. First, we had PE. And then we …

2 WORDS Where's the black cat?

a) *Where's the black cat? For each picture, say which answer is correct.*

1 behind the orange cat
2 in front of the orange cat

3 next to the cupboard
4 near the cupboard

5 under an armchair
6 between the armchairs

7 in the middle
8 on the right

9 outside
10 inside

11 at the top of the tree
12 at the bottom of the tree

b) **Extra** *Where's the orange cat? And where's the mouse?*

3 LISTENING Aliens at school

You're playing the computer game **Aliens at school**. *You have to find all the aliens in the picture.*

a) *Say where you see aliens in the picture.*
There are two aliens on the ...
There's one alien next to ...

b) *There are more aliens, but you can't see them. Listen to the CD and look at the picture.*

c) *Listen again. Draw the new aliens on a copy of the picture.*

d) **Extra** *Check with a partner. Don't show your picture. Talk like this:*
There's an alien behind/in front of/in the ...
There are two aliens ...

4 STUDY SKILLS Describing pictures

Partner B: Go to p. 108. Don't look at this page.

a) *Partner A: Choose picture* **1** *or* **2**. *Describe it to your partner:*

There's a house in the middle of my picture and two people ...

Your partner listens and draws the picture. Check your partner's picture. Is it correct?

b) *Now your partner describes a picture. Don't look at your partner's page. Listen and draw it. Show the picture to your partner. Is it correct?*

c) **Extra** *Now draw your own picture with two people, one house, two trees and a ball. (Don't show your partner your picture!)*
Describe your picture to your partner:

There's ...

Your partner listens and draws. Then compare your two pictures.

1

2

5 PRONUNCIATION (Vowel sounds)

a) *Say the words in these word lists. Then listen and check.*

bird ...
heard ...
hurt ...

fair ...
their ...
where ...

hear ...
here ...
year ...

b) *Make a copy of the word lists. Add these words to the correct list:*

hair • dear • ear • girl • first • her • near • share • they're

Then listen and check.

6 WRITING Linking words

Copy and complete the sentences from the flow chart. Put the verbs in the simple past.

STUDY SKILLS Linking words

*Wenn du beschreiben willst, in welcher Reihenfolge etwas passiert ist, helfen dir z. B. Zeitangaben (Englisch: **time phrases**) wie after breakfast, at 10 o'clock, after that, an hour later, then, in the afternoon usw.*

▸ *SF Linking words (p. 129)*

After breakfast Ms Travelot *rode* (ride) her ... to her ...

After that she ... (go) to Dover by ...

At 10 o'clock she ... (go) by ... to Dover station.

She ... (be) late, so she ... (run) to the train.

She ... (travel) by ... to London and ... (get off) there.

An hour later she ... (get on) a ... and ... (fly) to Leeds.

Then she ... (go) to Bristol by ... and ... (be) home for dinner.

DOSSIER ***Last Saturday***

Think about what you did last Saturday. Make a flow chart with at least four boxes. Here are some ideas:

have a nice breakfast • help my parents • listen to music • call my friend • play basketball • meet friends • ride my bike • go swimming • ...

At ... o'clock ... ▶ *Then ...* ▶ ... ▶ ...

Write a short text for your DOSSIER. Use some time phrases.

7 Extra REVISION The Grumbles (Simple present: negative statements)

a) *The Grumbles are very negative about everything. Write down their sentences.*

1 *Greg* My friend ☹ call me.
My friend doesn't call me.
2 *Grandma* No, Greg, but you ☹ call your friend.
3 *Griselda* I ☹ get any e-mails.
4 *Grandma* Griselda, you ☹ write any e-mails.
5 *Graham* Dad ☹ take me to school when I ask him.
6 *Griselda* No, Graham, but you ☹ say 'please' or 'thank you'
7 *Grandma* The neighbours ☹ talk to me.
8 *Griselda* Well, they ☹ like us!

b) *The Grumbles grumble when they go on holiday too. Make more sentences. Here are some ideas.*

the man at the pool – like me •
people at the shop – talk English •
bus – stop near our caravan

8 Grandma Grumble is grumbling (Simple past: positive and negative statements)

a) *Grandma Grumble went to London yesterday. Before she went, she made a list of nine jobs. Listen. Which three jobs did Graham, Greg and Griselda do? Write them down.*

b) *Say what the Grumbles did – and what they didn't do.*
Graham tidied the living room. But he didn't ...

c) Extra *What about you? Make two short lists.*

What I did last week	*What I didn't do last week*
I helped my dad in the garden. ...	*I didn't go shopping.* ...

9 Are you a good detective? (Simple past: positive and negative statements) ► D p. 113

Find the correct sentences. Look at pp. 12–13 to check.

1 Ananda didn't go to **London** in her holidays.
2 She didn't go by boat.
3 She didn't stay with her grandparents.
4 Dilip didn't go to Germany.
5 Sophie and Ananda didn't talk to the new boy.
6 Lesley didn't say 'Hi!'.
7 Sophie and Ananda didn't stay with Lesley.

She went by plane.
She stayed with her aunt and uncle.
He went to New York too.
Sophie and Ananda talked to the new girl.
She went to New York.
They went back to their friends.
She said 'Mind your own business'.

10 REVISION Is your partner a music person? (Simple present: yes/no questions)

a) *What do you think? Is your partner a music person? Fill in a copy of the chart.*

Does he/she ...

1. ... sometimes sing in the shower?
2. ... do his/her homework with music on?
3. ... play the piano or sing in a choir?
4. ... read about pop stars in magazines?
5. ... sometimes go out to listen to live music?
6. ... often take an MP3 player to school?

	I think	Partner's answer
1	Yes	No
2	No	...
3		
4		
5		
6		

b) *Now ask your partner the questions. Fill in his/her answers in the chart.*

A: Do you sometimes sing in the shower?

B: Yes, I do. / No, I don't.

Were you right or wrong?

○ 11 Did your father watch TV yesterday? (Simple past: yes/no questions)

Use the chart and ask a partner at least six questions. He/she gives short answers.

Did	you your father your mother your parents your pet your	watch TV do sport listen to ... play ... eat ... wear ... read ... go to	yesterday? two days ago? last Saturday? in the holidays?

A: Did you watch TV yesterday?

B: Yes, I did. / No, I didn't.
Did your grandparents do sport last Saturday?

A: Yes, they did. / No, they didn't. / I don't know. / I don't remember.

12 Find somebody who ... (Simple past: yes/no questions)

a) *Look at the questions.*

1. Did you go on a boat in the holidays?
2. Did you meet nice people in the holidays?
3. Did you see a good film in the holidays?
4. Did you learn to ride in the holidays?
5. Did you have a picnic in the holidays?

b) **Extra** *Write at least three more questions.*

c) *Find somebody in your class who did number **1**. Write down his/her name. Now find somebody who did number **2**, **3**, etc.*

d) *Report to a partner.*

Oliver went on a boat.

Anna met a nice girl in Spain.

...

//○ 13 Mum wants to know! (Simple past: wh-questions) ▸ D p. 113

Make correct questions in the simple past.

1 *Mum* What – do at school today – did you?
What did you do at school today?
Tom Not much.

2 *Mum* What – did you – lessons – have ?
Tom Well, we only had lessons in the morning.

3 *Mum* Really? What – in the afternoon – you – do – did?
Tom Our class went on a trip to the library.

4 *Mum* And what time – the trip – did – finish?
Tom At 3 o'clock.

5 *Mum* Where – go – after that – did – you?
Tom I went into town with some friends.

6 *Mum* What – do – did – there – you?
Tom I had a chicken burger.

7 *Mum* Why – you – did eat – a chicken burger?
Tom Because I don't like veggie burgers.

14 Yesterday afternoon (Simple past: wh-questions)

Partner B: Go to p. 108.

a) *Partner A: Ask your partner about the gaps in your chart. Fill in a copy of the chart. Then answer your partner's questions.*

	Where did ... go?	*How ... go there?*	*What ... do there?*
Ananda		*by bike*	*help her mum + watch TV*
Jo	*the swimming pool*	*by bike*	
Jack			
Sophie	*the library*		*read a book*
You			
Your partner			

b) *Swap your chart with your partner and check.*

c) **Extra** *Now write about you or your partner or one of the Bristol kids.*

15 GETTING BY IN ENGLISH At school today

a) *Can you say these things in English?*

1 Erzähl mir von New York. (p. 12)
2 Das geht dich nichts an. (p. 13)
3 Was ist passiert? (p. 13)
4 Das war unverschämt! (p. 13)
5 Auf keinen Fall! (p. 14)
6 Er ist wirklich böse auf dich. (p. 14)

● ***b)*** *Prepare a dialogue with a partner. Then act it out.*

Dialogue 1

A: Grüße B. Bitte ihn/sie, von seinem/ihrem Schultag zu erzählen.
B: Sag, dass ein neuer Junge in eurer Klasse ist. Er ist nicht sehr nett.
A: Frag, was passiert ist.
B: Sag, dass du den Jungen nach seinem Namen gefragt hast. Er sagte: 'Das geht dich nichts an.'
A: Sag, dass das wirklich unverschämt war.

Dialogue 2

B: Frag, wie es heute an der Schule war.
A: Sag, dein Mathelehrer war böse auf dich.
B: Frag, was passiert ist.
A: Sag, du hast deine Hausaufgabe nicht gemacht.
B: Sag, du kannst die Hausaufgabe heute Abend mit ihm/ihr machen.
A: Sag auf keinen Fall! – Du willst einen Film ansehen.

Saved!

Look at the pictures. Where are Dan and Jo in this story? When did this happen?

▸ *SF Understanding new words (p. 122)*

The sun came through the window of the caravan. Dan opened his eyes and looked round. His dad was still asleep. From the top bunk he could hear the 'bleep bleep' of a gameboy.
'Hi, Jo,' he whispered.
'Hi, Dan!' Jo said. 'Breakfast?'
'Good idea! ' said Dan.
Dan made the tea and some toast, Jo went and got milk.
'Mmm, is that breakfast?' Mr Shaw said.
'Morning, Dad. Can we pull out the table?'

'Yes, please!'
After breakfast they went to Hayle Beach.
'Do you want to go swimming, boys?' Mr Shaw asked.
'Yeah!' Jo said.
'Come on then. Let's go before the tide starts to go out – it's much too dangerous then.'

When they came out of the water, Dan saw Jody. He and Jo sometimes talked to her when they met her on the beach.
'Hi, Jody!' Dan called.
'Who's that?' Mr Shaw asked.
'That's Jody. She's really nice, Dad,' Dan said.
'She's staying in the village with her aunt,' Jo said. 'Do you want to play football with us, Jody?' he called.
'Maybe, but I want to go swimming first. See you!' She ran into the sea.

Jo went to get the football. Soon lots of other people came to play with the Shaws.
'Dan!' his dad shouted. But Dan didn't see the ball.

'Oh, Dan!' Jo grumbled.
'It's Jody,' said Dan. 'Look, she's so far away. And the tide is going out too.'
'Don't worry! She's a good swimmer.' Jo went back to the game. But Dan looked out to sea again. Suddenly Jody started to wave.
'Oh, no! She's in trouble,' Dan shouted.
'Dan, the ball!' It was Jo, but Dan didn't hear him.
'Dad! Dad!' Dan shouted, 'We have to do something. Look!'
Mr Shaw looked out to sea. Other people looked out to sea too. One man had binoculars.
'The boy's right. That swimmer is in trouble,' he said.
'Dad, where's your mobile? We have to call the lifeboat,' said Dan.
'Right,' Mr Shaw said. He called 999.
'Lifeboat, please,' he said.

A few minutes later the man with the binoculars shouted, 'There's the lifeboat! It's coming from St Ives, I can see it.'

'But where's Jody? I can't see Jody!' Dan was really scared.

'It's all right,' the man said. 'I can see her. But she isn't waving now. Maybe she's too tired. But the lifeboat is there ... it's there. Oh, I can't see her ... Wait ... they've got her, now they're pulling her out.'

'Dad, do you think Jody's OK?' asked Dan. 'Can we go to St Ives and see her? Please, Dad.'

'Come on then,' said Mr Shaw.

August ★ ST IVES TIMES

Bristol twins save girl

Photo: R. Cousins

On Tuesday, 21st August the St Ives lifeboat went out to save a young swimmer, Jody Brooks, 14, from London. 'I'm a good swimmer,' the teenager said. 'But I didn't know about the tides.'

'I saw her swim out,' said Jo Shaw, 13, from Bristol. 'And then I saw her wave. "She's in trouble because the tide is going out!" I said to my dad. So he called the lifeboat.'

The story had a happy ending: the lifeboat got to Jody in time.

'The lifeboatmen saved my life,' Jody said, 'And the twins!'

Working with the text

1 The story

Correct this text. Write it down.

Dan and Jo Shaw and their class were at a caravan park. After lunch they went to Duckpool Beach. They met Jody Brooks, 12, from Manchester.
Jody went surfing and the twins started to play volleyball. Then Jo saw Jody on the beach – she was OK. The teacher called 999. A few minutes later the police pulled the girl out of the water.

2 The newspaper report

Find differences between the story and the newspaper report.

	in the story	in the report
Who watched Jody?		
Who saw Jody wave?		
Who worried about Jody?		

DOSSIER *An exciting day*

Write your own story about an exciting day. Your story can be short or long, true or not true, funny or scary. But it ***must*** *be exciting!*

Before you start, look at the Study Skills box on p. ***18*** *again. Use time phrases to link your sentences.*

► *WB 20 (p. 14)*
► *SF Stop – Check – Go (p. 120)* **Checkpoint 1** ► *WB (p. 115)*

Extra A trip to Jamaica

1 Mr Kingsley's talk

a) *What do you know about Jamaica? Make notes. The pictures can give you ideas.*

Where is it?	*What's the weather like?*	*What can you see there?*
an island, near … in the … Sea	*sunny, hot, …*	*flowers, beaches, …*

b) *Listen to Mr Kingsley. Put the pictures in the right order.*

c) *Can you add to your notes?*

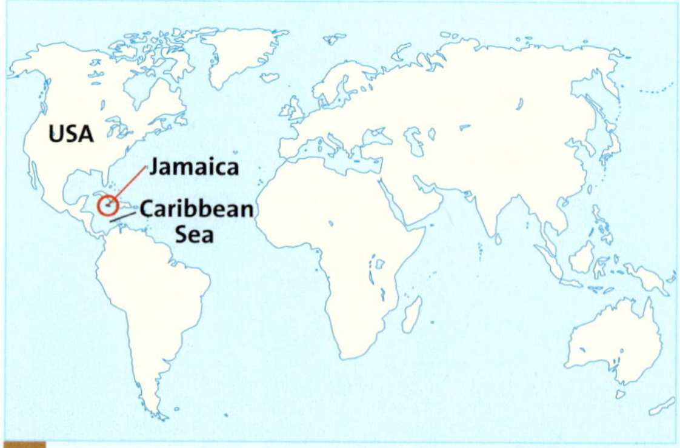

A

B A pretty Jamaican house

C A beautiful Jamaican beach

D There are hibiscus flowers all over the island. The birds love them.

E After a hurricane

2 Anansi the spider and the calabash of wisdom – an Afro-Caribbean legend

a) *What can you see in the picture? Use words from the box.*

a big brown spider • a little brown spider • a green and yellow calabash • a palm tree • a little old man and a little old woman

b) *Now listen. Who says what?*

Please give me all your wisdom!

Daddy, put the calabash on your back!

Of course.

My little son has got more wisdom than me!

Good idea!

c) *Now retell the story with your teacher.*

What money can buy

Where does your pocket money go?

Last month we asked our readers:

1 How do you spend your pocket money?
2 Do you save any of your pocket money?

Lots of readers answered our questions. Here are the results of the survey.

1 Our readers spend their money on ...

2 Most readers save some money

35%
I don't save any pocket money.

65%
I save some pocket money.

Other

1 Talking about shopping

a) *Talk about what you bought last week.*

A: What did you buy last week?
B: Well, I bought ... And what did you buy?

b) *Look at the magazine page. Then put the words from the box into groups.*

cap • chips • cinema ticket • comic • crisps • dress • jacket • magazine • make-up • pens and pencils • present • pullover • shirt • skirt • sports things • sweets • top • (pair of) trainers • (pair of) trousers

food and drink	free-time activities	clothes	other

Extra *Can you add more words to the lists?*

STUDY SKILLS Learning words – Step 2

Vokabeln kannst du dir besser merken, wenn du sie in ***Wortfeldern*** *lernst. Um ein* ***Wortfeld*** *zusammenzustellen, brauchst du einen Oberbegriff (Englisch:* ***group word****). Bei* ***cousin****,* ***aunt*** *und* ***married*** *ist der Oberbegriff* ***family****.*

► *SF Learning words – Step 2 (p. 121) • P 1 (p. 32) • WB 00 (p. 00)*

2 Where does *your* pocket money go?

a) *Ask your partner these questions.*

- Do you save any of your pocket money?
- What do you buy with your pocket money?
- What do your parents buy for you?

b) *Tell the class about your partner.*

My partner saves some/a bit/a lot of his/her pocket money.

He/She doesn't save any money.

His/Her mum/dad buys ... for him/her.

He/She usually/always buys ... with his/her pocket money.

► *P 2 (p. 32) • WB 1–3 (pp. 16–17)*

1 An awful day

Prunella — What's the matter, Sophie?
Sophie — I had an awful day!
Prunella — Mine was awful too. But tell me about yours first.
Sophie — Everybody was fed up. Jack's mum lost her job yesterday. So *he* was fed up. Then Ananda lost her lunch money and Dilip shouted at her ...
Prunella — Was it her money or his?
Sophie — Hers.
Prunella — So why did he shout at her?
Sophie — Good question.
Prunella — And why are you fed up, Sophie?
Sophie — Well, I've got to do a stupid project on 'Clothes without money'. How can you have clothes without money?
Prunella — Maybe I can help you later.
Sophie — Oh yes, please. Well, that was my day. Now tell me about yours.

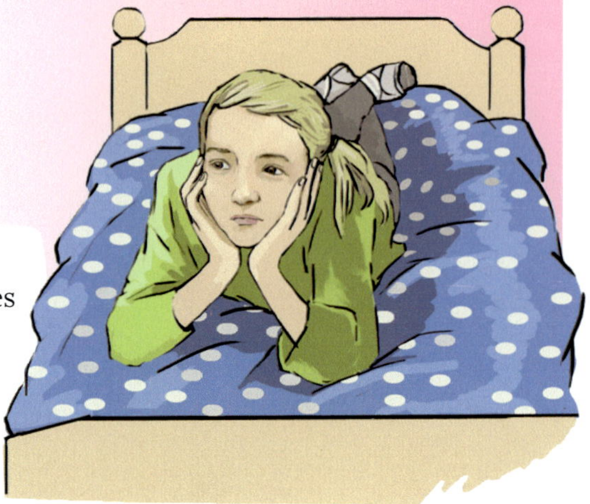

\> *1 Who lost her job?*
- *A Jack's mum*
- *B Sophie's mum*
- *C Ananda's mum*

2 Who lost their lunch money?
- *A Dilip*
- *B Ananda*
- *C Jack*

3 Who needs an idea for a project?
- *A Prunella*
- *B Sophie*
- *C Dilip*

2 SONG Chair rap

Do the rap in a group of four.

This chair is yours, that chair is mine.
Yeah, that's fine, yeah, that's fine!
This chair is hers, that chair is his.
Yes, it is, yes, it is!
These chairs are ours, those chairs are theirs.
Make new pairs, make new pairs!

Go on with a different partner. This bag/... is yours, that bag is ...

3 Extra Now you

Write a dialogue about a bad day at school. – Then act it out.

A: *What's the matter?*
B: *I had an awful day.*
A: *Tell me about it.*
B: ...
A: *Poor you!*
B: *And what about your day?*

I lost ... • I forgot ... • ... | I/... argued with ... • ... shouted at ...
We had a test in ... | I've got lots of English/... homework.

► P 3–6 (pp. 32–33) • WB 4–7 (pp. 17–19)

4 Money problems

'Can I have some money, Mum?' Jack asked. Mrs Hanson looked up from her newspaper. 'What for, Jack?' she asked.
'I'm sorry, Mum, but I need a new pair of trainers. My old ones are too small.'
'Don't be sorry, dear,' his mum said.
'But I know we haven't got much money right now,' Jack said.
'Yes, we had more money when I had a job. But we've still got more than lots of other people. And there's enough for most things.'
'Do you think you can find a new job, Mum?' Jack pointed to the newspaper.
'Well, there aren't many jobs in the paper this week. But I'm sure I can find something.'

1 What does Jack need?
2 What does Jack's mum need?

► P 7–8 (p. 34) • WB 8–11 (pp. 19–21)

5 Extra How much can you buy for £10?

Problem page

Q I get £10 pocket money – but it isn't enough. Everything is so expensive. What can I do?
– Kate, 14, Sussex

A Things don't have to cost a lot. Here's an example of what you can get for £10.

Rent a film with friends. Or try the library. Maybe films are free there.

Buy drinks at the supermarket and save money.

Buy a second-hand game at a jumble sale.

Share a big packet of popcorn with a friend.

£10 = £2.00 + £2.00 + £3.50 + £2.50

What do **Q** *and* **A** *mean?*
Which is the best idea here? Have you got any other ideas?

6 Now you

a) Think: *What things do you like to buy? Write a shopping list.*

b) Pair: *Compare lists with your partner. Agree on a shopping list for €10. Can you save money and buy more things?*

c) Share: *Compare your shopping list with another pair. Who can buy more for €10?*

DOSSIER ***My shopping diary***

Keep a shopping diary for one or two weeks. Write down what you buy and how much it costs.

7 Any ideas?

Jack I need some money for a new computer game and I can't ask mum and dad. Any ideas?
Jo I always have good ideas. It's easy. Find a job. I do a paper round and I get £10.50 every week.
Jack Yes, but it's easier for you. You're older than me. I'm only 12. I can't get a job.
Dan Really? So you are younger than Sophie and Ananda too.
Jo Ah! Jack is the youngest. The baby!
Jack Oh shut up, Jo. I'm not as old as you, but I'm smarter than you.
Jo You're wrong, Jack. I'm the smartest.
Dan No Jo, I'm the smartest and I've got a better idea. Jack, just sell some of your old games.
Jack Great idea, Dan! Why didn't I think of that? You're the best!

Right or wrong?
- *Dan and Jo are older than Jack.*
- *Jack is older than Sophie.*
- *Jo has got the best idea.*

Extra Background File

Jobs for kids

Q: When can kids start work in Britain?
A: You can start work when you're 13.
Q: What jobs can children do?
A: A paper round is a good job. Some kids do a paper round before school.
Q: Any other ideas?
A: Some kids do jobs for their family or neighbours. They wash the car, clean the windows or babysit. Or they go shopping for an older neighbour.

Looking at language

The boys compare a lot in **7**. *Copy and complete:*

easy	...	the easiest
young	...	the ...
...	...	the oldest
...	smarter	the ...
good	...	the ...

How do you say this in English?
Du bist älter als ich.
Ich bin nicht so alt wie du.
Er ist der Jüngste.

▸ *GF 4a, 4c, 4d: Comparison of adjectives (pp. 135–136) • P 9–11 (p. 35) • WB 12–13 (pp. 21–22)*

8 Now you

In groups of three make comparisons. Here are some ideas:

book • hair • hands • jacket • pencil • school bag • T-shirt • ...

big • cold • full • long • new • old • pretty • short • small • warm • ...

A: Philip's school bag is full.
B: My school bag is fuller.
C: But Mike's school bag is the fullest.

9 Project ideas

Ananda So, the project is 'Clothes without money'. Not very exciting.
Lesley No.
Ananda Why don't we do a report about clothes at a charity shop?
Lesley Boring.
Ananda Then what about a poster?
Lesley That's even more boring.
Ananda Maybe we can do something about clothes on the internet?
Lesley I thought your other ideas were boring. But that is the most boring.
Ananda OK, so what ideas have you got?
Lesley Recycling.
Ananda What about it?
Lesley You're so slow! Clothes from recycled things.
Ananda Like a dress from old newspapers?
Lesley Maybe.
Ananda Mmm, I like that.
Lesley So let's do it.

> *Make correct sentences.*
– Ananda/Lesley has got lots of ideas.
– Ananda/Lesley has got the best idea.

10 Now you

a) *What do you think is the most boring or the most exciting? Write three sentences.*

	the most boring	the most exciting
film		
pop star		
football team		
school subject		

b) **Extra** *Talk in your group. You can use sentences from the box.*

I think ... • I agree with you/Lisa. •
I don't agree with you/Lisa. •
I think ... is even more interesting/exciting/...

► *GF 4b–d: Comparison of adjectives (pp. 135–136) • P 12–13 (p. 36)*

11 Extra POEM Why is it?

Why is it some mornings
Your clothes just don't fit?
Your pants are too short
To bend over or sit,
Your sleeves are too long
And your hat is too tight –
Why is it some mornings
Your clothes don't feel right?

by Shel Silverstein

► *P 14–15 (p. 37) • WB 14–19 (pp. 22–25)*

○ 1 STUDY SKILLS Wortfelder

a) Which is the group word?

1 red • blue • *colour* • green
2 dance • hobby • models • music
3 Art • Geography • PE • subject
4 dog • hamster • parrot • pet
5 apple • banana • fruit • orange
6 fish • food • cheese • meat
7 clothes • jeans • shoes • socks
8 water • drink • juice • lemonade

b) Choose the right group word:

family • flat • holiday • school • sports

1 form, break, teacher, project, learn
2 sister, son, uncle, divorced, mum
3 kitchen, bathroom, living room, bedroom
4 tennis ball, win, player, football, match
5 go swimming, beach, by the sea, caravan

2 WORDS Clothes

a) Find the right words.

1 You wear them on your feet when you play football.
2 Girls wear them in summer – and sometimes to parties.
3 You wear them when it's hot or when you do sport.
4 Every boy and girl has got a pair of these – usually they're blue.
5 When it's cold you can wear this over a shirt or T-shirt.
6 Some kids wear shoes, but most kids wear these all the time.
7 You put your clothes in this.

b) Copy and complete the mind map. You can put it in your DOSSIER.

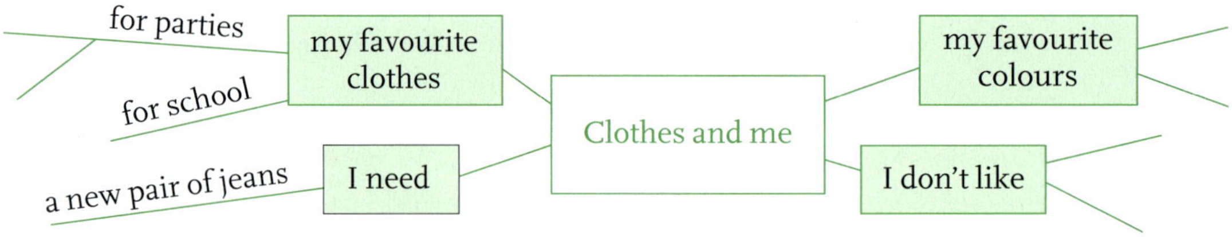

c) **Extra** *Make appointments with three different partners. Talk about your clothes. Use your mind maps.*

▸ *SF Mind maps (p. 122)*

//○ 3 A survey in Geography (Possessive pronouns) ▸ D p. 113

1 *Ananda* My new T-shirt is from China. Where's *yours/his* from, Sophie?
2 *Sophie* *Theirs/Mine* is from China too. What about Dan and Jo? Do you know where *theirs/his* are from?
3 *Dan + Jo* Oh, *hers/ours* are from Thailand. Our MP3 players are from Japan. *Yours/Hers* too, Tom?
4 *Tom* No, *mine/his* is from the USA. But my new mobile is from Japan.
5 *Dan* David has got a new mobile too. But *his/theirs* is from Taiwan.
6 *Jack* Ryan's trainers are from Vietnam. Where are *ours/yours* from, Kevin?
7 *Kevin* They're from Thailand. Ananda has got new ones too. *His/Hers* are from China.

4 REVISION Yes, but ... (Simple past)

Use the correct forms of the simple past.

1

- What (the children/find) *did the children find* in the kitchen?
- They (find) the dog. But they ~~(find)~~ their lunch.

2

- What (your Maths teacher/say) about your homework?
- Oh, she (like) *my* answers. But she ~~(like)~~ *yours*, Dad.

3

- (you/have) a good trip to Italy?
- Yes, we (see) a lot and (have) a very good trip. But all our bags (go) to Spain.

4

- (you/like) the food in Italy?
- Yes, I (like) it a lot. I (eat) lots of spaghetti. But I ~~(know)~~ it was so difficult!

5 Extra WORDS 'make' or 'do'?

a) *Fill in the right form of* ***make*** *or* ***do****.*

1 I often ... my bed before I go to school.
2 My brother usually ... a mess in his room.
3 We both ... our homework in the kitchen.
4 My homework today is to ... a poster.
5 We are ...ing a project on pocket money.
6 But my brother is ...ing a lot of noise.

b) *Do the words in the box go with* ***make*** *or with* ***do****? Write four sentences with these words.*

dinner • an exercise • a joke • a mistake • a sandwich • sport • tricks

6 PRONUNCIATION Is Bob's pet a cat or a dog? (Consonants at the end of words)

a) *What sound do you hear at the end of each word? Hold up a* ***red*** *or* ***blue*** *pen:*

[b] *or* [p] [g] *or* [k] [d] *or* [t]

b) *Say the words from the box. Are they* ***red*** *words or* ***blue*** *words? Listen and check.*

add • back • bag • bed • big • clock • club • date • dog • heard • hurt • job • plate • played • ride • right • sport • step • stop • web

c) *Say these tongue-twisters. Be careful with the ends of the words.*

– Bob's pet is in his bed.
– I've got a big bad bag on my big bad back.
– I heard you hurt your head and now your head hurts.

7 How much? How many? (much/many)

Remember?
much heißt „viel" und many heißt „viele":
- *how much + Singular, z.B. time, money*
- *how many + Plural, z.B. books, euros*

Make questions with How much or How many.

1 *A:* ... pairs of trainers have you got?
B: Oh, not many.

2 *A:* ... money do you save each month?
B: About two euros.

3 *A:* ... TV do you watch every day?
B: About an hour.

4 *A:* ... CDs do you buy?
B: Not many. I've got an MP3 player now.

5 *A:* ... water do you drink every day?
B: A lot. About two big bottles.

6 *A:* ... milk do you drink?
B: Milk? I don't like milk.

7 *A:* ... time do you need for breakfast?
B: Ten minutes. But sometimes I'm faster!

8 *A:* ... hours do you sleep at night?
B: About eight or nine.

1

2

3

4

5

6

7

8

8 How many computer games, how much time? (much/many – more – most)

a) *Partner B: Look at p. 109. Partner A: Read the information about Lennart. Then ask your partner about Christine. Write the answers in a copy of the chart. Now answer your partner's questions about Lennart.*

	Lennart	Christine	You	Your partner
books – read	one every month			
time – need for homework	60 minutes			
TV – watch every day	5 hours			
money – spend on sweets	€ 3 every week			
comics – buy every week	1			
computer games – know	10			

A: How many books does Christine read?
B: One every week.
A: How much time does she ...?

b) *Fill in the answers for You in your chart. Then ask your partner and add his/her answers.*
How many ... do you read?
How much ... do you ...?

c) **Extra** *Report to the class. Make comparisons. Use more and the most.*
My partner knows more computer games than Lennart. I know more computer games than my partner. But Christine knows the most.

9 Mr Bean is funnier than … (Comparison of adjectives)

a) What do you think? Make sentences like this:
1 I think Mr Bean is funnier than a clown.
But Prunella is the funniest.

b) Compare your answers.

1 funny

2 big

3 easy

4 pretty

5 nice

6 fast

7 cold

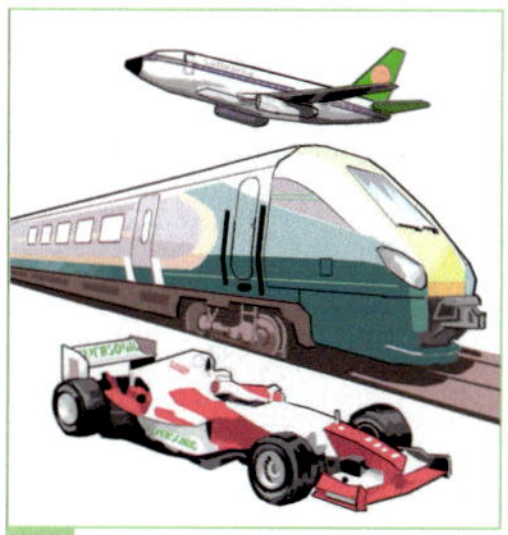
8 loud

10 As big as … (Comparison of adjectives) ▸ D p. 114

Two things are about the same. Make sentences.

1 big Belgium, the Netherlands, the USA
Belgium is about as big as the Netherlands.
2 sunny England, Germany, Turkey
3 sweet chocolate, banana, apple
4 cold April, January, October
5 warm Rome, Oslo, Stockholm
6 long a poem, a song, a book
7 small a mouse, a rabbit, a guinea pig

11 LISTENING Quiz show

a) Make two teams. One student from each team goes to the front. Listen to the first question. Do you know the answer? Who can buzz first? You've got ten seconds for your answer.
– What can you wear? Say three things.
– Buzz! – Shoes, trousers and a cap.
– That's right. One point for Team A. / That's wrong. One point for Team B. Next pair, please!

*b) **Extra** Make more questions and have your own quiz show.*

12 Jumble sale (Comparison of adjectives)

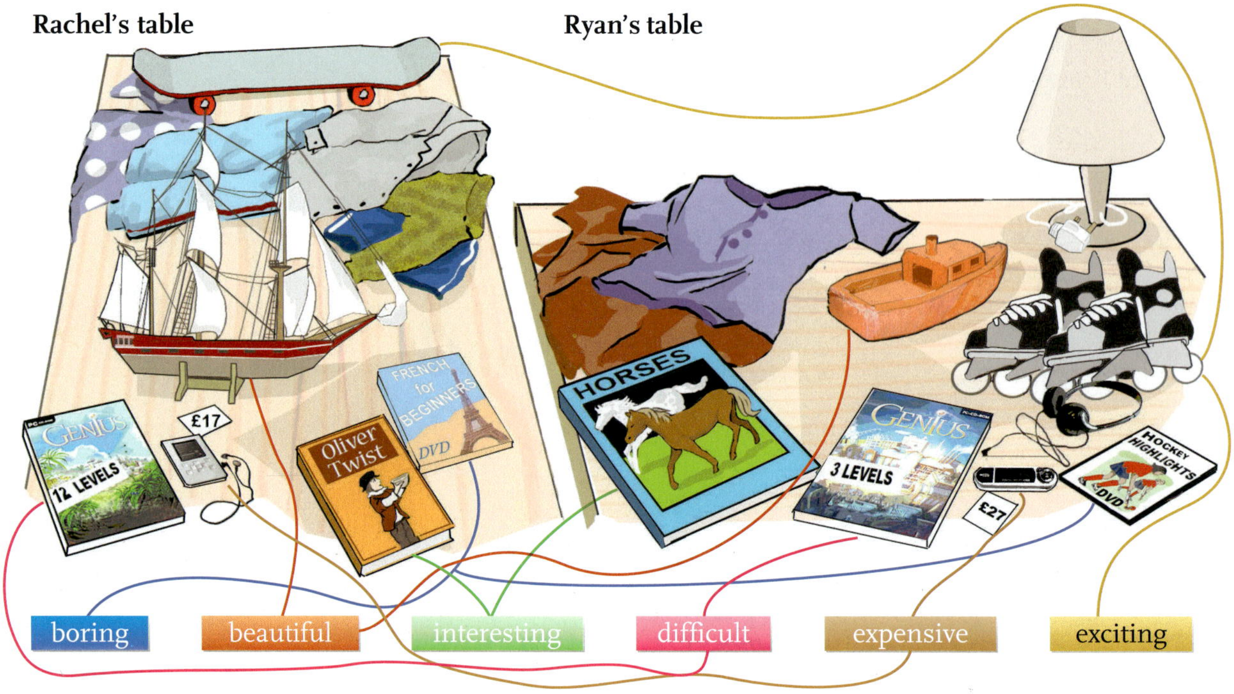

a) *Look at Rachel and Ryan's tables at the village jumble sale. Compare Rachel and Ryan's things:*
Rachel's computer game is more difficult than Ryan's.
Ryan's MP3 player is more …
Rachel's ship is …

b) *What do you think? Which table is better? Why? Which things are the most interesting?*
Rachel's/Ryan's table is better.
He/She has got the most interesting things.
The … on …'s table is the most expensive thing.

13 What do you think? (Comparison of adjectives)

What do you think?

a) Think: *Write questions for a group survey.*

1 difficult – Maths/English
What do you think is more difficult – Maths or English?
2 good – a pet rabbit/a pet dog
What do you think is better – …?
3 exciting – a computer game/a football match
4 interesting – a holiday by the sea/a holiday in the mountains
5 nice – a red pullover/a blue pullover
6 boring – three hours in the car/three hours shopping
7 funny – Bart Simpson/Donald Duck
8 dangerous – to travel by car/to travel by plane

b) Pair: *Ask your partner the questions. Take turns.*

c) Share: *Make a group of four. Compare your results. Prepare a report for your class.*
We all think Maths is more difficult than English. Two of us think a pet dog is better …

14 MEDIATION In a department store

STORE DIRECTORY

lower ground
technology hall
book shop
music
tv & video
shoe repair

ground floor
beauty hall
food hall
men's & women's accessories

first floor
men's wear
men's shoes
sports hall

second floor
women's wear
women's shoes
hats

third floor
kids' zone
hair salon

fourth floor
furniture
bed linen
bath shop
ice cream bar
car park access

fifth floor
café · sushi bar
car park access
travel
customer service
customer toilets

STUDY SKILLS Mediation

Manchmal musst du zwischen zwei Sprachen vermitteln. Übersetze nicht alles wörtlich, gib nur das Wesentliche weiter, z.B. hier: Wo werden die Wünsche deiner Eltern erfüllt?

▸ *SF Mediation (p. 131)*

Imagine you're shopping with your parents in Bristol. They want to find different things. Help them.

Mutter: Ärgerlich, mein Absatz fängt an, sich zu lösen. Kann man das hier reparieren lassen?

You: Bestimmt. Warte mal – *shoes* – *shoes*, ach, da steht es ja: *shoe repair*.

Mutter: Und wo ist das?

You: Im Untergeschoss.

1 *Vater* Aber dann möchte ich zur Stärkung einen Kaffee. Wo bekommen wir den?
You Es gibt ein Café …
2 *Mutter* Wo gibt's wohl ein Sweatshirt für deine kleine Schwester?
3 *Vater* Wo finde ich eine Toilette?
4 *Mutter* Und wo bekommen wir englische Bücher?
5 *Vater* Du wolltest doch englischen Tee kaufen. Aber wo?
6 *Mutter* Ich brauche unbedingt eine Hose für mich. Wo finde ich denn die?

15 GETTING BY IN ENGLISH Shopping for a birthday present

a) *Can you say these things in English?*

1 Wir haben im Moment nicht viel Geld. (p. 29)
2 Ich kann ganz bestimmt etwas finden. (p. 29)
3 Ich habe eine bessere Idee. (p. 30)
4 Warum habe ich nicht daran gedacht? (p. 30)
5 Warum machen wir nicht einen Bericht? (p. 31)
6 Hm, das finde ich gut. (p. 31)

b) *You and your partner want to buy a birthday present for your friend, Emma. Prepare a dialogue. Try and use phrases from a). Then act out your dialogue.*

Partner A | **Partner B**

Partner A: Du schlägst vor, einen Fußball zu kaufen.
→ Partner B: Du hast eine bessere Idee – eine Tasche.
→ Partner A: Du findest das gut, aber du hast nicht viel Geld im Moment.
→ Partner B: Du kennst einen Secondhandshop. Du schlägst vor, dahin zu gehen.
→ Partner A: Frag dich, warum du nicht daran gedacht hast.
→ Partner B: Du denkst, ihr findet ganz bestimmt etwas.

The Clothes Project

Part 1 At Sophie's house

Sophie and Jack are working on 8PK's 'Clothes Project'. Who is with them?

It was Tuesday afternoon, after school. Jack was at Sophie's house. They wanted to work on their clothes project.
'Clothes without money. What can we do?' Jack asked as he took another biscuit.
'I've got an idea,' Sophie said.
'Good!' Jack said.
'Well, Rachel and Tom want to do a fashion show. And Ananda and Lesley want to join them and I thought we ...'
'What?!' Jack said. 'Me in a fashion show? No way!'
'Not you. Me. You can be the presenter,' Sophie said.
'Oh – OK. So what's your idea?'
'Come up to the attic and see,' Sophie said.
Prunella floated over to Sophie, 'Oh good! We're going up to the attic!' she said.
'No, we aren't!' Sophie whispered. 'You're staying here.'
'What did you say?' Jack asked.
'Nothing,' Sophie said. 'Come on!'
Prunella was the first in the attic.
She went to the shelf with Grandma's plates.
'I love plates!' Prunella said. She took one.
Sophie and Jack came into the attic.
'Wow!' said Jack.
'Careful!' whispered Sophie.
'Oops!' said Prunella and dropped the plate.
Crash!
'What was that?' Jack said.
'Er ... nothing,' Sophie said. 'Come here and look.' She opened a wardrobe and took out a beautiful, long, blue dress.
'Isn't this beautiful? It was my grandma's dress. She designed it. And she made it too. And here's a hat ... It's all very old, but still beautiful. What do you think?'
'An outfit from grandma's wardrobe? That's a nice idea. We can say a bit about when she lived and ...'
Suddenly Prunella took the hat from Sophie and floated over to the mirror. She tried the hat on. Of course Jack couldn't see Prunella – he only saw the hat. He stood there with his mouth open.
'No! I don't like it!' Prunella said and dropped the hat on the floor.
'Ooops! The wind in here!' Sophie said as she went and got the hat. 'Come on, Jack. Let's take the stuff down and start work.' She hurried to the door.
'What about shoes?' asked Prunella.
'Oh, no!' said Sophie.
Crash! A pair of black shoes landed at Jack's feet. Bang! A pair of red shoes. Wallop! A pair of blue shoes.

'I don't understand,' Jack said. 'Hey, Sophie, maybe you've got a poltergeist? Maybe …' 'You and your mad ideas, Jack!' Sophie laughed. 'Now hurry up. We have to prepare our presentation. It has to be ready tomorrow.' 'Hee! Hee! Hee!' Prunella laughed as Sophie took a very puzzled Jack downstairs.

> Jack asks: 'Maybe you've got a poltergeist?' Why does he think so? Find three reasons in the text.

Part 2 The fashion show

Listen to the end of the story. There are two parts.

- The ball dress
- An outfit from the bin

Look at the pictures and find the mistakes.

Working with the text

1 Heads and tails

Match the heads and tails of these sentences.

1 Jack and Sophie needed …	… but he couldn't see Prunella.
2 Jack liked Sophie's idea but …	… Prunella tried on the hat.
3 When Sophie showed Jack the dress …	… he didn't want to be in a fashion show.
4 Jack could see the hat …	… a poltergeist in her house.
5 Jack thought Sophie had …	… an idea for their clothes project.

2 Jack's story

Imagine you are Jack. Describe the scene in the attic (p. 38, ll. 26–64).

I went up to the attic with Sophie. It was great.
There were lots of …
Then Sophie opened a …
She …, but suddenly …

3 Extra The outfits

Draw Sophie's or Ananda's outfit OR design a recycled outfit and present it to the class.

4 Extra ACTIVITY A fashion show

a) *Collect clothes words (for example **skirt**) and adjectives (for example **long**/**short**/…).*

b) *Prepare your show:*

- *collect clothes* • *choose music*
- *choose the model/presenter*
- *write the presentation*

Here are some ideas. Listen again for more ideas.

We want to show you … | He's/She's wearing …

We found this dress/… in …

We made this hat/… out of …

c) *Rehearse, then put on your show.*

► *WB 20 (p. 26)*
► *SF Giving a presentation (p. 124)*

Checkpoint 2 ► *WB (pp. 27–29)*

Extra Special days around the world

1 Special days

a) Work in groups of four. Answer these questions about one of the texts. Write down the answers in a chart.
– What is the special day?
– What country is the text about?
– When do people celebrate it?
– How do they celebrate it?

Special day	Where?	When?	How?
Guy Fawkes Day	England	5 Nov.	

b) Make a new group. Each student must know a different text. Use your chart to tell the others about the special day in your text.

► *SF Understanding new words (p. 122)*
► *SF Working with a dictionary (p. 123)*

A

▪ Fawkes, Guy (1570–1606)

Fawkes and his men were Catholics, and they did not want a Protestant king. On 5 Nov 1605 they put lots of gunpowder under the parliament building. They wanted to kill the king and his ministers. But the king's men found Fawkes and killed him.
Every year the English celebrate 'Guy Fawkes Day' on 5 November. They put a 'Guy' on big bonfires and have fireworks.

Guy Fawkes, or 'Bonfire Night', is very popular in England.

B

AN E-CARD FROM CATHERINE THOMPSON SHAW

To:
From:
Sent:

The card shows the 'New Zealand Christmas tree'. It's really the pohutukawa tree, and it gets lots of red flowers at Christmas – summertime here. So we aren't going to celebrate at home – we're going to the beach for a Christmas barbecue! Father Christmas comes on a surfboard every year. – Oh yes, did my parcel arrive in time for Christmas?
Lots of love – from Pat too!

C

3rd March

My dear Ananda

Thank you for your last letter. It's always nice to hear from my granddaughter.

The city is so quiet now after a week of Holi. Do you celebrate Holi in Bristol? Here in India the young people have a lot of fun! They go out in the morning in white clothes. Then in the street people throw gulal and kumkum (coloured water and powders).

At night there's singing and dancing in the streets. There are pretty colours everywhere. That's what Holi is – the Festival of Colour.

D

★ Queens Star Chronicle ★ July 5

Queens celebrates on a beautiful day

The people of Queens, New York, celebrated Independence Day yesterday with all the traditions: a morning parade, an afternoon barbecue, and evening fireworks.

"We had beautiful Fourth of July weather," said Mike Esker of the National Weather Service. The traditional parade started with a band from Benjamin Cardozo High School. Two open cars followed. They were full of young men – Cardozo's champion basketball team, including team captain Jay Gupta.

More on p. 3

Photo: Cardozo High School band at the Fourth of July Parade

2 Who sent the e-card?

Who sent the e-card? And the newspaper article? Who wrote the letter? How do you know?

I think ... sent the e-card.
She's got the same name as ..., and she lives ...
So it must be from her.

3 Now you

a) *Make notes about a special day in your family.*

24th December/Mother's day/... is a special day in our family.
We eat/drink/make/wear/visit ...

b) *Write about your special day. You can add pictures and put it in your DOSSIER.*

Animals in the city

Thursday 18 November

TV • Thursday

7.00 pm BBC 1

Animals in the City

The fox

New series of five programmes about wild animals in the city.
From the BBC's Natural History Unit in Bristol.

Tonight's programme:
The fox and how it survives in our cities

BBC 1

- 3.50 **Batman** Cartoon
- 4.10 **Dance Factory** Dance programme for kids
- 4.45 **Blue Peter** Zoe visits Japan for a lesson in origami
- 5.20 **Newsround** News for children
- 5.35 **Neighbours** Series
- 6.00 **BBC News**
- 6.30 **Points West** News, sport and weather
- 7.00 **Animals in the City**

BBC 2

- 3.30 FILM **The Man on the Train (2002)** Film about a bank robber and an old teacher
- 4.30 **Ready, Steady, Cook** Great food for parties
- 5.15 **Eggheads** Quiz show

ITV 1

- 3.50 **Art Attack** Art ideas for young Picassos
- 4.00 **Planet's Funniest Animals** Funny videoclips of pets and other animals

1 Now you

a) Which English TV programme would you like to watch? Why?

I'd like to watch …
… sounds interesting/funny/good/exciting/…

cartoons • sport programmes • quiz shows • music shows • films • action films • series • programmes about … • comedy shows • …

b) **Extra** *What TV programmes do you like?*

A: I like …
B: Really? / I don't like … – I love …
A: I love … too.
And my favourite … is …
B: …

Deer

Woodpecker

Grey squirrel

Mole

Frog

Hedgehog

2 Talking about animals

a) *Name as many animals as you can.*

b) *What's your favourite animal? Ask your classmates.*

3 A BBC radio interview

*Listen to the radio interview with the presenter of **Animals in the City**. Which animals does he name? Complete the notes.*

Programme	1	2	3	4	5
Animals	foxes				

► *P 1 (p. 48) • WB 1 (p. 30)*

STUDY SKILLS Listening

Bereite dich auf das Hören eines Textes vor:
- *Lies dir die Aufgabe gut durch. Worum wird es in dem Text gehen? Was sollst du herausfinden?*
- *Bereite deine Notizen vor, z.B. in Aufgabe 3 die Tabelle.*
- *Während des Hörens sollten deine Notizen kurz sein. Schreib z.B. nur die Anfangsbuchstaben der Stichwörter auf und ergänze sie hinterher.*

► *SF Listening (p. 125)*

1 Hello hedgehogs!

Ananda opened the back door, walked over to the dustbin and put the rubbish in. Suddenly she saw two baby hedgehogs.
'You poor little things. Where's your mum? You'll be very cold tonight without her.'
She looked round the yard. Their mother wasn't there. Ananda went inside.
'Sophie knows all about animals,' she thought. So she called her.

'You'll have to wait,' Sophie said. 'Maybe their mother will come later.'
'But maybe she won't come back tonight,' Ananda said. 'Then what? Tomorrow the babies will be hungry. Will they need milk?'
'No, they won't. Milk is bad for them. But they'll need water.'
'OK. What about food?'
'I'm not sure. They probably won't eat. They'll be too scared.'
'Oh, Sophie, will they survive without their mum?'
'Yes, I think they will. You know what? Mail that TV programme *Animals in the City*. Their Animal Hotline will help.'
So Ananda sat down and sent an e-mail to the Animal Hotline.

> *Write Ananda's e-mail to the Animal Hotline. You can use these ideas:*

I found some baby hedgehogs in our yard.

Yours
Ananda Kapoor

Will they be cold outside?

Thanks for your help.

I've got lots of questions about them. Can you help?

Will they survive without their mum?

Dear Animal Hotline

What about food?

Looking at language

a) *Collect sentences with 'll, will, won't from 1.*

+	–	?
– You'll be very cold tonight. – You'll …	– But maybe she won't … – …	– Will they …? – …

b) *Are Sophie and Ananda talking about the past (yesterday), the present (now) or the future (in a minute, tomorrow)?*

2 Now you

a) *Write sentences. Use ideas from the box.*
In 20 years I'll probably …
In 20 years I probably won't …

be a pop star • be married • have a family • have a horse • like the same music • live at home/in … • travel to the moon • …

b) *Compare with a partner.*

► *GF 5: will-future (p. 137) • P 2–4 (pp. 48–49) • WB 2–3 (p. 31)*

3 The Animal Hotline

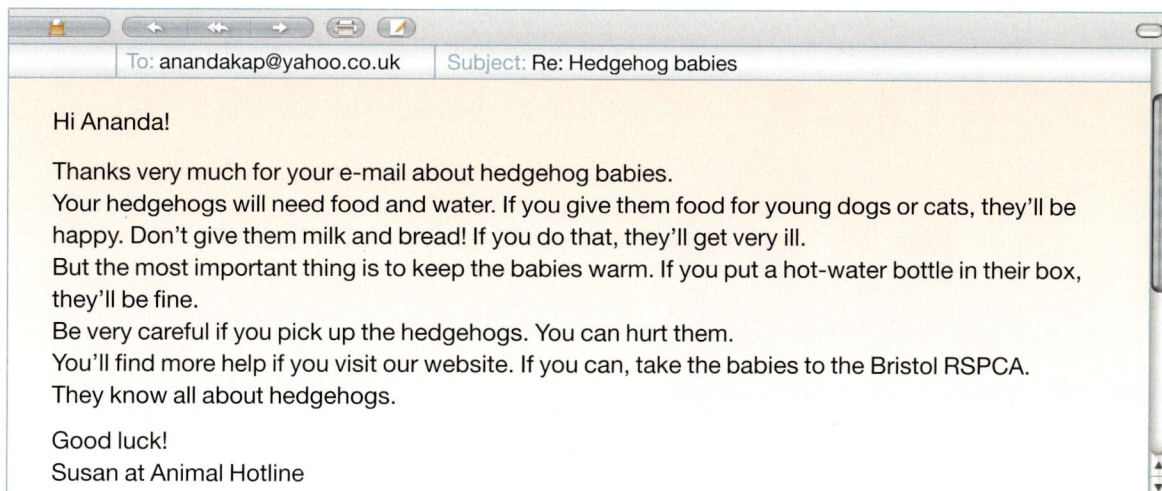

To: anandakap@yahoo.co.uk Subject: Re: Hedgehog babies

Hi Ananda!

Thanks very much for your e-mail about hedgehog babies.
Your hedgehogs will need food and water. If you give them food for young dogs or cats, they'll be happy. Don't give them milk and bread! If you do that, they'll get very ill.
But the most important thing is to keep the babies warm. If you put a hot-water bottle in their box, they'll be fine.
Be very careful if you pick up the hedgehogs. You can hurt them.
You'll find more help if you visit our website. If you can, take the babies to the Bristol RSPCA. They know all about hedgehogs.

Good luck!
Susan at Animal Hotline

> *Complete these notes:*

Tips for baby hedgehogs
Give them ... and ...
Don't give them ... or ...
Very important: Keep them ...
If you pick them up, be very ...
Take them to ...

Extra Background File

The Royal Society for the Prevention of Cruelty to Animals (RSPCA)

In 1824 a group of animal lovers started the Society for the Prevention of Cruelty to Animals. (The 'Royal' came later.) They wanted to help animals. Today the RSPCA is a big organization. People phone when they see animals in trouble.

For more information, visit their website at *www.rspca.org.uk.*

4 Extra Now you

What do you think will happen?
Finish these sentences.
Then tell the class.

If I get a '1' in my next English test, ...
If I go to bed at 1 o'clock in the morning, ...
If there's no homework tomorrow, ...

... I'll be very happy/tired/sad/angry/excited!

... everybody in the class will be happy!

... Mum and Dad will be very angry/happy!

What about you?

► GF 6: Conditional sentences (1) (p. 138) • P 5–8 (pp. 50–51) • WB 4–10 (pp. 32–35)

5 Dilip killed my hedgehogs

'... so,' Ananda explained, 'I took the box slowly and carefully back to the yard. Then, this morning, I went out very quietly with some water and ... the yard was empty.'
'Empty?' asked Sophie.
'Yes,' Ananda said sadly, 'Dilip put all the old boxes out for the rubbish collection. He killed my hedgehogs!'
'That's terrible!' said Jack.
'I'm sure there's an explanation,' said Dan.
'Look!' Sophie said loudly. 'There's Dilip!'
She walked over to him quickly.
'You horrible person!' Sophie shouted angrily.
'You killed Ananda's hedgehogs.'
'No, I didn't!' said Dilip. 'I put them in the garage. They're warm and safe.'

Who put the hedgehogs in the yard?
Who thinks Dilip killed the hedgehogs?
Who put the hedgehogs in the garage?

Ananda • Dan • Dilip • Jack • Jo • Sophie

Looking at language

a) *How do people do or say things?*
Write down sentences like this from **5**:
I took the box slowly and ...
I ...
Underline the **verb**.
What word describes **how** *somebody does something? Underline this word too.*

b) *Complete this chart of* **adjectives** *and* **adverbs**. *What's different?*

adjectives	adverbs
slow	slowly
...	carefully
...	quietly
...	...

► GF 7a–b: Adverbs of manner (p. 139) • P 9–11 (pp. 51–52) • WB 11–12 (p. 36)

6 GAME Act out the adverbs

a) *Write eight activities on blue cards and eight adverbs on orange cards. Here are some ideas:*

feed the dog	write an e-mail	slowly	quickly
sing	laugh	angrily	happily
clean the board	eat a sandwich	nervously	quietly
walk	dance	madly	sadly

b) *Put all the cards together. One person takes a blue card and an orange card and mimes what is on them. The others guess what he/she is doing.*

I think you're cleaning the board madly.

Yes, that's right. Your turn. / No, that's wrong. Try again.

7 Goodbye hedgehogs

'You did a good job with the hedgehogs,' said the woman at the RSPCA animal clinic.
'Really?' Ananda asked.
'Yes, the babies will be fine. You did well. So, would you like to see the clinic? This is Steve, one of our volunteers. He'll show you everything.'
Steve showed Ananda a small cat. 'She had a broken leg. She still can't run fast.'
'She's playing happily now,' said Ananda.
'Yes,' Steve said. 'She's playing more happily than last week.'
'I'd like to help animals too,' Ananda said. 'Is it hard work?'
'Well yes, I work hard,' Steve answered. 'But it's fun too. I'm afraid you have to be 16 to be a volunteer. But you can collect money for the RSPCA. There's a fun run next week.'
'A fun run?' Ananda asked.
'Yes,' Steve answered. 'You run, and for each mile, people give you money. Then you give the money to the RSPCA.'
'Oh, that's a good idea,' Ananda said.

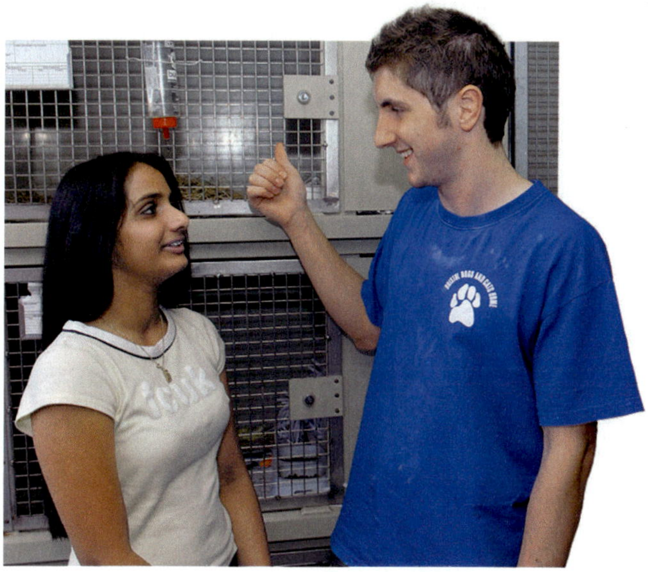

What does Ananda do with the hedgehogs?
Can Ananda help in the clinic like Steve?
Are there fun runs where you live?

Looking at language

Remember?
happy *is an adjective and* **happily** *is an adverb:*
A happy cat. – The cat is playing happily.

Look at these sentences from ***7****. Which are the adjectives and which are the adverbs?*

You did a good job. You did well.
Is it hard work? I work hard.

► *GF 7c–d: Adverbs of manner, irregular forms (pp. 139–140)* • *WB 13 (p. 37)*

► **Extra** *GF 7e: Comparison of adverbs (p. 140)*

8 More about animals

Complete the chart. You can scan these web pages for the missing information:
www.EnglishG.de/D2/fox
www.EnglishG.de/D2/squirrel
www.EnglishG.de/D2/hedgehog

	foxes	squirrels	hedgehogs
food			
number of babies			
enemies			

STUDY SKILLS Scanning

Wenn du in einem langen Text nach bestimmten Informationen suchst, brauchst du nicht den ganzen Text zu lesen.
Suche stattdessen nach Schlüsselwörtern und lies nur dort genauer, wo du sie findest.

► *SF Scanning (p. 126)* • *P 12 (p. 52)* • *WB 15 (p. 38)*

DOSSIER *Animals*

Write a short report about one of the animals from ***8****. These phrases can help you.*

They eat ...
They have one/two/... babies in the spring/...
They have no/a few/... enemies.
Their biggest enemies are ...

► *P 13–15 (p. 53)* • *WB 14, 16–18 (p. 37, pp. 39–40)*

1 WORDS Animals

a) *Write the animals in two lists: **pets** and **wild animals**. Which animals can go in both lists?*

budgies • cats • deer • dogs • fish • foxes • frogs • guinea pigs • hamsters • hedgehogs • horses • mice • moles • parrots • rabbits • snakes • squirrels • tortoises • woodpeckers

b) *Choose three or four animals from your lists. Match them with adjectives from the box.*

big • clever • fast • loud • pretty • quiet • slow • small • ...

I think parrots are pretty and clever.

I don't think parrots are pretty. – I think dogs are ...

c) *Compare your lists.*

2 In 2050 (will-future) ▸ D p. 115

a) *Choose a caption for each picture.*

In 2050 it will be warm in winter. In 2050 people will live on Mars.

In 2050 people won't read books. In 2050 animals will live in hotels.

In 2050 people will fly to work. In 2050 people probably won't need shops.

In 2050 some people will live under the sea. In 2050 babies will use computers.

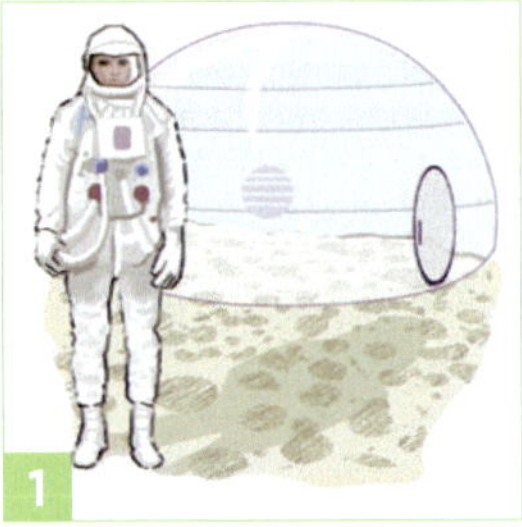
1

2

3

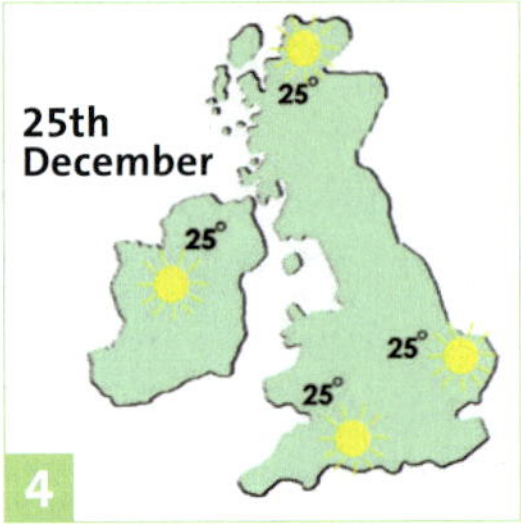

4

5

6

7

8

b) **Extra** *Do you and your partner agree with the captions?*

A: Caption **1** says: In 2050 people will live on Mars. What do you think?

B: I agree. / I don't agree – I think people *won't* live on Mars in 2050.

A: What about caption **2**?

3 Fifi the fortune-teller (will-future)

a) *Prunella wants to know about Sophie's future. So she goes to Fifi the fortune-teller. Fill in the correct forms of the* ***will****-future.*

1 P: *Will* Sophie *be* (be) a doctor, like her mum?
F: No, she *won't be* (be) a doctor. Maybe she*'ll be* (be) a teacher.
2 P: ... she ... (have) children?
F: Oh, yes. She ... (have) at least three children.
3 P: Where ... she (live)? ... she still ... (live) in this house in 20 years?
F: I don't know where she ... (live), but she ... (live) here.
4 P: How old ... she ... (be) then?
F: She ... (be) thirty.
5 P: Oh! But ... Sophie ... (remember) me?
F: Yes, she ... always ... (remember) you, Prunella.

b) **Extra** *Write five questions about your future. Your partner is a fortune-teller. Ask him/her your questions.*

4 READING A book: No Small Thing

Read about the book. Then answer the questions.

1 **No Small Thing** is a book about ...
A a newspaper. B a horse.
C the Queen. D a girl.

2 This book is a book for ...
A boys only. B girls only.
C young people. D old people.

3 The children live with ...
A their mum. B their dad.
C their aunt. D their mum and dad.

4 When the children tell their mother about the horse she says that ...
A they can't have a horse.
B she doesn't like horses.
C they can have the horse.
D horses are dangerous.

5 After the fire ...
A Smokey is dead. B Smokey isn't there.
C Smokey is ill. D Smokey is OK.

6 The article says this is ...
A a boring book. B a bad book.
C a good book. D a short book.

▸ *SF Multiple-choice exercises (p. 124)*

STUDY SKILLS **Multiple-choice exercises**

Lies bei Multiple-Choice-Aufgaben immer alle Lösungen genau durch, bevor du dich für die beste entscheidest.

No Small Thing ♦ by Natale Ghent
10–14 years, 256 pages

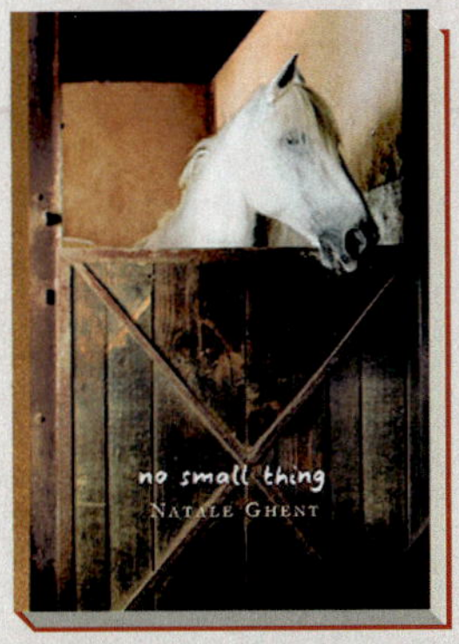

Life isn't easy for Nathaniel and his two sisters, Queenie and Cid. They live alone with their mother. One day the children see an ad for a horse in the newspaper. And the great thing is – it's free! At first they don't tell their mother. They are sure she will say no. But then they tell her, and she says yes. The children are happy again. They feed Smokey, ride him, and spend many happy hours together.
Then one day something terrible happens. There's a fire in the barn where Smokey lives. Luckily Smokey survives. But then the family has to sell their house. What will happen to Smokey?

No Small Thing is a great book about a horse. It is exciting and funny. You have to read it!

5 If you find a baby hedgehog … (Conditional sentences)

Make correct sentences.

1. If you find a baby hedgehog, → you'll have to keep it warm.
2. Be very careful
3. If you give it water and dog food,
4. The hedgehog will get very ill
5. If you write to the Animal Hotline,
6. If you ask your Biology teacher,

it will be happy.
you'll have to keep it warm.
they'll send you an e-mail.
he or she will tell you more about hedgehogs.
if you give it milk.
if you pick the hedgehog up.

6 Extra What will they do if …? (Conditional sentences)

a) *Partner B: Look at p. 109.*
Partner A: Ask your partner for the missing information.
Then answer his or her questions.

A: What will Maike do if she finds a baby squirrel?
B: She'll …
A: And what will Maike do if …?

	find a baby squirrel	get a 5 in English	need a new mobile
Maike		practise every day	
Jan	put it in a box		save his pocket money
Christoph	ask the Biology teacher for help	talk to his English teacher	
You			
Your partner			

b) *Write three sentences: one about Maike, Jan or Christoph, one about your partner and one about you.*
If Maike finds a baby squirrel, she'll take it to a clinic.
If my partner finds a baby squirrel, he'll / she'll …
If I find a baby squirrel, I'll …

7 REVISION Three cities (Comparison of adjectives)

There was a survey on British cities.
*Here are the results for London (**L**), Bristol (**B**) and Manchester (**M**).*

1. Is … pretty? — not pretty … M … L … B … very pretty
2. Is … green? — not green … M … L … B … very green
3. Is … exciting? — not exciting … B … M … L … very exciting
4. Is … dangerous? — not dangerous … B … M … L … very dangerous

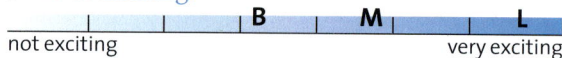

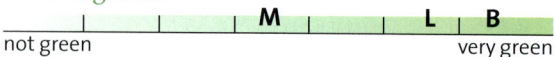

Compare the cities. Make statements like this:
Manchester isn't as pretty as London or Bristol. London is prettier than … Bristol is the prettiest.

8 WRITING An e-mail to *pet@petoftheday.com*

Partner B: Look at p. 108.
Partner A: Look at this page.

a) *Read the e-mail. Choose the correct words.*

b) **Partner check**
Read your text about Marley to your partner. Your partner will correct your mistakes.

This is Marley, my budgie. He's two years old and/because I love him very much. When/And I come home from school, he's very happy. I play with him because/before I have my tea. Before/After tea I always do my homework. Marley sits on my desk when/and watches me. But/When I open Marley's cage, he flies out. He sits on my head and/but sings to me.

c) **Partner check** *Now turn your book upside down.*

This is Rosie, my cat. She's seven months old and/~~but~~ she's very pretty. Every morning she comes to my room before/~~because~~ I get up. She comes in my bed because/~~after~~ she wants to play. I always feed Rosie before/~~after~~ I go to school. I feed her again when/~~before~~ I come home. I play with her before/~~because~~ I do my homework. Then she sits on my bed and/~~but~~ sleeps.

This is your partner's text. Listen to your partner and correct the mistakes.

DOSSIER *Pet of the day*

Write an e-mail to → *pet@petoftheday.com*
about a pet. Add a photo.
Write: ***the pet's name, what pet it is, how old it is, where the pet lives, what you like about the pet, …*** *Use words like:* ***and, when, so, but, because, after, before, then***

9 WORDS Fourth word

Find the fourth word.

1 this – that
these – ?

2 bird – birds
deer – ?

3 mouse – mice
fox – ?

4 house – yard
inside – ?

5 e-mail – write
TV programme – ?

6 left – right
background – ?

7 meet – met
find – ?

8 do – don't
will – ?

10 LISTENING She's talking loudly (Adverbs of manner)

a) *Make adverbs from these adjectives.*

angry • careful • happy • loud • quick • quiet • slow

b) *Listen to the CD. Write down how the people are talking. Use adverbs from a).*

1 *The first person is talking …*
2 *The second person is talking …*
3 …

//○ 11 Don't hit the dog! (Adverbs of manner) ▸ D p. 115

Complete the sentences with one of the adverbs in brackets.

Jack and Ananda walked (carefully/slowly) home from school.
'Tell me about your hockey match,' Jack said.
'Well, we didn't win,' said Ananda (happily/sadly).
'We played really (badly/quietly).'
Suddenly she stopped. 'Can you hear that noise?'
Jack listened (loudly/carefully).
'You're right,' he said (dangerously/quietly). 'It sounds like a dog. Come on!'
They ran (quickly/slowly). Soon they could hear the dog (cleverly/clearly). Then they saw a man.
'Don't hit the dog!' Ananda said (nervously/badly).
'Mind your own business,' the man answered (happily/rudely).
'Stop that!' Jack shouted (angrily/nicely). The man ran away.
'Poor little dog,' Ananda said, 'we'll take you to the RSPCA.'

12 STUDY SKILLS and MEDIATION Longleat Safari Park

a) *Can you see these animals at Longleat Safari Park? Scan quickly through the information and find out.*

monkeys • elephants • deer • snakes

▸ *SF Scanning (p. 126)*

Remember
Du brauchst nicht den ganzen Text zu lesen, sondern nur gezielt nach den Schlüsselwörtern zu suchen.

Welcome to Longleat

East Africa Reserve
Our herd of giraffes and zebras live happily together in this **25**-hectare reserve. Also look out for the camels.

Monkey Jungle
A drive through the Monkey Jungle is great fun. They are great entertainers!

Tiger Territory
Tigers are beautiful animals, but they can be very dangerous too! Close your car windows when you are in Tiger Territory!

Deer Park
Deer first came to Longleat in **1540**.
In our Deer Park you can feed the animals.

Open **10** am, last entry at **4** pm (**5** pm weekends)

Prices **£10** adult
£7 child (**3–14** yrs)

b) *Imagine you want to go to the Safari Park with your parents. Tell them in German:*
- *what animals you can see in the park*
- *how much it costs for you and your parents*
- *what you have to do in Tiger Territory*
- *when the park opens*

13 WORDS Word building

a) *Make nouns from the verbs.*

+ er	+ r	+ ner/ + mer	+ or
work	dance	run	act
sing	explore	swim	collect
listen	write	win	visit
paint	ride		
play	use		

b) *Complete the sentences with words from a).*

1 Johnny Depp is my favourite ... I try to see all his films.
2 Picasso was a famous ...
3 If I see a book by J. K. Rowling, I'll buy it. She's a really good ...
4 Jo is a good ... He goes to the pool every week with his dad.
5 You're a fantastic ...! Why aren't you in the choir?

c) Extra *Choose three more words from a) and make sentences like the ones in b). Swap. Can your partner find the missing words?*

14 PRONUNCIATION [f] – [v] – [w]

a) *What sound do you hear at the beginning of each word? Is the first letter f, v or w? Listen and write the words in your exercise book with the correct first letter.*

_ery • _eek • _illage • _ind • _eed • _ater • _isit • _ord • _ith • _iew • _irst • _alk • _ace • _oman • _olleyball • _hite • _ood • _ind • _oodpecker

b) *Say the words from a).*

c) Extra *Listen to these tongue-twisters. Then try them.*

Willy Walter won't wear white in winter, will he?
Fiona's got a very funny visitor from Valencia.
Where's the village with the very wild view?
Val fell on the floor when Vinny phoned Will.

15 GETTING BY IN ENGLISH We found a cat ...

You're on holiday in England in your family's caravan. Last night you found this cat under the caravan. You phone the RSPCA. Complete the dialogue.

RSPCA Good morning, RSPCA here. How can I help you?
You Grüße zurück und sag, dass du gestern eine Katze gefunden hast.
RSPCA Oh, OK. Can you give me your name, address and telephone number, please.
You Gib deinen Namen an. Sag, dass du im Urlaub in England bist.
RSPCA That's all right. Now what colour is the cat?
You Beantworte die Frage.
RSPCA Can you say how old the cat is?
You Schätze das Alter.
RSPCA OK. Now when did you find the cat?
You Sag, gestern Abend etwa um 21.00 Uhr.
RSPCA OK. And where?
You Sag, unter eurem Wohnwagen.
RSPCA All right, dear. Now, what would you like to do with the cat?
You Frag, ob ihr sie zur RSPCA bringen könnt.
RSPCA Yes, of course you can.

El's best friend

Look at the pictures and scan the text on p. 54. Who is El's 'best friend'?

▸ *SF Scanning (p. 126)*

Everybody called the four girls the Black Angels. They looked dangerous, but they weren't – they were OK. El was the youngest in the group. She was 12, but she looked older.

At their school in London, the Black Angels were always together – nobody bullied them! 'And if somebody tries to bully one of the little kids,' they said, 'we'll be there to help them.' At home El's best friend was her dog Scruffy. When her parents argued (and they argued a lot) she went to her room with Scruffy, and told him all her problems.

One day El came home from school and found two big suitcases in the hall. When she went to her bedroom her mother was there with a third suitcase.
'Quick, pack your things,' her mum said. 'We're leaving.'
'Leaving?' El didn't understand.
'Yes, I'm leaving your father! We'll go and stay with my friend Milly in Bristol. We'll find a flat there and a new school.'
'But what about my friends? What about Scruffy ... and Dad?'
'You'll find lots of new friends, dear. And Scruffy can come when we've got our own place.'
'I don't want new friends, I want my old friends,' El said angrily. 'And I don't want to ...'
'Just get your things, El. The train leaves in an hour.'
Her mum left the room. El sat down on the bed. Scruffy jumped up and sat next to her. She looked at him sadly.
'Oh, Scruffy, I'll miss you so much. But I'll come and get you, I promise.'

Tuesday, 27th November

Dear Dad

I hate the new school – it's full of boring kids – all neat and tidy in their school uniforms. I really want Scruffy – I need Scruffy! Please, please bring him to us.

Love
El

Hi, sweetheart!

I had to move out of our flat. I've got a nice room, but I'm afraid I can't have a pet. So I had to take Scruffy to Battersea Dogs Home. I'm sure he'll be OK there.
Sorry, sweetheart.
I'll write again soon.
Love
Dad

'Battersea Dogs Home?' thought El. 'But that's where people go when they want to give a dog a new home. Maybe somebody will want Scruffy – and then I'll never see him again! I have to save him. I'll call dad! He has to help me!'

What do you think El will do?

It was 5.30 in the morning. El's mum and her friend Milly were still asleep. But El had planned everything with her dad. She already had the return ticket. 'I'll need £4.90 for a travelcard in London,' El said and counted her money.
'Oh dear! I've only got £4.'
El looked in her jacket ... another 45p ... and in her jeans pocket she found another 50p. She left the house and closed the door very quietly.

On the trip back to Bristol, Scruffy was very good. He sat quietly at El's feet. When they got off the train at Temple Meads Station, he was really happy.
'Come on, Scruffy,' said El. 'I haven't got any more money, so we'll have to walk home.'
And so they started the long walk. After about 45 minutes they were near Milly's house. Suddenly El heard somebody call.
'Hey, Lesley!'
El turned. It was Jack from her new school.
'So you're a dog person, Lesley. I didn't know that.'
She smiled at Jack.
'Yes, I love dogs. This is my dog Scruffy.'
'Hello Scruffy,' said Jack. 'That's a nice name.'
El said shyly, 'In London all my friends called me El.'
'That's nice too. Can I call you El?' asked Jack.
'OK,' said Lesley.

Working with the text

1 The story in two sentences

Which sentences match the first part of the story (ll. 1–36) best?

1 When El and her mum came to Bristol, El tried to find new friends. She left her dog Scruffy with the Black Angels.
2 El's mum and dad argued a lot, so El and her mum moved to Bristol. She was sad because she had to leave her dog Scruffy in London.
3 El and her mum moved to Bristol. El hated it and went back to London to live with her dad and Scruffy.

2 The story in parts

a) *Match the titles to the parts of the story:*

1	ll. 1–8	El and the new school
2	ll. 9–12	Scruffy with El's dad
3	ll. 13–31	The Black Angels
4	ll. 32–36	Scruffy, El's best friend
5	letter 1	Leaving El's dad
6	letter 2	Goodbye Scruffy

b) **Extra** *Find titles for these parts of the story:*
ll. 37–41; ll. 42–51; ll. 52–59; ll. 60–71

3 How El felt

Find at least one part of the story when El felt:

afraid • angry • happy • sad

I think El felt afraid when she ...

4 Extra That evening

What will happen when El gets back to her mum? Do a) or b).

a) *Write a short dialogue.*

Mum ___ *Where were you?*
El ___ *In London, Mum. I'm sorry.*

b) *Write Lesley's diary page for the day.*

Checkpoint 3 ► *WB (p. 41)*

Extra Animal songs and poems

Read, listen to and enjoy these animal songs and poems. Then choose one task.

1 SONG I know an old lady who swallowed a fly

I know an old lady who swallowed a fly.
I don't know why she swallowed the fly –
Perhaps she'll die.

I know an old lady who swallowed a spider
That wriggled and jiggled and tickled inside her.
She swallowed the spider to catch the fly.
But I don't know why she swallowed the fly –
Perhaps she'll die.

I know an old lady who swallowed a bird.
How absurd – to swallow a bird.
She swallowed the bird to catch the spider
That wriggled and jiggled and tickled inside her.
She swallowed the spider to catch the fly.
But I don't know why she swallowed the fly –
Perhaps she'll die.

I know an old lady who swallowed a cat.
Imagine that. She swallowed a cat.
She swallowed the cat to catch the bird.
She swallowed the bird to catch the spider
That wriggled and jiggled and tickled inside her.
She swallowed the spider to catch the fly.
But I don't know why she swallowed the fly –
Perhaps she'll die.

I know an old lady who swallowed a dog.
What a hog! To swallow a dog!
She swallowed the dog to catch the cat.
She swallowed the cat to catch the bird.
...

I know an old lady who swallowed a goat.
Opened her throat and down went the goat!
She swallowed the goat to catch the dog.
She swallowed the dog to catch the cat.
...

I know an old lady who swallowed a horse –
She's dead of course!

by Rosemary Bedeau, Alan Mills

> *The old lady in the song swallowed the spider to catch the fly. Write one more verse for the song with a new animal.*

... who swallowed a duck | ... a fox

... a mouse | ... a mole

Oh how yuck, she swallowed a duck!

... she went in the house

... she opened a box

... she looked in a hole

2 POEM The frog on the log

There once
Was a green
Little frog, frog, frog –

Who played
In the wood
On a log, log, log!

A screech owl
Sitting
In a tree, tree, tree –

Came after
The frog
With a scree, scree, scree!

When the frog
Heard the owl –
In a flash, flash, flash –

He leaped
In the pond
With a splash, splash, splash

by Ilo Orleans

*Partner A: learn the green verses.
Partner B: learn the brown verses.
Act out the poem for the class. Which pair is best?*

3 POEM The song of a mole

All I did this afternoon was
Dig, dig, dig,
And all I'll do tomorrow will be
Dig, dig, dig,
And yesterday from dusk till dawn
I dug, dug, dug.
I sometimes think I'd rather be
A slug, slug, slug.

by Richard Edwards

Think of more verbs like 'dig' – there are some ideas in the box below. Then write your own poem. You can put another animal at the end. (It doesn't have to rhyme.)

drink/drank • fly/... • read/... • ride/... • sing/... • sit/... • write/...

All I did this afternoon was
Write, write, write.
And all I'll do tomorrow will be
Write, write, write
And yesterday from dusk till dawn
I wrote, wrote, wrote.
I sometimes think I'd rather be
A goat, goat, goat.

A weekend in Wales

1 Talking about your weekends

What do you like to do at the weekend?

I like to go …

to a park • for a walk • shopping in town • to the country • to the sea • to the mountains • to my grandparents' house • on trips • swimming • to a football match • …

… at the weekend.

I usually go by car/train/bus/bike.

2 Dan and Jo's trip to Wales

a) *Describe the photos. The words in the box can help you. Look up the words if you don't know them.*

beautiful • church • cinema • clean • cow • dirty • factory • farm • field • forest • green • hill • horse • house • people • traffic • noisy • quiet • river • sheep • shop • train station • tree • valley • village

b) Listen to Dan and Jo. They're going to their grandparents' new house in Wales. Match the dialogues A, B, C and D to the photos.

c) Choose one caption for each photo. Then listen again and check.

New country, new language!
Have you got your pyjamas?
Welcome to Crickhowell.
Towns all look the same!

3 Extra Town and country

What can you see or do in a town? And in the country? Which do you like better? Why?

There are lots of shops in towns. You can go shopping. That's fun.

I don't like shopping. I like animals. You can see lots of farms and animals in the country.

I like …

▸ SF Describing pictures (p. 123) • P1 (p. 64) • WB 1–2 (p. 42)

1 Friday dinner

It was late when the twins and their grandparents got to Crickhowell. 'Grandpa will show you your room, boys,' Grandma said. 'Dinner will be on the table in a few minutes.'
'It smells great,' Jo said when they came into the kitchen. 'What are you cooking?'
'Cawl mamgu,' Grandma answered. 'That's Welsh for "Granny's soup".'

'You're very quiet, Daniel,' Grandpa Thompson said. 'Are you all right?'
'Yes, I'm fine.'
'That's good,' Grandpa Thompson said. 'Because we're planning a trip to the Brecon Beacons in the morning. We want to go on the Brecon Mountain Railway. And we can have a picnic near Caerphilly Castle in the afternoon.'

▸ *GF 8: Word order (p. 141) • P 2–4 (pp. 64–65) • WB 3 (p. 43)*

What is it?
Crickhowell • Cawl mamgu • Caerphilly Castle

A

B

C

2 Tomorrow's plans

Famous WELSH sights

CAERPHILLY CASTLE
WALES

There are lots of reasons to visit **CAERPHILLY CASTLE**. It's one of the biggest castles in Europe. It has a famous **leaning tower**. It leans more than the Leaning Tower of Pisa! And the castle even has its own ghost – the Green Lady.

STUDY SKILLS Topic sentence

*In jedem Absatz (Englisch: **paragraph**) steckt ein Satz, der sagt, worum es in dem Absatz geht. Meistens ist das der erste Satz. Man nennt ihn **topic sentence**. Alle anderen Sätze geben weitere Informationen.*
*Nenne den **topic sentence** in dem Prospekt für Caerphilly Castle.*

3 Brecon Mountain Railway

Find the topic sentence. Then put it at the beginning to make a good paragraph.

It goes through beautiful mountains – the Brecon Beacons. From the train you have a fantastic view of the valley. Brecon Mountain Railway is one of the finest railways in Wales.

▸ *SF Topic sentence (p. 129) • P 5 (p. 65) • WB 4 (p. 44)*

4 Saturday morning

Grandma Daniel! Jonah! Breakfast is ready! I've cooked bacon and eggs for you. And Grandpa has already packed the picnic. Hurry up!

Grandpa It's OK, dear. I've checked the timetable. The first train is at 11.00 and the next one is at 12.15. Oh look, here's Gwyneth.

5 GAME I've packed my school bag

Play this game. Use ideas from the box.

- pack – my bag, the picnic, a suitcase
- wash – the car, my hair, the dog
- clean – the cage, my room, the board
- finish – my homework, my essay, my picture

A: I've packed my bag and now I can watch TV.
B: I've packed my bag and I've washed the car and now I can watch TV.
C: I've packed my bag and I've washed the car and I've ...

6 A visit from the neighbours

Gwyneth Bore da!
Grandma Bore da, Gwyneth! Hello, Emma.
Emma Look. We've just made this pie. It's for the twins.
Grandma Thank you, Emma. It smells great!
Emma But we haven't seen the twins yet.
Grandma Well, here's one twin now. Jonah, say hello to Emma and her mum. They're our neighbours.
Jo Hello ... er, sorry, Grandma, Dan hasn't come down because he doesn't feel well. Can you come up?
Grandma Oh, I'm sorry, Emma. See you later.

Right or wrong?

1 Grandma has made a pie.
2 Dan and Jo have had breakfast.
3 Emma has seen Dan.

Extra Background File

Croeso i Gymru!
That means 'Welcome to Wales' – in Welsh. And this is the Welsh flag. About 3 million people live in Wales. The capital of Wales is Cardiff. One in five people in Wales speaks Welsh at home. All school children in Wales learn Welsh as their first or second language.

► P 6 (p. 65)

Looking at language

What have they done? Grandma says:
I've cooked bacon and eggs for you.
(Deutsch: Ich habe für euch ... zubereitet.)

*Find other sentences with have or has from **4** and **6**. Underline the new form.*
Which verb does the new form come from?
I've cooked your breakfast. -> to cook

► GF 9, 10 a–b, 11: Present perfect (pp. 142–144) • P 7–11 (pp. 66–67) • WB 5–8 (pp. 45–47)

7 Poor Dan

'What's the matter, dear?' Grandma asked.
'I feel awful, Grandma,' said Dan. 'I have a terrible headache.'
'You look very hot.' Grandma touched Dan's face. 'I think you have a temperature too. Here, put the thermometer in your mouth. Do you have a sore throat?'
Dan nodded.
'Move your arms and legs. Do they hurt?'
Dan nodded.
'Oh dear,' said Grandma. 'Maybe Bryn can look at you later.'
'Who?' Jo asked.
'Bryn Evans, our neighbour, Emma's dad. He's a paramedic.'

*How many parts of the body can you find in **7**? Do you know more words for parts of the body?*

8 What's the matter?

a) *Say what's the matter with the boy in the pictures. Take turns. Use the words in the box.*

He has a cold. • He has an earache • He has a headache. • He has a stomach ache. • He has a temperature. • He has a toothache.

1

2

3

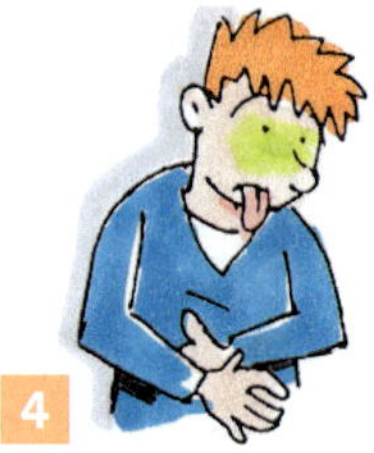
4

5

6

b) **Extra** *One student mimes something – a headache, a toothache, … The others guess what's the matter.*

A: Do you have a cold?
B: No, that's wrong.
C: Do you have a headache?
B: Yes, that's right. Your turn.

9 Extra Can you move your …?

Imagine you've fallen over your neighbour's dog. Your neighbour comes to help you. Listen to her. Move and bend and stretch when she tells you.

► *P 12–13 (p. 68) • WB 9 (p. 47)*

10 Grandma's new software

Grandma — Jonah, have you ever installed software?
Jo — Yes, of course I have, Grandma.
Grandma — Well, I'd like to try this photo software. Can you install it for me?
Jo — Sure, Grandma. No problem. I use that software for my photos too.
Grandma — Oh good. I've already read the instructions. It says here: 'Click on SETUP.' Have you done that, dear?
Jo — Yes, I have, Grandma.
Grandma — Good. Then it says: 'Read the instructions. Click on YES.' Have you done that?
Jo — Yes, I have, Grandma.

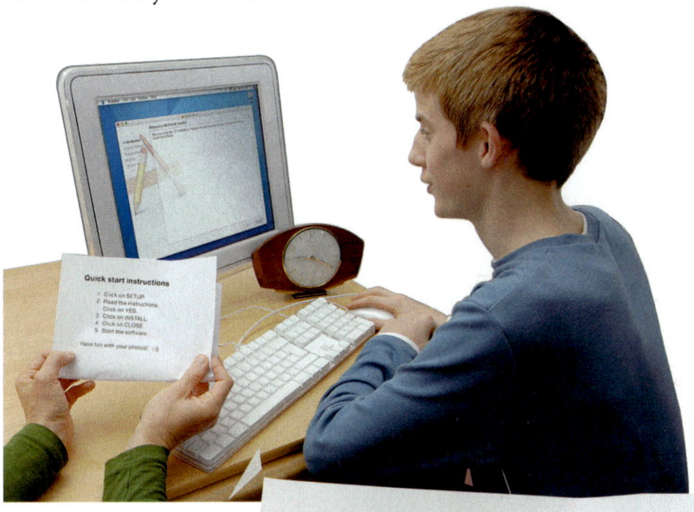

Go on with the dialogue. Use numbers 3–5 on the right.

Grandma — Good. Then it says: 'Click on ... ' Have you ...?
Jo — Yes, I ...
...
Jo — Yes, I have, Grandma. And by the way –
Grandma — Yes, dear?
Jo — There's an e-mail from Mum.

Quick start instructions

1 Click on SETUP.
2 Read the instructions. Click on YES.
3 Click on INSTALL.
4 Click on CLOSE.
5 Start the software.

Have fun with your photos! :-))

▸ GF 10c, 11: Present perfect – questions (p. 143) • P 14–15 (p. 68) • WB 10 (p. 48)

11 An e-mail from New Zealand

Hello Mum!
How are you? Have the boys arrived yet? How are they?
Love Cath

Who is 'Mum' in this e-mail? And who is Cath?

Dear Mum
It's me – Jo! Yes, we've arrived in Wales. Grandma and Grandpa are fine and their new house is cool :-)
But we can't go out because Dan is ill :-((
Love from Jo

Who is 'Mum' in this e-mail?

Hi Jo!
Mum, is Dan OK? Has he been to the doctor?

Who is 'Mum' in this e-mail? Who is the mail from?

Dear Catherine
Don't worry about Dan. It isn't that bad. He'll be fine tomorrow.

Who is this e-mail to? Who is it from?

▸ P 16–17 (p. 69) • WB 11–18 (pp. 48–52)

1 WORDS Travel

a) *Match the words to the sentences.*

bike • boat • bridge • bus • plane • road • station • train

1 Lots of kids take this to school everyday.
bus
2 You ride this to school or in your free time.
3 Cars travel on this between towns.
4 Trains stop here.
5 Cars and people go over a river on this.
6 If you go to an island, you can travel on this.
7 You can fly to New York on this.
8 It travels from one station to another, usually from town to town.

b) *Copy and complete the networks.*

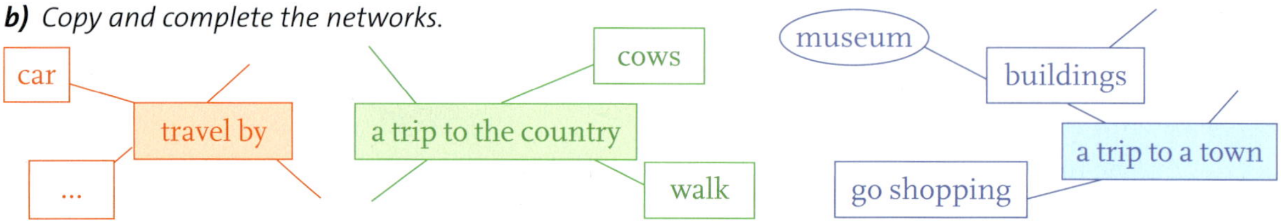

2 REVISION I can't go because … (Word order in subordinate clauses)

Finish the sentences. Use the words in brackets. Remember: S – V – O (subject – verb – object).

1 My dad always has a shower after … (he / sport / does)
My dad always has a shower after he does sport.
2 I have to finish my homework before … (TV / watch / I)
3 My mum gets angry with me when … (I / my homework / don't do)
4 I like English lessons because … (are / fun / the lessons)
5 I'll do well in my English test if … (more words / I / learn)
6 I'm always nervous when … (we / a test / have)

3 Where will they be tomorrow? (Word order: Place before time)

a) *Say where they'll be tomorrow morning, tomorrow afternoon or tomorrow evening.*

1 *afternoon* 2 *evening* 3 *morning* 4 *afternoon* 5 *evening*

I think Dan and Jo will be at Caerphilly Castle tomorrow afternoon. I think Ananda …

b) **Extra** *Write five sentences about where you'll be when.*

I'm sure	*I'll be*	*at home*	*on Friday*	*morning.*
I think		*at school*	*on Saturday*	*afternoon.*
		at football training	*tomorrow*	*evening.*
		at my friend's house	*at the weekend.*	

4 PRONUNCIATION Silent letters

In some English words you don't pronounce all the letters – they are silent.

a) *Read the words quietly. Then write them in your exercise book. Underline the silent letters.*

castle, two, knee, talk, know, write, would, climb, wrong, calm, sandwich, answer, half, who, could, walk, Christmas

b) *Check with your partner.*

c) *Listen and say the words.*

d) *Read the following sentences out loud:*

1 What's wrong with your knee?
2 Do you know the answer? Write it down.
3 Would you like to go for a walk to the castle?
4 Calm down! It's only half past two.

5 STUDY SKILLS Topic sentence

Find the topic sentence. Then put it at the beginning to make a good paragraph.

Big Pit Museum

It was a real coal mine till 1980. The *Big Pit* is a very special museum. A lot of the museum workers worked there when it was a coal mine.

Cardiff Castle

Each room is different, and the gardens are beautiful too. Cardiff Castle is one of the most famous sights of Wales. After your visit you can have tea in the Castle Tea Rooms.

DOSSIER *A special place*

Write a short paragraph about a place you like. Start with a topic sentence:
There are lots of reasons to visit (Berlin/Heidelberg/Friedewald/...).
Add two or three sentences. Add a photo if you have one.
It's a great place/a beautiful old village/...
You can see lots of things there. For example, ...

Extra *Read your paragraph to the class.*

6 LISTENING Accents

a) *Listen to four different people. Say where they are from: London, Scotland, Wales or the West Country.*

b) *Listen again. Are these sentences true?*

1 **A** Gwyneth can't speak English.
B She lives near Jo and Dan's grandparents.

2 **A** Thomas lives in Bristol.
B He doesn't like London.

3 **A** Angus lives on an island.
B He likes whisky.

4 **A** Caroline says she lives in a fantastic city.
B She doesn't like the river.

c) **Extra** *Correct the wrong sentences.*

► *SF Listening (p. 125)*

//○ 7 Mr Shaw has painted the kitchen door (Present perfect: regular verbs) ▸ D p. 115

1

2

3

4

5

6

7

8

a) *Make sentence about the pictures. Match the correct sentence parts.*

1 Mr Shaw has ...
2 The twins have ...
3 Jack has ...
4 Mr Kingsley has ...
5 The Kapoors have ...
6 Ananda and Sophie have ...
7 The Thompsons have ...
8 Prunella has ...

... watched a DVD. | ... dropped the plates. | ... painted the kitchen door. | ... tidied his desk. | ... finished his book. | ... counted the money. | ... cooked lunch. | ... packed their suitcases.

● **b)** *Match a sentence from a) to a sentence from the box.*

Now they can go up to the flat. • He really likes the new colour. • They're ready to go to the station. • The Carter-Browns will need new ones. • Today they're having chicken and chips. • Now he can go to bed. • Now he can find everything again. • They liked it a lot.

1 *Mr Shaw has painted the kitchen door. He really likes the new colour.*
2 *The twins have ...*

//○ 8 Grandma has made breakfast, so ... (Present perfect: irregular verbs) ▸ D p. 116

Put the verbs in the present perfect. Use the irregular forms in the box.

been (2x) • come • gone • made • seen • taken

1 Grandma ... (make) breakfast, so they can leave soon.
Grandma *has made* breakfast, so they can leave soon.
2 Jo ... (take) lots of photos because he wants to mail them to his mum.
3 Grandpa ... (go) out to the car because he wants to clean it.
4 Ananda and Jack ... (be) to the cinema and now they're sitting in a café.
5 Sophie ... (be) ill, so now she has to do lots of homework.
6 We ... (come) to see you today because we can't come to your party tomorrow.
7 I ... (see) the new film but I don't like it.

9 Mr and Mrs Kapoor make a list (Present perfect: negative sentences)

Complete the dialogue. Use haven't or hasn't and the correct form of the verbs in brackets.

Mr K   Let's go for a walk. It's a beautiful day.
Mrs K   But the children will be back soon and we ... (make) dinner.
Mr K   Ananda can do it. She likes cooking.
Mrs K   And we ... (change) the fruit prices.
Mr K   Don't worry. We can do that later.
Mrs K   And you ... (paint) the kitchen shelf. Why?
Mr K   Don't worry. I can do that tomorrow.

Mrs K   And what about the shop windows? I ... (clean) them.
Mr K   Maybe Dilip can do that too.
Mrs K   OK, OK. I'll make a list of jobs. Let's see – Ananda ... (tidy) her room.
Mr K   And Dilip's room is a mess too.
Mrs K   Look! They ... (make) their beds.
Mr K   And Dilip ... (take) out the rubbish.
Mrs K   Any other jobs?

10 They've already made their beds (Present perfect: already and not yet)

Mr and Mrs Kapoor are out, and Ananda and Dilip have lots of jobs.

a) *Say what they've already done.*
– Ananda and Dilip have already made their beds.
– Ananda has already ...
– Dilip has ...

b) *Now say what they haven't done yet.*
– Ananda and Dilip haven't tidied their rooms yet.
– Dilip ... yet.

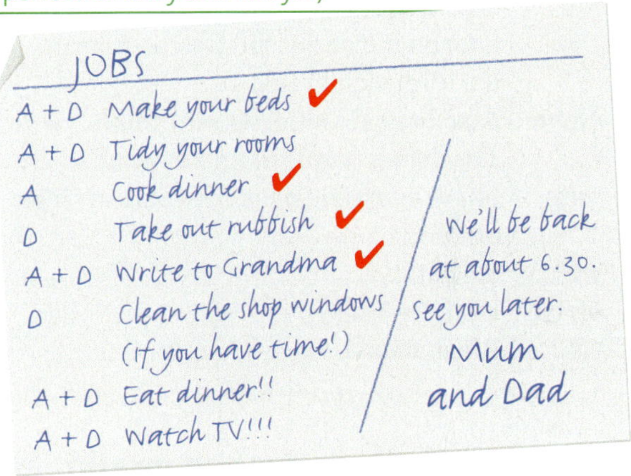

JOBS
A + D Make your beds ✔
A + D Tidy your rooms
A   Cook dinner ✔
D   Take out rubbish ✔
A + D Write to Grandma ✔
D   Clean the shop windows (if you have time!)
A + D Eat dinner!!
A + D Watch TV!!!

We'll be back at about 6.30. see you later.
Mum and Dad

11 👥 What's different? (Present perfect: just)

Partner B: Go to p. 110.
Partner A: Tell your partner about the people in the picture.
Ask about his/her picture. Take turns. Use ideas from the box.
A: In my picture Sophie has just made popcorn. What about your picture?
B: In my picture Sophie has just ... So our pictures are the same/different.

1 Sophie – make
2 Ananda – open
3 Dan – eat
4 Jo – take
5 Jack – drop
6 Prunella – find

12 WORDS The body

*Draw a **word body**. Use words from the box.*

arm • ear • eye • finger • foot • hair • hand • head • knee • leg • mouth • nose • shoulder • toe • tooth

13 MEDIATION Phoning a doctor

Imagine you've got an English guest, Sally, in your home. She feels ill, so you phone the doctor for her.

You — Guten Morgen, Frau Dr. Becker. Wir haben eine englische Gastschülerin. Sie fühlt sich krank.
Ärztin — Aha. Frag sie bitte, was ihr fehlt.
You — The doctor wants to know: what's …?
Sally — I have a terrible headache and my legs hurt.
You — Sie hat …
Ärztin — Und der Hals?
You — What about your …?
Sally — Well, I have a sore throat.
You — …
Ärztin — Hat sie auch Fieber?
You — And have you got …?
Sally — Yes, I think so.
You — …
Ärztin — Ich möchte sie sehen. Kann sie heute Nachmittag bei mir vorbeikommen?
You — Ja, das geht. Danke, Frau Dr. Becker. – Sally, she wants …

//○ 14 Have you done your homework? (Present perfect: questions) ▸ D p. 116

Jack is talking to his mother. Make questions. Use the words in brackets.

1 Mrs H — *Have you done* (you/have/done) your homework, Jack?
Jack — Yes, I have, Mum.

2 Mrs H — And … (Dan and Jo/finished/ have) that project yet?
Jack — No, they haven't.

3 Jack — What about dinner? … (cooked/dad/has) it yet?
Mrs H — No, he hasn't.

4 Jack — Well, … (you/have/read) Aunt Jenny's letter yet?
Mrs H — Yes, I have.

5 Jack — And … (fed/you/have) Polly?
Polly — No, she hasn't. Hurry up! Hurry up!

15 GAME Have you …? (Present perfect: questions)

***a)** Four students leave the room. The others change four things. For example, they open a window, write something on the board, move a bag, …*
Look at the box for help.

close • eat • move • open • put • take away • write

***b)** The four students come back in. They ask questions to find out what has changed.*

A: Have you opened the cupboard?
Class: No, we haven't.
B: Have you written on the board?
Class: Yes, we have. One point.

16 Extra WRITING Jo's e-mail

Dear Mum
Here are some photos of our weekend in Wales and a short report. I hope you can open them!
Love Jo

There are three sentences for each photo. Put them in the right order. Remember! Put the topic sentence first.

He had to stay in bed.
Dan was ill for most of our visit.
We visited Grandma and Grandpa at the weekend.

Poor Grandma and Dan had to stay at home.
We went to the Brecon Mountain Railway!
On Saturday afternoon I went out with Grandpa.

He wants to go back again soon. Me too.
We had to go back to Bristol on Sunday afternoon.
Dan felt better, but he still didn't feel well.

Dan ill.jpg

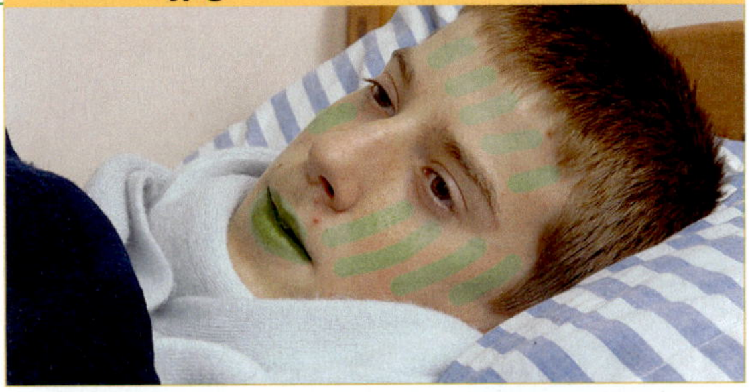

Brecon Beacons.jpg

Goodbye Crickhowell.jpg

DOSSIER ***Last weekend***

Write about your last weekend trip. Did you visit family or friends? Did you go to a town or the country? Think of good topic sentences.

▸ *SF Topic sentence (p. 129)*

17 GETTING BY IN ENGLISH How are you?

a) *Can you say these things in English?*

1 Ist bei dir alles in Ordnung? (p. 60)
2 Bis später. (p. 61)
3 Was fehlt dir? (p. 62)
4 Ich fühle mich schrecklich. (p. 62)
5 Ich habe Kopfschmerzen. (p. 62)
6 Oh je! (p. 62)
7 War er beim Arzt? (p. 63)
8 So schlimm ist es nicht. (p. 63)

b) *Partner A calls Sam, because he/she wasn't at school today. Prepare a dialogue. Then act it out.*

Partner A

Grüß Sam und frag, ob alles in Ordnung ist.

Partner B

Sag nein, du fühlst dich furchtbar.

Partner A

Frag, was ihr/ihm fehlt.

Partner B

Sag, du hast Ohrenschmerzen.

Partner A

Sag, oh je! Warst du schon beim Arzt?

Partner B

Sag, so schlimm ist es nicht. Du wirst morgen in der Schule sein.

Partner A

Sag, bis morgen.

All in a day's work

> *Look at the title and the pictures. What do you think the story is about?*

▸ *SF Understanding new words (p. 122)*

Bryn hated his mobile. It always rang when he was really tired – like this morning. He looked at the clock. It was 6.25.

'Morning, Bryn. Elaine here. We need you on the road to Tredegar – there has been a car accident. It's quite bad.'
Bryn put on his uniform and was in his car in four minutes. 'If Elaine says it's quite bad, it'll be very bad,' Bryn thought.
When Bryn got to the accident, he saw a red car on its side. Two policemen were with the driver, and Bryn could see that he wasn't hurt badly.
'They didn't call me for this,' he thought.
'Are you the paramedic?' It was one of the firemen. 'We've got a car down there.'
He pointed to the side of the hill. 'They need a paramedic down there – fast.'

Bryn followed the fireman. He could see that the car was in some trees about ten metres down. It was another 70 or 80 metres to the bottom.
'This is Beth. She'll go down with you,' the fireman told him.
'Hi,' said Beth. 'Are you ready?'
'I'm ready if you are,' he answered.
Bryn and Beth quickly climbed down to the car. There they found four very scared people:

a man, a woman and two children. 'We're here to help you,' Beth said. 'Is everybody OK?'
The man had a broken leg, but the others were fine. The trees were the problem. They weren't strong enough. Bryn and Beth had to work quickly.

Bryn worked on the man, and Beth started with the children. She took the little boy up the hill, then the girl. Then she came back for the woman.

'Beth,' Bryn said from the other side of the car, 'take her up fast. Then ...'

But before he could finish his sentence, the car started to fall. It stopped after three metres. When Beth and Bryn got to the car again, the man was unconscious. The woman didn't want to leave her husband, but Beth said, 'Think of the children. They need you.'

'The rescue helicopter is coming,' Beth said when she got back to Bryn and the man. 'Let's get him out and get him to hospital fast!'

'I'll have to go inside the car, Beth,' Bryn said. 'Or we won't get him out.'

'But, Bryn, with two people in the car ...' She didn't finish.

'I hope the trees will hold for just a few more minutes,' Bryn said.

Five minutes later the driver was out of the car. Bryn started to climb out. He had one foot in the tree when the car fell.

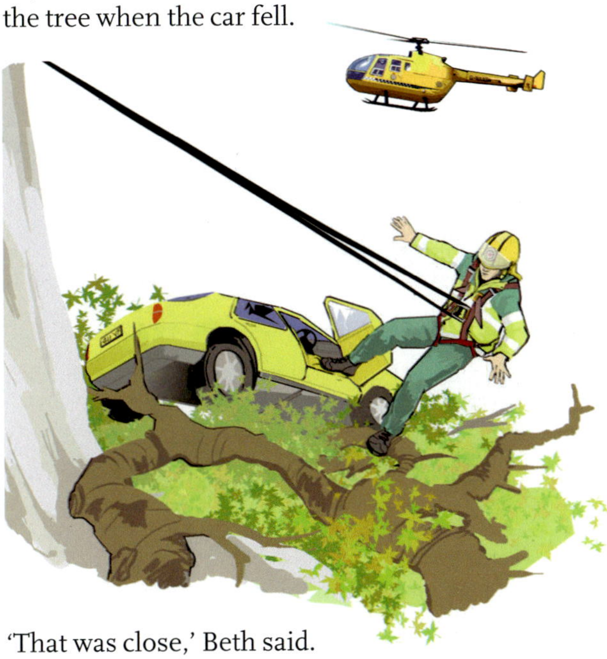

'That was close,' Beth said.

'Yeah,' said Bryn. 'Too close.'

That was just the start of Bryn's day. He got home at 5 pm – after one more car accident, a man with a broken arm, and a new baby. All in a day's work!

Working with the text

1 The rescue

Find seven mistakes in the picture.

The text says there is a red car on its side.
In the picture it's a blue car.
The text says there are two …

2 Extra Who said it?

Partner B: Go to p. 111.
Partner A: Test your partner and ask him/her who said these things.

1 'Morning, Bryn.' (Elaine: l. 4)
   A: Who said 'Morning, Bryn'?
   B: Elaine said it. It's in line …
2 'They need you.' (Beth: l. 50)
3 'I'll have to go inside the car.' (Bryn: l. 54)
4 'Yeah, too close.' (Bryn: l. 64)

Now listen to your partner's questions. Scan the text for the correct answers.

B: Who said 'They need a paramedic down there – fast.'
A: A fireman said it. It's in line/lines …

► *SF Scanning (p. 130)*

3 A radio report

a) *Prepare a 'live' radio report about the rescue. Look at lines 4 to 57. Answer these questions:*

– ***Where*** *are you?*
– ***What*** *can you see?*
– ***Who*** *can you see?*
– ***What*** *is happening now?*

Start like this:

This is … for Radio South Wales. I'm on the road to … There has been a terrible car …
I can see two cars. One car is on … The second car is in some trees about … metres down.
I can see a paramedic and a firewoman. They are climbing … Now they're talking to …
Now the firewoman is coming up with …
Now the paramedic has gone inside …
I'll have more for you in a few minutes.

b) **Extra** *Continue your report about the end of the rescue (ll. 58–68).*

Checkpoint 4 ► *WB (pp. 53–55)*

Extra Merlin and the dragons – or why the Welsh dragon is red

This story happened more than 1000 years ago. A Saxon army was in Wales and the king was worried. He called his wise men.

'You must build a strong castle on top of that mountain,' they said. The king liked the idea. But there was a problem. Every night the walls of the new castle fell down. Again the king called his wise men.

'Maybe the mountain is angry,' they said. 'You must give the mountain something.' 'What?' said the king. 'Blood. You need the blood of a special child, ... a child without a father.' 'OK,' the king said. 'Find me this child. But be quick. Or I will give the mountain your blood!'

The wise men found a boy and took him to the king. His name was Merlin. 'They say I must kill you,' the king said to the boy. 'What do you think?'

'Your wise men are wrong,' said Merlin. 'You don't need my blood. Look under the mountain. You will find a cave there. In the cave there are two dragons. One is a red Welsh dragon and the other is a white Saxon dragon. They're fighting. You must open the cave. The dragons must leave. Then you can build your castle.'

The king's men found the cave. They opened it and two terrible dragons flew out. One was red and one was white.

'Now you can build your castle,' said Merlin to the king. 'The dragons will fight for years and years. But don't worry. The red Welsh dragon will win in the end. And the Saxons will leave Wales.'

And that is why the Welsh dragon is red.

Teamwork

The Bristol game

Play the game in groups of four. You will need a dice and four counters. Use phrases from the box.

You can start. • Can I have the dice, please? • Great! I've got a six! • Whose turn is it? • It's my/your turn. • Hey, you had a three, not a four.

Bristol Tourist Information
Lots of good ideas for your time in Bristol!
Start here.

1 2 3

4

Explore-at-Bristol
This is an interesting museum. You learn about science here.
Move on one space.

5 6 7 8

Temple Meads Station
Stop and look at the station. Britain's greatest engineer, Brunel, built it.
Throw the dice again.

9 10 11 12

A pirate pub
You stop and look at this old pub (1664). Pirates drank here!
Miss a turn.

13 14 15

St Mary Redcliffe Church
You take a photo of this beautiful old church.
Move on one space.

16 17 18

Cotham School
You want to visit the school, but it's closed.
Move back two spaces.

19 20 21

St Nicholas Market
You have a healthy snack here.
Name two drinks.
Move on two spaces.

22 23 24 25 26 27

28

Pretty Polly B&B
You go back to your room and sleep.
Miss a turn.

29 30 31 32

47

British Empire and Commonwealth Museum
Many rich people in Bristol had land in the Caribbean.
Learn how slaves helped them to grow sugar and tobacco there.
Move on one space.

33

The Downs
You stop and sit in this beautiful park.
What do people do here?
Name two things.
Then move on two spaces.

34 35

36

Clifton Suspension Bridge
You walk over the River Avon on this famous bridge.
Move on three spaces.

37

River Avon
Oops! You've fallen into the water.
Sing a song in English or miss a turn.

38 39

40

Aardman Studios
You want to see where they make the Wallace and Gromit films, but they don't have tours.
Go back to Bristol Tourist Information!

41 42

43

Georgian House
The Pinney family lived here with their black slaves. Take the free tour.
Miss a turn.

44 45 46 47 48 49

50

Cabot Tower
Arrive here first, and you're the
winner!

▸ P 1–2 (p. 80) • WB 1–2 (p. 56)

1 Plans for the weekend

Mum What are you going to do this weekend?
Sophie I'm going to meet Ananda at the library on Saturday. We're going to do a quiz. Look.
Mum Mmm ... That looks fun. Are you going to make a brochure too?
Sophie Yes, we want to win the prize!
Mum Who is in your team?
Sophie Ananda and me. And I'm going to ask Jack and Dan. But I'm not going to ask Jo. He never wants to work. He just wants to take photos.
Mum He can take photos for your brochure then.
Sophie You're right, Mum. Our brochure is going to be great.

Who is Sophie going to have in her team?

BRISTOL

How well do you know your city? Do our Bristol quiz and find out!

- Put together a team of three or more people.
- Make a brochure. 'Our city: interesting people and places'
- **Win a great prize!**

For more details: Go to your local library or www.bristol-city.gov.uk/libraries

Looking at language

Sophie is talking to her mother about her plans for the weekend in **1**.
Find sentences with ***going to***.

What are you	going to	do	...?
I'm	going to	...	...
We're	...		
...			

How do you form the ***going to-future****?*

2 I'm going to play football

What are you going to do on Saturday afternoon? Talk to three partners.
A: I'm going to play football. What are you going to do?
B: I'm going to meet friends. / I'm going to play football too. / I'm ...

► *GF 12: going to-future (p. 145)* • *P 3–6 (pp. 81–82)* • *WB 3–5 (pp. 57–58)*

3 The quiz

The first questions of the quiz were quite easy.

BRISTOL

Question 1

You can find this **little monster** on a famous Bristol church. Which one?

BRISTOL

Question 2

It is **one of the oldest buildings** in Bristol (1664). Some bad people drank here. Who were they?

Can you answer these questions from the Bristol quiz? (Look at pp. 74–75 for help.)

4 Who is he?

The next Bristol quiz question was more difficult.

BRISTOL

Question 3

He did great things for Bristol. There's a statue of him outside a building near the station.

a) Who is he?
b) When did he live?
c) What things did he build in Bristol?
Find at least three.

▸ P 7–8 (pp. 82–83) • WB 6–7 (pp. 58–59)

'I've found out who it is,' said Jack. 'It's Brunel.'
'Of course,' said Dan. 'I'm sure he built the Clifton Suspension Bridge.'
'I think you're right,' said Sophie.
'I've heard that he built ships too,' said Ananda.
'Ships?' said Jo. 'I don't think you're right.'
'I think she's right,' said Sophie. 'But let's find out.'

Which questions have they already answered – 3a, 3b or 3c?

5 Brunel – Bristol's engineer

Sophie found this text and copied it.

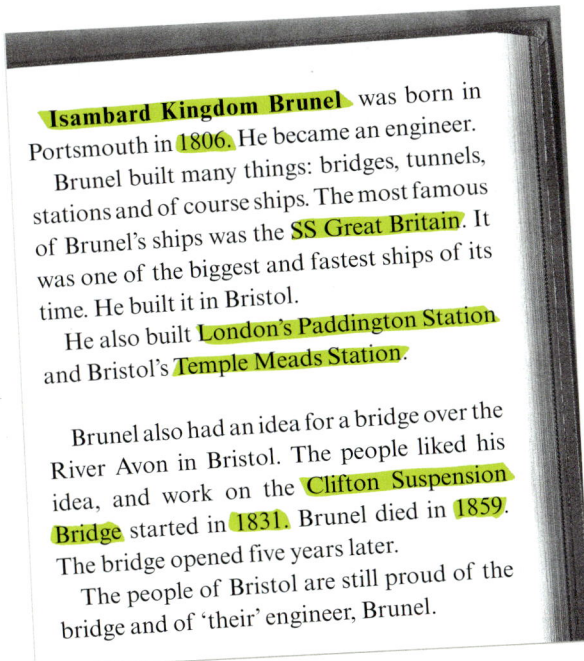

Isambard Kingdom Brunel was born in Portsmouth in 1806. He became an engineer.
Brunel built many things: bridges, tunnels, stations and of course ships. The most famous of Brunel's ships was the SS Great Britain. It was one of the biggest and fastest ships of its time. He built it in Bristol.
He also built London's Paddington Station and Bristol's Temple Meads Station.

Brunel also had an idea for a bridge over the River Avon in Bristol. The people liked his idea, and work on the Clifton Suspension Bridge started in 1831. Brunel died in 1859. The bridge opened five years later.
The people of Bristol are still proud of the bridge and of 'their' engineer, Brunel.

Sophie has marked too many facts here. She doesn't need two of them. Which two?

STUDY SKILLS **Marking up a text**

Wenn du einen Text mit vielen Fakten liest, wird es dir helfen, nur die für dich wichtigen Informationen zu markieren.

▸ SF Marking up a text (p. 127) • P 9 (p. 83) • WB 8 (p. 60)

6 Extra Project: ideas for your brochure (1) People and places

a) Think: *Think about your area. Make a list of interesting people and places.*

b) Pair: *Agree on one person or place with your partner.*
... was on TV/in the paper
... is famous/fun/very old
... is interesting for kids/tourists
You can see lots of ... there.
Let's take ... / What about ...? / Good idea.

c) Share: *Agree on one person or place with your group. Collect material about your person or place.*

7 Time for a break

The team went to St Nicholas Market to find an answer to the next question.

Question 4

You are in the centre of Bristol. Where can you get **a healthy and delicious snack**?

1
That's a hard question. Healthy and delicious?! That's impossible!
You're joking, aren't you? Of course it's possible.

2
This juice bar is a good place, isn't it?
It looks pretty healthy.

MENU Smoothies

apple	£1.55
banana	£1.25
kiwi	£1.55
strawberry	£1.55
cherry-banana	£2.05

3
How can I help you?
I'd like a smoothie, please.
What sort?
Strawberry, please.

4
The drinks are good, aren't they, Jo?
Yeah, healthy and delicious.
Delicious? You haven't tried the wheatgrass juice!

Extra ▸ *GF 13: Question tags (p. 146) • P 10 (p. 84) • WB 9 (p. 60)*

8 A role play – customer and waiter

a) *Who says what at the juice bar?*

What sort?
That's £..., please.
Can I have ..., please?
Here you are.
Small, medium or large?
How can I help you?
I'd like ..., please.
Have you got ...?

b) *Prepare a dialogue at a juice bar/an ice-cream place. Use some of these phrases. Act it out.*

▸ *P 11 (p. 84) • WB 10–11 (p. 61)*

9 Extra Project: ideas for your brochure (2) Time for a break

a) Think: *Where can you go for a break in your area (a park, an ice-cream place, a juice bar, ...)?*

b) Pair: *Agree on one place with your partner. Why is it a good place?*

You can get great ... there.
There are lots of different smoothies/...
The people are friendly.
It's pretty cheap there.
It's a good place for a picnic.

c) Share: *Agree on one place with your group. Collect material and/or take photos.*

10 The brochure

Ananda and Sophie wanted to write about Bristol pirates for the team's brochure.
'OK, we've got a title and we've got a good beginning. We've got something about the harbour. What next?' said Sophie.
'Let's write about Blackbeard,' said Ananda. 'I think he's the most famous Bristol pirate. Look at your notes.'
'Good idea. We have a picture of him too.'
Sophie thought for a minute and wrote something down.
'What do you think of that?' she asked.
'Great,' said Ananda. 'Now we need a nice end.'
'We can put in a photo of that pirate pub. Jo took one,' said Sophie.
'Let's see. What can we write?' Ananda said.
She added two more sentences.
'That's great, Ananda,' said Sophie. 'I think we're going to win that prize!'

A There aren't any pirates in Bristol today. But you can see this famous pirate pub.

B Bristol was an important harbour. There were lots of sailors there, and some famous pirates too.

C Blackbeard was probably the most famous Bristol pirate. He was born in Bristol in 1677.

D Bristol Pirates

Put Sophie and Ananda's text in the right order.

STUDY SKILLS Structuring a text

Wenn du einen Text schreibst, solltest du ihn gliedern:
***Beginning** (Einleitung)*
***Middle** (Mittelteil)*
***End** (Schluss).*

► SF Structuring a text (p. 129) • P 12 (p. 84) • WB 12 (p. 62)

11 Extra Project (3) Make your brochure

- *Make a page for a class brochure about your area. Write about a place, a person or a place for a break.*
- *Write at least five sentences.*
- *Structure your texts.*
- *Use your notes, photos and other material.*
- *Make the pages on a computer or write out your texts and add your material.*

You can get really good ... there.
... is a really nice place to visit.
... is probably the most famous person from ...
This is a picture of ...
It's very old/modern/...
The people are really friendly too.
You can see a statue of ...
... built/helped people/wrote books/...
You can find out more about ... in the library.
The best one is ...
If you need a break/a snack/..., go to ...
... was born in ...
It's a great place for ... too.

Which phrases can you use to talk about a place, a person or a place for a break?

► P 13–14 (p. 85) • WB 13–15 (pp. 62–63)

1 WORDS In Bristol

a) *Make a Bristol mind map. Use the ideas in the box.*

Explore-at-Bristol • a church • Clifton Suspension Bridge • the Downs • Bristol Tourist Information • Georgian House • Empire and Commonwealth Museum • a pirate pub • Cabot Tower • St Nicholas Market

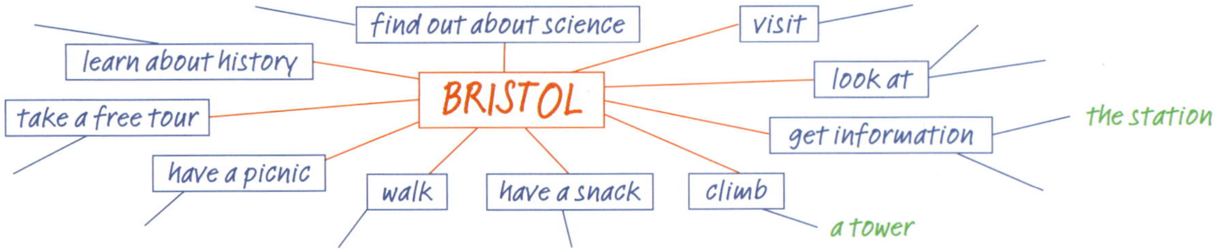

b) **Extra** *Would you like to visit Bristol? Why? Why not?*

You can do interesting things there. • It looks fun. • It looks boring. • I like/don't like cities. • ...

c) *Start a mind map for your area. Add to it as you go through the unit.*

2 LISTENING The slave girl's story

a) *Look at the pictures. Then listen to Binta's story and put the pictures in the right order.*

b) *Try and answer the questions. Listen and check.*

1 Where did Binta's family come from?
2 Where did Binta go next?
3 Where is she now?

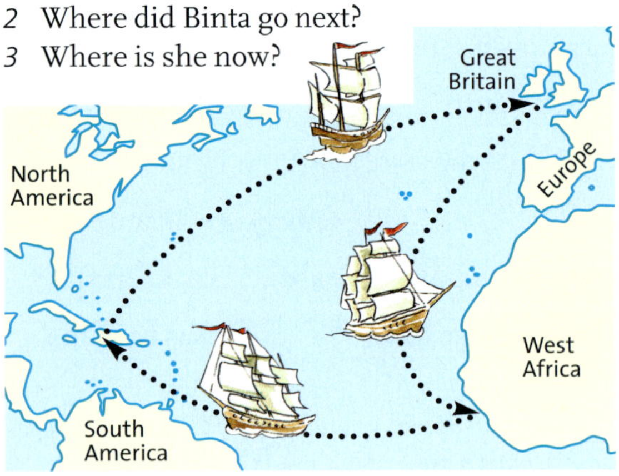

c) **Extra** *Listen, then choose the right answer.*

1 Binta was (6/11/30) years old when she left Africa.
2 She was on the ship for (30 days/6 weeks/11 months).
3 When the ship arrived in the Caribbean, the white men (sold animals/sold Binta/sold sugar).
4 Binta's new name was (Jane/Lucy/Mary).

//○ 3 Plans for this evening (going to-future) ▸ D p. 116

What are the people going to do this evening?

…	is are	going to	help Toby • write a letter • read a book • cook dinner • play cards • watch TV

1 Dan is going to …
2 Jo and his dad are going to …

1 Dan

2 Jo and his dad

3 Jack

4 Jack's parents

5 Sophie

6 Ananda

4 Your plans (going to-future)

a) *What are you going to do this evening? And tomorrow evening? Make notes like this:*

this evening	*tomorrow evening*
…	…

b) *Walk round the classroom. Try to find somebody with the same plans. Then tell the class.*

I'm going to play football this evening. What about you?
I'm going to play computer games.

What about tomorrow evening?
I'm going to do my homework.
Me too.

Ideas for plans (4 and 5)

buy new clothes/… •
do my homework/sport/… •
help my parents/my … •
listen to music/CDs/… •
play basketball/… •
read a book/… •
ride my bike/… •
sleep •
meet my friends/my … •
tidy my room •
visit my grandma/my … •
watch a film/TV/… •
write a letter/… •

5 Extra I'm not going to … (going to-future)

Everybody's plans for this evening are different.
Go round the class like this:

A: I'm going to tidy my room this evening.
B: I'm not going to tidy my room this evening. I'm going to visit my friend.
C: I'm not going to visit my friend. I'm going to …

If you repeat a plan, or if you can't think of a different plan, you are out.

6 What is he going to do? (going to-future: questions)

a) *Partner B: Look at p. 111.*
Partner A: Copy the chart. Then ask your partner about Jo, and about Sophie and Ananda. Write down the answers.
Then answer your partner's questions about Jack, and about Mr and Mrs Hanson.

Name	What is/are … going to do tomorrow?	Where is/are … going to …?
Jo		
Jack	read	in his room
Sophie and Ananda		
Mr and Mrs Hanson	clean cupboards	in the kitchen

b) **Extra** *Make a chart like this. Write down your plans. Then talk to different partners and complete the chart. Use your notes to report to the class.*

	What are you going to do at the weekend?	Where are you going to …?
You		
…		
…		

//○ 7 REVISION What has just happened? (Present perfect) ▸ D p. 117

Look at the picture. Say what has just happened: Three little men from Mars have just landed. Ananda has just …

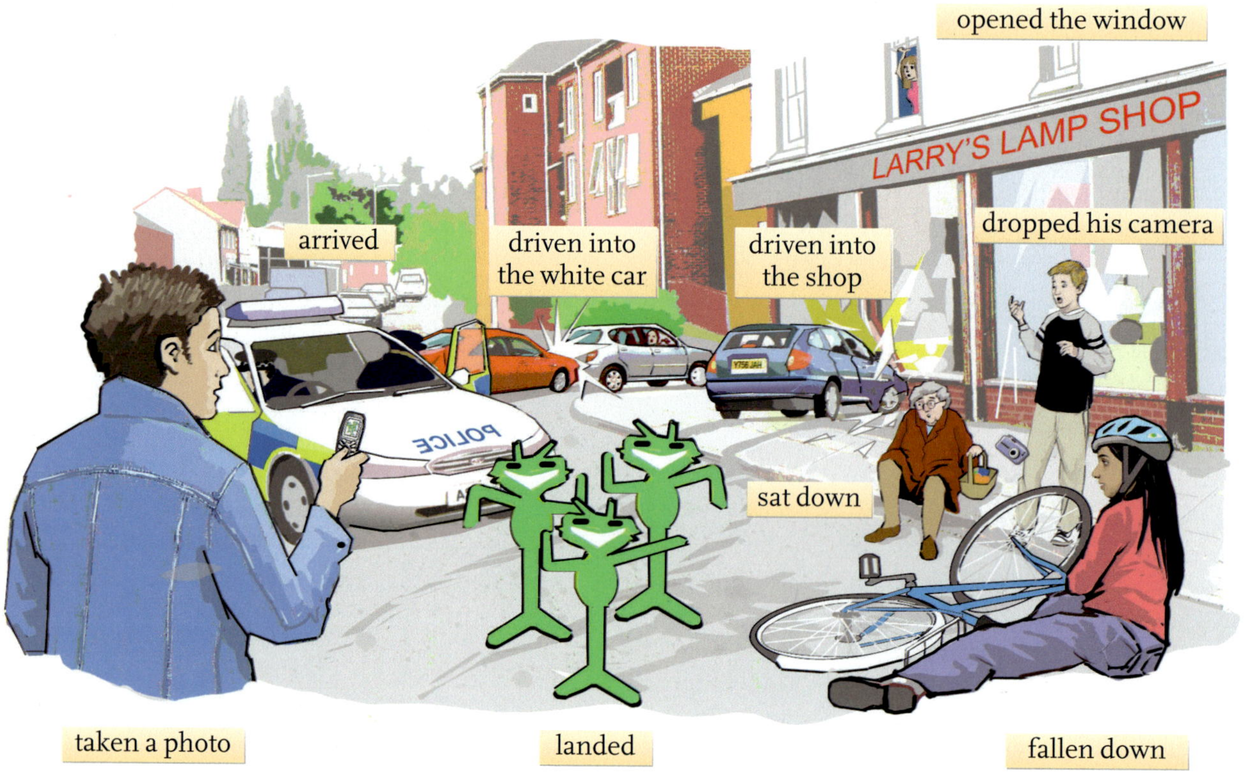

8 WORDS Discussion

Partner B: Go to p. 111.
Partner A: Look at this page. Swap after two turns.

Read out one of the statements to your partner ...

1 English is the most interesting subject.
2 Borussia Dortmund is a great team.
3 Pop songs are better in German than in English.
4 Bristol is an interesting city.

... and say what you think about the statement.

I agree with that.
I think that's right.

I don't agree with that.
I don't think that's right.

1 Maths/... is more interesting.
2 Schalke/... is better!
3 English sounds better.
4 It looks boring.

Then ask what your partner thinks.

What do you think?

9 STUDY SKILLS Marking up a text

Use a copy of the text.
a) *Look at another Bristol quiz question. Find the facts you need in the text and mark them up.*

BRISTOL

Question 5

Who are **Wallace and Gromit** and what are they like? Who is Nick Park? When did he make the first Wallace and Gromit film?

Wallace and Gromit

Nick Park works at Aardman Studios in Bristol. He is the 'father' of Wallace and Gromit. When Nick was a kid, he made models with plasticine. But he didn't throw his models away. He used a video camera and made films with them.
Later he went to film school. And in 1985 he started work at Aardman Studios.
The first Wallace and Gromit film was *A Grand Day Out*[1] (1989). The film was very popular. In 2005 Nick Park made the fourth Wallace and Gromit film, *The Curse of the Were-Rabbit*[2].

Wallace and Gromit are now big film stars! They have won Oscars! Everybody loves them because they are very funny. Wallace is a very nice man, but he isn't very smart. Gromit is his dog. He can't talk, but he is much smarter than Wallace. He even studied at 'Dogwarts University'! (Do you know 'Hogwarts' from the Harry Potter books?)
In 2005, there was a fire at the Aardman Studios, and they lost lots of the models from the old Wallace and Gromit films. But don't worry. It's easy to make new models! Wallace and Gromit live on!

b) *Work with a partner. Have you both marked all the facts? Have you marked too many?*

Deutsche Titel: [1]Alles Käse [2]Auf der Jagd nach dem Riesenkaninchen

10 Extra There's a juice bar in town, isn't there? (Question tags)

Add the correct question tag.

1 There's a juice bar in St Nicholas Market in Bristol, ... isn't it? / isn't there?
2 It's a good place, ... isn't it? / wasn't it?
3 The juices are delicious, ... weren't they? / aren't they?
4 Jack was at the juice bar last week, ... wasn't he? / wasn't she?
5 Jo, Dan, Sophie and Ananda were at the bar too, ... wasn't he? / weren't they?
6 The strawberry smoothie was very good, ... wasn't he? / wasn't it?
7 Sophie was unhappy with the wheatgrass juice, ... wasn't she? / wasn't it?

There's a juice bar in St Nicholas Market in Bristol, isn't there?

11 REVISION They found the answers quickly (Adverbs of manner)

a) *How did Sophie and her friends do it? Complete the sentences with the correct adverb.*
1 The first two Bristol quiz questions were easy, so the kids found the answers *quickly* (quick).
2 Sophie and her friends thought the quiz was fun, so they did it ... (happy).
3 Brunel is very famous, so they found information on him ... (easy).
4 At the juice bar they had to find a healthy and delicious drink, so they read the menu ... (careful).
5 They are going to work ... (hard) on their brochure.
6 They want to do it ... (good) because they want to win the prize.
7 They haven't got much time, so they have to work ... (fast).

b) Extra *Complete these sentences. Use adverbs.*
When I do my homework, I work ...
When I write a letter, I write ...
When I meet my friends, I talk ...
When I read, I read ...

12 STUDY SKILLS Structuring a text

a) *This is Jack's text for the Bristol brochure. Find the beginning, the middle and the end.*

A You can also be the star of your own TV show. I think that's the best thing in the museum.

B There's a lot to do there. For example, you can walk through a tornado or play volleyball with a computer.

C My favourite place in Bristol is Explore-at-Bristol. It's an exciting new museum. It opened in 2000. Museums are sometimes boring. But this one is really cool.

b) *Look at the text in a) again. Collect useful phrases for your own text about a place.*

//○ 13 MEDIATION A tour of Bristol

▸ D p. 117

The Meiers are on a tour of Bristol. But they don't understand much English. Answer their questions. But you don't have much time. Choose two important things each time.

Guide Hi, everybody. Welcome to our Bristol Open Top Bus Tour. My name is Carol and I'm your guide. I hope you have fun on our tour. OK, let's go.

You Sie sagt 'Hallo'. / Sie ist unsere Fremdenführerin. / Sie heißt Carol. / Sie wünscht uns viel Spaß.

Guide On the left you can see Bristol's famous harbour. The big ship over there is the *SS Great Britain*. This ship was the work of Bristol's great engineer Isambard Kingdom Brunel. It's open to visitors.

Frau M Was ist mit dem Schiff?

You Das Schiff ist *SS Great Britain* und man kann es besuchen. / Links ist der Hafen. / Der bekannte Ingenieur Brunel hat das Schiff gebaut. / Brunels vollständiger Name ist Isambard Kingdom Brunel.

Guide When we come to the top of the hill, the driver will turn left. Then, on your right, you'll see a large green area. We call this area *the Downs*. As you will see, people like to come here on a warm day. It's usually cooler than the city centre.

Herr M Wir biegen wohl ab, aber was ist dann?

You Die Leute kommen gern zum Park. / Der Fahrer wird links abbiegen. / Es ist hier kühler als im Stadtzentrum. / Der Park, den wir gleich sehen, wird the Downs genannt.

Guide Now we're in Clifton Village. There are lots of nice little shops and cafés in the village. We're going to stay here for thirty minutes. You can go to the shops or get something to drink but please don't be late. There's lots more to see.

Frau M Alle steigen aus. Ist die Fahrt schon zu Ende?

You Wir sind hier in Clifton Village. / Wir können hier in Clifton einkaufen oder etwas trinken gehen. / Nein, es geht in einer halben Stunde weiter. / Es gibt viel mehr zu sehen.

14 GETTING BY IN ENGLISH At the juice bar

Prepare the dialogue. You can look at p. 78 for help. Then act it out.

Partner A	Partner B
Wie kann ich Ihnen helfen?	Ich hätte gern einen Saft.
Welche Sorte? Apfel oder Kiwi oder …	Ich habe den *wheatgrass*-Saft noch nicht probiert. Ist der gut?
Das ist eine schwierige Frage. Er ist anders.	OK! Kann ich bitte einen Apfelsaft haben? – Groß.
Bitte schön. – Das macht £1.60.	Vielen Dank.

To catch a thief

'Well,' said Jack the next day, 'our teamwork on the brochure was good. Now we need good teamwork on the SHoCK Team's new case.'
'New case?' said Ananda.
'Yes,' Jack said. 'David can't find his mobile. It was in our classroom yesterday. And then it disappeared. Someone is stealing things from Form 8PK.'
'Well, it can only be one person,' Jo said.
'Who do you mean?' Sophie asked.
'Lesley, of course!' Jo said. 'Before she came, nothing disappeared in our class. Now things disappear all the time. I think it's Lesley.'
Jack was angry. 'That's not fair, Jo. There's no proof.'
'But Jack, you told us about Lesley and how her mum hasn't got much money,' said Ananda.
'So? We haven't got much money,' said Jack, 'but you don't think I'm a thief – or do you?'
'No, of course we don't think that,' said Dan. 'And I don't think Lesley's a thief!'
'Well, somebody is stealing things and we don't know who,' said Sophie.
'Right,' said Dan.
'So,' Sophie went on, 'we have to catch the thief and we need proof.'
'Right!' said Jack.
'And how are we going to get proof?' asked Jo.
Jack smiled. 'I have a plan. We're going to leave a purse with money in it in the classroom at break tomorrow. And then we're going to watch it.'
'But we have to go outside at break. So we can't watch it,' said Ananda.
'Hey,' said Sophie, 'I've got an idea. My mum always loses her keys. So my dad bought her a key ring – it bleeps when you whistle. So you can always find it.'
'Great idea!' said Jo. 'We put the key ring in the purse ...'
'... we leave the purse in the classroom,' Dan added.
'And after break we whistle and Lesley's school bag bleeps!' finished Jo.
'Shut up, Jo!' they all said.

The next day Ananda brought an old purse to school, and Sophie brought her mum's key ring. At break, Sophie left the purse on her desk and they all went outside.
'Have you left the purse?' asked Jack.
'Yes, I have,' said Sophie.

'And is the key ring in it?' asked Jo.
'Yes, it is,' said Sophie.
'And I put some money in the purse too. Five pounds,' said Ananda. 'Now we just have to wait.'

At the end of break, the SHoCK Team went to Sophie's desk.
'It has disappeared!' whispered Sophie.
'Right!' said Jo.
He started to whistle as he walked slowly towards Lesley's desk.

'What's wrong with you?' Lesley asked as Jo came nearer.
'Nothing. I'm just looking for Ananda's purse – somebody has stolen it,' said Jo.
'And you think this "somebody" is me,' said Lesley angrily. Jo whistled again. Nothing happened. No bleep.

'I told you it wasn't Lesley,' said Jack when Jo came back.
Just then Mr Kingsley came into the classroom.
'We'll have to look in other places at lunch break,' whispered Ananda.

So, at lunch break:

'Well?' asked Jack when they all met outside.
'Nothing,' said Jo.
'Nothing,' said Dan. He started to whistle again.
'Wait a minute,' said Sophie. 'Listen everybody.'
Jack smiled, 'A bleep! Whistle some more, Dan. Let's walk this way.'
They all walked towards the school. But there were no bleeps.
'We're walking the wrong way. Let's walk over there,' said Sophie.
They walked away from the school and ...
'Bleep! Bleep!' The bleeps got louder and louder.
'Look!' said Jack. 'We're following Mr Smith.'
'It can't be Mr Smith!' said Jo. 'He's the caretaker. He doesn't steal things!'
But, as they got nearer to Mr Smith, the bleeps got louder.
'Ah, there you are, Mr Kingsley!' The SHoCK Team stopped as Mr Smith started to talk to Mr Kingsley.
'Hello, Mr Smith,' said Mr Kingsley. 'What can I do for you?'
'It's your form – 8PK. They don't look after their things very well,' answered Mr Smith. He opened his bag and took out a mobile phone.
'The cleaners found this on the floor last night. And look ...' He took out a purse. Jo whistled.

'I found this purse when I went in to check the broken window at break this morning. Oh no, now it's bleeping!'

Jo stopped whistling. The rest of the SHoCK Team just stood there. Mr Kingsley turned.
'Ah, here's a group from 8PK. Does anybody know whose purse this is?'
'Er ... it's mine, Mr Kingsley,' said Ananda.
'And this mobile?'
'I think it's David's, Mr Kingsley,' said Jack.
'You really have to look after your things better, you know,' said Mr Smith.
'Mr Smith is right,' said Mr Kingsley. 'You have to look after your things better. I'm going to talk to the class about this later.'
Mr Kingsley and Mr Smith walked away together.
'Oh dear,' said Jack. 'Not one of the SHoCK Team's great cases, eh?'
'Well,' laughed Jo, 'You can't win them all!'
'No,' said Jack. 'But we have learned something.'
'Er ... have we?' asked Jo.
'Yes, we have,' said Sophie. 'We've learned that you always need proof before you go round and say people have stolen things, right Jo?'
'Er ... right.' Jo looked at the floor. 'I think I have to say sorry to Lesley.'
'Yes,' said Jack. 'She's over there.'

Working with the text

1 The story – what happened?

Put these sentences in the right order. Start with number 6.

1 At lunch break they tried again. The bleeps started when they were near Mr Smith.

2 At the end Jo had to say sorry to Lesley.

3 They put a purse in the classroom. There was a special key ring in the purse.

4 This was a new case for the SHoCK Team. They wanted to find the thief.

5 After break the purse wasn't there. There was no bleep from the key ring.

6 **Somebody was stealing things** in 8PK. Jo said it was Lesley.

7 Mr Smith gave the purse and a mobile to Mr Kingsley. There was no thief! The students had to look after their things better.

2 Extra The end of the story

Look at the pictures. Then write the end of the story. Here's some help:

Jo go to Lesley • want to say sorry •
Lesley very angry/not want to listen •
SHoCK Team try to help Jo •
want to be friends • at the end – 'It's OK.'

DOSSIER ***Lesley's diary***

Imagine you are Lesley. How was Lesley's day? Write 6–10 sentences for her diary.
Today something mad happened at school.
Jo Shaw came to me and whistled ...

► WB 16 (p. 64)

Checkpoint 5 ► WB (p. 65)

Extra EXTENSIVE READING Robinson Crusoe

> *1 Imagine you're going to live alone on an island. What five things do you want to take with you?*
> *2 Look at the pictures. What do you know about Robinson Crusoe?*

I was born in the year 1632 in the city of York. When I was 18, I told my parents that I wanted to be a sailor. They tried to stop me. But in 1651, when I was 19, I left home.

I travelled to lots of places. For two years I was a pirate's slave in Africa. I ran away and went on a ship to Brazil. I bought a farm there and became rich. But then some friends wanted my help. They wanted to go to Africa to get slaves. So I went with them.

Our ship left on 1 September 1659. After about ten days a terrible storm began. After two weeks we didn't know where we were.

Then one day, one of our men saw land. We tried to get closer to the island, but the water wasn't very deep. Soon the ship couldn't move. So we left the ship in a small boat. The wind and the waves were still very strong. A wave like a mountain came down on our small boat, and it threw us into the sea. I couldn't find the boat again, and I couldn't see the other men.

Again and again the waves pulled me under the water, but I was getting nearer to the island. Suddenly I felt land under me. But the waves pulled me out to sea again. This happened three more times before I was safe on land at last.

I was very afraid. I didn't know where I was, but I knew there were cannibals in this part of the world. 'How can I survive?' I thought. 'I've got nothing.'

I looked out to sea and saw the wreck of my ship. It was very far away. I needed food and water, and I needed a place to sleep. I was scared, but I walked round a bit, and I found a little river and drank. There was a tree near the river, so I climbed it and slept there.

The next morning I saw that the storm was over. But the biggest surprise was that my ship was now only about a mile away, on some rocks. It was on its side, but it was still in one piece.

When the tide went out, I could walk most of the way to the ship. I swam the rest of the way. When I got there, I climbed up. I found food, guns, tools and clothes. I took a sail from the ship too because I wanted to make a tent with it. But how could I get everything to the island? I had to make a raft.

I used some of the tools from the ship. It wasn't a very good raft, but it helped me to take my things to the beach.

I went to the ship eleven times in my first thirteen days and I brought back lots of things. When I went for the last time, I found silver in the captain's cabin.

I wanted to take more things, but I saw that there were clouds in the sky, and the wind was getting stronger.

I got back to the island before the storm and took everything to my tent. The storm went on all night. And when I woke up the next morning, the ship wasn't there.

I still didn't know where I was. About a mile from my tent there were some hills. One was higher than the others, so I walked up to the top. It was hard work.

There I could see all of the island. There were no houses or farms, just trees and wild animals. 'I'll probably be here a long time,' I thought. So I had to build a house. And my house had to be a fort. It was difficult to find a good place: I needed water, shelter from the sun and rain, and a place where I was safe from wild animals or cannibals. And I wanted to see the sea. 'If a ship comes, I have to see it and send a signal.' It was hard work, but with the tools from the ship, I built my fort. Now I felt safe when I slept at night.

Over the next months and years I learned many things. I went to different parts of my island and found the best place for fruit. I learned to catch the wild goats on the island. I made clothes and candles from them. I made tables and chairs too. And I became a farmer.

When I ate, I sat down with my pets. I had a parrot, a dog and two cats from the ship, and I had a baby goat. I wanted real friends, but my pets were better than nothing.

I even taught Poll – that was my name for the parrot – to talk. He learned to say his name.

Fifteen years came and went. And then ... one day, as I was walking round my island, I suddenly saw a footprint! A man's footprint in the sand. I was very scared. I looked for more footprints, but there was only one.

I walked very quickly back to my fort – I looked behind me all the time. When I got back, I thought, 'How is this possible? Where is the man's ship? Why is there only one footprint?'

After some time, I started to think that the footprint was really mine. I felt much better. But I had to go back and see. I went to the place, and the footprint was still there. I put my own foot next to it. My foot was much smaller!

In my fifteen years on the island, I was the only person there. Who was this other man? What was he doing on my island? I went back to my house and started work to make my fort stronger and safer.

Then one day, when I was looking after my goats, I found something terrible: a place with bones – people's bones – round a fire. Cannibals! They weren't there now, but I thought, 'Maybe they'll come back! I don't want to be food for cannibals.'

I often went back to the place to look for the cannibals. I always had my guns with me.

Then one day, the cannibals came back. There were twenty or more, and they had two prisoners. They killed one and started to cook him. Just then the other prisoner ran. He ran, and three of the cannibals followed him. When the prisoner got to the little river near my house, he quickly swam to the other side. Two of the cannibals followed. The prisoner was faster than the other men, and soon I was between him and the cannibals.

I had to kill one of the cannibals before he could kill me. The prisoner killed the other cannibal. Then he came towards me and spoke to me. I couldn't understand his language, but I knew he wanted to say thank you and be my servant.

I gave my servant the name Friday because that was the day when I saved him. Friday became a friend. I taught him to speak our language, to use a gun and to eat meat, not people. Yes, he was a cannibal too before I saved him.
The time with Friday was my best time on the island.
Then one day, he hurried into the fort. 'They have come,' he shouted. 'They have come!'
I followed Friday. We saw an English ship. And there was a small boat. But something wasn't right. The men in the boat were English, but they had three prisoners. Friday thought the men were cannibals, but I told him they weren't.
The men brought the prisoners to the island. When the prisoners sat down under some trees, not far from us, I talked to them quietly from behind the trees. They were very surprised. Then they told me their story.
One of the prisoners was the captain of the ship. But a group of mutineers was now in control of his ship. 'I will help you,' I told the captain, 'if you promise to take me and my man Friday to England.' He quickly agreed.
I gave the captain and his men guns, and they killed one of the mutineers and injured another. The others agreed to help the captain to take back his ship.
And so it happened. The captain took control of his ship again. Then he sent a boat for me and Friday.
I took with me a few souvenirs and the silver from my ship. It was 19 December 1686 when I left my island – after 28 years, two months and 19 days.

Background File

The real Robinson Crusoe
Daniel Defoe's book Robinson Crusoe came out in 1719.
Most people agree that the 'real' Robinson Crusoe was Alexander Selkirk. Selkirk was born in Scotland in 1676. He became a sailor when he was 19.
When Selkirk argued with his captain, the captain left him on an island near Chile.
He was there for four and a half years. A rich Englishman brought Selkirk back to Bristol. Selkirk met Defoe in a pub and told him his story. You can still visit the pub today. It's name is the Llandoger Trow.

1 What happened when?

Continue the sentences.

In 1632 Robinson was born in York.
In 1651 …
On 1 Sep 1659 …
In his first thirteen days …
After fifteen years …
After twelve more years …
On 19 Dec 1686 …

2 You are Robinson Crusoe

Imagine Robinson writes a message in a bottle and asks for help. Write his message.
OR
Draw a picture of Robinson Crusoe's island.

A trip to Bath

1 The Roman Baths

Talk about the picture of the Roman Baths. What can you see? What are the people doing?
In the picture on the left/...

I can see ...	The people are ...
water • stairs • mosaics • Roman clothes • a cold/... room • a big/round/... pool • ...	swimming • chatting • having a sauna • shouting • relaxing • playing games • ...

▸ *SF Describing pictures (p. 123)*

2 Travel through time

a) *You're going to walk through the Roman Baths. Close your eyes. Relax and enjoy the walk. Think about the things you see, hear, feel and smell.*

b) *Look at the picture again. What rooms did you visit? What was it like there?*
First we went to the ... / Then we ...

It was ... warm • hot • dark • cold • cool • funny • noisy • nice • ... there.

▸ *WB 1 (p. 66)*

Extra Background File

The city of Bath

Bath is about 20 km southeast of Bristol. It is a beautiful old city, and it is famous for the Roman Baths there.
The Romans were in the area for over 400 years till about the year 450. The map shows the Roman Empire in the early second century.

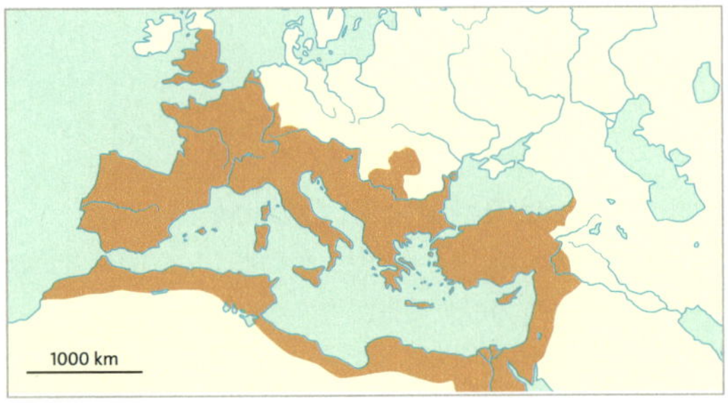

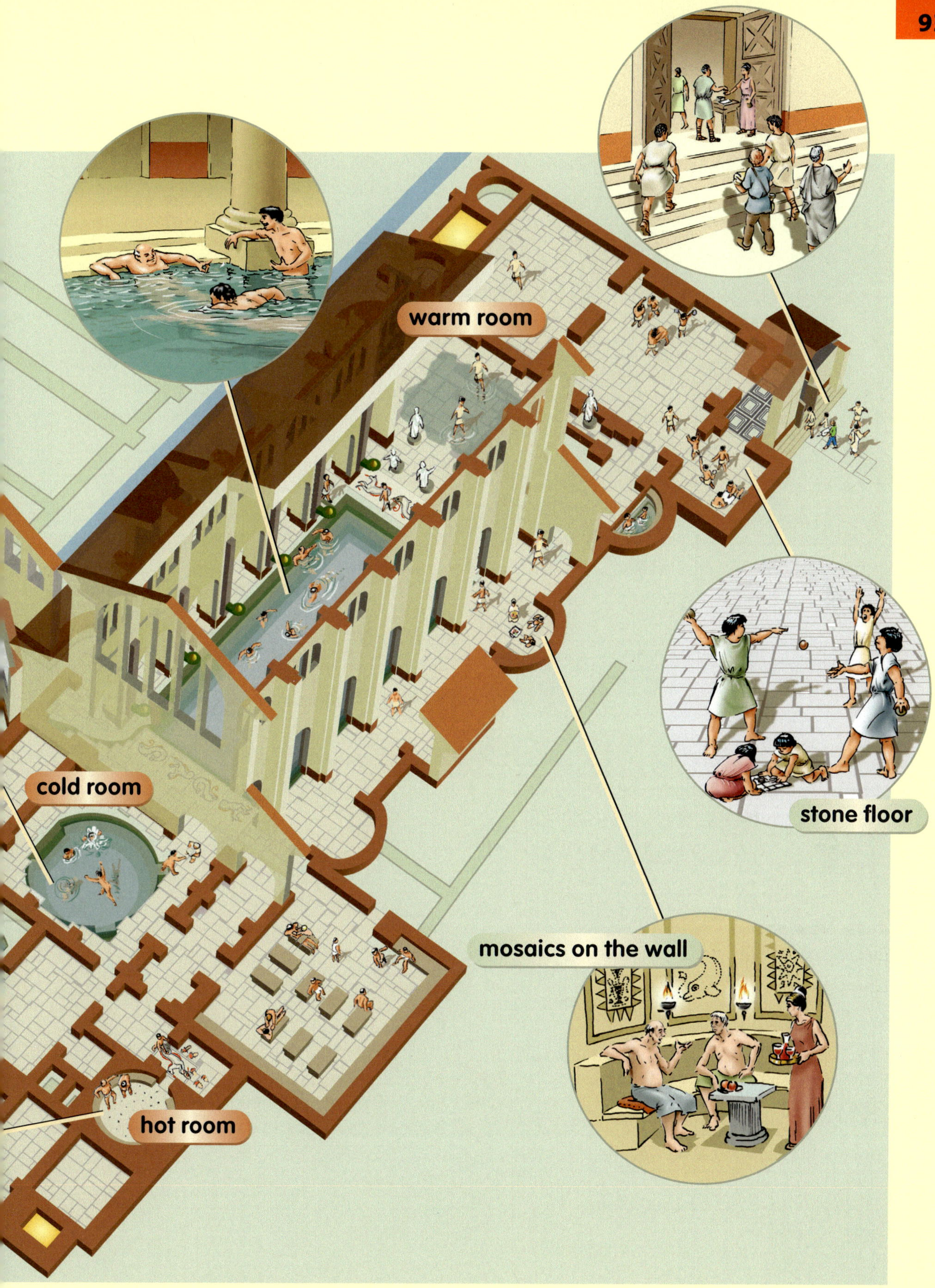
warm room
cold room
hot room
stone floor
mosaics on the wall

1 8PK's school trip to Bath

It was a great day for a bike ride. Form 8PK were on the Bristol and Bath Railway Path.

▸ P 1–2 (p. 98) • P 3 (p. 98) • WB 2 (p. 67)

Jack Hi Lesley. How are you?
Lesley Oh, hi Jack. I'm OK. And you?
Jack I'm a bit tired.
Lesley Me too. How far is it to Bath?
Jack About fourteen miles. But we only have to cycle seven. Then we're going to take the bus. Oh, hi Jo.
Jo Hi! Can I cycle with you?
Jack Sure.
Jo I know we all have to go to the Roman Baths in the morning. But in the afternoon we can choose. What are you going to do then?
Lesley I'm going to visit the Museum of Costume with Mr Kingsley. What about you, Jack?
Jack I'm going to visit that museum about planets and stars with Miss White.
Jo The Herschel Museum? Yes, that sounds good. Well, see you later.
Jack OK. See you.
Lesley See you.

▸ *Complete the programme for the trip.*

Morning:
Cycle to Warmley (7 miles),
then take ... to Bath
Visit ...
Afternoon
Group 1: to ... with ...
Group 2: to ... with ...

STUDY SKILLS Talking to people

Hier einige Regeln für ein freundliches Gespräch:
1) Fang nett an: **Hello! Can I sit with you?**
2) Zeig, dass du wissen willst, was die anderen denken oder fühlen: **What do you think?**
3) Verabschiede dich freundlich: **Bye then!**
Finde weitere nützliche Redewendungen in **1**.

▸ SF Talking to people (p. 128) • P 3 (p. 98) • WB 3 (p. 67)

2 Now you

Talk to a partner like this:

Partner A	Partner B
Hi! OK? / Hello, how are you?	I'm fine. / I'm OK. / I'm a bit tired. What about you?
I'm OK. / I'm really tired. / I'm fine. Can I sit with you?	Sure. / OK. / If you like. / Of course. What are you going to do this afternoon?
I'm going to ... What about you?	I'm going to ...
That sounds fun/interesting/great. Well, see you later!	OK, see you.

3 Which way?

When they got to Bath, they went to the Roman Baths first. After lunch Mr Kingsley said, 'Let's make two groups. Everybody for the Herschel Museum, go with Miss White. The others stay with me.'

I want to go to the costume museum. Jo, can you tell Miss White, please?
Sure, Dan, no problem.

'Please look at your maps,' Mr Kingsley went on. 'We're at the Abbey. That's number 1, in the middle. The Museum of Costume is number 5, at the top. Who can find the way? Lesley?'
'OK,' said Lesley. 'It looks easy.' – But it wasn't that easy.
'Can I help you?' asked a man.
'Yes, please,' said Lesley. 'Can you tell us the way to the Museum of Costume?'
'Oh yes,' the man said. 'Well, first turn left into Cheap Street and walk to Union Street. Then turn right into Union Street and go straight on. There's a post office on the right. Go past the post office and walk to the end of Milsom Street.'
'OK,' said Lesley. 'And then?'
'Then turn right into George Street, then left into Bartlett Street. Then cross Alfred Street, and the museum is on the corner.'
'OK,' said Lesley. 'Thanks very much!'

> *Follow Mr Kingsley's group on the map.*

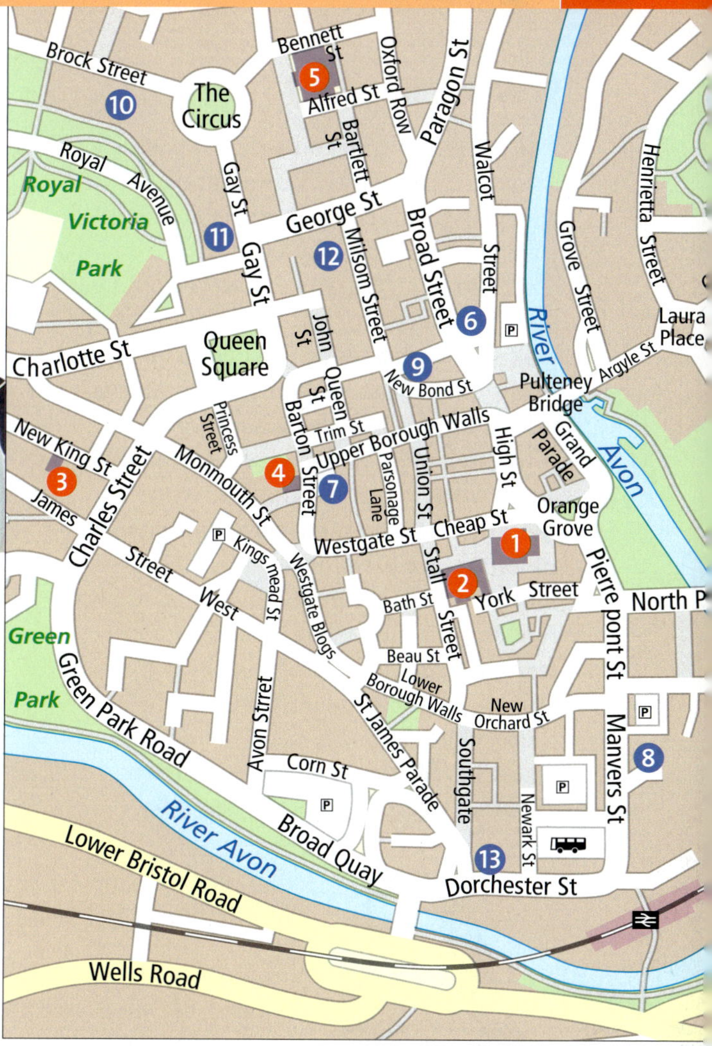

1 Bath Abbey 2 Roman Baths
3 Herschel Museum 4 Theatre Royal
5 Museum of Costume 6 church
7 hospital 8 police station 9 post office
10 chemist 11 café/restaurant
12 department store 13 supermarket

4 Can you tell us the way to ...?

a) *Match the phrases and the pictures.*

Turn left. • Go straight on. • Turn right into King Street. • Cross the next street. • Go past the church. • It's on the corner on the right.

b) *Say how to get to the Herschel Museum. Start at Bath Abbey.*

c) **Extra** *Choose a place on the map. Start from the Abbey. Make notes, then tell your partner how to get there. (Don't say what it is.) Can he/she find the place?*

A: ... and then go straight on. The place is on the left.
B: Oh, it's the supermarket!
A: That's right. Your turn.

▸ P 4–5 (p. 99) • WB 4–6 (pp. 68–69)

5 Who's missing?

At 1.30 Miss White and her group were walking through Bath. Miss White stopped. 'I must check that everybody's here,' she said. 'Where's your brother?' she asked Jo.
'Dan?' Jo said. 'Oh, er ... we were going past a shop a minute ago, and Dan stopped and looked in the window. You needn't worry, Miss White ... oh, I can see him. He's coming.'
'All right then, but please stay together.'
A bit later, Miss White was checking the group again when Jo came round the corner.
'Jo!' she said, 'We must stay together! You mustn't leave the group!'
'Sorry, Miss. But I'm not Jo. I'm Dan. I was looking in a shop window, and suddenly you weren't there.'
'You're Dan? But then where's Jo?'
'I don't know, Miss.'
The other kids were laughing quietly.
'This isn't funny!' Miss White said.

Hello, Paul?
This is Isabel. I've lost Jo!
Oh dear.
We were walking along the street and then he disappeared. Dan told me ...
Did you say Dan? But Dan is with me. It's a trick, Isabel. Your 'Dan' is really Jo!
A trick? Jo! You're in trouble now!

Are Dan and Jo with Miss White or with Mr Kingsley?

Looking at language

a) *What were Miss White and her group doing at 1.30?*
They were walking through Bath.
What were they doing when 'Dan' stopped?
They ... ... past a shop.
What was Miss White doing when Jo came?
She ... ... the group again.
Find other examples of this new verb form in **5**.

b) *How do you make this verb form?*

6 Now you

Talk to different partners.

A:	What were you doing ...?	at 8 o'clock on Saturday night at 3.30 yesterday afternoon ...
B:	I was ...	watching .../talking to .../ listening to .../eating/ doing my homework/ reading/tidying .../...

What about you?

► *GF 14–15: Present and past progressive (pp. 146–147)* • *P 6–8* • *(p. 100–101)* • *WB 7–9 (pp. 70–72)*

7 Extra What planets can you name?

Miss White was in the museum with her group. Nicola, from the museum, was talking to the students.
'... and please don't touch anything. Right, let's see what you know about astronomy. First, what planets can you name?'
'Mars!' called Jo. 'And Saturn, Venus ... and Jupiter.'
'Wow!' said Ananda. 'You really know about astronomy.'
'Well, astronomy is interesting!' said Jo.
'Not bad,' said Nicola to Jo. 'Now, the man who lived in this house was William Herschel. Can you name the planet which Herschel discovered?'

'Uranus!' said Jo.
'Very good! OK then, let's look at Herschel's telescope, but please remember: you mustn't touch it. This way!'

Extra ▸ *GF 16: Relative clauses (pp. 147–148)* • *P 9 (p. 101)*

8 Extra William and Caroline

a) *At the museum the students heard about William and Caroline Herschel.*
Listen. Look at the notes. Are they about William or Caroline Herschel?

Born: 1750, in Hanover
Interests: music and astronomy
Moved: to Bath
Discovered: 8 comets

b) *Listen again. Write some short notes like the ones in a) about the other Herschel.*

9 Jo's report

Our school trip to Bath
We went on a school trip to Bath yesterday. First we cycled a bit and then we took a bus.

When we arrived, we went to the Roman Baths. They were OK. Then we had lunch. After that we made two groups. My group went to the Herschel Museum. It was really interesting – all about stars and planets. I really enjoyed that.

Before we left Bath, Miss White bought us all an ice cream. And the sun was still shining when we got home at six o'clock. It was a great day.

▸ *P 10–12 (p. 102)* • *WB 10–12 (pp. 73–74)*

DOSSIER *A school trip*

Write about a school trip. First collect ideas.
Where did you go? Who did you go with? What happened? Was it a nice trip?

Beginning: Start with a sentence like this:
Last year / When I was in Class .../... I went on a school trip to ...
Middle: Report on the trip.
First we ... / Then we ... / Before we left I ...
End: Finish with a sentence like this:
It was a great/... trip and I'll remember it for a long time.

Read your report to the class.

▸ *SF Structuring a text (p. 129)*

1 REVISION On the cycle path (going to-future)

Sophie and Ananda are chatting about their plans for the weekend.
*Complete the dialogue. Use **going to**.*

S: What (you, do) *are you going to do* at the weekend, Ananda?
A: I ... (play) hockey on Saturday morning and in the evening we ... (visit) my grandparents. What about you, Sophie?
S: I ... (buy) some new dance shoes in the morning. Mum ... (take) me to the new shopping centre. We ... (look) for a birthday present for Hannah too.
A: That sounds fun. And in the evening?
S: Mum and Dad ... (visit) some friends. And Emily ... (stay) with a friend. So I ... (look after) Hannah.
A: I ... (do) my homework on Sunday morning.
S: Me too. What (you, do) ... on Sunday afternoon? Do you want to come to my house?
A: Great idea.

2 WORDS Word building

a) *Which words go together?*

family tree, form ...

family	machine
form	bag
jumble	room
living	tree
pocket	teacher
school	money
washing	sale

dishwasher, ...

dish	board
dust	shirt
rail	ache
skate	bin
sweat	washer
time	way
tooth	table

b) *Use words from a) to fill in the gaps in the story.*
It was 8 o'clock. Mr Kingsley jumped out of bed. He was a ... at Cotham, so he had to be at school on time. Oh, no! His favourite trousers and red ... were in the ... (He always did his washing at night!) And all his glasses and plates were in the ... Oh well, no breakfast. What was his first lesson? He checked his ...: Oh yes, Sport with 7IW. It's 8.15 already – time to go – Ouch! he fell over his old ... – 'That's an idea!' he thought. 'I can skate to school today.'

3 STUDY SKILLS Talking to people

a) *Listen to two more dialogues on the cycle path to Bath. Which sounds better? Why?*

b) Extra *Finish this dialogue.*
Use the phrases in the box. Listen again and check.

Partner A	Partner B
Hello.	Oh hi!
Are you enjoying the trip?	...
Oh, yes. I really like long bike rides.	Do you often cycle in your free time?
...	...

Yes, it's great. What about you? •
That's nice. How many brothers and sisters have you got? •
Just one sister. What about you? •
Yes, sometimes, with my sister. •
I've got one brother. •
Yeah, see you later. • Well, see you later.

4 WORDS Can you tell me the way to ..., please?

a) *Partner B: Go to p. 112. Partner A: Look at your map. The names of some places are missing. Ask your partner where they are:* tourist information • internet café • department store • church • post office
Now answer your partner's questions. Use these phrases.

It's in ... Street/Road/... • in front of/behind ... • near/next to/... • between ... and ... • on the corner of ... and ...

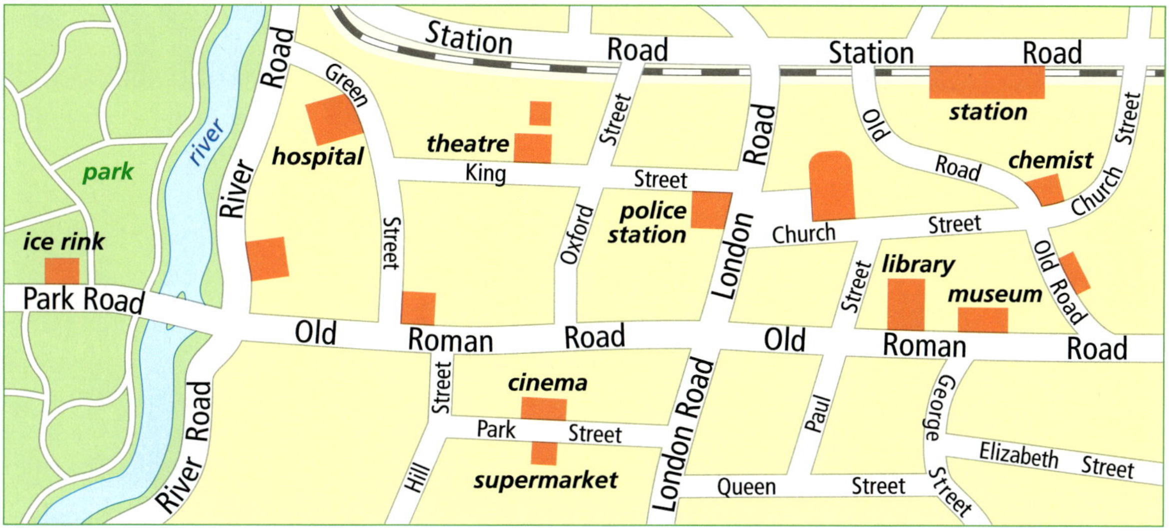

b) **Extra** *Now label the places in a copy of the map. Compare your maps.*

c) *You're in front of the ice rink. A tourist (your partner) asks you the way to three places on the map.*
Tourist Excuse me, please. Can you tell me the way to ...?
You First go past ... Then turn left/right into ... Cross/Go straight on/... The ... is on the left/right/corner of ...

d) *Now you're the tourist. Ask your partner the way to three places too.*

5 MEDIATION The way to the Roman Baths

Imagine you're on holiday in Bristol with your family. You're driving to Bath to see the Roman Baths. You know the way. Answer the questions.

By car from Bristol
Take the A4 into Bath. For a day visit to Bath go to *Newbridge Park and Ride,* which is on the A4 just after the bridge across the River Avon. Park your car there and then take a bus to the centre. To park in the city centre, go along the A4 to Charlotte Street car park. This is the biggest car park in Bath and it is easy to find. When you leave your car, follow the black pedestrian finger signposts to the Baths.

Mother Also, welche Straße nehmen wir nach Bath?
You ...
Mother Steht da, wo wir parken können?
You ...
Mother Park and Ride? Das heißt, wir nehmen dann einen Bus?
You ...
Mother Das ist nicht so schön. Können wir mehr im Zentrum parken?
You ...
Mother Und wie geht's dann zu den Römischen Bädern?
You ...

6 REVISION Dan is listening ... (Present progressive)

a) *Look at the pictures and say what the people are doing.*

1 Dan – listen to – MP3 player

Dan is listening to his MP3 player.

2 Jack and Lesley – walk – together

Jack and Lesley ...

3 Sophie – sit – next to Ananda

4 Mr Kingsley – talk to – group

5 Jo – take – photo

6 Miss White and Ananda – look at – building

b) **Extra** *Now write down what they are doing. Be careful with the spelling of the -ing forms.*

//○

7 Yesterday they were working (Past progressive) ▸ D p. 118

Look at the pictures. What were the people doing at 10 o'clock yesterday? And at ...?

1 At ten o'clock yesterday Sophie was making a poster. Jo ... a report.

2 At eleven o'clock yesterday ...

//○ 8 What were they doing when Mrs Harper came home? (Past progressive) ► D p. 119

Write down what the different people in the picture where doing when Mrs Harper came home. The words in the box will help you.

build a tower • do judo • feed the dog • play badminton • read the paper • ride a bike • sleep • take photos • talk on the phone • watch TV

When Mrs Harper came home, Adam was building a tower.
When Mrs Harper came home, ...

9 Extra The man who ... (Relative clauses)

Complete the captions.

A

That's the teacher who ...

B

That's the museum which ...

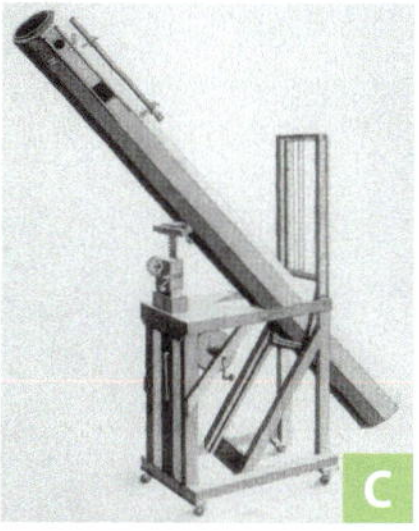
C

That's the telescope which ...

D

That's William Herschel. He's the man who ...

discovered Uranus.

Herschel made.

the students visited.

went to the Herschel Museum.

10 WORDS A school trip

a) *Find words and phrases in the word snake. You can use all of them when you write a text about a school trip.*

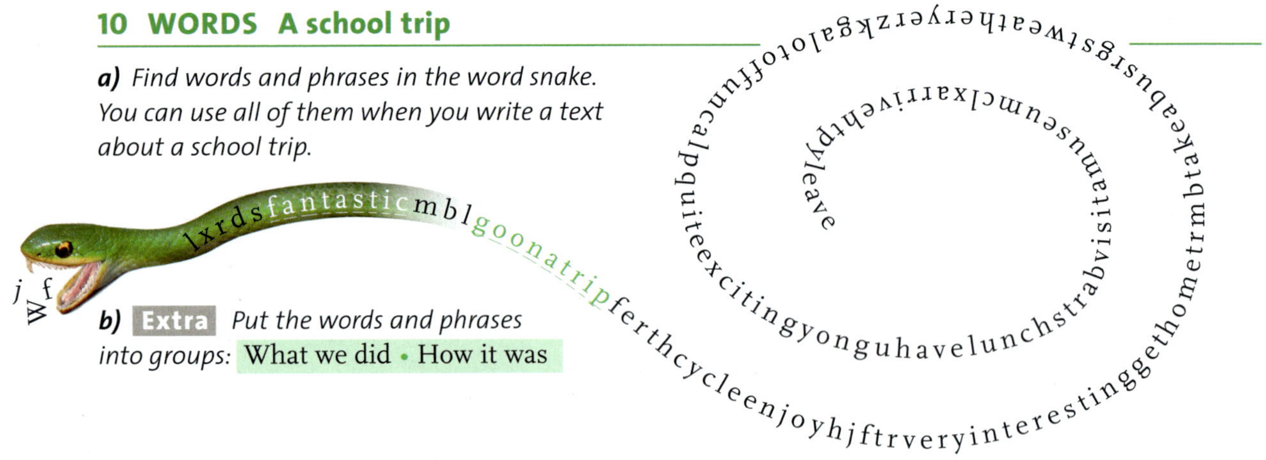

b) Extra *Put the words and phrases into groups:* What we did • How it was

11 STUDY SKILLS Correcting mistakes

a) *Mr Kingsley is correcting one of the student's texts. There are* ***four more spelling mistakes*** *in this text. Can you find them and correct them?*

STUDY SKILLS Correcting mistakes

Ein Text ist noch nicht „fertig", wenn du ihn zu Ende geschrieben hast. Du solltest ihn immer mehrmals durchlesen: einmal, um zu sehen, ob er vollständig und gut verständlich ist; und dann erneut, um ihn auf Fehler zu überprüfen.

▸ *SF Correcting mistakes (p. 130)*

b) *Check with a partner.*

8PK's trip to Bath

On a beautiful suny morning 8PK cycled happyly from Bristol to a village on the way to Bath. There they left their bikes and took the bus into Bath. First they visited the Roman Baths. They were there for about ninety minutes. Most of them enjoied the Baths. Then they had lunch at a great sanwich place. Later Miss White was takeing her group of students to the Herschel Museum when Jo disapeared. Miss White got worryd. She stoped and phoned Mr Kingsley. He told her, 'Jo is playing a trick on you.'

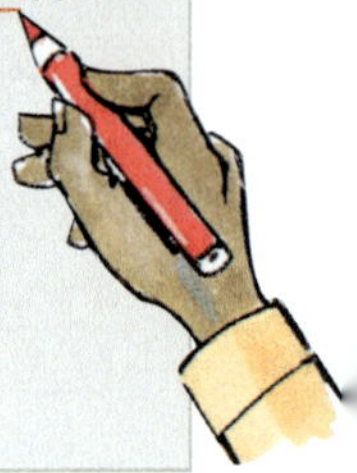

//○ 12 WORDS Prepositions ▸ D p. 118

Choose the right preposition.

1. Dan and Jo live in/at/near 7 Hamilton Street.
2. They are students at/on/in Cotham School.
3. They're both under/on/in Form 8PK.
4. They usually go to school with/by/on bike.
5. They don't like to wait on/for/with the bus.
6. School starts at/on/for 8.45 and finishes at/on/for 3.30.
7. They've got PE with/under/behind Mr Kingsley.
8. Jo plays football at/on/for Mondays.
9. At/In/By the weekends he often goes to/on/after the pool with his brother Dan.
10. He listens at/on/to music too.

Dan and Jo aren't students on Cotham School, they are students at Cotham School!

A trip to Bath – a play for the end of term

Look quickly at pp. 103–105. How many people are there in this play? Who are they? What are they doing?

Jack Hello, I'm Jack …

Lesley I'm Lesley …

Jo I'm Jo …

Ananda I'm Ananda …

Dan I'm Dan …

Sophie And I'm Sophie. We're all students at Cotham School in Bristol.

Jack Welcome to our little play:

Lesley 'A trip to Bath'.

Jo Not 'bath' as in 'I have a bath every evening' … *(He mimes.)*

Ananda Do you really have a bath every evening, Jo? I only have a bath every second evening. But I like a shower better anyway. I …

Jack When you two have finished, maybe we can go on?

Ananda Oh, sorry. Right.

Dan The city of Bath is just 14 miles from Bristol, so our teacher …

Sophie Mr Kingsley, our teacher, *(she points)* said:

'Mr Kingsley' Let's cycle to Bath! *(All grumble.)*

Sophie Luckily our Music teacher, Miss White, *(she points)* had a good idea. *('Miss White' walks over to 'Mr Kingsley'.)*

'Miss White' Paul, dear, let's cycle to Warmley. That's only seven miles. We can leave our bikes there and take the bus into Bath.

'Mr Kingsley' What a good idea, Isabel.

All Good idea!

'Mr Kingsley' Everybody here? Then let's go! *(Each actor sits on a chair and mimes cycling.)*

Jack We cycled … *(very fast)*

Lesley … and cycled *(fast)*

Jo … and cycled *(slower)*

Ananda … and cycled *(and slower)*

Dan … and … cycled … *(He stops and falls off.)*

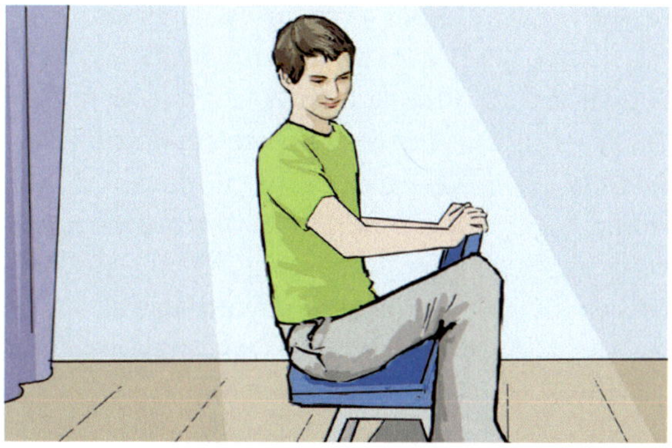

Sophie And then we arrived in Warmley … *(all get up)* … and got on the bus.

(All sit the other way round on their chairs. They mime the movement of the bus and wave. The bus stops and all jump up and take their chairs to the back. They make a group round 'Mr Kingsley'.)

'Mr Kingsley' Now here we are in the Roman Baths. The Romans built them almost two thousand years ago. They were a bit like our leisure centres – you know, swimming pools, saunas, cold pools ...

Sophie *(She shivers.)* Very healthy!

Ananda Very nice.

Dan Very interesting.

Jo Very old! *(He yawns, then turns to audience.)* We were in there for two hours! And then, at last, Miss White said:

'Miss White' Time for lunch, Paul?

All Yes! Hooray! Lunch!

'Mr Kingsley' I know a great sandwich place. Follow me!
(They walk, they choose, they pay, they sit down on the floor and eat.)

Lesley There were sandwiches with brown bread with salad ...

Sophie Very healthy!

Lesley ... tomato, cheese and lettuce ...

Ananda Very nice!

Lesley ... chicken tikka in a brown roll ...

Dan Very interesting ...

Lesley ... tuna and mayonnaise ...

Jo Very old! Hey Dan, that bread really looks very old!

Dan It's a Roman sandwich!
(They all get up and make two groups, Miss White's group walks to one corner.)

Jack After lunch we divided into two groups ... and we walked ... *(fast)*

Lesley ... and walked ... *(slower)*

Dan ... and walked ... *(very slowly)*

Jack ... and walked ... *(He falls to the floor.)*

'Mr Kingsley' Come on, everybody!

Lesley We went to the Museum of Costume ...

Sophie And that's when things started to get interesting.

'Mr Kingsley' Now, let's start here with the clothes from the 18th century.

Lesley There was so much work in these dresses – look.

Dan Hey, what are those things? Look!

Sophie They're corsets.

Dan Corsets?

Lesley Yes, corsets. In those days all the women wore corsets under their clothes, poor things.

Dan But not the men, right!

Sophie No, not the men.

Dan I wonder what they feel like ...
(Dan tries to put on a corset. Jack helps him, then moves back to look at Dan. They all laugh.)

Dan Lesley is right: the poor women. Get me out of here!

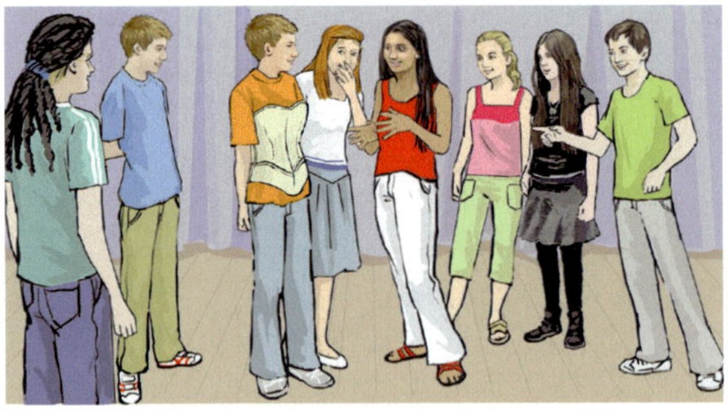

(He tries to get out of the corset.)

Dan Help!
(Jack tries to help.)

'Mr Kingsley' Come on there! Hurry up!

Lesley We're coming, Mr Kingsley!

Dan You can't leave me here!

Lesley *(She smiles.)* Can't we?

Dan Please! Jack, Lesley, Sophie ...

Sophie — *(She turns to audience.)* Did we leave Dan? Well... *(She laughs.)* ... No, we didn't. Here's the rest of the story – in pictures – Jo's pictures, of course. *(Jo on stage with his camera. Lesley is opening Dan's corset. They freeze.)*

Jo — Click!
Sophie — 'Lesley saves Dan.'
Dan — Thank you, Lesley.
Lesley — You're welcome, Dan.
Sophie — After the museum there was ice cream ... *(All come on stage and cheer.)*
All — Hooray! Chocolate for me! I'd like strawberry!
Jo — OK, say ice CREEEEAM! *(They freeze.)*
All — Ice CREEEEEEAM!
Jo — Click!
Sophie — And then we all took the bus back to Warmley. Miss White sat with Mr Kingsley.

('Mr Kingsley' looks into 'Miss White's' eyes.)
'Mr Kingsley' — Tired, Isabel?
'Miss White' — Yes, Paul.
Sophie — Sweet. *(They freeze.)*
Jo — Click!
'Mr Kingsley' — Jo Shaw!
Sophie — And then we cycled home ... Click!
Jo — End of trip!
Lesley — Click!
Jo — End of term!
Jack — Click!
Jo — Happy holidays!
All — *(They sing.)*

We're all going on a summer holiday.
No more working for a week or two.
Fun and laughter on a summer holiday.
No more worries for me and you.
For a week or two.
We're going where the sun shines brightly.
We're going where the sea is blue.
We've seen it in the movies.
Now let's see if it's true.

by Bruce Welch, Brian Bennett

Working with the text

1 One play, seven scenes

a) *Read the play. Divide it into seven scenes. Choose a title for each scene from the box.*

b) *Work in a group. Take a part. Read the play out loud.*

- Welcome to 'A trip to Bath'
- Sandwiches
- On the way to Bath
- Hooray! The summer holidays
- This group for clothes and corsets!
- The end in photos
- At the Roman Baths

2 Extra Act out the play

Make groups of 8. Think about what you need for the play: costumes, chairs, a corset, ...
Learn the words.
Act out the play or your favourite scene(s).

Checkpoint 6 ▸ *WB (pp. 75–77)*

Extra Dan and Jo's summer holidays in New Zealand

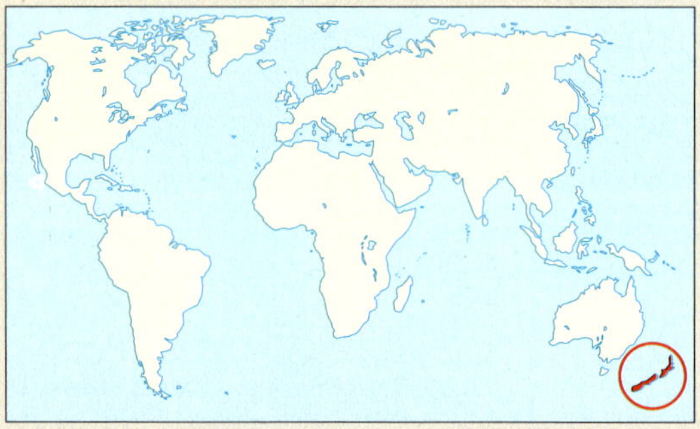

1 Plans for the trip

Dan and Jo are going to spend their summer holidays with their mum. Look at their desk and try to answer these questions.

1. *Where does their mum live?*
2. *What city are they going to fly to?*
3. *What do you think they want to do in New Zealand? The ideas below will help you.*

climb a mountain • fly in a helicopter • go bungee jumping • go kayaking • go swimming • watch dolphins • watch *The Lord of the Rings*

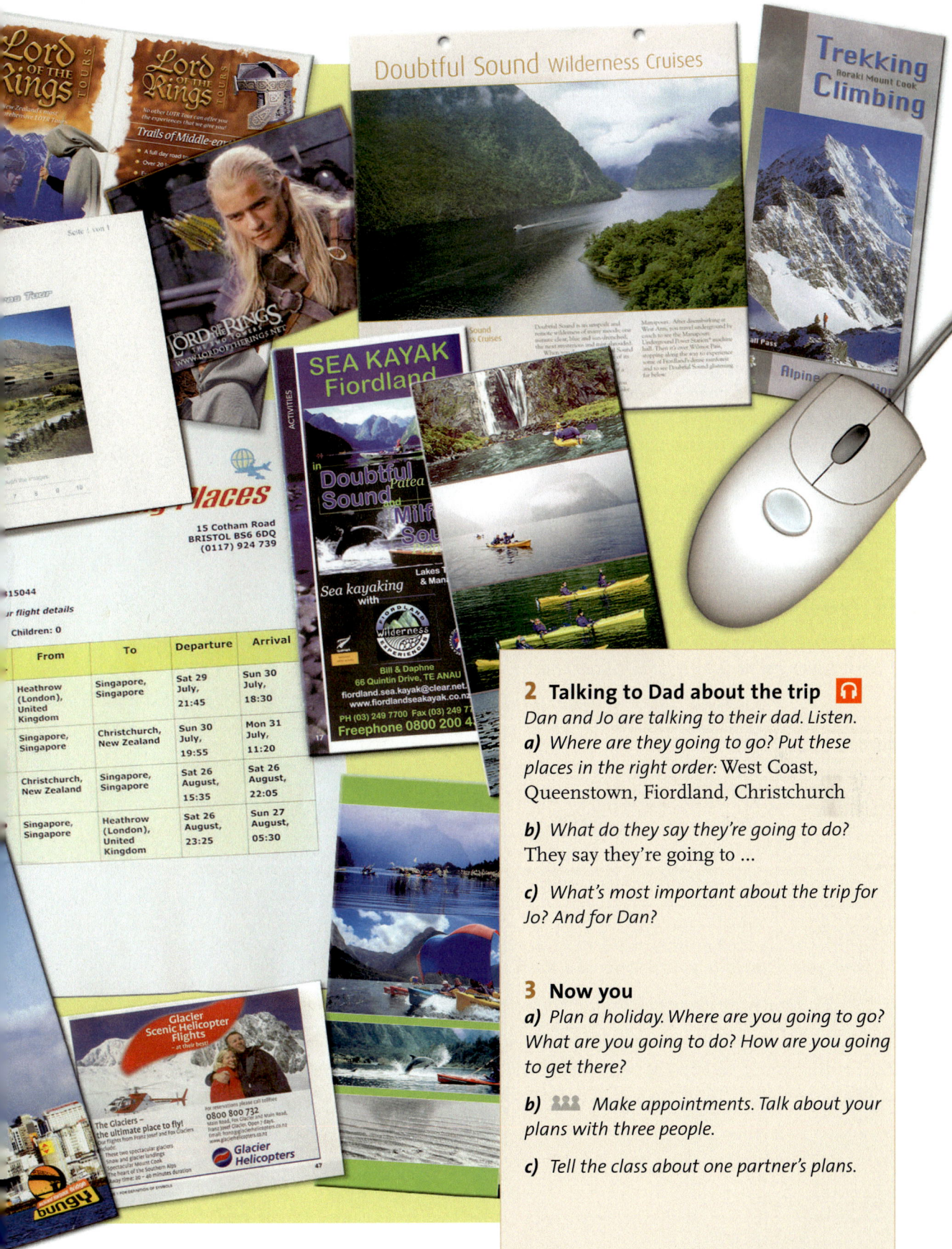

Lord of the Rings Tours
Trails of Middle-earth
Doubtful Sound Wilderness Cruises
Trekking
Aoraki Mount Cook
Climbing
SEA KAYAK Fiordland
Doubtful Sound
Sea kayaking with
Bill & Daphne
66 Quintin Drive, TE ANAU
Places
15 Cotham Road
BRISTOL BS6 6DQ
(0117) 924 739
Children: 0
From | To | Departure | Arrival
Heathrow (London), United Kingdom | Singapore, Singapore | Sat 29 July, 21:45 | Sun 30 July, 18:30
Singapore, Singapore | Christchurch, New Zealand | Sun 30 July, 19:55 | Mon 31 July, 11:20
Christchurch, New Zealand | Singapore, Singapore | Sat 26 August, 15:35 | Sat 26 August, 22:05
Singapore, Singapore | Heathrow (London), United Kingdom | Sat 26 August, 23:25 | Sun 27 August, 05:30

Glacier Scenic Helicopter Flights
The Glaciers – the ultimate place to fly!
0800 800 732
Glacier Helicopters
bungy

2 Talking to Dad about the trip

Dan and Jo are talking to their dad. Listen.

a) *Where are they going to go? Put these places in the right order:* West Coast, Queenstown, Fiordland, Christchurch

b) *What do they say they're going to do?* They say they're going to …

c) *What's most important about the trip for Jo? And for Dan?*

3 Now you

a) *Plan a holiday. Where are you going to go? What are you going to do? How are you going to get there?*

b) *Make appointments. Talk about your plans with three people.*

c) *Tell the class about one partner's plans.*

Unit 1

4 STUDY SKILLS Describing pictures

a) *Partner B: Don't look at your partner's page. He/She describes a picture and you draw it. Show your picture to your partner. Is it correct?*

b) *Now it's your turn. Choose picture **3** or **4**. Describe it to your partner:*

> ***There's a table and a chair in the foregound of my picture and a wardrobe …***

Your partner listens and draws the picture. Check your partner's picture. Is it correct?

c) **Extra** *Now draw your own picture with one person, a table and a chair, a cupboard and a tortoise. (Don't show your partner your picture!) Describe your picture to your partner:*

> ***There's …***

Your partner listens and draws. Then compare your two pictures.

3

4

14 Yesterday afternoon (Simple past: wh-questions)

a) *Partner B: Answer your partner's questions. Then ask him/her about the gaps in your chart. Fill in a copy of the chart.*

	Where did … go?	How … go there?	What … do there?
Ananda	home		
Jo			play football
Jack	home	by bus	do his homework + write a story
Sophie		by car	
You			
Your partner			

b) *Swap your chart with your partner and check.*

c) **Extra** *Now write about you or your partner or one of the Bristol kids.*

Unit 2

8 How many computer games, how much time? (much/many – more – most)

a) Read the information about Christine. Answer your partner's questions about her. Then ask your partner about Lennart. Write the answers in a copy of the chart.

	Lennart	Christine	You	Your partner
books – read		one every week		
time – need for homework		90 minutes		
TV – watch every day		4 hours		
money – spend on sweets		€ 5 every week		
comics – buy every week		2		
computer games – know		15		

B: How many books does Lennart read?
A: One every month.
B: How much time does …?

b) *Fill in the answers for* **You** *in your copy of the table. Then ask your partner and add his/her answers.*
How many … do you read?
How much … do you …?

c) **Extra** *Report to the class. Make comparisons. Use* **more** *and* **the most**.
My partner knows more computer games than Lennart. I know more computer games than my partner. But Christine knows the most.

Unit 3

6 Extra What will they do if …? (Conditional sentences)

a) *Answer your partner's questions.*
Then ask him or her for the missing information.
B: What will Jan do if he finds a baby squirrel?
A: He'll …
B: And what will Jan do if …?
A: …

	find a baby squirrel	get a 5 in English	need a new mobile
Maike	take it to a clinic		ask her parents
Jan		get help from his dad	
Christoph			wait till his birthday
You			
Your partner			

b) *Write three sentences: one about Maike, Jan or Christoph, one about your partner and one about you.*
If Maike finds a baby squirrel, she'll take it to a clinic.
If my partner finds a baby squirrel, he'll / she'll …
If I find a baby squirrel, I'll …

Unit 3

8 WRITING An e-mail to *pet@petoftheday.com*

a) *Read this e-mail. Choose the correct words.*

This is Rosie, my cat. She's seven months old and/but she's very pretty. Every morning she comes to my room before/because I get up. She comes in my bed because/after she wants to play. I always feed Rosie before/after I go to school. I feed her again when/before I come home. I play with her before/because I do my homework. Then she sits on my bed and/but sleeps.

b) **Partner check** *Turn you page upside down.*

This is Marley, my budgie. He's two years old and/~~because~~ I love him very much. When/~~And~~ I come home from school, he's very happy. I play with him ~~because~~/before I have my tea. ~~Before~~/After tea I always do my homework. Marley sits on my desk ~~when~~/and watches me. ~~But~~/When I open Marley's cage, he flies out. He sits on my head and/~~but~~ sings to me.

This is your partner's text. Listen to your partner and correct the mistakes.

c) **Partner check**

Now read your text about Rosie to your partner. Your partner will correct your mistakes.

Unit 4

11 What's different? (Present perfect: just)

Partner B: Answer your partner's question about the people in the picture. Then ask about his/her picture. Take turns. Use ideas from the box.

A: In my picture Sophie has just made popcorn. What about your picture?

B: In my picture Sophie has just ... So our pictures are the same/different.

1 Sophie – make
2 Ananda – open
3 Dan – eat
4 Jo – take
5 Jack – drop
6 Prunella – find

Unit 4

Working with the text

2 Who said it?

Listen to your partner's questions. Scan the text for the correct answers.

A: Who said 'Morning, Bryn'?
B: Elaine said it. It's in line ... ▸ *SF Scanning (p. 130)*

Now test your partner and ask him/her who said these things.

1 'They need a paramedic down there – fast.' (a fireman: ll. 14–15)
B: Who said 'They need a paramedic down there – fast.'
A: A fireman said it. It's in lines ...
2 'I'm ready if you are.' (Bryn: l. 25)
3 'Is everybody OK?' (Beth: ll. 29)
4 'I hope the trees will hold for just a few more minutes.' (Bryn: ll. 58–59)

Unit 5

6 What is he going to do? (going to-future: questions)

a) *Look at the chart. Answer your partner's questions about about Jo, and about Sophie and Ananda. Then ask your partner about Jack, and about Mr and Mrs Hanson. Write down the answers.*

Name	What is/are ... going to do tomorrow?	Where is/are ... going to ...?
Jo	play football	on the Downs
Jack		
Sophie and Ananda	watch a DVD	at Sophie's house
Mr and Mrs Hanson		

8 WORDS Discussion

Your partner is going to talk about one of these statements. Listen carefully.

1 English is the most interesting subject.
2 Borussia Dortmund is a great team.
3 Pop songs are better in German than in English.
4 Bristol is an interesting city.

Say what you think when your partner asks you ...

I think you're right.	Sorry, I don't think you're right.
I agree with you.	I don't agree with you.

... and say why.

I think ... is very/more interesting.	I think English/German sounds cool.
I think ... is the best team.	I think/don't think Bristol looks great/ boring.

Unit 6

4 WORDS Can you tell me the way to ..., please?

a) *Answer your partner's questions. The phrases in the box can help.*

> It's in ... Street/Road/... • near/next to/... • in front of/behind ... • between ... and ... • on the corner of ... and ...

Then look at your map. The names of some buildings are missing:
supermarket • hospital • police station • chemist • library
Ask your partner where they are.

b) **Extra** *Now label the buildings in a copy of the map. Compare your maps.*

c) *You're a tourist. You're in front of the ice rink. Ask your partner the way to three places on the map.*

Tourist Excuse me please, can you tell me the way to ...?

d) *Now your partner is the tourist. Help him/her.*

You First go past ...
Then turn left/right into ...
Cross/Go straight on/...
The ... is on the left/right/corner of ...

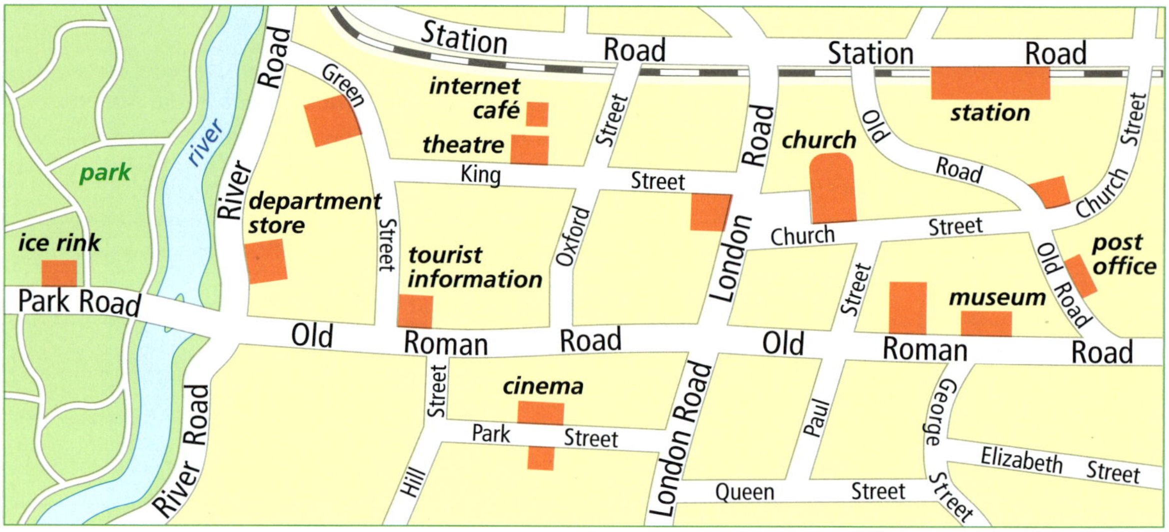

Unit 1

// ● 9 Are you a good detective? (Simple past: positive and negative statements)

Find out what's wrong with these sentences. You can look at p. 12–13 for help.

1 Ananda went to London in her holidays.
Ananda didn't go to London. She went to New York.
2 She went by boat.
3 She stayed with her grandparents.
4 Dilip went to Germany.
5 Ananda and Sophie talked to the new boy.
6 Lesley said 'Hi!'.
7 Sophie and Ananda stayed with Lesley.

// ● 13 Mum wants to know! (Simple past: wh-questions)

Ask questions in the simple past. Use question words **(what, where, when, why)**

1 *Mum* *What did* you *do* (do) at school today?
Tom Not much.
2 *Mum* *What* lessons ... you ... (have)?
Tom Well, we only had lessons in the morning.
3 *Mum* Oh really? ... you ... (do) in afternoon?
Tom Our class went on a trip to the library.
4 *Mum* And ... time ... the trip ... (finish)?
Tom At 3 o'clock.

5 *Mum* ... you ... (go) after that?
Tom I went into town with some friends.
6 *Mum* ... you ... (do) there?
Tom I had a chicken burger.
7 *Mum* ... you ... (eat) a chicken burger?
Tom Because I don't like veggie burgers.

Unit 2

// ● 3 A survey in Geography (Possessive pronouns)

Complete the sentences with the right pronouns: mine • yours • his • hers • ours • theirs

1 *Ananda* My new T-shirt is from China. Where's ... from, Sophie?
2 *Sophie* ... is from China too. What about Dan and Jo? Do you know where ... are from?
3 *Dan + Jo* Oh, ... are from Thailand. Our MP3 players are from Japan. ... too, Tom?
4 *Tom* No, ... is from the USA. But my new mobile is from Japan.
5 *Dan* David has got a new one too. But ... is from Taiwan.
6 *Jack* Ryan's trainers are from Vietnam. Where are ... from, Kevin?
7 *Kevin* They're from Thailand. Ananda has got new ones, too. ... are from China.

Unit 2

// 10 As big as ... (Comparison of adjectives)

Two things are about the same. Make sentences.

1 big — Belgium, the Netherlands, the USA
Belgium is about as big as the Netherlands.
The USA is the biggest.
2 sunny — England, Germany, Turkey
3 sweet — chocolate, banana, apple
4 cold — April, January, October
5 warm — Rome, Oslo, Stockholm
6 long — a poem, a song, a book
7 small — a mouse, a rabbit, a guinea pig

Unit 3

// 2 In 2050 (will-future)

a) *Write a caption for each picture. Use* **will** *or* **won't**.

In 2050 babies (use) computers.
In 2050 people (fly) to work.
In 2050 animals (live) in hotels.
In 2050 it (be) warm in winter.
In 2050 people (read) books.
In 2050 people probably (need) shops.
In 2050 some people (live) under the sea.
In 2050 people (live) on Mars.

1

2

3

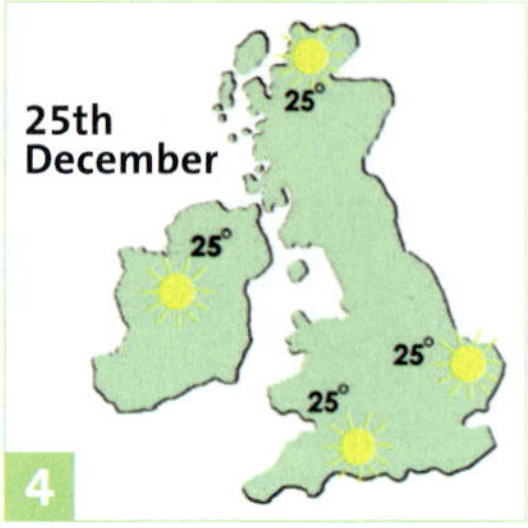

4

5

6

7

8

b) Extra *Are your captions the same?*

A: My caption **1** says: In 2050 people will live on Mars. What do you think?
B: I agree. / I don't agree – I think people won't live on Mars in 2050.
A: What about caption **2**?

Unit 3

// ● 11 Don't hit the dog! (Adverbs of manner)

Complete the sentences with an adverb.

Jack and Ananda walked (careful/slow) home from school.
'Tell me about your hockey match,' Jack said.
'Well, we didn't win,' said Ananda (happy/sad).
'We played really (bad/quiet).'
Suddenly she stopped. 'Can you hear that noise?'
Jack listened (loud/careful).
'You're right,' he said (dangerous/quiet). 'It sounds like a dog. Come on!'
They ran (quick/slow). Soon they could hear the dog (clever/clear). Then they saw a man.
'Don't hit the dog!' Ananda said (nervous/bad).
'Mind your own business,' the man answered (happy/rude).
'Stop that!' Jack shouted (angry/nice). The man ran away.
'Poor little dog,' Ananda said, 'we'll take you to the RSPCA.'

Unit 4

// ● 7 Mr Shaw has painted the kitchen door (Present perfect: regular verbs)

a) *Write about the pictures.*

1 Mr Shaw
paint – kitchen door

2 The twins
pack – suitcases

3 Jack
tidy – desk

4 Mr Kingsley
finish – book

5 The Kapoors
count – money

6 Ananda and Sophie
watch – DVD

7 The Thompsons
cook – lunch

8 Prunella
drop – plate

1 *Mr Shaw has painted the kitchen door.*
2 *The twins have ...*

Unit 4

//● 8 Grandma has made breakfast, so ... (Present perfect: irregular verbs)

Put the verbs in the present perfect. You can look up the irregular forms on pp. 210–211.

1 Grandma ... (make) breakfast, so they can leave soon.
Grandma *has made* breakfast, so they can leave soon.
2 Jo ... (take) lots of photos because he wants to mail them to his mum.
3 Grandpa ... (go) out to the car because he wants to clean it.
4 Ananda and Jack ... (be) to the cinema and now they're sitting in a café.
5 Sophie ... (be) ill, so now she has to do lots of homework.
6 We ... (come) to see you today because we can't come to your party tomorrow.
7 I ... (see) the new film, but I don't like it.

//● 14 Have you done your homework? (Present perfect: questions)

Complete the questions with the verbs in brackets. Then complete the answers.

1 Mrs H — *Have you done* (you/do) your homework, Jack?
Jack — Yes, I *have*, Mum.
2 Mrs H — And ... (Dan and Jo/finish) that project yet?
Jack — No, they ...
3 Jack — What about dinner? ... (dad/cook) it yet?
Mrs H — No, he ...
4 Jack — Well, ... (you/read) Aunt Jenny's letter yet?
Mrs H — Yes, I ...
5 Jack — And ... (you/feed) Polly?
Polly — No, she ... – Hurry up! Hurry up!

Unit 5

//● 3 Plans for this evening (going to-future)

Say what the people are going to do this evening.

1 Dan

2 Jo and his dad

3 Jack

4 Jack's parents

5 Sophie

6 Ananda

1 Dan is going to ...
2 Jo and his dad are going to ...

Unit 5

// ● 7 REVISION What has just happened? (Present perfect)

Look at the picture. Say what has just happened. Use these verbs.

arrive • drive into (2x) • drop • fall down • land • open • sit down • take

Three little men from Mars have just landed. Ananda has just …

// ● 13 MEDIATION A tour of Bristol

The Meiers are on a tour of Bristol. But they don't understand much English.
Answer their questions. But you don't have much time. Tell them only the important things each time.

Guide Hi, everybody. Welcome to our Bristol Open Top Bus Tour. My name is Carol and I'm your guide. I hope you have fun on our tour. OK, let's go.

You …

Guide On the left you can see Bristol's famous harbour. The big ship over there is the *SS Great Britain*. This ship was the work of Bristol's great engineer Isambard Kingdom Brunel. It's open to visitors.

Frau M Was ist mit dem Schiff?

You …

Guide When we come to the top of the hill, the driver will turn left. Then, on your right, you'll see a large green area. We call this area the Downs. As you will see, people like to come here on a warm day. It's usually cooler than the city centre.

Herr M Wir biegen wohl ab, aber was ist dann?

You …

Guide Now we're in Clifton Village. There are lots of nice little shops and cafés in the village. We're going to stay here for thirty minutes. You can go to the shops or get something to drink but please don't be late. There's lots more to see.

Frau M Alle steigen aus. Ist die Fahrt schon zu Ende?

You …

Unit 6

// ● 7 Yesterday they were working (Past progressive)

Look at the pictures. What were the people doing at 10 o'clock yesterday? And at ...?

1 At ten o'clock yesterday Sophie was making a poster. Jo ... a report.
2 At eleven o'clock yesterday ...

// ● 12 WORDS Prepositions

a) *Complete with the correct prepositions.*

1 Dan and Jo live ___ 7 Hamilton Street.
2 They are students ___ Cotham School.
3 They're both ___ Form 8PK.
4 They usually go to school ___ bike.
5 They don't like to wait ___ the bus.
6 School starts ___ 8.45 and finishes ___ 3.30.
7 They've got PE ___ Mr Kingsley.
8 Jo plays football ___ Mondays.
9 ___ the weekends he often goes ___ the pool with his brother Dan.
10 He listens ___ music too.

Dan and Jo aren't students on Cotham School, they are students at Cotham School!

Unit 6

// 8 What were they doing when Mrs Harper came home? (Past progressive)

Write down what the different people in the picture where doing when Mrs Harper came home. The verbs in the box will help you.

build • do • feed • play • read • ride • sleep • take • talk • watch

When Mrs Harper came home, Adam was building a tower.
When Mrs Harper came home, …

Inhalt **Seite**

Im **Skills File** findest du Hinweise zu Arbeits- und Lerntechniken. Was du in den Skills-Kästen der Units gelernt hast, wird hier näher erläutert.

Was du bereits aus Band 1 von English G 21 kennst, ist mit **REVISION** gekennzeichnet.

Viele neue Hinweise helfen dir bei der Arbeit mit Hör- und Lesetexten, beim Sprechen, beim Schreiben von eigenen Texten, bei der Sprachmittlung und beim Lernen von Methoden.

STUDY AND LANGUAGE SKILLS

SF REVISION Stop – Check – Go

Fehler bei den Hausaufgaben? Falsche oder keine Antworten im Unterricht? Die nächste Englischarbeit steht bevor? – Höchste Zeit für STOP – CHECK – GO!

Stop
Mindestens einmal pro Unit, besser häufiger.

Check
Überprüfe, ob du den Stoff der Unit verstanden hast. Was zum Stoff einer Unit gehört, kannst du z.B. im Inhaltsverzeichnis sehen oder deine/n Lehrer/in fragen. Der **Checkpoint** ▸ im *Workbook* hilft dir am Ende jeder Unit bei der Überprüfung. Dort findest du Testaufgaben.

Go
Überlege, was du besser machen kannst. Du könntest
- deine/n Lehrer/in um Rat fragen,
- dir das, was du nicht verstanden hast, von einem Mitschüler/einer Mitschülerin erklären lassen,
- Übungen im Buch wiederholen,
- dir einzelne Abschnitte im *Grammar File* oder *Skills File* anschauen,
- die *Listening*-CD zum Schülerbuch oder das *Workbook* benutzen.

REVISION Learning words – Step 1

Worauf solltest du beim Lernen und Wiederholen von Vokabeln achten?

- Führe dein Vokabelverzeichnis, dein Vokabelheft oder deinen Karteikasten aus Klasse 5 weiter.
- Lerne immer 7–10 Vokabeln auf einmal.
- Lerne neue und wiederhole alte Vokabeln regelmäßig – am besten jeden Tag 5–10 Minuten.
- Es macht mehr Spaß, wenn du die Vokabeln mit jemandem zusammen lernst. Fragt euch gegenseitig ab.
- Finde heraus, wie du am besten Vokabeln lernen kannst: durch Hören, durch Bilder, am Computer mit deinem *e-Workbook* oder dem *English Coach*. Vielleicht kannst du dir auch eigene Geschichten um die neuen Vokabeln ausdenken.

round the car

SF Learning words – Step 2

Wörter kannst du besser behalten, wenn du sie in Wortgruppen sammelst und ordnest. Dazu gibt es verschiedene Möglichkeiten.

Du kannst

- **Gegensatzpaare** sammeln, z.B. sunny – rainy, happy – sad, top – bottom, foreground – background;

- Wörter in **Wortfamilien** sammeln, z.B. (to) sing – song – singer;
- Wörter in **Wortfeldern** sammeln – dabei schreibst du alle Wörter unter Oberbegriffen (**group words**) auf;

SCHOOL

subjects	sports	things
Maths	tennis	book
Art	football	pencil
Geography	...	...
...		

- Wörter in **Wortnetzen** (*networks*) sammeln und ordnen.

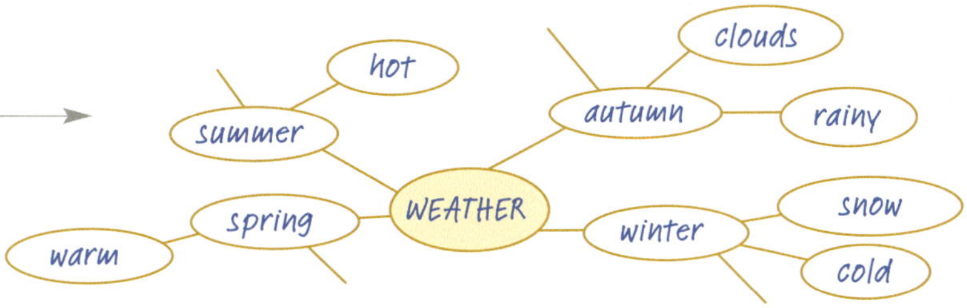

SF REVISION Mind maps

Wozu dienen Mindmaps?

Mithilfe von Mindmaps kannst du Ideen sammeln und ordnen, wenn du etwas vortragen sollst oder einen Text vorbereiten willst.

Wie mache ich eine Mindmap?

1. Schreib das Thema in die Mitte eines leeren, unlinierten Blattes Papier. Male einen Kreis oder eine Wolke drum herum.
2. Überlege dir, welche Oberbegriffe zu deiner Sammlung von Ideen passen. Verwende unterschiedliche Farben.
3. Ergänze jede Idee, die zu einem Oberbegriff passt, auf einem Nebenast. Nimm dafür nur wichtige Schlüsselwörter.
Du kannst statt Wörtern auch Symbole verwenden und Bilder ergänzen.

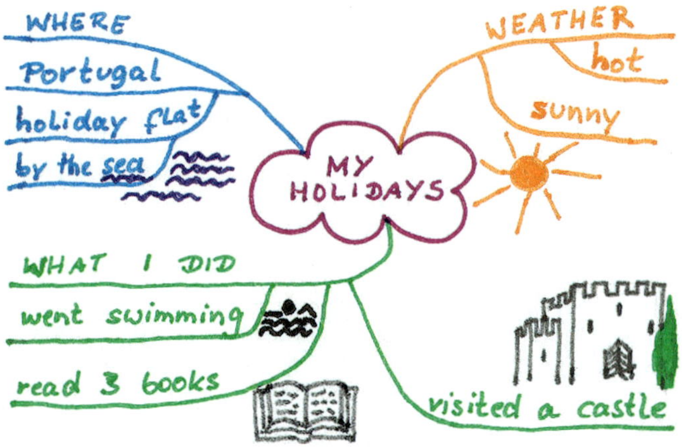

SF REVISION Understanding new words

Immer gleich im Wörterbuch nachschlagen?

Das Nachschlagen unbekannter Wörter im Wörterbuch kostet Zeit und nimmt auf Dauer den Spaß am Lesen. Oft kannst du die Bedeutung von Wörtern ohne Wörterbuch herausfinden.

Was hilft mir, unbekannte Wörter zu verstehen?

1. Bilder sind eine große Hilfe. Sie zeigen oft die Dinge, die du im Text nicht verstehst. Schau sie dir deshalb vor dem Lesen genau an.
2. Oft helfen dir die Wörter, die vor oder nach dem unbekannten Wort stehen. Erschließe die Bedeutung eines Wortes aus dem Textzusammenhang, z.B. *We must hurry. Our train* **departs** *in ten minutes.*
3. Viele englische Wörter werden ähnlich wie im Deutschen geschrieben oder klingen ähnlich, z.B. **discussion**, **statue**, **margarine**.
4. Manchmal stecken in unbekannten Wörtern bekannte Teile, z.B. **sunshine**, **bottle opener**, **skater**.

- Alles klar? Dann überlege, was diese Wörter bedeuten.
energy • **discovery** • **builder** • **winner** • **telescope** • **unfair** • **friendly** • **milkshake** • **sprinter**

SF REVISION Working with a dictionary

Du verstehst ein Wort nicht? Du brauchst ein englisches Wort, das du nicht kennst? Dann hilft Dir ein Wörterbuch weiter.
In diesem Buch findest du das **English-German dictionary** auf den Seiten 173–191 und das **German-English dictionary** auf den Seiten 192–206.

Wörter nachschlagen: Wie benutze ich ein Wörterbuch?

Denk daran:
- Stichwörter sind alphabetisch geordnet: **f** vor **g**, **fa** vor **fe** und **fle** vor **fli** usw.
- Zusammengesetzte Wörter und längere Ausdrücke findest du oft unter mehr als einem Stichwort, z.B. **ask sb. the way** unter **ask** und unter **way** und **Geh ein Feld vor** unter **gehen** und unter **Feld**.
- In eckigen Klammern steht, wie das Wort ausgesprochen und betont wird. (→ Englische Laute: S. 191)
- Die Ziffern 1., 2. usw. zeigen, dass ein Stichwort mehrere Bedeutungen hat.

- Suche im *Dictionary* (Seiten 173–191 und 192–206) die Bedeutung der Wörter rechts heraus ...
- ... und sprich sie deinem Partner/deiner Partnerin oder der Klasse richtig vor.

bottom • rude • service • Flug • gefährlich • Insel

Dictionary (English – German)

art [ɑːt] Kunst I
as [əz, æz]
1. als, während II 2 (38)
2. as old as so alt wie II 2 (30)
ask [ɑːsk] fragen I • **ask about sth.** nach etwas fragen I • **ask questions** Fragen stellen I • **ask sb. the way** jn. nach dem Weg fragen II 6 (95/170)

Dictionary (German – English)

Feld **1.** field [fiːld] • **auf dem Feld** in the field
2. *(bei Brettspielen)* **Geh ein Feld vor.** Move on one space. [speɪs] • **Geh ein Feld zurück.** Move back one space.
Fleisch meat [miːt]
fliegen fly [flaɪ]
Flug flight [flaɪt]

SF Describing pictures

Wenn du ein Bild beschreibst, geht es viel besser, wenn du die folgenden Dinge beachtest.

Was hilft mir beim Bilder beschreiben?

Wo?
- Um zu sagen, wo etwas abgebildet ist, benutze:
  at the top/bottom • **in the foreground/background** • **in the middle** • **on the left/right**
- Diese Präpositionen sind auch hilfreich:
  behind • **between** • **in front of** • **next to** • **under**

Wie?
Geh bei der Beschreibung in einer bestimmten Reihenfolge vor, z.B. von links nach rechts, von oben nach unten oder vom Vordergrund zum Hintergrund.

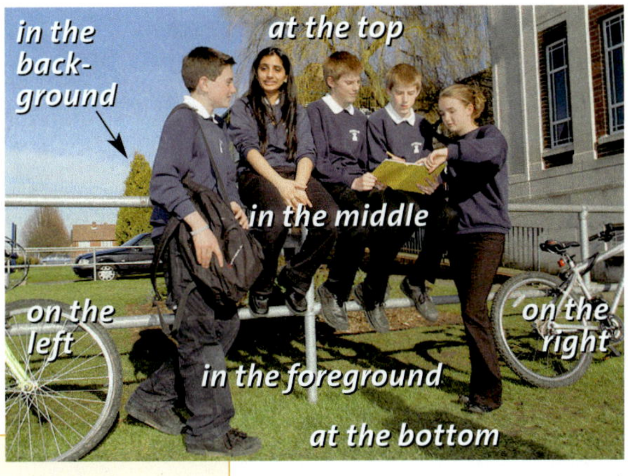

Tipp

Um zu sagen, was gerade passiert, benutze das **present progressive**.
Sophie ***is showing*** *Jo a book. Ananda* ***is talking*** *to Jack.*

- Alles klar? Dann beschreib das Foto oben rechts und mach Übung 4 auf S. 17.

SF Multiple-choice exercises

Was sind Multiple-Choice-Aufgaben?

Bei Multiple-Choice-Aufgaben gibt es mehrere Antworten (meist sind es drei oder vier). Meistens ist nur **eine** davon richtig, und die musst du auswählen.

Worauf sollte ich bei Multiple-Choice-Aufgaben achten?

- Lies die Frage sehr genau durch.
- Bevor du dir die Lösungsangebote anschaust, deck sie mit Papier ab. Überlege dir, was die richtige Antwort sein könnte. Wenn das dann auch als eine Lösungsmöglichkeit angeboten wird, ist es meistens richtig.
- Lies immer alle vorgegebenen Lösungen, bevor du dich entscheidest.
- Sprich die Sätze mit den verschiedenen Lösungsmöglichkeiten leise nach. Oft hört man heraus, was richtig ist.
- Wenn es heißt, dass nur eine der Antworten richtig ist, dann achte darauf, dass du nur **eine** ankreuzt.
- Mach erst alle Aufgaben und geh zum Schluss zu den Fragen zurück, bei denen du unsicher bist.

• Nun probier die Aufgabe 4 auf Seite 49.

1 What did Ananda find in her yard?
A two cats
B one fox
C two hedgehogs
D three mice

2 Hedgehog babies can drink …
A orange juice.
B water.
C milk.
D ice tea.

SF REVISION Giving a presentation

Wie mache ich eine gute Präsentation?

Vorbereitung
- Schreib die wichtigsten Gedanken als Notizen auf, z.B. auf nummerierte Karteikarten oder als Mindmap (vgl. SF **Mind maps**, S. 122).
- Bereite ein Poster oder eine Folie vor. Schreib groß und für alle gut lesbar.
- Übe deine Präsentation zu Hause vor einem Spiegel. Sprich laut, deutlich und langsam.

Durchführung
- Bevor du beginnst, häng das Poster auf bzw. leg deine Folie auf den ausgeschalteten Projektor und sortiere deine Vortragskarten.
- Warte, bis es ruhig ist. Schau die Zuhörer an.
- Erkläre zu Anfang, worüber du sprechen wirst. Lies nicht von deinen Karten ab, sondern sprich frei.

My presentation is about … First, I'd like to talk about … Second, …

This picture/photo/… shows …

Schluss
- Sag, dass du fertig bist.
- Frag die Zuhörenden, ob sie Fragen haben. Bedanke dich fürs Zuhören.

That's the end of my presentation. Have you got any questions?

LISTENING AND READING SKILLS

SF Listening

Du brauchst nicht jedes Wort zu verstehen!

Bei einem Hörtext sollst du oft nur allgemein verstehen, worum es geht.

1. Bevor es losgeht, frag dich: Was weiß ich schon über das Thema? Worum wird es in dem Hörtext gehen?
2. Denk daran: *Wie* jemand etwas sagt, verrät dir viel darüber, *was* die Person sagt. Klingt er oder sie fröhlich, traurig, aufgeregt, gelangweilt ...?
3. Auch Nebengeräusche sind eine Hilfe: Eine Erkennungsmelodie verrät, dass es um eine Radiosendung geht. Oder du hörst einen pfeifenden Teekessel? Dann weißt du, dass sich der Dialog, den du hörst, in der Küche abspielt.
4. Vor allem: Lass dich nicht verunsichern, wenn du mal einen Satz nicht verstehst. Das geht jedem so.

Was sollte ich noch beim *Listening* beachten?

Oft willst du aus einem Hörtext Einzelinformationen heraushören, z.B. auf S. 43, in welcher Reihenfolge die Fernsehsendungen ausgestrahlt werden. Das ist nicht so schwer, wenn du die folgenden Tipps beachtest.

1. **Bereite dich gut vor**
   Lies die Aufgabe zum Hörtext gut durch und bereite deine Notizen vor. Leg z.B. eine Tabelle oder Liste an.
2. **Und wenn ich eine wichtige Information nicht verstehe?**
   Auch hier gilt: keine Panik! Oft werden wichtige Informationen auch wiederholt. Denk an die Aufgabe und hör weiter zu.
3. **Stimme und Betonung helfen dir**
   Achte darauf, was der/die Sprecher/in besonders betont – das ist wichtig!
4. **Aufgepasst!**
   Die Informationen, die du suchst, kommen vielleicht in einer anderen Reihenfolge vor, als du erwartest.
5. **Notizen machen: gewusst wie**
   Mach während des Hörens nur kurze Notizen oder verwende Symbole. Du kannst sie hinterher ergänzen. (Vgl. SF **Taking notes**, S. 127).

SF Scanning

Texte nach Informationen absuchen

Du brauchst einen ganzen Text nicht genau zu lesen, wenn du nur bestimmte Informationen benötigst. Suche nach Schlüsselwörtern (**key words**) und lies nur dort genauer, wo du sie findest.

Wie gehe ich vor?

Schritt 1: Bevor du auf den Text schaust

Denk an das Schlüsselwort, nach dem du suchst. Es hilft dir, wenn du es aufschreibst.

Schritt 2: Das Schlüsselwort finden

Geh mit deinen Augen sehr schnell durch den Text. Dabei hast du das Schriftbild oder das Bild des Wortes, nach dem du suchst, vor Augen. Das gesuchte Wort wird dir sofort „ins Auge springen". Du kannst auch mit dem Finger in breiten Schlingen oder Bewegungen wie bei einem „S" durch die Mitte des Texts von oben bis unten gehen.
Wenn du das Schlüsselwort gefunden hast, lies nur dort weiter, um Näheres zu erfahren.

- Probier das *Scanning* am Text über Maulwürfe aus.
  Suche nach der ersten fehlenden Information (*food*) und vervollständige die Tabelle auf einem Blatt Papier.
  Suche dann nach der zweiten und nach der dritten fehlenden Information.

	moles
food	
number of babies	
enemies	

MOLES

Moles are about 17 cm long and weigh about 100 grams. They have sharp teeth, very small eyes and ears, and a hairless snout. They live underground – in tunnels in gardens, parks and woods. They don't usually come out during the day.
But at night they come out to look for food. Every day they eat 70 to 100 grams of worms and insects. They can't see colours very well, but they can see when something moves. And they can smell and hear very well. So it isn't difficult for them to find something to eat.
Female moles usually have three to five babies a year. The babies are born without any fur and are quite helpless. At first they stay underground. Then, at the age of three months, they are almost as large as their parents and are able to leave the tunnel. Moles can live up to three years. They have only a few enemies, like dogs and cats. These animals catch and kill them, but they don't eat them.

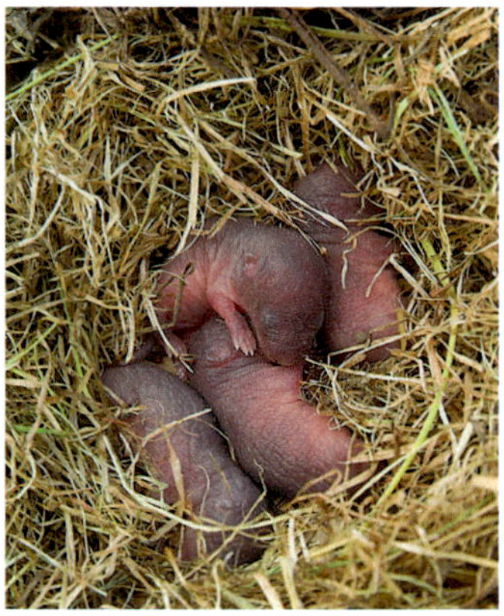

- Alles klar? Dann mach die Aufgabe 8 auf Seite 47.

SF REVISION Taking notes

Worum geht es beim Notizen machen?

Wenn du beim Lesen oder Zuhören Notizen machst, kannst du dich später besser daran erinnern, wenn du etwas vortragen, nacherzählen oder einen Bericht schreiben sollst.

Hmm, da hab ich wohl ein paar Symbole zu viel benutzt ...

Wie mache ich Notizen?

In Texten oder Gesprächen gibt es immer wichtige und unwichtige Wörter. Die wichtigen Wörter werden Schlüsselwörter (**key words**) genannt und nur die solltest du notieren. Meist sind das Substantive und Verben, manchmal auch Adjektive oder Zahlen.

Tipp

- Verwende Ziffern (z.B. „7“ statt „seven“).
- Verwende Symbole und Abkürzungen, z.B. ✔ (für Ja) und + (für und) oder GB für Great Britain, A. für Ananda.
  Du kannst auch eigene Symbole erfinden.
- Verwende not oder ✕ statt „doesn't“ oder „don't“.

SF Marking up a text

Wann sollte ich einen Text markieren?

Du hast einen Text mit vielen Fakten vor dir liegen und sollst später über bestimmte Dinge berichten. Dann wird es dir helfen, die für dich wichtigen Informationen im Text zu markieren.

Wie gehe ich am besten vor?

Lies den Text und markiere nur die für dein Thema wichtigen Informationen. Nicht jeder Satz enthält für deine Aufgabe wichtige Wörter, und oft reicht es aus, nur ein oder zwei Wörter in einem Satz zu markieren.

- Du kannst wichtige Wörter einkreisen.
- Du kannst sie unterstreichen.
- Du kannst sie mit einem Textmarker hervorheben.

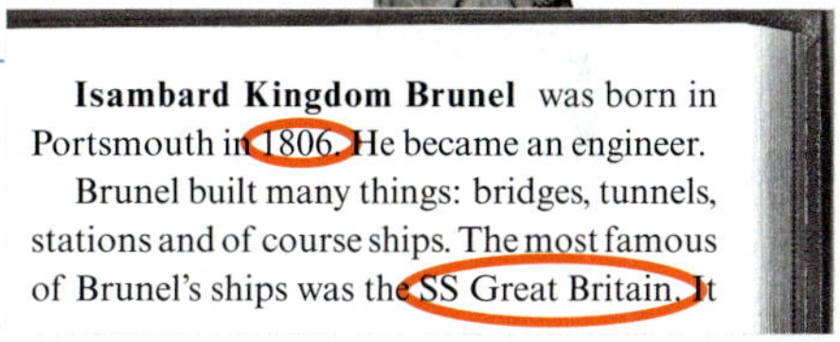

Isambard Kingdom Brunel was born in Portsmouth in 1806. He became an engineer. Brunel built many things: bridges, tunnels, stations and of course ships. The most famous of Brunel's ships was the SS Great Britain. It

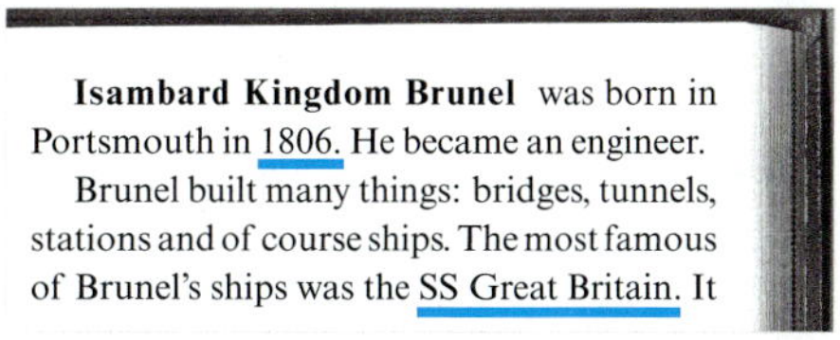

Isambard Kingdom Brunel was born in Portsmouth in 1806. He became an engineer. Brunel built many things: bridges, tunnels, stations and of course ships. The most famous of Brunel's ships was the SS Great Britain. It

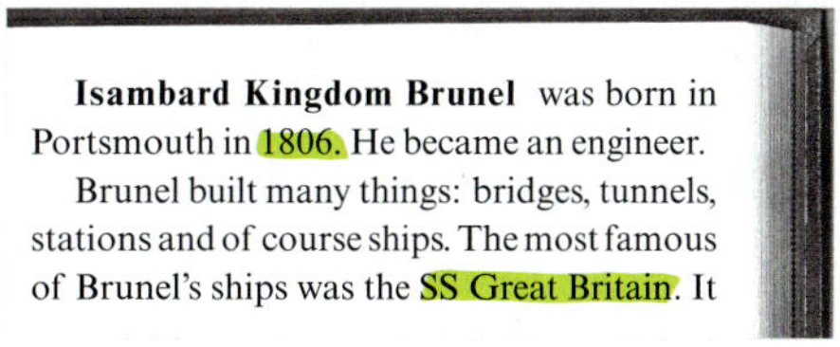

Isambard Kingdom Brunel was born in Portsmouth in 1806. He became an engineer. Brunel built many things: bridges, tunnels, stations and of course ships. The most famous of Brunel's ships was the SS Great Britain. It

ABER:
Markiere nur auf Fotokopien von Texten oder in deinen eigenen Büchern.

- Alles verstanden? Dann probier Aufgabe 9 auf S. 83.

SPEAKING AND WRITING SKILLS

SF Talking to people

Wie kann ich mich freundlich auf Englisch unterhalten?

Wenn du dich auf Englisch unterhalten willst, helfen dir ein paar einfache Redewendungen:

1. Fang nett an ...	**2.** ... und antworte nicht nur mit einem Wort.	**3.** Zeig, dass du wissen willst, was die anderen denken ...	**4.** ... und erzähle etwas von dir.	**5.** Verabschiede dich freundlich.
Hello! **How are you?** **Can I sit with you?**	**Fine, thank you.** **Yes, of course.** **Yes, it is.** **No, I can't.** **Yes, thank you.**	**What about you?** **And you?** **What do you think?** **Do you like...?**	**I'm interested in ...** **I often ...** **I like ... very much**	**Bye then.** **See you later.** **See you tomorrow.** **Goodbye.**

Am folgenden Beispiel kannst du sehen, welchen Unterschied es macht, ob man diese Redewendungen verwendet oder nicht.

a) Jan aus Mainz ist Austauschschüler in England und spricht mit Jenny, der Tochter seiner Gasteltern.

Jenny Hi Jan.
Jan Hi.
Jenny Is this your first time in England?
Jan Yes.
Jenny When did you arrive?
Jan Yesterday.
Jenny Mmm ... Do you like music and dancing?
Jan Yes.
Jenny Well, ... would you like to come to the student disco this evening?
Jan OK.
Jenny Well, let's meet at 7 pm then.
Jan OK.
Jenny Bye then, Jan.
Jan Bye.

b) Malte ist auch zum ersten Mal in England.

Debbie Hi Malte.
Malte Oh, hi Debbie.
Debbie Is this your first time in England?
Malte Yes, it is. It's really great here.
Debbie When did you arrive?
Malte We arrived yesterday. So I'm a bit tired.
Debbie Do you like music and dancing?
Malte Oh yes, I like music a lot. What about you?
Debbie Me too! Well, ... would you like to come to the student disco this evening?
Malte Yes, that sounds great.
Debbie Well, let's meet at 7 pm then.
Malte OK. Thank you.
Debbie See you later.
Malte Bye, Debbie. See you.

- Nun probier das **Now you** auf S. 94 und Übung 3 auf S. 98.

SF Linking words

Eine Geschichte klingt viel interessanter, wenn man die Sätze mit **linking words** miteinander verbindet. Eine Möglichkeit dazu sind **time phrases** wie **at 7 o'clock, a few minutes later, suddenly, then, next, ...**

At 2 o'clock in the morning David walked downstairs and opened the front door. Tim was outside. 'Follow me,' he whispered. A few minutes later the two boys were in the garden of the old house. 'We can hide behind these trees,' Tim said. They waited and watched. Suddenly somebody opened one of the windows. Then they saw a man and a woman. First the woman climbed out and jumped down. Next the man threw out a big box before he jumped down too. 'What are they doing?' David asked.

SF Topic sentence

Wofür sind *topic sentences* gut?

Wenn du einen Text schreibst, sind kurze, einleitende Sätze (**topic sentences**) am Anfang jedes Absatzes gut, weil sie den Lesern sofort sagen, worum es geht. So lesen sie mit mehr Interesse weiter, wovon du berichten willst.
Folgende Wendungen können dir helfen, einen topic sentence zu formulieren:

1. Orte: **Bristol is famous for ... / ... is a great place. / There are lots of reasons to visit ...**
2. Personen: **... is/was one of the greatest/most interesting ...**
3. Aktivitäten: **... is great fun. / Lots of people ... every day.**

• Alles verstanden? Dann probier Übung 5 auf S. 65.

SF Structuring a text

Warum sollte ich meine Texte gliedern?

Ein Text ist viel besser zu verstehen, wenn er nicht einen „Textbrei", sondern mehrere Absätze enthält.

Wie sollte ich meine Texte gliedern?

Unterteile deinen Text in:

- eine Einleitung (**beginning**) – hier schreibst du, worum es in dem Text geht (vgl. SF **Topic sentence**).
- einen Mittelteil (**middle**) – hier schreibst du mehr über dein Thema.
- einen Schluss (**end**) – hier bringst du den Text zu einem interessanten Ende.

Wuppertal is famous for its overhead monorail, the 'Schwebebahn'.

The 'Schwebebahn' is over 100 years old. It's 13.5 km long and follows the River Wupper. The people of Wuppertal built it over the river because there wasn't much room in the Wupper valley. The 'Schwebebahn' isn't very fast, but it's very safe. Lots of people use it every day.

When you're in Wuppertal, travel by 'Schwebebahn'. It's great fun!

• Nun probier Übung 12 auf S. 84.

SF Correcting mistakes

Warum sollte ich einen Text überarbeiten?

Ein Text ist noch nicht „fertig“, wenn du ihn zu Ende geschrieben hast. Du solltest ihn immer mehrmals durchlesen:
Lies ihn noch einmal, um zu sehen, ob er vollständig und gut verständlich ist.

Lies ihn erneut, um ihn auf Fehler zu überprüfen. Das können unterschiedliche Fehler sein, z.B. **Wortfehler** – du hast vielleicht eine falsche **Präposition** benutzt.

um drei Uhr	– **at** three o'clock
im Moment	– **at** the moment
zu Hause	– **at** home

Tipp

- Lerne Wörter immer mit der dazugehörigen **Präposition**, z.B. nicht nur **wait**, sondern **wait for**, oder **am** Abend – **in** the evening.

- Alles klar? Dann probier Aufgabe 12 auf S. 102.

Häufig sind es aber auch Rechtschreibfehler (**spelling mistakes**).

Wie erkenne ich Rechtschreibfehler?

Lies deinen Text langsam, Wort für Wort, Buchstabe für Buchstabe. Wenn du unsicher bist, hilft dir ein Wörterbuch.
Einige **spelling mistakes** kannst du vermeiden, wenn du folgende Regeln beachtest.

tomato [tə'mɑːtəʊ], *pl* **tomatoes**
Tomate II 6 (104)

wife [waɪf], *pl* **wives** [waɪvz]
Ehefrau II 4 (71)

drop (-pp-) [drɒp] fallen lassen I

forget (-tt-) [fə'get] vergessen I

Tipp

Einige Wörter haben Buchstaben, die geschrieben, aber nicht gesprochen werden,
z.B. **walk**, **grandma**.

Manchmal ändert sich die Schreibweise, wenn ein Wort eine Endung erhält,
z.B. **take** —> **taking**,
grumble —> **grumbled**,

z.B. **happy** —> **happily**,
fly —> **flies**,
ABER **stay** —> **stays**,

z.B. **sit** —> **sitting**,
plan —> **planned**.

Beim Plural reicht manchmal ein *-s* als Endung nicht aus, es muss noch ein *-e* dazu,
z.B. **box** —> **boxes**,
potato —> **potatoes**.

- Alles verstanden? Dann probier auch Aufgabe 11 auf S. 102.

MEDIATION SKILLS

SF Mediation

Wann muss ich zwischen zwei Sprachen vermitteln?

Manchmal musst du zwischen zwei Sprachen vermitteln. Das nennt man **mediation**.

Was sagt er?

1. Du gibst englische Informationen auf Deutsch weiter: Du fährst z.B. mit deiner Familie nach Großbritannien und deine Eltern oder Geschwister wollen wissen, was jemand in einem Café gesagt hat oder was an einer Informationstafel steht.

2. Du gibst deutsche Informationen auf Englisch weiter: Vielleicht ist bei dir zu Hause eine Austauschschülerin aus England oder Dänemark zu Gast, die kein Deutsch spricht und Hilfe braucht.

Willst Du auch Würstchen?
Sorry, Niklas, what is your grandma saying?
Would you like sausages too?

3. In schriftlichen Prüfungen musst du manchmal in einem englischen Text gezielt nach Informationen suchen und diese auf Deutsch wiedergeben.

Worauf muss ich bei *mediation* achten?

Übersetze nicht alles wörtlich, gib nur das Wesentliche weiter.
Du kannst Unwichtiges weglassen und Sätze anders formulieren.

Well, let's go to the show by car. We can't walk there because of the children. They can't walk so far.
Er will mit dem Auto fahren. Die Kinder können nicht so weit laufen.

Tipp

- Verwende kurze und einfache Sätze.
- Wenn du ein Wort nicht kennst, umschreibe es oder ersetze es durch ein anderes mit ähnlicher Bedeutung.

- Alles verstanden? Dann probier die Aufgabe 14 auf S. 37.

Im **Grammar File** (S. 132–149) wird zusammengefasst, was du in den sechs Units über die englische Sprache lernst.

In der **linken Spalte** findest du **Beispielsätze** und **Übersichten**, z.B.

How did Dan **help** her?

Fragen

Merke:

Simple present Do you **get up** early? Does Lesley **get**

Simple past Did you **get up** earl

In der **rechten Spalte** stehen **Erklärungen** und nützliche **Hinweise**. Das rote **Ausrufezeichen** (**!**) macht dich auf besondere Fehlerquellen aufmerksam.

Hinweise wie ► *Unit 1 (p. 13)* • *P 8–9 (p. 19)* zeigen dir, zu welcher Unit und welcher Seite ein **Grammar-File**-Abschnitt gehört und welche Übungen du dazu im Practice-Teil findest.

Die **grammatischen Fachbegriffe** *(grammatical terms)* kannst du auf S. 149 nachschlagen.

Am Ende der Abschnitte stehen wieder kleine Aufgaben zur Selbstkontrolle. Schreib die Lösungen in dein Heft. Überprüfe sie auf S. 148.

Grammar File – Inhalt

Seite

Unit 1

GF 1 REVISION The simple past: positive statements

Die einfache Form der Vergangenheit: bejahte Aussagesätze

We were in Spain **last summer**.
It was great. We went swimming a lot and played volleyball on the beach.
Wir waren letzten Sommer in Spanien / sind letzten Sommer in Spanien gewesen ...

Mit dem *simple past* kannst du über Vergangenes berichten, z.B. wenn du eine Geschichte erzählst. Das *simple past* steht häufig mit Zeitangaben wie *last summer, yesterday, three weeks ago, in 2004.*

a) (to) be and regular verbs

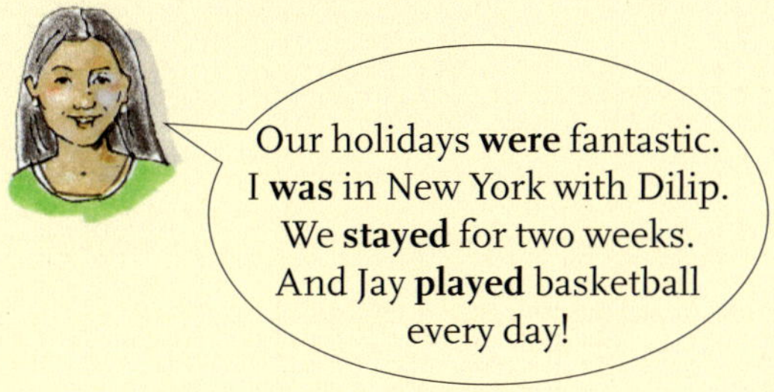

Our holidays **were** fantastic. I **was** in New York with Dilip. We **stayed** for two weeks. And Jay **played** basketball every day!

(to) be und regelmäßige Verben

- Beim *simple past* von ***be*** gibt es nur zwei Formen:
  I, he/she/it *was*
  you, we, they *were*
- Bei **regelmäßigen Verben** bildest du das *simple past* durch Anhängen von ***ed*** an den Infinitiv:
  stay → stayed, play → played

  Es gibt für **alle** Personen nur eine Form.

! Merke aber:

1 It was great for Prunella without the Carter-Browns. Nobody grumbled.
Dan and Jo argued a lot.

1 Ein stummes ***e*** fällt weg:
grumble → grumbled, argue → argued.

2 Prunella dropped Emily's CDs on the floor.

2 Einige Konsonanten werden verdoppelt:
drop → dropped, plan → planned.

3 Prunella tried on Emily's clothes too.

3 ***y*** nach einem Konsonanten wird zu ***ied***:
try → tried.
(Aber ***y*** nach einem **Vokal** bleibt: *play → played.*)

4 In August the Shaws painted their kitchen.
After that they needed a holiday.

4 Nach ***t*** und ***d*** wird die ***ed***-Endung [ɪd] ausgesprochen: *painted, needed.*

b) Irregular verbs

The Carter-Browns went to Majorca.
(Infinitiv: **go**)

Dan and Jo met a nice girl in Cornwall.
(Infinitiv: **meet**)

The Carter-Browns had a very nice holiday.
(Infinitiv: **have**)
They had a house with a swimming pool.
(Infinitiv: **have got**)

▸ *Unit 1 (p. 12)* • *P 6 (p. 18)*

Unregelmäßige Verben

Wie im Deutschen gibt es auch im Englischen eine Reihe von unregelmäßigen Verben, deren *simple past*-Formen du einzeln lernen musst.

▸ *Unregelmäßige Verben (pp. 210–211)*

! *had* ist die *simple past*-Form von *have* und von *have got*.

Welche dieser Formen sind simple past-*Formen?*

1 has • 2 met • 3 sit • 4 go • 5 travelled • 6 heard
7 were • 8 hear • 9 had • 10 sat • 11 went • 12 meet

GF 2 The simple past: negative statements
Die einfache Form der Vergangenheit: verneinte Aussagesätze

Sophie — Lesley didn't **want** to come to Bristol.

Ananda — She didn't **say** much.
But we didn't **ask** her much.

Eine Aussage im *simple past* verneinst du immer mit ***didn't*** + **Infinitiv** (Langform: *did not*).

Verneinte Aussagesätze

Merke:			
	Simple present	I don't **get up** early.	Lesley doesn't **get up** early.
	Simple past	I didn't **get up** early.	Lesley didn't **get up** early.

▸ *Unit 1 (p. 13) • P 8–9 (p. 19)*

Sieh dir die Bilder an und vervollständige die Sätze im simple past.

1  This morning Jo **didn't** ... his bed. (not – make)

2  Last week Dan ... ... his bike. (not – clean)

3  Yesterday Jack ... ... his homework. (not – do)

GF 3 The simple past: questions and short answers
Die einfache Form der Vergangenheit: Fragen und Kurzantworten

Did Jo **help** Jody?
– Yes, he did. / No, he didn't.

Did the girls **talk** to Lesley?
– Yes, they did. / No, they didn't.

Why did Jody **need** help?
How did Dan **help** her?

Fragen im *simple past* bildest du mit ***did***:
Did Jo help?
! (Nicht: *Did Jo ~~helped~~?*)

Das Fragewort steht wie immer am Anfang.

Fragen

Merke:			
	Simple present	Do you **get up** early?	Does Lesley **get up** early?
	Simple past	Did you **get up** early?	Did Lesley **get up** early?

▸ *Unit 1 (p. 14) • P 11–14 (pp. 20–21)*

Unit 2

GF 4 The comparison of adjectives Die Steigerung der Adjektive

a) Comparison with *-er/-est*

How old are the Carter-Brown children?
– Well, Sophie is young. She's twelve.
Toby is younger. He's nine.
Baby Hannah is the youngest,
and Emily is the oldest.

Prunella thinks Sophie is nicer **than** Emily.
Emily is bigger, but is she prettier?

► *Unit 2 (p. 30) • P 9 (p. 35)*

Steigerung mit *-er/-est*

Steigerungsformen verwendest du, um Personen oder Dinge miteinander zu vergleichen, z.B.:

young [jʌŋ]	jung
younger ['jʌŋgə]	jünger
(the) youngest ['jʌŋgɪst]	der/die/das jüngste ...; am jüngsten
old	alt
older	älter
(the) oldest	der/die/das älteste ...; am ältesten

Die Steigerung mit ***-er/-est*** verwendest du für
– einsilbige Adjektive *(young, full, nice, big, ...)* und
– zweisilbige Adjektive mit der Endung ***-y*** *(pretty, funny, easy, ...)*.

! Merke:

nice	– *nicer*	– *nicest*
big	– *bigger*	– *biggest*
pretty	– *prettier*	– *prettiest*

b) Comparison with *more/most*

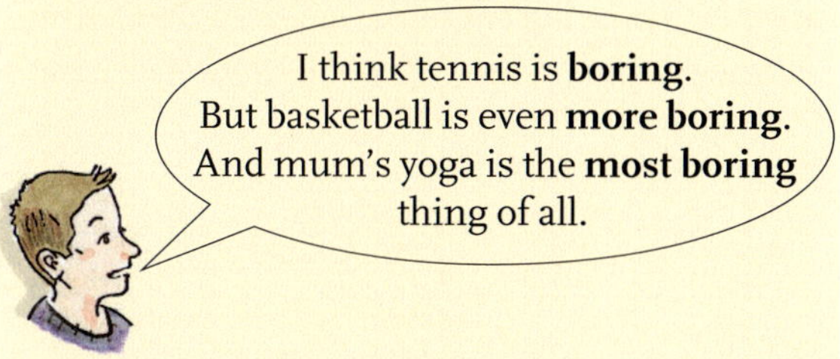

I think tennis is **boring**.
But basketball is even **more boring**.
And mum's yoga is the **most boring** thing of all.

► *Unit 2 (p. 31) • P 12 (p. 36)*

Steigerung mit *more/most*

Andere Adjektive werden mit ***more*** und ***most*** gesteigert:

boring	langweilig
more boring	langweiliger
(the) most boring	der/die/das langweiligste ...; am langweiligsten

Weitere Beispiele:

expensive	– *more expensive*	– *most expensive*
difficult	– *more difficult*	– *most difficult*

c) Irregular comparison

Ananda has got a good idea, but Sophie's idea is better. Lesley has got the best idea.

Jo hasn't got much money this week. Dan has got more, but Dilip has got the most.
Jo hat diese Woche nicht viel Geld. Dan hat mehr, aber Dilip hat das meiste/am meisten.

► *Unit 2 (p. 30)*

Unregelmäßige Steigerung

Einige Adjektive werden unregelmäßig gesteigert:

good	– *better*	– *best*
bad	– *worse* [wɜːs]	– *worst* [wɜːst]
much/many	– *more*	– *most*

Die Steigerung der Adjektive

Mit *-er/-est*:	Mit *more/most*:	Unregelmäßig:
Einsilbige Adjektive: *old – older – oldest* Adjektive auf *-y*: *happy – happier – happiest*	Andere zwei- und mehrsilbige Adjektive: *boring – more boring – most boring* *terrible – more terrible – most terrible* *exciting – more exciting – most exciting*	*good – better – best* *bad – worse – worst* *much/many – more – most*

d) bigger than – as big as

„größer als" – „so groß wie"

Sophie, Hip is so big. I think your rabbit is **bigger than** my cat.
But your cat is **faster than** Hip.

◂ Wenn Personen oder Dinge **unterschiedlich** groß/schnell/alt/... sind, vergleichst du sie mit der 1. Steigerungsform + ***than*** („als"):

Your rabbit is *bigger* *than* *my cat.* (... größer als ...)
Your cat is *faster* *than* *Hip.* (... schneller als ...)

↑ 1. Steigerungsform

! (Nicht: ... *bigger/faster* ~~*as*~~ ...)

Is your cat as **fast** as my rabbit?
Ist deine Katze so schnell wie mein Kaninchen?

She's faster. But she is**n't** as **big** as your rabbit.
... Aber sie ist nicht so groß wie dein Kaninchen.

◂ Wenn Personen oder Dinge **gleich** groß/schnell/alt/... sind, vergleichst du sie mit ***as*** *big/fast/old/...* ***as***.
(Verneint: *not as big/fast/old/... as*)

Sophie is twelve. Emily is **older than** her.
Sophie ist zwölf. Emily ist älter als sie.

Is Sophie as old as Dan and Jo?
No, she isn't **as old as** them.
... Nein, sie ist nicht so alt wie sie.

! Merke:
Nach Vergleichen mit ***than*** und ***as ... as*** stehen die Personalpronomen *me/him/her* usw. (nicht: ~~*I/he/she*~~ usw.):
older than me/him/her/us/them
älter als **ich/er/sie/wir/sie**

▸ *Unit 2 (pp. 30–31)* • *P 10, 13 (pp. 35–36)*

Sieh dir an, wie alt die drei Jungen in der Zeichnung sind. Schreib Vergleiche mit old *auf.*

1 Ali is ... ... Ben and Chris. He is the ...
2 Ben is ... ... Chris, but he isn't ... ... Ali.

Ali (13) Ben (12) Chris (12)

I'm faster than them.

Unit 3

GF 5 The *will*-future Das Futur mit *will*

The hedgehogs **will be** cold tonight. **I'll have to** take them inside.

Maybe their mother **will come**. But maybe she **won't**.

Um auszudrücken, was in der Zukunft geschehen wird, benutzt du ***will*** + **Infinitiv**.
Es gibt für **alle** Personen nur eine Form.
Die Kurzform von *will* ist *'ll*: *I'll, you'll* usw.

Das *will-future* steht häufig mit Zeitangaben wie *tomorrow, next month, soon, in a few weeks.*

Die **verneinte Form** von *will* heißt ***won't***.
(Langform: *will not*).

Ananda — **What will they need?**
Will they want milk?
Sophie — **No, they won't.**

Fragen kannst du **mit Fragewort** *(What will they ...?)* oder **ohne Fragewort** *(Will they ...?)* stellen.

Die Kurzantworten lauten: *Yes, I will / No, I won't* usw.

Mit *will* kannst du eine **Vermutung** oder eine **Vorhersage** ausdrücken:

Sophie — **I think** they'll need water.
Ich glaube, sie werden Wasser brauchen. / Ich glaube, sie brauchen Wasser.
(Vermutung)

◂ Eine **Vermutung** fängt oft mit *I think, I'm sure* oder *maybe* an.

Ananda — It will be cold tonight.
Es wird heute Nacht kalt (werden).
(Vorhersage)

◂ Bei einer **Vorhersage** geht es oft um Dinge, die man nicht beeinflussen kann, z.B. um das Wetter.

! Im Deutschen benutzen wir oft das Präsens, wenn wir über die Zukunft sprechen:
Vielleicht kommt ihre Mutter bald.

Im Englischen steht das *will-future*:
Maybe their mother will come soon.

Ananda — I want to help the hedgehogs.
I will send an e-mail to the Animal Hotline.
Ich will den Igeln helfen. Ich werde eine E-Mail an die *Animal Hotline* schicken.

▸ *Unit 3 (p. 44) • P 2–3 (pp. 48–49)*

! Nicht verwechseln:
- *I want to* heißt „ich will".
- *I will* heißt „ich werde".

Ergänze diese Vorhersagen und Vermutungen. Verwende will *oder* 'll *und diese Verben:*

be – like – be – survive

1 I... ... 13 next month.
2 Come and visit me! I think you... ... it here.
3 I'm sure the weather ... ... fine in August.
4 What do you think? ... the baby hedgehogs ...?

GF 6 Conditional sentences (type 1) Bedingungssätze (Typ 1)

If you **give** a hedgehog water, it'**ll be** happy.

Wenn du einem Igel Wasser gibst, wird er zufrieden sein.

If you **don't keep** it warm, it **won't survive**.

Wenn du ihn nicht warm hältst, wird er nicht überleben.

Bedingungssätze (Typ 1) sind „Was ist, wenn …"-Sätze: Sie beschreiben, was unter bestimmten Bedingungen geschieht oder nicht geschieht.

Die Bedingung steht im *if*-Satz, die Folge davon steht im Hauptsatz:

***if*-Satz (Bedingung)** ↓	**Hauptsatz (Folge für die Zukunft)** ↓
*If you **give** a hedgehog water,*	*it'**ll be** happy.*
*If you **don't keep** it warm,*	*it **won't survive**.*
Im *if*-Satz steht das *simple present.*	Im Hauptsatz steht meist das *will-future*.

You'll find more help **if you visit our website**.
If you visit our website, you'll find more help.

◄ Wenn der Hauptsatz am Anfang steht, brauchst du kein Komma.

If I **see** Jack, I'**ll show** him the babies.

Ananda:
When I see Jack, I'll tell him about the babies.
Sobald ich Jack sehe, …

If I see Jack, I'll tell him about the babies.
Falls ich Jack sehe, …

! Verwechsle nicht *when* und *if*:
– *when* = „sobald", „dann wenn"
– *if* = „falls", „wenn"

If you visit Ananda, you **can help** her with the hedgehogs.
If you need more information, **write** to the Animal Hotline.

► *Unit 3 (p. 45) • P 5–6 (p. 50)*

◄ Im Hauptsatz können auch *can, must* oder ein Imperativ (Befehl, Aufforderung) stehen.

Schreib die Sätze mit der richtigen Verbform in dein Heft.

1 If Jack sees the babies, he **(wants / will want)** to help them too.
2 What will happen if their mum **(won't come / doesn't come)** back?
3 If Ananda **(keeps / will keep)** the babies warm, they **(be / will be)** fine.

Extra If you add blue to yellow, you **get** green.
If the bus is late, I always **walk** home.
Immer dann, wenn …

Wenn etwas immer so ist, kann im Hauptsatz auch das *simple present* stehen.

GF 7 Adverbs of manner Adverbien der Art und Weise

a) Use — Gebrauch

Hedgehogs are **slow** and **quiet**.
This is Sleepy. He's a very **slow** hedgehog.
You have to be **careful** when you pick him up.

◀ Ein **Adjektiv** beschreibt ein **Nomen** näher.
Es sagt aus, wie etwas oder jemand **ist**.

Hedgehogs walk slowly and quietly.
Igel gehen langsam und leise.

You have to pick up a hedgehog very carefully.
Du musst einen Igel sehr vorsichtig hochheben.

◀ Ein **Adverb der Art und Weise** beschreibt ein **Verb** näher.
Es sagt aus, wie jemand etwas **tut** oder wie etwas **geschieht**.

b) Regular forms — Regelmäßige Formen

Adjektiv			Adverb
slow	→	slowly	
quiet	→	quietly	
careful	→	carefully	

Die meisten Adverbien der Art und Weise entstehen durch Anhängen von ***-ly*** an das Adjektiv.

Ananda was **angry** with Dilip. (Adjektiv)
Sophie shouted at Dilip angrily. (Adverb)

! Merke aber:
1. ***y*** wird zu ***i***: *angry* → *angrily*, *happy* → *happily*
2. ***le*** wird zu ***ly***: *terrible* → *terribly*, *horrible* → *horribly*
3. Nach ***ic*** wird ***ally*** angehängt: *fantastic* → *fantastically*

▸ *Unit 3 (p. 46)* • *P 10–11 (pp. 51–52)*

c) Irregular forms — Unregelmäßige Formen

Einige Adverbien haben eine unregelmäßige Form, die du auswendig lernen musst:

She did a **good** job with the babies. (Adjektiv)
She did the job well. (Adverb)

– Das Adverb zu *good* heißt *well*.

Jo The rabbits are very **fast**. (Adjektiv)
Dan Of course! All rabbits can run fast. (Adverb)

– Bei *fast* und *hard* sind Adjektiv und Adverb gleich.

Ananda It's **hard** work at the clinic. (Adjektiv)
Steve That's right. The volunteers at the clinic work very hard. (Adverb)

▸ *Unit 3 (p. 47)*

d) Word order — Wortstellung

'You killed the hedgehogs,' she shouted angrily.

Das Adverb der Art und Weise steht direkt **nach dem Verb**.

Steve fed **the babies** carefully.
Steve fütterte vorsichtig die Babys.

! In Sätzen mit Objekt steht es **nach dem Objekt**.

Welches Wort ist richtig, Adjektiv oder Adverb?

1. When you pick up a small animal, you have to be very **careful / carefully**.
2. Squirrels and rabbits can run very **quick / quickly**.
3. Hedgehogs walk **slow / slowly** and **quiet / quietly**.
4. Ananda did a **good / well** job with the hedgehogs.
5. The woman at the animal clinic said Ananda did **good / well**.

e) Extra The comparison of adverbs of manner

Die Steigerung der Adverbien der Art und Weise

Du kannst nicht nur Adjektive, sondern auch Adverbien steigern:

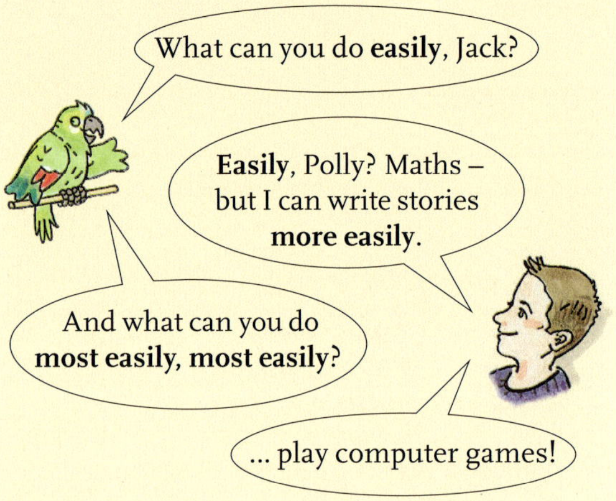
What can you do easily, Jack?
Easily, Polly? Maths – but I can write stories more easily.
And what can you do most easily, most easily?
... play computer games!

◄ Adverbien, die auf ***-ly*** enden, steigerst du mit ***more/most***:

quickly	*more quickly*	*most quickly*
schnell	schneller	am schnellsten

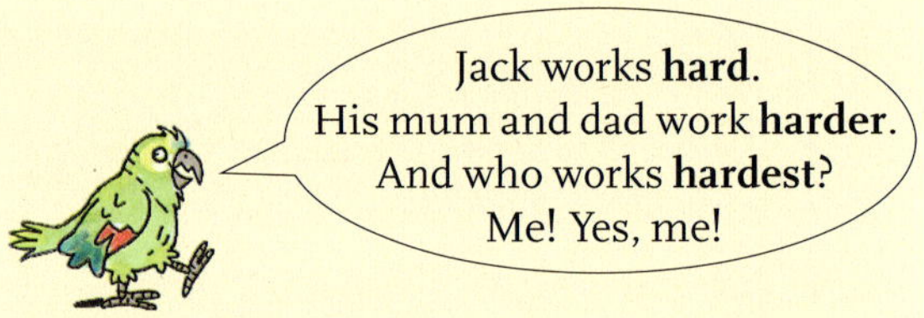
Jack works hard.
His mum and dad work harder.
And who works hardest?
Me! Yes, me!

◄ Einsilbige Adverbien *(fast, hard)* steigerst du mit ***-er/-est***:

fast	*faster*	*fastest*
schnell	schneller	am schnellsten

I sing badly.
I think Jo sings worse.
But we all know
who sings worst!

◄ Die Steigerungsformen von *well* und *badly* lernst du am besten auswendig:

well	*better*	*best*
gut	besser	am besten
badly	*worse*	*worst*
schlecht, schlimm	schlechter, schlimmer	am schlechtesten, am schlimmsten

▸ *Unit 3 (p. 47)*

Unit 4

GF 8 Word order Wortstellung

a) REVISION S – V – O

S – V – O

Die Wortstellung im Aussagesatz lautet
S – V – O (**S**ubjekt – **V**erb – **O**bjekt): *Jack writes stories.*

! Beachte die folgenden Unterschiede zum Deutschen:

1 Jack often **writes stories.**
Jack **schreibt** oft **Geschichten**.

1 Ein Häufigkeitsadverb *(often)* steht nie zwischen Verb und Objekt.

2 Dilip **can play** the guitar.
Dilip **kann** Gitarre **spielen**.

2 Hilfsverb *(can)* und Vollverb *(play)* dürfen nicht durch ein Objekt *(the guitar)* getrennt werden.

3 After school Jo **plays** football.
Nach der Schule **spielt** Jo Fußball.

When Jack comes home, he **feeds** Polly.
Wenn Jack nach Hause kommt, **füttert** er Polly.

3 Das Subjekt *(Jo, he)* steht auch dann vor dem Verb, wenn der Satz mit einer Zeitangabe *(after school)* oder einem Nebensatz *(when Jack comes home)* beginnt.

4 What do you do **when you** come **home**?
Was machst du, **wenn du nach Hause** kommst?

4 Auch im Nebensatz ist die Wortstellung **S – V – O**.

Denk dabei an die **Straßen-Verkehrs-Ordnung**, an die du dich immer halten musst!

▸ Unit 4 (p. 60) • P 2 (p. 64)

b) Place before time

We can go **to the mountains in the morning.**

Wir können morgen Vormittag in die Berge fahren.

Great! And we can have a picnic **near the castle in the afternoon.**

... Und am Nachmittag können wir in der Nähe der Burg ein Picknick machen.

▸ Unit 4 (p. 60) • P 3 (p. 64)

Ort vor Zeit

Wenn Ortsangaben *(to the mountains)* und Zeitangaben *(in the morning)* zusammen am Satzende stehen, dann gilt: **Ort vor Zeit**.

1 Ort	**2** Zeit
... to the mountains	*in the morning.*
... near the castle	*in the afternoon.*

Welcher Satz ist richtig, **1** *oder* **2**?

1 We have to be at six o'clock at the station.

2 We have to be at the station at six o'clock.

GF 9 The present perfect: use Das *present perfect*: Gebrauch

Hurry up, boys!
I've cooked bacon and eggs and Grandpa has packed a picnic.
Dan! Grandma has made breakfast. We can eat now. Hurry up!

▸ *Unit 4 (p. 61)*

◂ Mit dem *present perfect* drückst du aus, dass jemand etwas getan hat oder dass etwas geschehen ist. Dabei ist **nicht wichtig**, **wann** es geschehen ist. Deshalb wird auch kein genauer Zeitpunkt genannt.

Wenn du aber den genauen Zeitpunkt angeben willst *(yesterday, last week, two years ago, in 2004)*, musst du das *simple past* verwenden.
(Zum *simple past* siehe GF 1–3, S. 133–134).

◂ Oft hat die Handlung Auswirkungen auf die Gegenwart oder die Zukunft:
Im Beispiel links hat Grandma das Frühstück gemacht.
Ergebnis: Jetzt können alle frühstücken.

GF 10 The present perfect: form Das *present perfect*: Form

a) The past participle

Das Partizip Perfekt

Das *present perfect* wird mit *have/has* und der 3. Form des Verbs gebildet. Die 3. Form des Verbs heißt **Partizip Perfekt** *(past participle)*.

1 Grandpa **has** packed a picnic.

They **have** planned a day in the mountains.
Dan and Jo **haven't** tidied their room.

1 Bei regelmäßigen Verben hängst du ***ed*** an den Infinitiv an: *pack* + *ed* → *packed*.

◂ Beachte die Besonderheiten der Schreibung und der Aussprache (siehe GF 1, S. 133).

2 The twins **haven't** seen Caerphilly Castle.
Dan doesn't feel well, so he **hasn't** eaten his breakfast.

2 Unregelmäßige Verben haben eigene Formen, die du einzeln lernen musst.
Unregelmäßige Verben werden immer so angegeben: *(to) see, saw,* ***seen***
(to) eat, ate, ***eaten***.
Die 3. Form ist das *past participle*.

▸ *Unit 4 (p. 61)*

▸ *Unregelmäßige Verben (pp. 210–211)*

Welche dieser Formen sind past participles?

1 eaten • 2 went • 3 gone • 4 did • 5 ate • 6 done • 7 taken • 8 took

b) Positive and negative statements

Bejahte und verneinte Aussagesätze

1 The neighbours have made a pie for the Thompsons.
Die Nachbarn haben einen Obstkuchen für die Thompsons gemacht.

1 Bejahte Aussagesätze im *present perfect*:
***have/has* + Partizip Perfekt**.

2 Grandpa hasn't cleaned the car yet.
Opa hat das Auto noch nicht sauber gemacht.

2 Verneinte Aussagesätze im *present perfect*:
***haven't/hasn't* + Partizip Perfekt**.

Dan hasn't come down.
Dan ist nicht nach unten gekommen.

! Beim *present perfect* musst du immer ***have/has*** verwenden, egal ob im Deutschen „haben" oder „sein" steht.

Present perfect

Positive statements		Negative statements		Long forms
I've packed		I haven't seen		I/You/We/They have (not) packed
You've packed		You haven't seen		He/She has (not) packed
He's packed		He hasn't seen		
She's packed	a picnic.	She hasn't seen	Dan.	I/You/We/They have (not) seen
We've packed		We haven't seen		He/She has (not) seen
You've packed		You haven't seen		
They've packed		They haven't seen		

► *Unit 4 (p. 61) • P 7–9 (pp. 66–67)*

Polly has cleaned her cage. Now she can watch TV.

c) Questions and short answers

Fragen und Kurzantworten

Have the twins been to the Brecon Beacons?
– Yes, they have. / No, they haven't.

Bei Fragen im *present perfect* werden Subjekt und *have/has* vertauscht.

Has Jo installed the software?
– Yes, he has. / No, he hasn't.

Kurzantworten werden mit *have/has* gebildet.

Why has Grandma printed out the instructions?

Fragewörter stehen wie immer am Satzanfang.

! Merke:
Im *present perfect* gibt es **keine Fragen mit *when***.
When fragt nach einem Zeitpunkt – und dafür verwendest du das *simple past*: *When did ...?*

► *Unit 4 (p. 63) • P 14–15 (p. 68)*

GF 11 The present perfect with adverbs of indefinite time
Das *present perfect* mit Adverbien der unbestimmten Zeit

I've **already** packed the car.

Ich habe schon das Auto beladen.

Oh, good. Have the twins had breakfast **yet?**

Haben ... schon gefrühstückt?

I've **just** seen Jo in the kitchen. But Dan has**n't** come down **yet**.

Ich habe gerade Jo ... gesehen. Aber Dan ist noch nicht nach unten gekommen.

I've **always** wanted to visit Caerphilly Castle. Grandma, Grandpa, have you **ever** been there?

Ich wollte schon immer ... besuchen. Oma, Opa, seid ihr jemals dort gewesen?

▸ *Unit 4 (p. 61/p. 63) • P 10–11 (p. 67)*

Das *present perfect* drückt aus, dass etwas **irgendwann** geschehen ist.
Daher findest du oft **Adverbien der unbestimmten Zeit** in *present perfect*-Sätzen:

already	schon, bereits
always	(schon) immer
just	gerade (eben), soeben
never	(noch) nie
not ... yet	noch nicht
often	(schon) oft
ever?	jemals? / schon mal?
yet?	schon?

Die Adverbien der unbestimmten Zeit stehen **direkt vor** dem *past participle*.

! Ausnahme: *yet* steht am Satzende.

Sieh dir die Bilder an. Wie lauten die dazu passenden Sätze im present perfect?

1 

Grandpa – just – wash – car

2 

Dan – not eat – his breakfast – yet

3 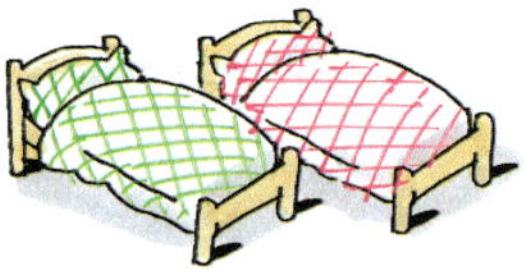

The twins – already – make – their beds

Unit 5

GF 12 The *going to*-future Das Futur mit *going to*

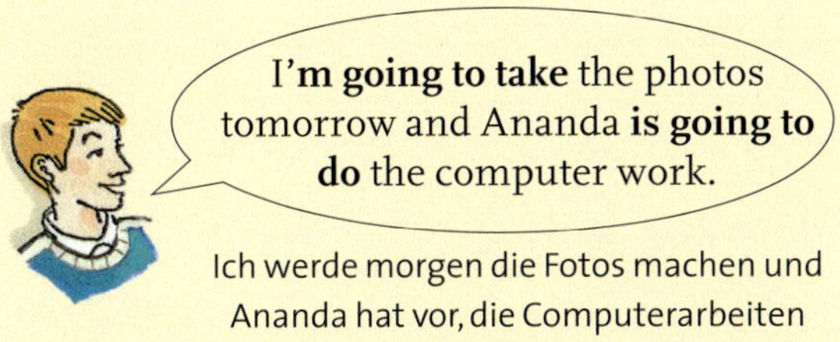
I'm **going to take** the photos tomorrow and Ananda **is going to do** the computer work.

Ich werde morgen die Fotos machen und Ananda hat vor, die Computerarbeiten zu erledigen.

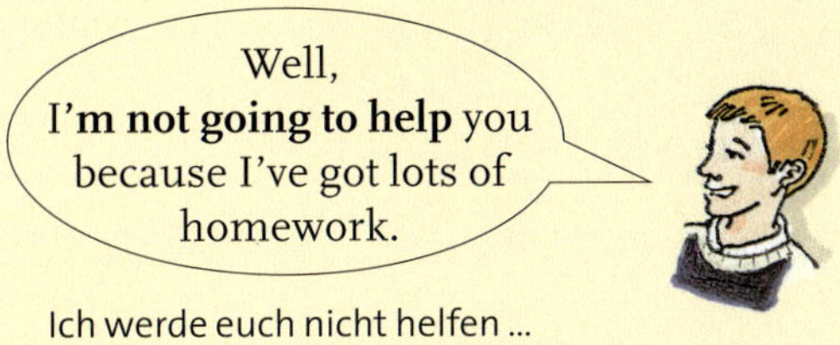
Well, I'm **not going to help** you because I've got lots of homework.

Ich werde euch nicht helfen ...

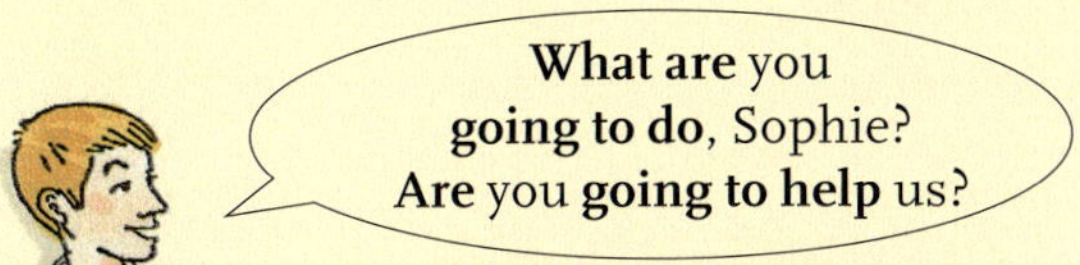
What are you **going to do**, Sophie? **Are** you **going to help** us?

Was hast du vor, Sophie? Wirst/Willst du uns helfen?

Yes, I am. Of course!

Das kennst du schon:
Du verwendest das *will-future*, wenn du Vorhersagen oder Vermutungen über die Zukunft äußern willst (siehe GF 5, S. 137).

◄ Wenn du aber über **Absichten** und **Pläne** für die Zukunft sprechen willst, verwendest du das Futur mit ***going to***. Es wird mit ***am/are/is*** **+** ***going to*** **+ Infinitiv** gebildet. Die Kurzformen heißen *I'm/you're/he's going to* usw.

! *going to* hat hier nichts mit „gehen“ zu tun. Es bedeutet „werden“, „wollen“, „vorhaben“.

◄ Die verneinten Formen heißen *I'm not going to/ you aren't going to/he isn't going to* usw.

◄ Fragen kannst du **mit Fragewort** *(What ...?)* oder **ohne Fragewort** *(Are you ...?)* stellen.

◄ Die Kurzantworten sind *Yes, I am / No, I'm not* usw.

The *going to*-future

Positive statements		Negative statements		Questions and short answers
I'm going to	read.	I'm not going to	play.	Are you going to watch TV?
You're going to		You aren't going to		– Yes, I am. / No, I'm not.
He's/She's going to		He/She isn't going to		Is Jo going to watch TV?
We're going to		We aren't going to		– Yes, he is. / No, he isn't.
You're going to		You aren't going to		
They're going to		They aren't going to		

► *Unit 5 (p. 76)* • *P 3–6 (pp. 81–82)*

Sieh dir die Bilder an. Was haben Sophie, Jo und Dan heute Abend vor? Was werden sie nicht tun? Schreib zwei Sätze mit going to *und zwei Sätze mit* not going to *in dein Heft.*

1  (read a book)
Sophie is ... this evening.

2  (watch TV)
She isn't ...

3  (play football)
Dan and Jo ... this evening.

4  (take photos)
They ...

GF 13 Extra **Question tags with *be*** Frageanhängsel mit *be*

Jo — **The new pizza place is** near here, isn't it? Let's go there.
Die neue Pizzeria ist doch hier in der Nähe, nicht? ...

Dan — Wow! **The pizzas are** really big here, aren't they?
Die Pizzas sind wirklich groß hier, oder?

Jo — That's great, because **we're** hungry, aren't we? Can you see an empty table?

Wenn du von jemandem Zustimmung zu einer Aussage erwartest, benutzt du oft ein Frageanhängsel *(isn't it?, aren't they?, weren't they?).*
Deutsche Frageanhängsel sind zum Beispiel „nicht wahr?", „oder?", „ne?", „gell?" oder „woll?".

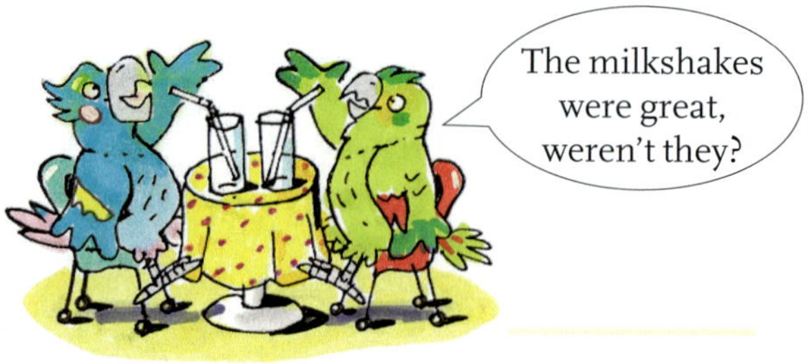
The milkshakes were great, weren't they?

bejaht — verneint
There's a table in the corner, isn't there?

◀ Wenn der Aussagesatz bejaht ist, ist das Frageanhängel verneint.

verneint — bejaht
It isn't too expensive here, is it?
Look at the prices before we sit down.

◀ Wenn der Aussagesatz verneint ist, ist das Frageanhängel bejaht.

▸ *Unit 5 (p. 78) • P 10 (p. 84)*

Ordne die Frageanhängsel den Aussagen zu.

1 We're late for school, ...
2 The boys are hungry, ...
3 Jo is in the pizza place, ...
4 There was a good film on TV last night, ...
5 The pizzas were great, ...

A aren't they?
B wasn't there?
C aren't we?
D weren't they?
E isn't he?

Unit 6

GF 14 REVISION **The present progressive** Die Verlaufsform der Gegenwart

What **are** you **doing**, Jo?
Was machst du gerade, Jo?

I'm not doing anything.
I'm just **waiting** for Dan.

Ich mache nichts.
Ich warte gerade auf Dan.

▸ *Unit 6 (p. 96) • P 6 (p. 100)*

Du benutzt das *present progressive*, um auszudrücken, dass etwas gerade in diesem Moment geschieht.

Das *present progressive* wird mit *am/are/is* + *-ing*-Form des Verbs gebildet.
Die *-ing*-Form ist der Infinitiv + *-ing*:
do → ***doing***, ***wait*** → ***waiting***.
Beachte: ***have*** → ***having***, ***plan*** → ***planning***

GF 15 The past progressive Die Verlaufsform der Vergangenheit

Yesterday at one o'clock ...

Yesterday at one o'clock Form 8PK and their teachers were having lunch.
Gestern um ein Uhr aßen die Klasse 8PK und ihre Lehrer gerade zu Mittag.

Du benutzt das *past progressive*, um auszudrücken, dass etwas zu einem bestimmten Zeitpunkt in der Vergangenheit gerade im Gange war.

Das *past progressive* wird mit *was/were* + *-ing*-Form gebildet.

Jack was telling jokes, but Jo wasn't listening.
Jack erzählte Witze, aber Jo hörte nicht zu.

◄ Die verneinten Formen heißen *I wasn't listening/ you weren't listening/he wasn't listening* usw.

What was Jo doing? Was he talking to Ananda?
Was machte Jo gerade? Redete er gerade mit Ananda?
– No, he wasn't. He was planning a trick.
– Nein. Er war gerade dabei, einen Streich zu planen.

◄ Fragen kannst du **mit Fragewort** *(What ...?)* oder **ohne Fragewort** *(Was he ...?)* stellen.
Die Kurzantworten sind *Yes, I was / No, I wasn't* usw.

The others were still eating and chatting when Jo suddenly **started** to laugh.
Die anderen waren noch dabei zu essen und sich zu unterhalten, als Jo plötzlich anfing zu lachen.

Das *past progressive* wird oft benutzt, um auszudrücken, was gerade vor sich ging *(the others were still eating ...)*, als eine andere Handlung einsetzte *(Jo started to laugh)*.
! Die zweite Handlung steht im *simple past*.

► *Unit 6 (p. 96) • P 7–8 (pp. 100–101)*

Welche Sätze drücken aus, dass jemand gerade dabei war, etwas zu tun?

1 At 6 o'clock yesterday evening Jack was reading a spy story.
2 Two days ago Sophie played tennis with Lesley.
3 At 8.30 this morning Lesley was cycling to school.
4 Last week Jo read two detective stories.
5 Emily cycled to school last Wednesday.
6 At 6.15 Jo and Dan were playing football in the park.

GF 16 Extra Relative clauses Relativsätze

Mit Relativsätzen sagst du genauer, wen oder was du meinst:

Nicola **The man** who lived in this house was William Herschel.
Der Mann, der in diesem Haus lebte, war William Herschel.

◄ In Relativsätzen, die **Personen** beschreiben, verwendest du ***who***:
the man/woman/people *who ...*
der Mann, der ... / die Frau, die ... / die Leute, die ...

Nicola What's the name of **the planet** which Herschel discovered?
Wie heißt der Planet, den Herschel entdeckt hat?

◄ In Relativsätzen, die **Dinge** (und Tiere) beschreiben, verwendest du ***which***:
the planet/bag/animal *which ...*
der Planet, der ... / die Tasche, die ... / das Tier, das ...

The woman **who** **helped** us ...

Die Frau, **die** uns **geholfen hat** ...

! Beachte die unterschiedliche Wortstellung in englischen und deutschen Relativsätzen.

► *Unit 6 (p. 97) • P 9 (p. 101)*

Wo brauchst du who, *wo brauchst du* which?

1 Nicola was the woman ... told the students about Herschel.
2 Uranus was the planet ... Herschel discovered.

Lösungen der Grammar-File-Aufgaben

p. 134/1 **2, 5, 6, 7, 9, 10, 11**

p. 134/2
1 This morning Jo **didn't make** his bed.
2 Last week Dan **didn't clean** his bike.
3 Yesterday Jack **didn't do** his homework.

p. 136
1 Ali is **older than** Ben and Chris. He is the **oldest**.
2 Ben is **as old as** Chris, but he isn't **as old as** Ali.

p. 137
1 I'**ll be** 13 next month.
2 Come and visit me! I think you'**ll like** it here.
3 I'm sure the weather **will be** fine in August.
4 ... **Will** the baby hedgehogs **survive**?

p. 138
1 If Jack sees the babies, he **will want** to help them too.
2 What will happen if their mum **doesn't come** back?
3 If Ananda **keeps** the babies warm, they **will be** fine.

p. 140
1 When you pick up a small animal, you have to be very **careful**.
2 Squirrels and rabbits can run very **quickly**.
3 Hedgehogs walk **slowly** and **quietly**.
4 Ananda did a **good** job with the hedgehogs.
5 The woman at the animal clinic said Ananda did **well**.

p. 141 2 (We have to be at the station at six o'clock.)

p. 142 **1, 3, 6, 7**

p. 144
1 Grandpa **has just washed** the car.
2 Dan **hasn't eaten** his breakfast yet.
3 The twins **have already made** their beds.

p. 145
1 Sophie is **going to read a book** this evening.
2 She isn't **going to watch TV**.
3 Dan and Jo **are going to play football** this evening.
4 They **aren't going to take photos**.

p. 146 **1C, 2A, 3E, 4B, 5D**

p. 147 **1, 3, 6**

p. 148
1 Nicola was the woman **who** told the students about Herschel.
2 Uranus was the planet **which** Herschel discovered.

Grammatical terms (Grammatische Fachbegriffe)

adjective ['ædʒɪktɪv]	Adjektiv	*good, red, new, boring, ...*
adverb of frequency [,ædvɜ:b_əv 'fri:kwənsi]	Häufigkeitsadverb	*always, often, never, ...*
adverb of indefinite time [ɪn,defɪnət 'taɪm]	Adverb der unbestimmten Zeit	*already, ever, just, never, ...*
adverb of manner ['mænə]	Adverb der Art und Weise	*badly, happily, quietly, well, ...*
comparison [kəm'pærɪsn]	Steigerung	*old – older – oldest*
conditional sentence [kən,dɪʃənl 'sentəns]	Bedingungssatz	*If I see Jack, I'll tell him.*
future ['fju:tʃə]	Zukunft, Futur	
***going to*-future**	Futur mit *going to*	***I'm going to watch** TV tonight.*
imperative [ɪm'perətɪv]	Imperativ (Befehlsform)	*Open your books. Don't talk.*
infinitive [ɪn'fɪnətɪv]	Infinitiv (Grundform des Verbs)	*(to) open, (to) see, (to) read, ...*
irregular verb [ɪ,regjələ 'vɜ:b]	unregelmäßiges Verb	*(to) go – went – gone*
negative statement [,negətɪv 'steɪtmənt]	verneinter Aussagesatz	*I don't like bananas.*
noun [naʊn]	Nomen, Substantiv	*Sophie, girl, brother, time, ...*
object ['ɒbdʒɪkt]	Objekt	*My sister is writing **a letter**.*
object form ['ɒbdʒɪkt fɔ:m]	Objektform (der Personalpronomen)	*me, you, him, her, it, us, them*
past [pɑ:st]	Vergangenheit	
past participle [,pɑ:st 'pɑ:tɪsɪpl]	Partizip Perfekt	*cleaned, planned, gone, seen, ...*
past progressive [,pɑ:st prə'gresɪv]	Verlaufsform der Vergangenheit	*At 7.30 I **was having** dinner.*
person ['pɜ:sn]	Person	
personal pronoun [,pɜ:sənl 'prəʊnaʊn]	Personalpronomen (persönliches Fürwort)	*I, you, he, she, it, we, they; me, you, him, her, it, us, them*
plural ['plʊərəl]	Plural, Mehrzahl	
positive statement [,pɒzətɪv 'steɪtmənt]	bejahter Aussagesatz	*I like oranges.*
possessive determiner [pə,zesɪv dɪ'tɜ:mɪnə]	Possessivbegleiter (besitzanzeigender Begleiter)	*my, your, his, her, its, our, their*
possessive form [pə,zesɪv fɔ:m]	*s*-Genitiv	*Jo's brother; my sister's room*
possessive pronoun [pə,zesɪv 'prəʊnaʊn]	Possessivpronomen	*mine, yours, his, hers, ours, theirs*
preposition [,prepə'zɪʃn]	Präposition	*after, at, in, next to, under, ...*
present ['preznt]	Gegenwart	
present perfect [,preznt 'pɜ:fɪkt]	*present perfect*	***We've made** a cake for you.*
present progressive [,preznt prə'gresɪv]	Verlaufsform der Gegenwart	*The Hansons **are having** lunch.*
pronoun ['prəʊnaʊn]	Pronomen, Fürwort	
pronunciation [prə,nʌnsi'eɪʃn]	Aussprache	
question ['kwestʃən]	Frage(satz)	
question tag ['kwestʃən tæg]	Frageanhängsel	*This place is great, **isn't it?***
question word ['kwestʃən wɜ:d]	Fragewort	*what?, when?, where?, how?, ...*
regular verb [,regjələ 'vɜ:b]	regelmäßiges Verb	*(to) help – helped – helped*
relative clause [,relətɪv 'klɔ:z]	Relativsatz	*The man **who lived here** ...*
short answer [,ʃɔ:t_'ɑ:nsə]	Kurzantwort	*Yes, I am. / No, I don't. / ...*
simple past [,sɪmpl 'pɑ:st]	einfache Form der Vergangenheit	*Jo **wrote** two letters yesterday.*
simple present [,sɪmpl 'preznt]	einfache Form der Gegenwart	*I always **go** to school by bike.*
singular ['sɪŋgjələ]	Singular, Einzahl	
spelling ['spelɪŋ]	Schreibweise, Rechtschreibung	
subject ['sʌbdʒɪkt]	Subjekt	***My sister** is writing a letter.*
subject form ['sʌbdʒɪkt fɔ:m]	Subjektform (der Personalpronomen)	*I, you, he, she, it, we, they*
subordinate clause [sə,bɔ:dɪnət 'klɔ:z]	Nebensatz	*I like Scruffy **because I like dogs**.*
verb [vɜ:b]	Verb	*hear, open, help, go, ...*
***will*-future**	Futur mit *will*	*I think it **will be** cold tonight.*
word order ['wɜ:d_ɔ:də]	Wortstellung	
yes/no question	Entscheidungsfrage	*Are you 13? Do you like comics?*

Diese Wörterverzeichnisse findest du in deinem Englischbuch:

- Das **Vocabulary** (Vokabelverzeichnis – S. 150–172) enthält alle Wörter und Wendungen, die du lernen musst. Sie stehen in der Reihenfolge, in der sie in den Units vorkommen.
- Das **Dictionary** besteht aus zwei alphabetischen Wörterlisten zum Nachschlagen: Englisch – Deutsch: S. 173–191 / Deutsch – Englisch: S. 192–206.

So ist das Vocabulary aufgebaut:

- Hier siehst du, wo die Wörter vorkommen.
  p. 31/A 11 = Seite 31, Abschnitt 11
  p. 35/P 11 = Seite 35, Übung 11
- Die Lautschrift zeigt dir, wie ein Wort ausgesprochen und betont wird. (→ Englische Laute: S. 191)
- Eingerückte Wörter lernst du am besten zusammen mit dem vorausgehenden Wort, weil die beiden zusammengehören.
- Diese Kästen solltest du dir besonders gut ansehen.

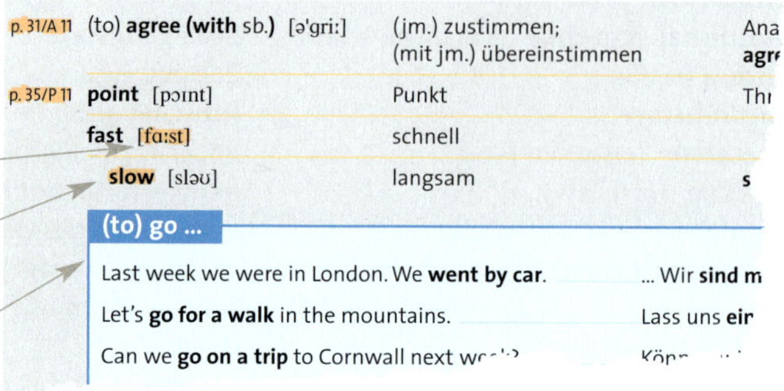

p. 31/A 11	(to) **agree (with** sb.) [əˈgriː]	(jm.) zustimmen; (mit jm.) übereinstimmen	Ana agr
p. 35/P 11	**point** [pɔɪnt]	Punkt	Thi
	fast [fɑːst]	schnell	
	slow [sləʊ]	langsam	s

(to) go ...

Last week we were in London. We **went by car**.	... Wir **sind** m
Let's **go for a walk** in the mountains.	Lass uns **ein**
Can we **go on a trip** to Cornwall next we	

Tipps zum Wörterlernen findest du im Skills File auf Seite 121.

Abkürzungen:

n	= *noun*	*v*	= *verb*
adj	= *adjective*	*adv*	= *adverb*
prep	= *preposition*	*conj*	= *conjunction*
pl	= *plural*	*no pl*	= *no plural*
p.	= page	pp.	= pages
sb.	= somebody	sth.	= something
jn.	= jemanden	jm.	= jemandem

Symbole:

◂▸ ist das „Gegenteil"-Zeichen: **slow** ◂▸ **fast** (**slow** ist das Gegenteil von **fast**)

! Hier stehen Hinweise auf Besonderheiten, bei denen man leicht Fehler machen kann.

Welcome back – After the holidays

Remember?

p. 6

The weather[1]

the sun

It's hot and sunny. heiß und sonnig

a cloud

It's cloudy. bewölkt

rain

It's rainy. regnerisch

wind

It's windy. windig

a storm[2]

It's stormy. stürmisch

snow

snow on a mountain Schnee auf einem Berg

It's raining.

It's very cold.

It's warm.

It's too hot.

[1]weather [ˈweðə] *Wetter* • [2]storm *Sturm; Gewitter*

(to) **travel** ['trævl] **(-ll-)**[1]	reisen	Last year we **travelled** to Turkey in the holidays.
caravan ['kærəvæn]	Wohnwagen	
by the sea [baɪ]	am Meer	a **caravan by the sea**  ! **by** = **1.** an essay **by** J. Hanson („von") **2.** a party **by** the pool („an"; „(nahe) bei")

Irregular simple past forms

(to) drink	**drank** [dræŋk]	trinken	(to) read [ri:d]	**read** [red]	lesen
(to) eat	**ate** [et, eɪt]	essen	(to) ride	**rode** [rəʊd]	reiten; *(Rad)* fahren
(to) meet	**met** [met]	(sich) treffen	(to) swim	**swam** [swæm]	schwimmen
(to) put	**put** [pʊt]	legen, stellen, *(wohin)* tun	(to) throw	**threw** [θru:]	werfen

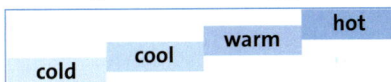

on the beach [bi:tʃ]	am Strand	
(to) **stay** [steɪ]	bleiben; wohnen, übernachten	It rained all day so I **stayed** at home. In the holidays we **stayed** at a B&B.
anyway ['eniweɪ]	trotzdem	It was cold, but we went swimming **anyway**.
theatre ['θɪətə]	Theater	! Betonung auf der 1. Silbe: **theatre** ['θɪətə]
cool [ku:l]	kühl	**cold** – **cool** – **warm** – **hot**
(to) **go for a walk** [wɔ:k]	spazieren gehen, einen Spaziergang machen	
country ['kʌntri]	Land *(auch als Gegensatz zur Stadt)*	! The Millers live **in the country**. (= auf dem Land)
(to) **fly** [flaɪ], *simple past:* **flew** [flu:]	fliegen	
view [vju:]	Aussicht, Blick	
plane [pleɪn]	Flugzeug	! **im** Flugzeug = **on** the plane
round [raʊnd]	um ... (herum); in ... umher	**round** the car  Walk **round** the classroom and talk to different partners.
(to) **shine** [ʃaɪn], *simple past:* **shone** [ʃɒn]	scheinen *(Sonne)*	
island ['aɪlənd]	Insel	
p. 7 **sky** [skaɪ]	Himmel	
our **own** pool [əʊn]	unser eigenes Schwimmbad	! I've got **my own** room. (*Never:* ~~an own~~ room)
(to) **go by car/train/bike/...**	mit dem Auto/Zug/Rad/... fahren	

(to) go ... (*simple past:* went)

Last week we were in London. We **went by car**.	... Wir **sind mit dem Auto gefahren**.
Let's **go for a walk** in the mountains.	Lass uns **einen Spaziergang** in den Bergen **machen**.
Can we **go on a trip** to Cornwall next week?	Können wir ... **einen Ausflug** nach Cornwall **machen**?
We **went on holiday** to Italy this summer.	Wir sind diesen Sommer nach Italien **in Urlaub gefahren**.

[1] Die Angabe **(-ll-)** zeigt, dass der Endkonsonant bei der Bildung von *-ing*-Form und *-ed*-Form verdoppelt wird: **travel** – **travelling / travelled**.

	something ['sʌmθɪŋ]	etwas	Hockey again? No, I want to do **something** new.
	(to) **go together**	zusammenpassen, -gehören	
	What was the weather like?	Wie war das Wetter?	
p. 8	**degree** [dɪ'gri:]	Grad	It's 14 **degrees** (14°) and very cloudy in England.
	foggy ['fɒgi]	neblig	
	fog [fɒg]	Nebel	noun: **fog** – adjective: **foggy**
p. 9	**sad** [sæd]	traurig	**sad** ◄► **happy**
	nobody ['nəʊbədi]	niemand	
	(to) **speak (to)** [spi:k], *simple past:* **spoke** [spəʊk]	sprechen (mit), reden (mit)	
	clothes *(pl)* [kləʊðz, kləʊz]	Kleider, Kleidung(sstücke)	! **clothes** ist ein Pluralwort: **Kleidung ist** teuer. = **Clothes are** expensive.
	lake [leɪk]	(Binnen-)See	 ! the **lake** = der See • the **sea** = die See, das Meer
	(to) **visit** ['vɪzɪt]	besuchen	

Unit 1: Back to school

p. 10	**canteen** [kæn'ti:n]	Kantine, Schulmensa	Students can buy lunch in the school **canteen**.
	(to) **describe** sth. **(to** sb.**)** [dɪ'skraɪb]	(jm.) etwas beschreiben	! **Describe** the picture **to your partner**. = **Beschreibe** das Bild **deinem Partner**.
	description [dɪ'skrɪpʃn]	Beschreibung	
	background ['bækgraʊnd]	Hintergrund	 Dan and Jo are in the **foreground**. In the **background** you can see a lake.
	foreground ['fɔ:graʊnd]	Vordergrund	

left – right

Do you write with your **left** or your **right** hand? — Schreibst du mit der **linken** oder mit der **rechten** Hand?

Jack looks **left** and **right**, but he can't see the man. — Jack schaut **nach links** und **nach rechts**, aber ...

On the left, you can see Morris, my cat. — **Links/Auf der linken Seite** ...

My dog Emma is **on the right**. — ... **rechts/auf der rechten Seite**.

at the bottom (of) ['bɒtəm]	unten, am unteren Ende (von)	Now do the exercise **at the bottom of** the page. ↓ **at the bottom (of)** ◄► **at the top (of)** ↑

Where's the rabbit? (Prepositions)

behind[1] the cage · **in front of** the cage · **in** the cage · **between**[2] the girls · **near** the cat · **next to**[3] the cat

[1] **behind** [bɪ'haɪnd] hinter

[2] **between** [bɪ'twi:n] zwischen

[3] **next to** neben

p. 12/A 1	**flight** [flaɪt]	Flug	verb: (to) **fly** – noun: **flight**
	time(s) [taɪm(z)]	Mal(e); -mal	We went surfing four **times** last week.
	a bit [ə 'bɪt]	ein bisschen, etwas	The tea was **a bit** hot, so I added some cold milk.
	the underground ['ʌndəgraʊnd]	die U-Bahn	*American English:* **the subway** ['sʌbweɪ]

Irregular simple past forms

(to) forget	**forgot** [fə'gɒt]	vergessen		(to) give	**gave** [geɪv]	geben
(to) get	**got** [gɒt]	gelangen, (hin)kommen		(to) hear	**heard** [hɜːd]	hören
				(to) know	**knew** [njuː]	wissen; kennen
(to) get on/off	**got on/off**	ein-, aussteigen		(to) teach	**taught** [tɔːt]	unterrichten, lehren

	dangerous ['deɪndʒərəs]	gefährlich	
	fast [fɑːst]	schnell	
	slow [sləʊ]	langsam	
	What was **the best thing about ...?**	Was war das Beste an ...?	**The best thing about** the film was the music.
	building ['bɪldɪŋ]	Gebäude	**buildings** 
	lift [lɪft]	Fahrstuhl, Aufzug	*American English:* **elevator** ['elɪveɪtə] 
	amazing [ə'meɪzɪŋ]	erstaunlich, unglaublich	
	for miles [maɪlz]	meilenweit	You can see **for miles** from this tower.
	mile [maɪl]	Meile *(= etwa 1,6 km)*	
p. 13/A 2	**Mind your own business.** [ˌmaɪnd jər‿ˌəʊn 'bɪznəs]	Das geht dich nichts an! / Kümmere dich um deine eigenen Angelegenheiten!	
	Come on. [ˌkʌm‿'ɒn]	Na los, komm.	**Come on**, let's go. We're late.
	rude [ruːd]	unhöflich, unverschämt	
p. 14/A 4	**Do you really think so?**	Meinst du wirklich? / Glaubst du das wirklich?	
	No way! [ˌnəʊ 'weɪ]	Auf keinen Fall! / Kommt nicht in Frage!	Mum, can you give me £20 for a new T-shirt? – £20? **No way!** You can have £10.
	Come on. [ˌkʌm‿'ɒn]	Ach komm! / Na hör mal!	Oh **come on** – you know that's wrong!
	(to) **calm down** [ˌkɑːm 'daʊn]	sich beruhigen	
	angry (about sth.**/with** sb.**)** ['æŋgri]	wütend, böse (über etwas/auf jn.)	Let's be friends again. Or are you still **angry with** me?
	(to) **get angry/hot/... (-tt-)**, *simple past:* **got**	wütend/heiß/... werden	It's **getting hot** in here. Can you open the window, please?

	nothing ['nʌθɪŋ]	nichts	**nothing** (nichts) · **something** (etwas) · **everything** (alles)
p. 15/A 6	**role play** ['rəʊl pleɪ]	Rollenspiel	
p. 18/P 6	**linking word** ['lɪŋkɪŋ wɜːd]	Bindewort	
	Ms Travelot [mɪz, məz]	Frau Travelot	**!** An der Anrede **Ms ...** ist nicht zu erkennen, ob eine Frau verheiratet ist oder nicht. (**Mrs ...** = verheiratet; **Miss ...** = unverheiratet)
	hour ['aʊə]	Stunde	
p. 20/P 10	**person** ['pɜːsn]	Person	**!** Betonung auf der 1. Silbe: **person** ['pɜːsn]
	(to) **be on**	eingeschaltet sein, an sein *(Radio, Licht usw.)*	I can't do my homework when the radio **is on**.
p. 20/P 12	**Find/Ask somebody who ...**	Finde/Frage jemanden, der ...	I've got no idea. **Ask somebody who** knows more about Bristol.

Saved!

p. 22	(to) **save** [seɪv]	retten	
	through [θruː]	durch	He's climbing **through** the window. 
	bunk (bed) [bʌŋk]	Etagenbett, Koje	**bunk beds**  the top **bunk**
	he **could ...** [kəd, kʊd]	er konnte ...	My brother **could** ride a bike when he was four. I **couldn't** watch TV last night. I had lots of homework.
	(to) **get (-tt-)**, *simple past:* **got**	holen, besorgen	

(to) get (*simple past:* got)

1. **holen, besorgen**	Can you **get** the tickets for the theatre?	
2. **gelangen, (hin)kommen**	How can I **get** to the station, please?	
3. **werden**	My mother **got** very angry last night.	
4. **bekommen, kriegen**	Did you **get** nice birthday presents?	

Remember:

(to) **get dressed**	sich anziehen
(to) **get on/off**	ein-/aussteigen
(to) **get up**	aufstehen

out („hinaus, heraus", „draußen")

There's a little cat in the water. We have to pull her **out**.	... Wir müssen sie **heraus**ziehen.
Dan saw a girl swim **out**.	Dan sah ein Mädchen **hinaus**schwimmen.
Where's Sheeba? – She's **out** there in the garden.	... Sie ist da **draußen** im Garten.

before [bɪ'fɔː]	bevor	**!** **before** = 1. bevor – **before** we eat; 2. vor – **before** lunch
after ['ɑːftə]	nachdem	**!** **after** = 1. nachdem – **after** I came home; 2. nach – **after** school

	far [fɑː]	weit (entfernt)	Is it **far** to the station? – Yes, it is. It's too **far** to walk.
	(to) **wave** [weɪv]	winken	She's **waving**.

	(to) **be in trouble** ['trʌbl]	in Schwierigkeiten sein; Ärger kriegen	My friends helped me when I **was in trouble**. Jo **is in trouble**. He hasn't got his homework.
p. 23	**a few** [fjuː]	ein paar, einige	
	all right [ɔːl 'raɪt]	gut, in Ordnung	
	(to) **see** sb. [siː], *simple past:* **saw** [sɔː]	jn. besuchen, jn. aufsuchen	Why don't you come and **see** us next Sunday?
	(to) **know about** sth., *simple past:* **knew** [njuː]	von etwas wissen; über etwas Bescheid wissen	I didn't **know about** the party, so I couldn't go.
	happy ending [ˌhæpi‿'endɪŋ]	Happyend	! In English you say **happy ending**. (*Not:* ~~happy end~~)
	in time [ɪn 'taɪm]	rechtzeitig	We didn't get home **in time**, so we couldn't watch the film.
	(to) **go surfing** ['sɜːfɪŋ]	wellenreiten gehen, surfen gehen	(to) **go surfing**

Unit 2: What money can buy

p. 26	**pocket money** ['pɒkɪt mʌni]	Taschengeld	
	pocket ['pɒkɪt]	Tasche *(an einem Kleidungsstück)*	
	(to) **spend money/time (on)** [spend], *simple past:* **spent** [spent]	Geld ausgeben (für) / Zeit verbringen (mit)	My brother **spends** a lot of money **on** clothes. We **spent** the weekend at my grandma's house in Rostock.
	(to) **save** [seɪv]	sparen	
	survey (on) ['sɜːveɪ]	Umfrage, Untersuchung (über)	

Irregular simple past forms

p. 27	(to) buy	**bought** [bɔːt]	kaufen	(to) understand	**understood** [ˌʌndə'stʊd]	verstehen
	(to) find	**found** [faʊnd]	finden	(to) wear	**wore** [wɔː]	tragen *(Kleidung)*
	(to) think	**thought** [θɔːt]	glauben, meinen, denken	(to) win	**won** [wʌn]	gewinnen

(baseball) cap [kæp]	(Baseball-)Mütze	a **(baseball) cap**
jacket ['dʒækɪt]	Jacke, Jackett	! Betonung auf der 1. Silbe: **jacket** ['dʒækɪt]
make-up ['meɪkʌp]	Make-up	**make-up** ['meɪkʌp]
pullover ['pʊləʊvə]	Pullover	**pullover** ['pʊləʊvə]
skirt [skɜːt]	Rock	
a pair (of) [peə]	ein Paar	a **pair of trainers**
trainers *(pl)* ['treɪnəz]	Turnschuhe	

trousers *(pl)* ['traʊzəz]	Hose		! **Are** your **trousers** new? – Yes, **they are**. (= **Ist** deine **Hose** neu?)

Plural words: *glasses, jeans, shorts, trousers*

She wears **glasses**.	Sie trägt **eine Brille**.	! Wörter wie **glasses, jeans, shorts, trousers** sind Pluralwörter – also nie ~~a glasses~~, ~~two jeans~~, ~~this trousers~~!
Why does he need **two pairs of glasses**?	... **zwei Brillen**?	
Those trousers are great. Can I have **them**?	**Die Hose da ist** toll. Kann ich **sie** haben?	
I need **a new pair of trousers/some new trousers**.	... **eine neue Hose**.	

p. 28/A 1	**What's the matter?** ['mætə]	Was ist los? / Was ist denn?	
	awful ['ɔ:fl]	furchtbar, schrecklich	very bad, terrible
	mine [maɪn]	meiner, meine, meins	

Possessive pronouns (Possessivpronomen)

mine	This isn't my pencil. **Mine** is green.	**meiner, meine, meins**
yours	My pen doesn't write. Can I use **yours**?	**deiner, deine, deins**
his	Where are Mike's shoes? Those aren't **his**.	**seiner, seine, seins**
hers	That isn't Kate's book. **Hers** is on her desk.	**ihrer, ihre, ihrs**
ours	Your dog is black, **ours** is brown.	**unserer, unsere, unseres**
yours	Dan, Jo, what about these CDs? Are they **yours**?	**eurer, eure, eures**
theirs	That wasn't the Millers' car. **Theirs** is red.	**ihrer, ihre, ihrs**

	everybody ['evribɒdi]	jeder, alle	**nobody** (niemand) – **somebody** (jemand) – **everybody** (jeder, alle)
	(to) **be fed up (with** sth.**)** [ˌfed‿'ʌp]	die Nase voll haben (von etwas)	I'**m fed up with** comics. I think they're boring.
	(to) **lose** [lu:z], *simple past:* **lost** [lɒst]	verlieren	(to) **lose money** ◂▸ (to) **find money** (to) **lose a match** ◂▸ (to) **win a match**
	stupid ['stju:pɪd]	blöd, dämlich	**stupid** ◂▸ **clever**
	(to) **have** [həv, hæv], *simple past:* **had** [həd, hæd]	haben, besitzen	! **haben, besitzen** = **1.** have got; **2.** (to) have (Im *simple present* wird *have got* häufiger verwendet. Das *simple past* von beiden ist *had*.)
p. 28/A 2	**fine** [faɪn]	gut, schön; in Ordnung	
p. 29/A 4	**problem** ['prɒbləm]	Problem	
	(to) **look up (from)**	hochsehen, aufschauen (von)	She heard a noise and **looked up from** her book.
	What for? [ˌwɒt 'fɔ:]	Wofür?	
	my old **ones** [wʌnz]	meine alten	There are three CDs: a new **one** (= a new CD) and two old **ones** (= two old CDs).
	more than ['mɔ: ðən]	mehr als	! **more than** <u>**me**</u> = **mehr als** <u>**ich**</u>: My sister has got **more** CDs **than** <u>**me**</u>.

	(to) **point (at/to** sth.**)** [pɔɪnt]	zeigen, deuten (auf etwas)	He **pointed at/to** the clock. 'We're late,' he said. 
	(to) **be sure** [ʃʊə, ʃɔː]	sicher sein	
p. 30/A 7	**easier (than)** ['iːziə]	leichter (als), einfacher (als)	Do you think English is **easier than** Maths?

Steigerung

easy einfach	**easier** einfacher	**(the) easiest** der/die/das einfachste ...; am einfachsten
old alt	**older** älter	**(the) oldest** der/die/das älteste ...; am ältesten
young jung	**younger** jünger	**(the) youngest** der/die/das jüngste ...; am jüngsten

! älter als ich/er/sie = **older than me/him/her**

	Shut up. [ˌʃʌt‿'ʌp] (*simple past:* **shut**)	Halt den Mund!	
	as old/big **as**	so alt/groß wie	Bristol is not **as big as** New York.
	smart [smɑːt]	clever, schlau	
	(to) **be wrong**	sich irren, Unrecht haben	Sophie is 14. – **You're wrong.** She's 12.

good – better – best • bad – worse – worst

good	gut	**bad**	schlecht, schlimm
better	besser	**worse** [wɜːs]	schlechter, schlimmer
(the) best	am besten; der/die/das beste ...	**(the) worst** [wɜːst]	am schlechtesten, schlimmsten; der/die/das schlechteste, schlimmste ...

My computer is **better** than yours, but Mr Scott's computer is **the best**.
Our school uniform is **bad**, but theirs is **worse**.
What do you think: What's **the best** pop group? What's **the worst**?

	(to) **sell** [sel], *simple past:* **sold** [səʊld]	verkaufen	(to) **sell** ◄► (to) **buy**
p. 31/A 9	**even** ['iːvn]	sogar	Everybody tried to help, **even** the children.
	more boring **(than)**	langweiliger (als)	My home town is smaller and **more boring than** New York.
	(the) most boring [məʊst]	der/die/das langweiligste ...; am langweiligsten	This village must be **the most boring** place in Britain.
	recycling [ˌriː'saɪklɪŋ]	Wiederverwertung, Recycling	
	recycled [ˌriː'saɪkld]	wiederverwertet, wiederverwendet, recycelt	
p. 34/P 7	**about** [ə'baʊt]	ungefähr	There were **about** 300 people in the park. ! **about** = **1.** über – a book **about** pets **2.** ungefähr – **about** 300 people
p. 35/P 11	**point** [pɔɪnt]	Punkt	Three **points** for the right answer!
p. 37/P 14	**department store** [dɪ'pɑːtmənt stɔː]	Kaufhaus	

The Clothes Project

p. 38	**as** [əz, æz]	als, während	I ate my sandwiches **as** I waited for the bus.
	fashion ['fæʃn]	Mode	
	(to) **join** sb. [dʒɔɪn]	sich jm. anschließen; bei jm. mitmachen	We're going shopping. Do you want to **join** us? I like computers, so I **joined** the computer club.
	presenter [prɪ'zentə]	Moderator/in	
	over to …	hinüber zu/nach …	Dan saw Jo in the park and walked **over to** him.
	(to) **love** [lʌv]	lieben, sehr mögen	(to) **love** ◄► (to) **hate**
	love	Liebe	
	careful ['keəfl]	vorsichtig; sorgfältig	Please be **careful** – this road is very dangerous. The poster looks great, Ananda. Thank you for your **careful** work.
	(to) **design** [dɪ'zaɪn]	entwerfen, gestalten	
	hat [hæt]	Hut	a **hat** 
	mirror ['mɪrə]	Spiegel	a **mirror** 
	(to) **stand** [stænd], *simple past:* **stood** [stʊd]	stehen; sich (hin)stellen	 Tom **is standing** on the chair. 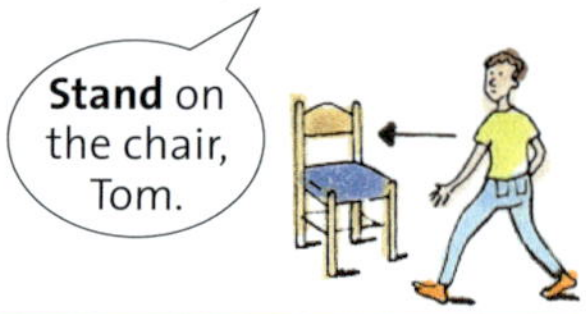
	stuff [stʌf]	Zeug, Kram	What's that red **stuff** on your T-shirt? Ketchup?
	(to) **hurry** ['hʌri]	eilen; sich beeilen	It was very cold so we **hurried** to the car. **Hurry (up)**, we haven't got much time.
	(to) **land** [lænd]	landen	
p. 39	(to) **prepare** [prɪ'peə]	vorbereiten; sich vorbereiten	(to) **prepare** a presentation / a show / a report ! **sich vorbereiten auf = (to) prepare for**: I have to **prepare for** a test.
	puzzled ['pʌzld]	verwirrt	
	bin [bɪn], **dustbin** ['dʌstbɪn]	Mülltonne	a **dustbin** 

Unit 3: Animals in the city

p. 42	**animal** ['ænɪml]	Tier	
	fox [fɒks]	Fuchs	a **fox** 
	series, *pl* **series** ['sɪəri:z]	(Sende-)Reihe, Serie	
	wild [waɪld]	wild	! Pronunciation: **wild** [waɪld]

tonight's programme – Zeitangaben mit s-Genitiv

tonight's programme	das Programm von heute Abend; das heutige Abendprogramm
yesterday's homework	die Hausaufgaben von gestern
tomorrow's weather	das Wetter von morgen

(to) **survive** [sə'vaɪv]	überleben	

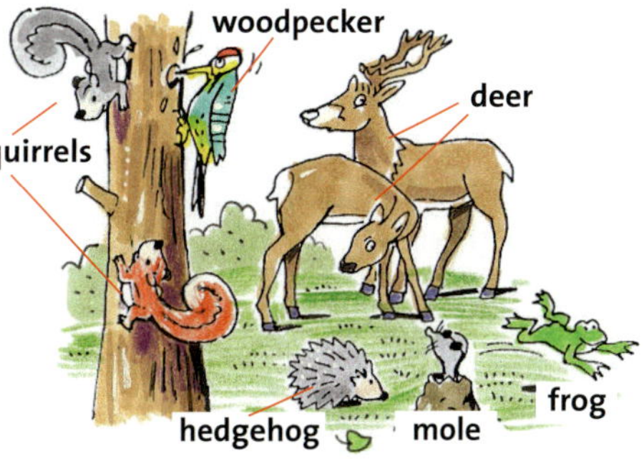

p. 43	**deer**, *pl* **deer** [dɪə]	Reh, Hirsch	
	woodpecker ['wʊdpekə]	Specht	
	grey [greɪ]	grau	
	squirrel ['skwɪrəl]	Eichhörnchen	
	mole [məʊl]	Maulwurf	
	hedgehog ['hedʒhɒg]	Igel	
	frog [frɒg]	Frosch	
p. 44/A 1	**rubbish** ['rʌbɪʃ]	(Haus-)Müll, Abfall	Where's my old cap? – Dad put it in the **rubbish**.
	you**'ll be cold** (= you **will be cold**) [wɪl]	du wirst frieren; ihr werdet frieren	! I**'ll** (= I **will**) help Dan. = Ich **werde** Dan helfen. I **want to** help Dan. = Ich **will** Dan helfen.
	you **won't be cold** [wəʊnt] (= you **will not be cold**)	du wirst nicht frieren; ihr werdet nicht frieren	
	yard [jɑːd]	Hof	! After school we always play **in the yard**. (= auf dem Hof)
	probably ['prɒbəbli]	wahrscheinlich	
	(to) **mail** sb. [meɪl]	jn. anmailen	
	(to) **sit down** (-tt-), *simple past:* **sat down**	sich hinsetzen	
	(to) **send (to)** [send], *simple past:* **sent** [sent]	schicken, senden (an)	Yesterday I **sent** Sarah a birthday card. I always **send** birthday cards to my friends.

Irregular simple past forms

(to) bring	**brought** [brɔːt]	(mit-, her)bringen	(to) lay the table	**laid** [leɪd]	den Tisch decken
(to) choose	**chose** [tʃəʊz]	(aus)wählen, (sich) aussuchen	(to) let	**let** [let]	lassen
(to) feed	**fed** [fed]	füttern	(to) sing	**sang** [sæŋ]	singen
(to) hide	**hid** [hɪd]	(sich) verstecken	(to) sleep	**slept** [slept]	schlafen
			(to) write	**wrote** [rəʊt]	schreiben

p. 44/A 2	**moon** [muːn]	Mond	
p. 45/A 3	**Thanks very much!**	Danke sehr! / Vielen Dank!	(to) like/love sth. **very much** = etwas **sehr** mögen/**sehr** lieben
	if [ɪf]	falls, wenn	! **If** I see him, I'll ask him. (**Falls** ich ihn sehe ...) **When** I see him, ... (**Dann wenn** ... / **Sobald** ...)
	ill [ɪl]	krank	Susan is **ill**. 
	important [ɪm'pɔːtnt]	wichtig	
	(to) **keep** sth. warm/cool/open/... [kiːp], *simple past:* **kept** [kept]	etwas warm/kühl/offen/... halten	It's important to **keep** hedgehog babies **warm**. **Keep** your eyes **open** when you're on the road.
	fine [faɪn]	*(gesundheitlich)* gut	! I'm/He's **fine**. = Es geht mir/ihm gut.
	(to) **pick** sth. **up** [ˌpɪk_'ʌp]	etwas hochheben, aufheben	Who dropped this paper on the floor? Come and **pick it up**, please.

p. 46/A 5	(to) **explain** sth. **to** sb. [ɪk'spleɪn]	jm. etwas erklären, erläutern	❗ Kannst du **mir** das **erklären**? = Can you **explain** that **to me**? (*Not:* Can you ~~explain me~~ ...)
	explanation [ˌeksplə'neɪʃn]	Erklärung	
	horrible ['hɒrəbl]	scheußlich, grauenhaft	a **horrible** day; **horrible** weather
	garage ['gærɑːʒ]	Garage	❗ Betonung auf der 1. Silbe: **garage** ['gærɑːʒ]
	safe (from) [seɪf]	sicher, in Sicherheit (vor)	
p. 47/A 7	(to) **do a good job**	gute Arbeit leisten	I like your essay. You **did a** really **good job**.
	clinic ['klɪnɪk]	Klinik	
	You did **well**. *(adv)* [wel]	Das hast du gut gemacht.	adjective: **good** – adverb: **well**
	broken *(adj)* ['brəʊkən]	gebrochen; zerbrochen, kaputt	a **broken** arm   a **broken** plate
	hard [hɑːd]	hart; schwer, schwierig	**hard** work; a **hard** piece of bread This exercise isn't **hard**. You can do it.
	(to) **work hard**	hart arbeiten	
	I'm afraid [ə'freɪd]	leider	❗ • I have to go now, **I'm afraid**. = **Leider** muss ich jetzt gehen. • My sister **is afraid of** dogs. = Meine Schwester **hat Angst** vor Hunden.
p. 47/A 8	**enemy** ['enəmi]	Feind/in	**enemy** ◄► **friend**
	(to) **scan** a text [skæn] **(-nn-)**	einen Text schnell nach bestimmten Wörtern/ Informationen absuchen	
	(to) **have a baby**	ein Baby/Kind bekommen	❗ ein Kind **bekommen** = (to) **have** a baby
p. 49/P 4	**fire** ['faɪə]	Feuer, Brand	
p. 52/P 11	(to) **hit** [hɪt] **(-tt-)**, *simple past:* **hit**	schlagen	Jo often argues with Dan, but he never **hits** him.

Remember?

p. 52/P 12

1 **crocodile** ['krɒkədaɪl]
2 **monkey** ['mʌŋki]
3 **camel** ['kæml]
4 **zebra** ['zebrə]
5 one **wolf** [wʊlf], two **wolves** [wʊlvz]
6 **tiger** ['taɪgə]
7 **giraffe** [dʒə'rɑːf]
8 **lion** ['laɪən]
9 **rhino** ['raɪnəʊ]
10 **hippo** ['hɪpəʊ]
11 **bear** [beə]
12 **elephant** ['elɪfənt]
13 **kangaroo** [ˌkæŋgə'ruː]

p. 53/P 13	**word building** ['wɜːd ˌbɪldɪŋ]	Wortbildung	
	famous (for) ['feɪməs]	berühmt (für, wegen)	
p. 53/P 15	**address** [ə'dres]	Adresse, Anschrift	! English: **address** – German: **Adresse**

El's best friend

p. 54	**angel** ['eɪndʒl]	Engel	an **angel**
	(to) **bully** ['bʊli]	einschüchtern, tyrannisieren	
	suitcase ['suːtkeɪs]	Koffer	a **suitcase** 
	(to) **pack** [pæk]	packen, einpacken	
	(to) **leave** [liːv], *simple past:* **left** [left]	gehen, weggehen; abfahren	I said 'Goodbye' and **left**.

(to) leave (*simple past:* left)

1. (weg)gehen; abfahren	Get your suitcase. We**'re leaving**.	Hurry up, the train **leaves** in an hour.
2. verlassen	El's mum wanted to **leave** her dad.	I took my bags and **left** the room.
3. zurücklassen	He **left** his dog in the car when he went into the shop.	

	(to) **jump** [dʒʌmp]	springen	
	(to) **miss** [mɪs]	vermissen	It was great in England, but I **missed** my friends.
	(to) **promise** ['prɒmɪs]	versprechen	I'll come and visit you. I **promise**. ! Ich **verspreche es**! = I **promise**! (*not:* I promise ~~it~~)
	neat and tidy [niːt], ['taɪdi]	schön ordentlich	My room is always **neat and tidy**.
	neat	gepflegt	Your hair looks very **neat**, but isn't it a bit short?
	tidy	ordentlich, aufgeräumt	
	sweetheart ['swiːthɑːt]	Liebling, Schatz	
	heart [hɑːt]	Herz	a **heart** 
	(to) **move out** [ˌmuːv_'aʊt]	ausziehen	(to) **move out** ◄► (to) **move in**
	(to) **move (to)**	umziehen (nach, in)	We had to **move out** of our house, so we **moved to** London, **to** a small flat in Camden.
p. 55	**already** [ɔːl'redi]	schon, bereits	Jo was still on the beach, but Dan was **already** in the water.
	return ticket [rɪ'tɜːn ˌtɪkɪt]	Rückfahrkarte	
	(to) **count** [kaʊnt]	zählen	Jack **counted** his money. He had £6.50.
	Oh dear!	Oje!	
	good	brav	! **good** = **1.** gut – a **good** film/story **2.** brav – a **good** boy/dog
	(to) **turn** [tɜːn]	sich umdrehen	
	shy [ʃaɪ]	schüchtern, scheu	
	line [laɪn]	Zeile	I don't know the second word in **line** 12. Abkürzung: **l.** 5 = **line** 5 • **ll.** 5–9 = **lines** 5–9
	letter (to) ['letə]	Brief (an)	a **letter** 
	(to) **feel** [fiːl], *simple past:* **felt** [felt]	sich fühlen; fühlen	I always **feel** good when I hear that song. Take my hand. Can you **feel** how cold it is?

Unit 4: A weekend in Wales

p. 58	**clean** [kli:n]	sauber	verb: (to) **clean** – adjective: **clean**
	cow [kaʊ]	Kuh	
	dirty ['dɜ:ti]	schmutzig	**dirty** ◂▸ **clean**
	factory ['fæktri]	Fabrik	
	farm [fɑ:m]	Bauernhof, Farm	
	field [fi:ld]	Feld, Acker, Weide	! <u>auf</u> dem Feld = <u>**in**</u> **the field**
	forest ['fɒrɪst]	Wald	
	hill [hɪl]	Hügel	
	traffic ['træfɪk]	Verkehr	Look at all those cars. The **traffic** here is terrible.
	noisy ['nɔɪzi]	laut, lärmend	noun: **noise** – adjective: **noisy**

	river ['rɪvə]	Fluss	
	sheep, *pl* **sheep** [ʃi:p]	Schaf	
	valley ['væli]	Tal	

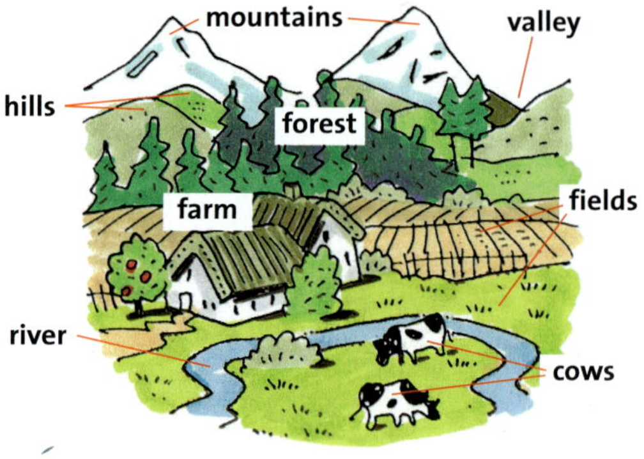

p. 59	**pyjamas** *(pl)* [pə'dʒɑ:məz]	Schlafanzug	! Where <u>**are**</u> my **pyjamas**? (= Wo <u>**ist**</u> mein **Schlafanzug**?)
p. 60/A 1	(to) **smell** [smel]	riechen	I could **smell** Mum's cake in the kitchen. 'Mmm, that **smells** great,' I said.

Verbs and nouns with the same form

(to) **glue**	(auf-, ein)kleben	(to) **list**	auflisten, aufzählen	(to) **smell**	riechen
glue	Klebstoff	**list**	Liste	**smell**	Geruch
(to) **interview**	interviewen, befragen	(to) **name**	nennen; benennen	(to) **smile**	lächeln
interview	Interview	**name**	Name	**smile**	Lächeln
(to) **joke**	scherzen, Witze machen	(to) **report (to)**	berichten	(to) **visit**	besuchen
joke	Witz	**report**	Bericht, Reportage	**visit**	Besuch

	(to) **cook** [kʊk]	kochen, zubereiten	
	Welsh [welʃ]	walisisch; Walisisch	Some people in Wales speak English and **Welsh**.
	soup [su:p]	Suppe	

	railway ['reɪlweɪ]	Eisenbahn	
p. 60/A 2	**sights** *(pl)* [saɪts]	Sehenswürdigkeiten	
	castle ['kɑ:sl]	Burg, Schloss	a **castle** 
	ghost [gəʊst]	Geist, Gespenst	

	topic sentence [ˌtɒpɪk 'sentəns]	*Satz, der in das Thema eines Absatzes einführt*	
	paragraph ['pærəgrɑ:f]	Absatz *(in einem Text)*	
p. 61/A 4	**bacon** ['beɪkən]	Schinkenspeck	**bacon** and **eggs** 
	egg [eg]	Ei	
	timetable ['taɪmteɪbl]	Fahrplan	! **timetable** = **1.** Stundenplan; **2.** Fahrplan
p. 61/A 6	**just** [dʒʌst]	gerade (eben), soeben	

The present perfect: statements

In Aussagesätzen im *present perfect* findet man oft diese unbestimmten Zeitangaben:

already	Please tidy your room. – But I've **already** tidied it.	**schon**
not ... yet	I've tidied my room, but I have**n't** finished my homework **yet**.	**noch nicht**
never	I often play football but I've **never** played basketball.	**(noch) nie**
just	Your room looks great. – Yes, I've **just** tidied it.	**gerade (eben), soeben**

made [meɪd]	*3. Form von „make"*	(to) make – made – **made**
pie [paɪ]	Obstkuchen; Pastete	
seen [si:n]	*3. Form von „see"*	(to) see – saw – **seen**
come [kʌm]	*3. Form von „come"*	(to) come – came – **come**

Irregular past participles[1]

(to) be	was/were	**been** [bi:n]	sein
(to) do	did	**done** [dʌn]	tun, machen
(to) eat	ate	**eaten** ['i:tn]	essen
(to) find	found	**found** [faʊnd]	finden
(to) forget	forgot	**forgotten** [fə'gɒtn]	vergessen
(to) go	went	**gone** [gɒn]	gehen, fahren
(to) have (have got)	had	**had** [hæd]	haben, besitzen
(to) take	took	**taken** ['teɪkən]	nehmen, (weg-, hin)bringen
(to) write	wrote	**written** ['rɪtn]	schreiben

[1] Die dritte Form des Verbs heißt *past participle* (Partizip Perfekt).

	well *(adj)*	*(gesundheitlich)* gut; gesund, wohlauf	! **well** = **1.** gut – She sang **well**. **2.** gesund – He doesn't feel **well**. I'm **well** again.
p. 62/A 7	**headache** ['hedeɪk]	Kopfschmerzen	I have a **headache**. I often get **headaches**.
	(to) **touch** [tʌtʃ]	berühren, anfassen	Don't **touch** the plates! They're hot.
	(to) **have a temperature** ['temprətʃə]	Fieber haben	I feel very hot. I think I **have a temperature**.
	temperature	Temperatur	
	thermometer [θə'mɒmɪtə]	Thermometer	
	(to) **have a sore throat** [sɔ: 'θrəʊt]	Halsschmerzen haben	She **has a sore throat**.
	throat	Hals, Kehle	
	(to) **nod** [nɒd] **(-dd-)**	nicken (mit)	! Er **nickte** <u>**mit**</u> **dem Kopf**. = He **nodded his head**.

	(to) **move** [muːv]	bewegen; sich bewegen	Don't **move**. 
	paramedic [ˌpærə'medɪk]	Sanitäter/in	**!** Im Englischen stehen Berufsangaben immer mit dem unbestimmtem Artikel: My mum is **a** paramedic / **a** teacher. (Meine Mutter ist Sanitäterin / Lehrerin.)

I don't feel well.

(to) have **a headache / a toothache / an earache / a stomach[1] ache**	Kopfschmerzen / Zahnschmerzen / Ohrenschmerzen / Magenschmerzen haben
(to) have **a cold**	eine Erkältung haben, erkältet sein

I don't feel well. / I feel ill.	Ich fühle mich nicht gut. / Ich fühle mich krank.
– What's the matter?	– Was ist denn los?
I have a terrible headache and a sore throat.	Ich habe schreckliche Kopfschmerzen und Halsschmerzen.
– Maybe you have a cold. Do you have a temperature too?	– Vielleicht hast du eine Erkältung / bist du erkältet. Hast du auch Fieber?

Statt *I **have** a cold / a headache / a temperature* usw. kannst du auch *I**'ve got** a cold / a headache / a temperature* usw. sagen.

[1] stomach ['stʌmək] *Magen*

p. 63/A 10	**ever** ['evə]	je, jemals, schon mal	Have you **ever** visited England?

The present perfect: questions

In Fragen im *present perfect* findet man oft diese unbestimmten Zeitangaben:

ever?	Have you **ever** played tennis? – No, never.	**schon mal? / jemals?**
yet?	Have you done your homework **yet**? – Yes, I have.	**schon?**

(to) **install** [ɪn'stɔːl]	installieren, einrichten	
instructions *(pl)* [ɪn'strʌkʃnz]	(Gebrauchs-)Anweisung(en), Anleitung(en)	
It says here: ...	Hier steht: ... / Es heißt hier: ...	

The text says ...

The text says (that) the castle is 700 years old.	Im Text steht, dass ...
It says here / in line 4 / on page 3 that London is older than Berlin.	Hier / In Zeile 4 / Auf Seite 3 steht, dass ...
The poster says (that) it's only £1 for children.	Auf dem Poster steht, dass ...

(to) **click on** sth. [klɪk]	etwas anklicken	What do I do next? – Just **click on** 'OK'.
by the way [ˌbaɪ ðə 'weɪ]	übrigens	

Irregular past participles

(to) buy	bought	**bought** [bɔːt]	kaufen	(to) put	put	**put** [pʊt]	legen, stellen
(to) feed	fed	**fed** [fed]	füttern	(to) say	said	**said** [sed]	sagen
(to) give	gave	**given** ['gɪvn]	geben	(to) send	sent	**sent** [sent]	schicken, senden
(to) know	knew	**known** [nəʊn]	wissen; kennen	(to) think	thought	**thought** [θɔːt]	denken, glauben

p. 65/P 4	**silent letter** [ˌsaɪlənt 'letə]	„stummer" Buchstabe *(nicht gesprochener Buchstabe)*	You can't hear the 'w' in 'answer' – it's a **silent letter**.
p. 65/P 6	**accent** ['æksənt]	Akzent	

All in a day's work

p. 70	(to) **ring** [rɪŋ], **rang** [ræŋ], **rung** [rʌŋ]	klingeln, läuten	Listen – I think the phone **is ringing**.
	accident ['æksɪdənt]	Unfall	
	quite bad/quick/good ... [kwaɪt]	ziemlich schlimm/schnell/gut/...	You'll need a pullover – it's **quite** cold today.
	(to) **put** sth. **on** (-tt-)	etwas anziehen *(Kleidung)*	
	(to) **take** sth. **off**	etwas ausziehen *(Kleidung)*	(to) **take off** a pullover ◄► (to) **put on** a pullover
	side [saɪd]	Seite	How can we get to the other **side** of the river? ! Seite (im Buch) = **page**
	policeman [pə'li:smən] **/ policewoman** [pə'li:swʊmən]	Polizist/Polizistin	
	driver ['draɪvə]	Fahrer/in	
	(to) **drive** [draɪv], **drove** [drəʊv], **driven** ['drɪvn]	*(ein Auto/mit dem Auto)* fahren	Does your mother **drive** to work? – No, she usually goes by bike.
	hurt [hɜ:t]	verletzt	! **hurt** = **1.** *(v)* verletzen; wehtun; **2.** *(adj)* verletzt
	fireman ['faɪəmən] **/ firewoman** ['faɪəˌwʊmən]	Feuerwehrmann/-frau	He's very **strong**.  He's **weak**.
	metre ['mi:tə]	Meter	
	strong [strɒŋ]	stark	
	weak [wi:k]	schwach	
p. 71	(to) **fall** [fɔ:l], **fell** [fel], **fallen** ['fɔ:lən]	fallen, stürzen; hinfallen	Oh no! Toby **has fallen** into the pool. I **fell** and hurt my leg yesterday.
	husband ['hʌzbənd]	Ehemann	! mein **Mann** = my **husband** *(not:* ~~my man~~)
	wife [waɪf], *pl* **wives** [waɪvz]	Ehefrau	! meine **Frau** = my **wife** *(not:* ~~my woman~~)

(to) think

think	I **think** you're right.	**denken, glauben, meinen**
think about	**Think about** these questions: ...	**nachdenken über**
think of	**Think of** the children. They need you. **Think of** a word with five letters.	**denken an** **sich ausdenken**
think about/of	What do you **think about / think of** the story?	**denken über, halten von**

rescue helicopter ['reskju: ˌhelɪkɒptə]	Rettungshubschrauber	
hospital ['hɒspɪtl]	Krankenhaus	
(to) **hope** [həʊp]	hoffen	John is late. I **hope** he hasn't had an accident.
(to) **hold** [həʊld], **held**, **held** [held]	halten	Can you **hold** the baby for a minute, please? That bridge looks dangerous. It won't **hold**.
That was close. [kləʊs]	Das war knapp.	

Unit 5: Teamwork

p. 74	**dice,** *pl* **dice** [daɪs]	Würfel	
	Whose turn is it? [huːz]	Wer ist dran / an der Reihe?	
	whose?	wessen?	**Whose** CDs are these? Are they yours, Sophie? And **whose** are these? (= Wem gehören diese?)
	Move on one space.	Geh ein Feld vor.	
	Move back one space.	Geh ein Feld zurück.	
	Miss a turn.	Einmal aussetzen.	
	engineer [ˌendʒɪˈnɪə]	Ingenieur/in	
	(to) **build** [bɪld], **built, built** [bɪlt]	bauen	
	pub [pʌb]	Kneipe, Lokal	
	closed [kləʊzd]	geschlossen	**closed** ◂▸ **open**
	market [ˈmɑːkɪt]	Markt	
	healthy [ˈhelθi]	gesund	
	snack [snæk]	Snack, Imbiss	
p. 75	**slave** [sleɪv]	Sklave, Sklavin	
	British [ˈbrɪtɪʃ]	britisch; Brite, Britin	There's a lot of **British** music on German radio. I'm German, but my mother is **British**.
	rich [rɪtʃ]	reich	**rich** ◂▸ **poor**
	land [lænd]	Land, Grund und Boden	! Land/Staat = **country**
	(to) **grow** [grəʊ], **grew** [gruː], **grown** [grəʊn]	*(Getreide usw.)* anbauen, anpflanzen	We have a garden and **grow** our own potatoes. ! (to) **grow** = **1.** wachsen; **2.** anbauen, anpflanzen
	sugar [ˈʃʊgə]	Zucker	
	tobacco [təˈbækəʊ]	Tabak	
	(to) **arrive** [əˈraɪv]	ankommen, eintreffen	(to) **arrive** ◂▸ (to) **leave**
p. 76/A 1	**brochure** [ˈbrəʊʃə]	Prospekt, Broschüre	
	detail [ˈdiːteɪl]	Detail, Einzelheit	! Betonung auf der 1. Silbe: **detail** [ˈdiːteɪl]
	local [ˈləʊkl]	Orts-, örtlich	What's the name of Bristol's **local** newspaper?
p. 77/A 4	**statue** [ˈstætʃuː]	Statue	

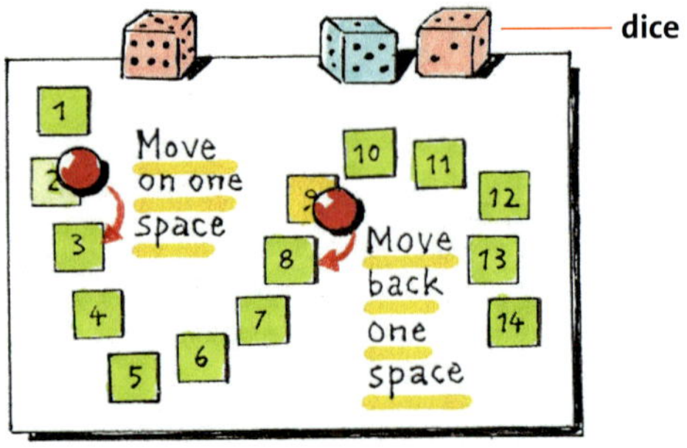

Irregular past participles

(to) hear	heard	**heard** [hɜːd]	hören
(to) leave	left	**left** [left]	(weg)gehen, abfahren; verlassen; zurücklassen
(to) meet	met	**met** [met]	(sich) treffen
(to) run	ran	**run** [rʌn]	rennen, laufen
(to) sell	sold	**sold** [səʊld]	verkaufen
(to) sit	sat	**sat** [sæt]	sitzen; sich setzen
(to) sleep	slept	**slept** [slept]	schlafen

p. 77/A 5	(to) **copy** [ˈkɒpi]	kopieren; abschreiben
	copy [ˈkɒpi]	Kopie

	(to) **be born** [bi 'bɔ:n]	geboren sein/werden	! I **was** born in 1997. = Ich **bin** 1997 geboren. Never: I ~~am born~~ in 1997.
	(to) **become** [bɪ'kʌm], **became** [bɪ'keɪm], **become**	werden	Kate Walker **became** a singer five years ago. ! Nicht verwechseln: (to) **become** = **werden** (to) **get** = **bekommen**
	tunnel ['tʌnl]	Tunnel	
	also ['ɔ:lsəʊ]	auch	Jack had an idea and Ananda had an idea too. = Ananda **also** had an idea.
	(to) **die (of)** [daɪ]	sterben (an)	! -ing form: **dying** – This tree is **dying**.
	proud (of sb./sth.**)** [praʊd]	stolz (auf jn./etwas)	Our daughter is the best student in her class. We're very **proud of** her.
	(to) **mark** sth. **up** [ˌmɑ:k_'ʌp]	etwas markieren, kennzeichnen	
p. 78/A 7	**delicious** [dɪ'lɪʃəs]	köstlich, lecker	What's the pizza like? – Mmm. It's **delicious**.
	impossible [ɪm'pɒsəbl]	unmöglich	
	possible ['pɒsəbl]	möglich	**possible** ◄► **impossible**
	You're joking, aren't you?	Du machst Witze, nicht wahr? / Das ist nicht dein Ernst, oder?	I don't want to go on holiday. – **You're joking, aren't you?**
	pretty healthy/good/... ['prɪti]	ziemlich gesund/gut/...	! **pretty** = **1.** hübsch – Polly is a **pretty** parrot. **2.** ziemlich – This place looks **pretty** good.
	menu ['menju:]	Speisekarte	There's pizza on the **menu**, but no spaghetti.
	kiwi ['ki:wi:]	Kiwi	
	strawberry ['strɔ:bəri]	Erdbeere	
	cherry ['tʃeri]	Kirsche	
	sort [sɔ:t]	Art, Sorte	The menu's great – there are 45 **sorts** of pizza.
p. 78/A 8	**customer** ['kʌstəmə]	Kunde, Kundin	
	waiter ['weɪtə]	Kellner	
	waitress ['weɪtrəs]	Kellnerin	
	medium ['mi:diəm]	mittel(groß)	We sell this T-shirt in three sizes: small, **medium** and **large**. 
	large [lɑ:dʒ]	groß	

big – large – great

big / large	**big** und **large** sind oft austauschbar.	▶ a **big/large** family, a **big/large** house
	large wird in der Regel nicht verwendet, um Menschen zu beschreiben.	▶ a very **big** man 
great	**great** drückt aus, dass jemand oder etwas **wichtig, bedeutend, großartig** ist.	▶ a **great** actor/singer/engineer; a **great** CD; a **great** idea/time

p. 79/A 10	**beginning** [bɪ'gɪnɪŋ]	Beginn, Anfang; Einleitung	**beginning** ◄► **end**
	harbour ['hɑːbə]	Hafen	
	sailor ['seɪlə]	Seemann, Matrose	
	(to) **structure** ['strʌktʃə]	strukturieren, aufbauen	
p. 80/P 1	**information (about/on)** *(no pl)* [ˌɪnfə'meɪʃn]	Information(en) (über)	! • Hier sind die **Informationen** über die Show. = Here's the **information** about/on the show. *Nie:* ... the information~~s~~ • **eine** interessante Information = **some** interesting information
p. 83/P 8	**discussion** [dɪ'skʌʃn]	Diskussion	
	(to) **agree with** sb./sth. [ə'griː]	jm./etwas zustimmen; mit jm./etwas übereinstimmen	Ananda thinks sport is fun but Jack doesn't **agree with** her.
p. 84/P 12	**tornado** [tɔː'neɪdəʊ]	Tornado, Wirbelsturm	

To catch a thief

p. 86	(to) **catch** [kætʃ], **caught, caught** [kɔːt]	fangen; erwischen	You throw the ball and I'll **catch** it. The police are trying to **catch** a bank robber.
	thief [θiːf], *pl* **thieves** [θiːvz]	Dieb/in	
	case [keɪs]	Fall	'This will be a difficult **case**,' the detective said.
	(to) **disappear** [ˌdɪsə'pɪə]	verschwinden	
	(to) **steal** [stiːl], **stole** [stəʊl], **stolen** ['stəʊlən]	stehlen	

Irregular past participles

(to) bring	brought	**brought** [brɔːt]	(mit-, her)bringen	(to) speak	spoke	**spoken** ['spəʊkən]	sprechen
(to) choose	chose	**chosen** ['tʃəʊzn]	(aus)wählen, (sich) aussuchen	(to) swim	swam	**swum** [swʌm]	schwimmen
(to) drink	drank	**drunk** [drʌŋk]	trinken	(to) teach	taught	**taught** [tɔːt]	unterrichten, lehren
(to) hit	hit	**hit** [hɪt]	schlagen	(to) tell	told	**told** [təʊld]	erzählen

who?	wen? / wem?

who? = „wer?" / „wen?" / „wem?"

„wer?"

„Wer?"-Fragen werden ohne *do/does/did* gebildet:

Who loves Polly? – Jack.
Wer liebt Polly? – Jack.

Who helped Toby? – Emily.
Wer half Toby? – Emily.

Jack loves Polly.

Emily helped Toby.

„wen?" / „wem?"

„Wen?"-Fragen und „Wem?"-Fragen werden im *simple present* mit *do/does* und im *simple past* mit *did* gebildet:

Who does Jack love? – Polly.
Wen liebt Jack? – Polly.

Who did Emily help? – Toby.
Wem half Emily? – Toby.

(to) **mean** [miːn], **meant, meant** [ment]	meinen	I hate that man. – Who do you **mean**? I said Tuesday, but I **meant** Thursday.
proof *(no pl)* [pruːf]	Beweis(e)	Is she really a thief? We need **proof**. ! Never: ~~a proof~~

	So?	Und? / Na und?	It's very cold today. – **So?** You can wear a pullover when you go out.
	purse [pɜːs]	Geldbörse	a **purse** 
	at break	in der Pause *(zwischen Schulstunden)*	
	key [kiː]	Schlüssel	I can't open the door. I can't find my **keys**.
	ring [rɪŋ]	Ring	
	(to) **bleep** [bliːp]	piepsen	
	bleep [bliːp]	Piepton	
	(to) **whistle** ['wɪsl]	pfeifen	
p. 87	**towards** sb./sth. [tə'wɔːdz]	auf jn./etwas zu	Jo turned and walked slowly **towards** the door. 'Bye,' he said.
	(to) **look for** ['lʊk fɔː]	suchen	I'm **looking for** my purse. Do you know where it is?
	Wait a minute.	Warte mal! / Moment mal!	
	this way ['ðɪs weɪ]	hier entlang, in diese Richtung	Excuse me. Where's 8PK's classroom? – **This way**, please. It's on the right.
	the wrong way	in die falsche Richtung	Stop! You're going **the wrong way.**
	caretaker ['keəteɪkə]	Hausmeister/in	
	(to) **look after** sth./sb. [ˌlʊk_'ɑːftə]	auf etwas/jn. aufpassen; sich um etwas/jn. kümmern	Emily often **looks after** Baby Hannah.
	cleaner ['kliːnə]	Putzfrau, -mann	
p. 88	**rest** [rest]	Rest	
	Does **anybody** know whose purse this is**?** ['enibɒdi]	Weiß (irgend)jemand, wessen Geldbörse das ist?	

somebody – anybody / something – anything / somewhere – anywhere

Für die Zusammensetzungen mit **some-** und **any-** gelten dieselben Regeln wie für **some** und **any**:

– **somebody, something, somewhere** stehen vor allem in bejahten Aussagesätzen,

– **anybody, anything, anywhere** stehen vor allem in verneinten Aussagesätzen und in Fragen.

+	Listen. There's **somebody** at the door.	... Da ist **jemand** an der Tür.
–	I heard a noise in the garden, but I ca**n't** see **anybody**.	... aber ich kann **niemanden** sehen.
?	Can you see **anybody** in the garden**?**	Kannst du **(irgend)jemanden** im Garten sehen**?**
+	Let's go to the shops and get **something** to eat.	... **etwas** zu essen
–	I'm too nervous – I ca**n't** eat **anything** at the moment.	... ich kann im Moment **nichts** essen.
?	Do you need **anything** from the shops**?**	Brauchst du **(irgend)etwas** ...**?**
+	This summer I'd like to go **somewhere** where it's hot.	... **irgendwohin**, wo es warm ist.
–	I do**n't** want to go **anywhere**, I want to stay at home.	Ich möchte **nirgendwohin** fahren ...
?	Are you going to go **anywhere** this summer**?**	Fährst du diesen Sommer **irgendwohin?**

Unit 6: A trip to Bath

p. 92	**Roman** ['rəʊmən]	römisch; Römer, Römerin	
	bath [bɑːθ]	Bad, Badewanne	! (to) **have a bath** = baden, ein Bad nehmen
	round [raʊnd]	rund	
	(to) **chat** [tʃæt] **(-tt-)**	plaudern; chatten	We sat in the park and **chatted** for a few hours.
	(to) **have a sauna** ['sɔːnə]	in die Sauna gehen	
	(to) **relax** [rɪ'læks]	(sich) entspannen, sich ausruhen	
	wall [wɔːl]	Wand; Mauer	
	stone [stəʊn]	Stein	
p. 94/A 1	**(bike) ride**	(Rad-)Fahrt	
	path [pɑːθ]	Pfad, Weg	a **cycle path**
	How are you? [ˌhaʊ_'ɑː jʊ]	Wie geht es dir/Ihnen/euch?	**How are you**, Mr Kingsley**?** – I'm fine, thank you.
	(to) **cycle** ['saɪkl]	(mit dem) Rad fahren	(to) ride a bike
	planet ['plænɪt]	Planet	
	star [stɑː]	Stern	a **star** 
p. 95/A 3	**map** [mæp]	Landkarte, Stadtplan	
	(to) **tell** sb. **the way**	jm. den Weg beschreiben	
	(to) **ask** sb. **the way**	jn. nach dem Weg fragen	

way („Richtung", „Weg")

Stop. You're going **the wrong way**. We have to go **this way**.	Halt! Du gehst **in die falsche Richtung**. Wir müssen **hier entlang / in diese Richtung**.
Which way is the station, please?	**In welcher Richtung liegt** der Bahnhof, bitte? / **Wo geht's** zum Bahnhof, bitte?
I don't know where we are. Let's **ask** somebody **the way**. 'Excuse me. Can you **tell** us **the way** to Bath?'	... Lass uns jemanden **nach dem Weg fragen**. „... Können Sie uns **den Weg** nach Bath **beschreiben**?"
The group had a lot of fun **on their way** to Bath.	... **auf ihrem Weg** nach Bath.

(to) **turn left/right**	(nach) links/rechts abbiegen	**Turn left.**   **Turn right.**

(to) turn

The way to the station? No problem – **turn left** at the church, then **turn right** into Elm Street.	**abbiegen**
Suddenly the woman **turned** and looked at me.	**sich umdrehen**
Mrs Hanson **turned to** Jack and asked, 'Why?'	**sich jm. zuwenden; sich an jn. wenden**

straight on [streɪt_'ɒn]	geradeaus weiter	The way to the hospital? Turn left here, and then go **straight on**.
post office ['pəʊst_ɒfɪs]	Postamt	
past [pɑːst]	vorbei (an), vorüber (an)	We walked **past** theatres, cafés and shops.

	(to) **cross** ['krɒs]	überqueren	Don't **cross** the road here. It's too dangerous.
	corner ['kɔːnə]	Ecke	! **on the corner of** Green Street and London Road (= Green Street, Ecke London Road)
	police station [pə'liːs steɪʃn]	Polizeiwache, Polizeirevier	
	restaurant ['restrɒnt]	Restaurant	! Betonung auf der 1. Silbe: **restaurant** ['restrɒnt]
	chemist ['kemɪst]	Drogerie, Apotheke	
p. 96/A 5	(to) **be missing** ['mɪsɪŋ]	fehlen	Almost all my friends were at the party. Only Robbie **was missing**.
	needn't do ['niːdnt]	nicht tun müssen, nicht zu tun brauchen	I can do the exercise. You **needn't** help me. **needn't** ◄► **must**
	mustn't do ['mʌsnt]	nicht tun dürfen	You can go out, but you **mustn't** be back late.

must – needn't – mustn't

must (müssen)	**needn't** (nicht müssen)	**mustn't** (nicht dürfen)
Mit **must** drückt man aus, dass jemand etwas tun muss:	Mit **needn't** drückt man aus, dass jemand etwas nicht zu tun braucht:	Mit **mustn't** drückt man aus, dass jemand etwas nicht tun darf:
I **must** clean the hamster's cage today. It's very dirty.	I **needn't** clean the rabbits' cage. It isn't dirty.	You **mustn't** give hedgehogs milk. It's bad for them.
(Ich muss ... sauber machen.)	(Ich muss ... nicht sauber machen / brauche ... nicht sauber zu machen.)	(Du darfst Igeln keine Milch geben.)

This is Isabel.	Hier spricht Isabel. / Hier ist Isabel. *(am Telefon)*	*(on the phone)* Am I speaking to Laura? – No, **this is** Emma.

Irregular past participles

(to) feel	felt	**felt** [felt]	(sich) fühlen	(to) read [riːd]	read [red]	**read** [red]	lesen
(to) fly	flew	**flown** [fləʊn]	fliegen	(to) ride	rode	**ridden** ['rɪdn]	reiten; *(Rad)* fahren
(to) get	got	**got** [gɒt]	bekommen; holen; werden; (hin)kommen	(to) sing	sang	**sung** [sʌŋ]	singen
(to) hide	hid	**hidden** ['hɪdn]	(sich) verstecken	(to) throw	threw	**thrown** [θrəʊn]	werfen
(to) lose	lost	**lost** [lɒst]	verlieren	(to) win	won	**won** [wʌn]	gewinnen

	along the street [ə'lɒŋ]	entlang der Straße / die Straße entlang	We walked **along** the river and then crossed the bridge.
	trick [trɪk]	Streich	
p. 97/A 9	(to) **enjoy** [ɪn'dʒɔɪ]	genießen	Lunch was very good. I really **enjoyed** it.
p. 99/P 4	**ice rink** ['aɪs rɪŋk]	Schlittschuhbahn	
p. 102/P 11	(to) **correct** [kə'rekt]	berichtigen, korrigieren	

A trip to Bath – a play for the end of term

p. 103	**term** [tɜːm]	Trimester	The school year has three **terms** in Britain.
	(to) **mime** [maɪm]	pantomimisch darstellen, vorspielen	Can you say a poem or **mime** something for me?
	(to) **like** sth. **better**	etwas lieber mögen	Tim's favourite sport is tennis, but I **like** football **better**.

	luckily ['lʌkɪli]	zum Glück, glücklicherweise	
	actor ['æktə]	Schauspieler/in	
	(to) **fall off** [ˌfɔːl‿'ɒf]	herunterfallen (von)	Liz **fell off** her horse, but luckily she wasn't hurt.
p. 104	**the other way round**	anders herum	So your name is John James. – No, **the other way round**: James John.
	movement ['muːvmənt]	Bewegung	verb: (to) **move** – noun: **movement**
	leisure centre ['leʒə sentə]	Freizeitzentrum, -park	
	(to) **yawn** [jɔːn]	gähnen	She**'s yawning**. 
	audience ['ɔːdiəns]	Publikum; Zuschauer/innen, Zuhörer/innen	
	Hooray! [hu'reɪ]	Hurra!	
	(to) **pay (for)** [peɪ], **paid, paid** [peɪd]	bezahlen	**!** (to) **pay for a sandwich** (ein Sandwich bezahlen)
	tomato [tə'mɑːtəʊ], *pl* **tomatoes**	Tomate	 **tomatoes**
	lettuce ['letɪs]	(Kopf-)Salat	 **lettuce**
	century ['sentʃəri]	Jahrhundert	
	(to) **wonder** ['wʌndə]	sich fragen, gern wissen wollen	Do you know that boy over there? I **wonder** who he is.
p. 105	(to) **cheer** [tʃɪə]	jubeln, Beifall klatschen	At the end of the play, the audience **cheered** loudly.
	laughter ['lɑːftə]	Gelächter	
	worry ['wʌri]	Sorge, Kummer	
	bright [braɪt]	hell, leuchtend	It's a very **bright** room. It gets the sun all day.
	if	ob	**!** **if** = **1**. I don't know **if** I can come to your party. (ob) **2**. But I'll come **if** I can. (falls, wenn)
	true [truː]	wahr	The twins' mother lives in Australia. – That's not **true**. She lives in New Zealand.

Irregular past participles

(to) hurt	hurt	**hurt** [hɜːt]	wehtun; verletzen
(to) keep	kept	**kept** [kept]	*(warm/offen/...)* halten
(to) lay the table	laid	**laid** [leɪd]	den Tisch decken
(to) let	let	**let** [let]	lassen
(to) shine	shone	**shone** [ʃɒn]	scheinen *(Sonne)*
(to) show	showed	**shown** [ʃəʊn]	zeigen
(to) spend	spent	**spent** [spent]	*(Geld)* ausgeben; *(Zeit)* verbringen
(to) stand	stood	**stood** [stʊd]	stehen; sich (hin)stellen
(to) understand	understood	**understood** [ˌ-'stʊd]	verstehen
(to) wear	wore	**worn** [wɔːn]	tragen *(Kleidung)*

Das Dictionary besteht aus zwei alphabetischen Wörterlisten:

Englisch – Deutsch (S. 173–191)
Deutsch – Englisch (S. 192–206).

Das **English – German Dictionary** enthält den Wortschatz der Bände 1 und 2 von *English G 21*.
Wenn du wissen möchtest, was ein Wort bedeutet, wie man es ausspricht oder wie es genau geschrieben wird, kannst du hier nachschlagen.

Im **English – German Dictionary** werden folgende **Abkürzungen** und **Symbole** verwendet:

jm. = jemandem	sb. = somebody	*pl* = *plural* (Mehrzahl)	*AE* = *American English*
jn. = jemanden	sth. = something	*no pl* = *no plural*	

° Mit diesem Kringel sind Wörter markiert, die nicht zum Lernwortschatz gehören.
▸ Der Pfeil verweist auf Kästchen im Vocabulary (S. 150–172), in denen du weitere Informationen zu diesem Wort findest.

Die **Fundstellenangaben** zeigen, wo ein Wort zum ersten Mal vorkommt.
Die Ziffern in Klammern bezeichnen Seitenzahlen:

I	= Band 1
II Welc (6)	= Band 2, Welcome back, Seite 6
II Welc (6/151)	= Band 2, Welcome back, Seite 151 (im Vocabulary, zu Seite 6)
II 1 (22)	= Band 2, Unit 1, Seite 22
II 1 (22/154)	= Band 2, Unit 1, Seite 154 (im Vocabulary, zu Seite 22)

Tipps zur Arbeit mit dem Dictionary findest du im Skills File auf Seite 123.

A

a [ə] ein, eine I • **a bit** ein bisschen, etwas II 1 (12) • **a few** ein paar, einige II 1 (23) • **a lot (of)** eine Menge, viel, viele II 2 (27)
He likes her a lot. Er mag sie sehr. I
°**abbey** ['æbi] Abtei
about [ə'baʊt]
1. über I
2. ungefähr II 2 (34)
ask about sth. nach etwas fragen I
This is about Mr Green. Es geht um Mr Green. I • **What about ...?** **1.** Was ist mit ...? / Und ...? I; **2.** Wie wär's mit ...? I • **What are you talking about?** Wovon redest du? I
What was the best thing about ...? Was war das Beste an ...? II 1 (12)
°**absurd** [əb'sɜːd] absurd, lächerlich
accent ['æksənt] Akzent II 4 (65)
accident ['æksɪdənt] Unfall II 4 (70)
act [ækt] aufführen, spielen I
°**Act out ...** Spiele/Spielt ... vor.
activity [æk'tɪvəti] Aktivität, Tätigkeit I
actor ['æktə] Schauspieler/in II 3 (53) / II 6 (103)
add (to) [æd] hinzufügen, ergänzen, addieren (zu) I
address [ə'dres] Adresse, Anschrift II 3 (53)
afraid [ə'freɪd]
1. be afraid (of) Angst haben (vor) I
2. I'm afraid leider II 3 (47)
°**Afro-Caribbean** [ˌæfrəʊˌkærə'biːən] afro-karibisch
after ['ɑːftə] nach *(zeitlich)* I
after that danach I
after ['ɑːftə] nachdem II 1 (22/154)
afternoon [ˌɑːftə'nuːn] Nachmittag I • **in the afternoon** nachmittags, am Nachmittag I • **on Friday afternoon** freitagnachmittags, am Freitagnachmittag I
again [ə'gen] wieder; noch einmal I
ago [ə'gəʊ]: **a minute ago** vor einer Minute I
agree (on) [ə'griː] sich einigen (auf) I • **agree with sb./sth.** jm./etwas zustimmen; mit jm./etwas übereinstimmen II 5 (83)
°**alien** ['eɪliən] Außerirdische(r)
all [ɔːl] alle; alles I • **all day** den ganzen Tag (lang) I • °**all I did** alles, was ich tat • °**All in a day's work.** *etwa:* Mach ich doch gern. °**all over the island** auf der ganzen Insel • **all right** gut, in Ordnung II 1 (23) • **all the time** die ganze Zeit I • **This is all wrong.** Das ist ganz falsch. I
alone [ə'ləʊn] allein I
along the street [ə'lɒŋ] entlang der Straße / die Straße entlang II 6 (96)
alphabet ['ælfəbet] Alphabet I
°**alphabetical** [ˌælfə'betɪkl] alphabetisch
already [ɔːl'redi] schon, bereits II 3 (55)
▸ S.163 The present perfect: statements
also ['ɔːlsəʊ] auch II 5 (77)
always ['ɔːlweɪz] immer I
am [ˌeɪ_'em]: **7 am** 7 Uhr morgens/vormittags I
amazing [ə'meɪzɪŋ] erstaunlich, unglaublich II 1 (12)
American football [əˌmerɪkən 'fʊtbɔːl] Football I
an [ən] ein, eine I
and [ənd, ænd] und I
angel ['eɪndʒl] Engel II 3 (54)
angry (about sth./with sb.) ['æŋgri] wütend, böse (über etwas/auf jn.) II 1 (14)
animal ['ænɪml] Tier II 3 (42)
another [ə'nʌðə] ein(e) andere(r, s); noch ein(e) I • **another 45p** weitere 45 Pence, noch 45 Pence II 3 (55)
answer ['ɑːnsə] antworten; beantworten I
answer (to) ['ɑːnsə] Antwort (auf) I
any ['eni]: **any ...?** (irgend)welche ...? I • **not (...) any** kein, keine I
anybody ['enibɒdi] (irgend)jemand II 5 (88) • **not (...) anybody** niemand II 5 (88/169)
▸ S.169 somebody – anybody

anything ['eniθɪŋ] (irgend)etwas II 5 (88/169) • **not (...) anything** nichts II 5 (88/169)
▶ S.169 something – anything
anyway ['eniweɪ]
1. sowieso I
2. trotzdem II Welc (6)
anywhere ['eniweə] irgendwo(hin) II 5 (88/169) • **not (...) anywhere** nirgendwo(hin) II 5 (88/169)
▶ S.169 somewhere – anywhere
apple ['æpl] Apfel I
appointment [ə'pɔɪntmənt] Termin, Verabredung I
April ['eɪprəl] April I
are [ɑː] bist; sind; seid I • **How are you?** Wie geht es dir/Ihnen/euch? II 6 (94) • **The pencils are 35p.** Die Bleistifte kosten 35 Pence. I • **You're joking, aren't you?** Du machst Witze, nicht wahr? / Das ist nicht dein Ernst, oder? II 5 (78)
°**area** ['eəriə] Gegend, Gebiet
argue ['ɑːgjuː] sich streiten, sich zanken I
arm [ɑːm] Arm I
armchair ['ɑːmtʃeə] Sessel I
°**army** ['ɑːmi] Armee
°**around the world** [ə'raʊnd] in/auf der ganzen Welt
arrive [ə'raɪv] ankommen, eintreffen II 5 (75)
art [ɑːt] Kunst I
as [əz, æz]
1. als, während II 2 (38)
2. as old/big as so alt/groß wie II 2 (30)
ask [ɑːsk] fragen I • **ask about sth.** nach etwas fragen I • **ask questions** Fragen stellen I • °**ask sb. for sth.** jn. um etwas bitten **ask sb. the way** jn. nach dem Weg fragen II 6 (95/170)
asleep [ə'sliːp]**: be asleep** schlafen I
°**astronomy** [ə'strɒnəmi] Astronomie
at [ət, æt]**: at 7 Hamilton Street** in der Hamiltonstraße 7 I • **at 8.45** um 8.45 I • **at break** in der Pause *(zwischen Schulstunden)* II 5 (86) **at home** daheim, zu Hause I • **at last** endlich, schließlich I • **at least** zumindest, wenigstens I **at night** nachts, in der Nacht I **at school** in der Schule I • **at that table** an dem Tisch (dort) / an den Tisch (dort) I • **at the bottom (of)** unten, am unteren Ende (von) II 1 (10) • **at the end (of)** am Ende (von) I • **at the Shaws' house** im Haus der Shaws / bei den Shaws zu Hause I • **at the station** am Bahnhof I • **at the top (of)** oben, am oberen Ende, an der Spitze (von) I • **at the weekend** am Wochenende I • **at work** bei der Arbeit / am Arbeitsplatz I
ate [et, eɪt] *siehe* **eat**
°**attic** ['ætɪk] Dachboden
audience ['ɔːdiəns] Publikum; Zuschauer/innen, Zuhörer/innen II 6 (104)
August ['ɔːgəst] August I
aunt [ɑːnt] Tante I • **auntie** ['ɑːnti] Tante II 2 (30)
autumn ['ɔːtəm] Herbst I
away [ə'weɪ] weg, fort I
awful ['ɔːfl] furchtbar, schrecklich II 2 (28)

B

baby ['beɪbi] Baby I • **have a baby** ein Baby/Kind bekommen II 3 (47)
°**back** [bæk] Rücken
back (to) [bæk] zurück (nach) I
°**Jo went back to the game.** Jo wandte sich wieder dem Spiel zu.
back door [ˌbæk 'dɔː] Hintertür II 3 (44)
background ['bækgraʊnd] Hintergrund II 1 (10) • **background file** *etwa:* Hintergrundinformation II (3)
bacon ['beɪkən] Schinkenspeck II 4 (61)
bad [bæd] schlecht, schlimm I
badminton ['bædmɪntən] Badminton, Federball I
bag [bæg] Tasche, Beutel, Tüte I
ball [bɔːl] Ball I
°**ball dress** ['bɔːl dres] Ballkleid
banana [bə'nɑːnə] Banane I
band [bænd] Band, (Musik-)Gruppe I
°**Bang!** [bæŋ] Peng!
bank [bæŋk] Bank, Sparkasse I
bank robber ['bæŋk ˌrɒbə] Bankräuber/in I
bar [bɑː] Bar II 5 (78)
°**barbecue** ['bɑːbɪkjuː] Grillparty
baseball ['beɪsbɔːl] Baseball I
baseball cap Baseballmütze II 2 (27)
basket ['bɑːskɪt] Korb I • **a basket of apples** ein Korb Äpfel I
basketball ['bɑːskɪtbɔːl] Basketball I
bath [bɑːθ] Bad, Badewanne II 6 (92)
have a bath baden, ein Bad nehmen II 6 (92/170)
bathroom ['bɑːθruːm] Badezimmer I
be [biː]**, was/were, been** sein I
beach [biːtʃ] Strand II Welc (6) • **on the beach** am Strand II Welc (6)
bear [beə] Bär II 3 (52/160)
beautiful ['bjuːtɪfl] schön I
became [bɪ'keɪm] *siehe* **become**
because [bɪ'kɒz] weil I
become [bɪ'kʌm]**, became, become** werden II 5 (77)
bed [bed] Bett I • **Bed and Breakfast (B&B)** [ˌbed_ən 'brekfəst] Frühstückspension (*wörtlich:* Bett und Frühstück) I • **go to bed** ins Bett gehen I
bedroom ['bedruːm] Schlafzimmer I
been [biːn] *siehe* **be**
before [bɪ'fɔː] vor *(zeitlich)* I
before [bɪ'fɔː] bevor II 1 (22)
beginning [bɪ'gɪnɪŋ] Beginn, Anfang; Einleitung II 5 (79)
behind [bɪ'haɪnd] hinter II 1 (10)
°**below** [bɪ'ləʊ] unten
°**bend (over)** [ˌbend_'əʊvə] sich bücken
best [best] am besten II 2 (30)
the best ... der/die/das beste ...; die besten I • °**like sth. best** etwas am liebsten mögen • **What was the best thing about ...?** Was war das Beste an ...? II 1 (12)
better ['betə] besser I • **like sth. better** etwas lieber mögen II 6 (103)
between [bɪ'twiːn] zwischen II 1 (10)
big [bɪg] groß I
▶ S.167 big – large – great
bike [baɪk] Fahrrad I • **bike ride** (Rad-)Fahrt II 6 (94) • **ride a bike** Rad fahren I
bin [bɪn] Mülltonne II 2 (39)
°**binoculars** *(pl)* [bɪ'nɒkjələz] Fernglas
biology [baɪ'ɒlədʒi] Biologie I
bird [bɜːd] Vogel I
birthday ['bɜːθdeɪ] Geburtstag I
Happy birthday. Herzlichen Glückwunsch zum Geburtstag. I • **My birthday is in May.** Ich habe im Mai Geburtstag. I • **My birthday is on 13th June.** Ich habe am 13. Juni Geburtstag. I • **When's your birthday?** Wann hast du Geburtstag? I
biscuit ['bɪskɪt] Keks, Plätzchen I
bit: a bit [ə 'bɪt] ein bisschen, etwas II 1 (12)
black [blæk] schwarz I
bleep [bliːp] piepsen II 5 (86)
bleep [bliːp] Piepton II 5 (87)
°**blood** [blʌd] Blut
blue [bluː] blau I
board [bɔːd] (Wand-)Tafel I • **on the board** an der/die Tafel I

notice board Anschlagtafel, schwarzes Brett I
boat [bəʊt] Boot, Schiff I
body ['bɒdi] Körper I
°**bone** [bəʊn] Knochen
°**bonfire** ['bɒnfaɪə] (Freuden-)Feuer
book [bʊk] Buch I
boot [buːt] Stiefel I
boring ['bɔːrɪŋ] langweilig I
born [bɔːn]**: be born** geboren sein/werden II 5 (77)
both [bəʊθ] beide I
bottle ['bɒtl] Flasche I • **a bottle of milk** eine Flasche Milch I
bottom ['bɒtəm] unteres Ende II 1 (10) • **at the bottom (of)** unten, am unteren Ende (von) II 1 (10)
bought [bɔːt] *siehe* **buy**
bowl [bəʊl] Schüssel I • **a bowl of cornflakes** eine Schale Cornflakes I
box [bɒks] Kasten, Kästchen, Kiste I
sandwich box Brotdose I
boy [bɔɪ] Junge I
bread *(no pl)* [bred] Brot I
break [breɪk] Pause I • **at break** in der Pause *(zwischen Schulstunden)* II 5 (86)
breakfast ['brekfəst] Frühstück I
have breakfast frühstücken I
bridge [brɪdʒ] Brücke I
bright [braɪt] hell, leuchtend II 6 (105)
bring [brɪŋ]**, brought, brought** (mit-, her)bringen I
British ['brɪtɪʃ] britisch; Brite, Britin II 5 (75)
brochure ['brəʊʃə] Prospekt, Broschüre II 5 (76)
broken ['brəʊkən] gebrochen; zerbrochen, kaputt II 3 (47)
brother ['brʌðə] Bruder I
brought [brɔːt] *siehe* **bring**
brown [braʊn] braun I • °**brown bread** Mischbrot
budgie ['bʌdʒi] Wellensittich I
°**buffet** ['bʊfeɪ] Büfett
build [bɪld]**, built, built** bauen II 5 (74)
building ['bɪldɪŋ] Gebäude II 1 (12)
built [bɪlt] *siehe* **build**
bully ['bʊli] einschüchtern, tyrannisieren II 3 (54)
°**bungee jumping** ['bʌndʒi dʒʌmpɪŋ] Bungeejumping
bunk (bed) [bʌŋk] Etagenbett, Koje II 1 (22)
bus [bʌs] Bus I
business ['bɪznəs]**: Mind your own business.** Das geht dich nichts an!/ Kümmere dich um deine eigenen Angelegenheiten! II 1 (13)
but [bət, bʌt] aber I
buy [baɪ]**, bought, bought** kaufen I
°**buzz** [bʌz] *hier:* den Summer/die Glocke betätigen
by [baɪ]
1. von I
2. an; (nahe) bei II Welc (6)
3. by car/train/bike/... mit dem Auto/Zug/Rad/... II Welc (7) • **by the way** übrigens II 4 (63)
Bye. [baɪ] Tschüs! I

C

°**cabin** ['kæbɪn] Kajüte
café ['kæfeɪ] *(kleines)* Restaurant, Imbissstube, Café II 4 (66)
cage [keɪdʒ] Käfig I
cake [keɪk] Kuchen, Torte I
°**calabash** ['kæləbæʃ] Kalebasse *(aus einem Kürbis hergestelltes Gefäß)*
calendar ['kælɪndə] Kalender I
call [kɔːl] rufen; anrufen; nennen I
call [kɔːl] Anruf, Telefongespräch I
calm down [ˌkɑːm 'daʊn] sich beruhigen II 1 (14)
came [keɪm] *siehe* **come**
camel ['kæml] Kamel II 3 (52/160)
camera ['kæmərə] Kamera, Fotoapparat I
can [kən, kæn]
1. können I
2. dürfen I
Can I help you? Kann ich Ihnen helfen?/ Was kann ich für Sie tun? *(im Geschäft)* I
°**candle** ['kændl] Kerze
°**cannibal** ['kænɪbl] Kannibale, Kannibalin
canteen [kæn'tiːn] Kantine, Schulmensa II 1 (10)
cap [kæp] Mütze, Kappe II 2 (27)
°**capital** ['kæpɪtl] Hauptstadt
°**captain** ['kæptɪn] Kapitän/in
°**caption** ['kæpʃn] Bildunterschrift
car [kɑː] Auto I
caravan ['kærəvæn] Wohnwagen II Welc (6)
card [kɑːd] (Spiel-, Post-)Karte I
careful ['keəfl]
1. vorsichtig II 2 (38)
2. sorgfältig II 2 (38)
caretaker ['keəteɪkə] Hausmeister/in II 5 (87)
°**Caribbean** [ˌkærə'biːən]**: in the Caribbean** in der Karibik
carrot ['kærət] Möhre, Karotte I
cartoon [kɑː'tuːn] Cartoon (Zeichentrickfilm; Bilderwitz) II 3 (42)
case [keɪs] Fall II 5 (86)
castle ['kɑːsl] Burg, Schloss II 4 (60)
cat [kæt] Katze I
catch [kætʃ]**, caught, caught** fangen; erwischen II 5 (86)
°**Catholic** ['kæθlɪk] katholisch; Katholik/in
caught [kɔːt] *siehe* **catch**
°**cave** [keɪv] Höhle
CD [ˌsiː'diː] CD I • **CD player** CD-Spieler I
°**celebrate** ['selɪbreɪt] feiern
cent (c) [sent] Cent I
centre ['sentə] Zentrum, Mitte I
city centre Stadtzentrum, Innenstadt I • **sports centre** Sportzentrum I
century ['sentʃəri] Jahrhundert II 6 (104)
chair [tʃeə] Stuhl I
champion ['tʃæmpiən] Meister/in, Champion I
change [tʃeɪndʒ] Wechselgeld I
°**chant** [tʃɑːnt] Sprechchor
°**charity** ['tʃærəti] Wohltätigkeitsorganisation • °**charity shop** *Geschäft, in dem Sachen für eine Wohlfahrtsorganisation verkauft werden*
°**chart** [tʃɑːt] Schaubild, Diagramm, Tabelle
chat (-tt-) [tʃæt] plaudern; chatten II 6 (92)
cheap [tʃiːp] billig I
check [tʃek] (über)prüfen, kontrollieren I
checkpoint ['tʃekpɔɪnt] Kontrollpunkt *(hier: zur Selbstüberprüfung)* I
cheer [tʃɪə] jubeln, Beifall klatschen II 6 (105)
cheese [tʃiːz] Käse I
chemist ['kemɪst] Drogerie, Apotheke II 6 (95)
cherry ['tʃeri] Kirsche II 5 (78)
chicken ['tʃɪkɪn] Huhn; (Brat-)Hähnchen I • °**chicken tikka** [ˌtʃɪkɪn 'tɪkə] *indisches Gericht (mariniertes gegrilltes Hühnerfleisch)*
child [tʃaɪld]**,** *pl* **children** ['tʃɪldrən] Kind I
chips *(pl)* [tʃɪps] Pommes frites I
chocolate ['tʃɒklət] Schokolade I
°**choice** [tʃɔɪs] (Aus-)Wahl
choir ['kwaɪə] Chor I
choose [tʃuːz]**, chose, chosen** (sich) aussuchen, (aus)wählen I
°**chorus** ['kɔːrəs] Refrain
chose [tʃəʊz] *siehe* **choose**
chosen ['tʃəʊzn] *siehe* **choose**
Christmas ['krɪsməs] Weihnachten I
church [tʃɜːtʃ] Kirche I
cinema ['sɪnəmə] Kino I • **go to the cinema** ins Kino gehen II 1 (14)

city ['sɪti] (Groß-)Stadt I • **city centre** Stadtzentrum, Innenstadt I
class [klɑːs] (Schul-)Klasse I
class teacher Klassenlehrer/in I
classmate ['klɑːsmeɪt] Klassenkamerad/in, Mitschüler/in I
classroom ['klɑːsruːm] Klassenzimmer I
clean [kliːn] sauber II 4 (58)
clean [kliːn] sauber machen, putzen I • **I clean my teeth.** Ich putze mir die Zähne. I
cleaner ['kliːnə] Putzfrau, -mann II 5 (87)
clear [klɪə] klar, deutlich I
clever ['klevə] schlau, klug I
click on sth. [klɪk] etwas anklicken II 4 (63)
climb [klaɪm] klettern; hinaufklettern (auf) I • **Climb a tree.** Klettere auf einen Baum. I
clinic ['klɪnɪk] Klinik II 3 (47)
clock [klɒk] (Wand-, Stand-, Turm-) Uhr I
close [kləʊs]**: That was close.** Das war knapp. II 4 (71)
close [kləʊz] schließen, zumachen I
closed [kləʊzd] geschlossen II 5 (74)
clothes *(pl)* [kləʊðz, kləʊz] Kleider, Kleidung(sstücke) II Welc (9)
cloud [klaʊd] Wolke II Welc (6/150)
cloudy ['klaʊdi] bewölkt II Welc (6/150)
clown [klaʊn] Clown/in II 2 (35)
club [klʌb] Klub; Verein I
°**coal mine** ['kəʊl maɪn] Kohlenbergwerk
°**coast** [kəʊst] Küste
cola ['kəʊlə] Cola I
cold [kəʊld] kalt I • **be cold** frieren I
cold Erkältung II 4 (62/164) • **have a cold** erkältet sein, eine Erkältung haben II 4 (62/164)
► S.164 I don't feel well
collect [kə'lekt] sammeln I
collector [kə'lektə] Sammler/in II 3 (53)
colour ['kʌlə] Farbe I • **What colour is ...?** Welche Farbe hat ...? I
°**coloured** ['kʌləd] farbig, bunt
°**combine** [kəm'baɪn] kombinieren, verbinden
come [kʌm]**, came, come** kommen I
°**come after sb.** hinter jm. herkommen • **come home** nach Hause kommen I • **come in** hereinkommen I • **Come on.** **1.** Na los, komm. II 1 (13); **2.** Ach komm! / Na hör mal! II 1 (14)
°**comet** ['kɒmɪt] Komet
comic ['kɒmɪk] Comic-Heft I

°**Commonwealth** ['kɒmənwelθ]**: the Commonwealth** *Gemeinschaft der Länder des ehemaligen britischen Weltreichs*
°**compare** [kəm'peə] vergleichen
comparison [kəm'pærɪsn] Steigerung; Vergleich II 2 (30) / II 2 (135)
°**make comparisons** Vergleiche anstellen, vergleichen
°**complete** [kəm'pliːt] vervollständigen, ergänzen
computer [kəm'pjuːtə] Computer I
°**context** ['kɒntekst]**: from the context** aus dem Zusammenhang, aus dem Kontext
°**control** [kən'trəʊl]**: be in control of sth.** etwas unter Kontrolle haben; die Gewalt über etwas haben
°**take control** die Kontrolle/Gewalt übernehmen
°**conversation** [ˌkɒnvə'seɪʃn] Gespräch, Unterhaltung
cook [kʊk] kochen, zubereiten II 4 (60)
cooker ['kʊkə] Herd I
cool [kuːl]
1. kühl II Welc (6)
2. cool I
copy ['kɒpi] kopieren; abschreiben II 5 (77)
copy ['kɒpi] Kopie II 5 (77/166)
corner ['kɔːnə] Ecke I • **on the corner of Green Street and London Road** Green Street, Ecke London Road II 6 (95/171)
°**corner shop** ['kɔːnə ʃɒp] *etwa:* Tante-Emma-Laden (*wörtlich:* Eck-Geschäft)
cornflakes ['kɔːnfleɪks] Cornflakes I
correct [kə'rekt] berichtigen, korrigieren II 6 (102)
°**correct** [kə'rekt] richtig, korrekt
°**corset** ['kɔːsɪt] Korsett
°**cost** [kɒst]**, cost, cost** kosten
°**costume** ['kɒstjuːm] Kostüm
could [kəd, kʊd]**: he could ...** er konnte ... II 1 (22)
count [kaʊnt] zählen II 3 (55)
°**counter** ['kaʊntə] Spielstein
country ['kʌntri] Land *(auch als Gegensatz zur Stadt)* II Welc (6)
in the country auf dem Land II Welc (6/151)
course: of course [əv 'kɔːs] natürlich, selbstverständlich I
cousin ['kʌzn] Cousin, Cousine I
cover ['kʌvə] (CD-)Hülle I
cow [kaʊ] Kuh II 4 (58)
°**Crash!** [kræʃ] Krach!
crisps *(pl)* [krɪsps] Kartoffelchips I

crocodile ['krɒkədaɪl] Krokodil II 3 (52/160)
cross [krɒs] überqueren II 6 (95)
cross [krɒs]**: be cross (with)** böse, sauer sein (auf) I
°**cruel** ['kruːəl]**: be cruel to animals** Tiere quälen
°**cruelty to animals** ['kruːəlti] Tierquälerei
cupboard ['kʌbəd] Schrank I
°**curse** [kɜːs] Fluch
customer ['kʌstəmə] Kunde, Kundin II 5 (78)
cycle ['saɪkl] (mit dem) Rad fahren II 6 (94) • **cycle path** Radweg II 6 (94/170)

D

dad [dæd] Papa, Vati; Vater I
dance [dɑːns] tanzen I • **dancing** Tanzen I • **dancing lessons** Tanzstunden, Tanzunterricht I
dance [dɑːns] Tanz I
dancer ['dɑːnsə] Tänzer/in II 3 (53)
dangerous ['deɪndʒərəs] gefährlich II 1 (12)
dark [dɑːk] dunkel I
date [deɪt] Datum I
daughter ['dɔːtə] Tochter I
°**dawn** [dɔːn] (Morgen-)Dämmerung
day [deɪ] Tag I • **one day** eines Tages I • **days of the week** Wochentage I
dead [ded] tot I
dear [dɪə] Schatz, Liebling I
Oh dear! Oje! II 3 (55)
dear [dɪə]**: Dear Jay ...** Lieber Jay, ... I
December [dɪ'sembə] Dezember I
°**decide (on)** [dɪ'saɪd] sich entscheiden (für), beschließen
°**deep** [diːp] tief
deer, *pl* **deer** [dɪə] Reh, Hirsch II 3 (43)
degree [dɪ'griː] Grad II Welc (8)
delicious [dɪ'lɪʃəs] köstlich, lecker II 5 (78)
department store [dɪ'pɑːtmənt stɔː] Kaufhaus II 2 (37)
describe sth. (to sb.) [dɪ'skraɪb] (jm.) etwas beschreiben II 1 (10)
description [dɪ'skrɪpʃn] Beschreibung II 1 (10/152)
design [dɪ'zaɪn] entwerfen, gestalten II 2 (38)
desk [desk] Schreibtisch I
detail ['diːteɪl] Detail, Einzelheit II 5 (76)
detective [dɪ'tektɪv] Detektiv/in I
°**dialogue** ['daɪəlɒg] Dialog

diary ['daɪəri] Tagebuch; Terminkalender I • °**keep a diary** ein Tagebuch führen
dice, *pl* **dice** [daɪs] Würfel II 5 (74)
dictionary ['dɪkʃənri] Wörterbuch, *(alphabetisches)* Wörterverzeichnis I
did [dɪd] *siehe* **do** • **Did you go ...?** Bist du ... gegangen? / Seid ihr ... gegangen? I • **we didn't sing** ['dɪdnt] wir sangen nicht / wir haben nicht gesungen I
die (of) *(-ing form:* **dying***)* [daɪ] sterben (an) II 5 (77)
°**difference** ['dɪfrəns] Unterschied
different (from) ['dɪfrənt] verschieden, unterschiedlich; anders (als) I
difficult ['dɪfɪkəlt] schwierig, schwer I
°**dig (-gg-)** [dɪg], **dug, dug** graben
dining room ['daɪnɪŋ ru:m] Esszimmer I
dinner ['dɪnə] Abendessen, Abendbrot I • **have dinner** Abendbrot essen I
dirty ['dɜ:ti] schmutzig II 4 (58)
disappear [ˌdɪsə'pɪə] verschwinden II 5 (86)
disco ['dɪskəʊ] Disko I
°**discover** [dɪ'skʌvə] entdecken; herausfinden
°**discuss** [dɪ'skʌs] besprechen; diskutieren (über)
discussion [dɪ'skʌʃn] Diskussion II 5 (83)
dishwasher ['dɪʃwɒʃə] Geschirrspülmaschine I
°**divide (into)** [dɪ'vaɪd] auf-, einteilen (in)
divorced [dɪ'vɔ:st] geschieden I
do [du:], **did, done** tun, machen I
Do you like ...? Magst du ...? I
do a good job gute Arbeit leisten II 3 (47) • °**do a paper round** Zeitungen austragen • **do a project** ein Projekt machen, durchführen II 1 (16) • **do an exercise** eine Übung machen II 2 (33) • **do sport** Sport treiben I
doctor ['dɒktə] Doktor; Arzt/Ärztin II 3 (49)
dog [dɒg] Hund I
°**dolphin** ['dɒlfɪn] Delfin
done [dʌn] *siehe* **do**
don't [dəʊnt]**: Don't listen to Dan.** Hör/Hört nicht auf Dan. I • **I don't know.** Ich weiß es nicht. I
I don't like ... Ich mag ... nicht. / Ich mag kein(e) ... I
door [dɔ:] Tür I
doorbell ['dɔ:bel] Türklingel I

dossier ['dɒsieɪ] Mappe, Dossier *(des Sprachenportfolios)* I
double ['dʌbl] zweimal, doppelt, Doppel- I
down [daʊn] hinunter, herunter, nach unten I • **down there** dort unten II 4 (70) • **fall down** hinfallen II 5 (82)
downstairs [ˌdaʊn'steəz] unten; nach unten I
°**Down Under** [ˌdaʊn‿'ʌndə] *umgangssprachliche Bezeichnung für Australien und Neuseeland*
°**dragon** ['drægən] Drache
drama ['drɑ:mə] Schauspiel, darstellende Kunst I
drank [dræŋk] *siehe* **drink**
°**draw** [drɔ:] zeichnen
dream [dri:m] Traum I • **dream house** Traumhaus I
dress [dres] Kleid I
dressed [drest]**: get dressed** sich anziehen I
drink [drɪŋk] Getränk I
drink [drɪŋk], **drank, drunk** trinken I
drive [draɪv], **drove, driven** *(ein Auto/mit dem Auto)* fahren II 4 (70/165)
driven ['drɪvn] *siehe* **drive**
driver ['draɪvə] Fahrer/in II 4 (70)
drop (-pp-) [drɒp] fallen lassen I
drove [drəʊv] *siehe* **drive**
drunk [drʌŋk] *siehe* **drink**
°**duck** [dʌk] Ente
°**dug** [dʌg] *siehe* **dig**
°**dusk** [dʌsk] (Abend-)Dämmerung
dustbin ['dʌstbɪn] Mülltonne II 2 (39)
DVD [ˌdi: vi:' di:] DVD I

E

each [i:tʃ] jeder, jede, jedes (einzelne) I
ear [ɪə] Ohr I
earache ['ɪəreɪk] Ohrenschmerzen II 4 (62/164)
► S.164 I don't feel well
early ['ɜ:li] früh I
earring ['ɪərɪŋ] Ohrring I
easier (than) ['i:ziə] leichter (als), einfacher (als) II 2 (30)
easiest ['i:ziəst] der/die/das leichteste ..., einfachste ...; am leichtesten, einfachsten II 2 (30)
easy ['i:zi] leicht, einfach I
eat [i:t], **ate, eaten** essen I
eaten ['i:tn] *siehe* **eat**
egg [eg] Ei II 4 (61)
elephant ['elɪfənt] Elefant I
elevator ['elɪveɪtə] *(AE)* Fahrstuhl, Aufzug II 1 (12)

e-mail ['i:meɪl] E-Mail I
°**empire** ['empaɪə] (Welt-)Reich
empty ['empti] leer I
end [end] Ende, Schluss I • **at the end (of)** am Ende (von) I
enemy ['enəmi] Feind/in II 3 (47)
engineer [ˌendʒɪ'nɪə] Ingenieur/in II 5 (74)
English ['ɪŋglɪʃ] Englisch; englisch I
enjoy [ɪn'dʒɔɪ] genießen II 6 (97)
enough [ɪ'nʌf] genug I
essay (about, on) ['eseɪ] Aufsatz (über) I
°**etc.** [et'setərə] usw.
euro (€) ['jʊərəʊ] Euro I
even ['i:vn] sogar II 2 (31)
evening ['i:vnɪŋ] Abend I • **in the evening** abends, am Abend I
on Friday evening freitagabends, am Freitagabend I
ever? ['evə] je? / jemals? / schon mal? II 4 (63)
► S.164 The present perfect: questions
every ['evri] jeder, jede, jedes I
everybody ['evribɒdi] jeder, alle II 2 (28)
everything ['evriθɪŋ] alles I
°**everywhere** ['evriweə] überall
°**example** [ɪg'zɑ:mpl] Beispiel
°**for example** zum Beispiel
exciting [ɪk'saɪtɪŋ] aufregend, spannend I
Excuse me, ... [ɪk'skju:z mi:] Entschuldigung, ... / Entschuldigen Sie, ... I
exercise ['eksəsaɪz] Übung, Aufgabe I • **exercise book** Schulheft, Übungsheft I
expensive [ɪk'spensɪv] teuer I
explain sth. to sb. [ɪk'spleɪn] jm. etwas erklären, erläutern II 3 (46)
explanation [ˌeksplə'neɪʃn] Erklärung II 3 (46)
explore [ɪk'splɔ:] erkunden, erforschen I
explorer [ɪk'splɔ:rə] Entdecker/in, Forscher/in II 3 (53)
°**extensive reading** [ɪk'stensɪv] extensives Lesen *(das Lesen längerer Texte mit dem Ziel des allgemeinen Verständnisses, nicht des Detailverständnisses)*
extra ['ekstrə] zusätzlich I
eye [aɪ] Auge I

F

face [feɪs] Gesicht I
factory ['fæktri] Fabrik II 4 (58)
fair [feə] fair, gerecht II 1 (18)

fall [fɔːl], **fell, fallen** fallen, stürzen; hinfallen II 4 (71) • **fall down** hinfallen II 5 (82) • **fall off** herunterfallen (von) II 6 (103)
fallen ['fɔːlən] *siehe* **fall**
family ['fæməli] Familie I • **family tree** (Familien-)Stammbaum I
famous (for) ['feɪməs] berühmt (für, wegen) II 3 (53)
fan [fæn] Fan I
fantastic [fæn'tæstɪk] fantastisch, toll I
far [fɑː] weit (entfernt) II 1 (22)
farm [fɑːm] Bauernhof, Farm II 4 (58)
°**farmer** ['fɑːmə] Bauer, Bäuerin
fashion ['fæʃn] Mode II 2 (38)
fast [fɑːst] schnell II 1 (12) / II 3 (47)
father ['fɑːðə] Vater I • °**Father Christmas** der Weihnachtsmann
favourite ['feɪvərɪt] Lieblings- I **my favourite colour** meine Lieblingsfarbe I
February ['februəri] Februar I
fed [fed] *siehe* **feed** • **be fed up (with sth.)** [ˌfed_'ʌp] die Nase voll haben (von etwas) II 2 (28)
feed [fiːd], **fed, fed** füttern I
feel [fiːl], **felt, felt** sich fühlen; fühlen II 3 (55); sich anfühlen II 6 (104)
► S.164 I don't feel well
feet [fiːt] *Plural von „foot"* I
fell [fel] *siehe* **fall**
felt [felt] *siehe* **feel**
felt tip ['felt tɪp] Filzstift I
°**festival** ['festɪvl] Fest, Festival
few [fjuː]: **a few** ein paar, einige II 1 (23)
field [fiːld] Feld, Acker, Weide II 4 (58) **in the field** auf dem Feld II 4 (58/162)
°**fight** [faɪt], **fought, fought** kämpfen
file [faɪl]: **background file** *etwa:* Hintergrundinformation II (3) **grammar file** *Grammatikanhang* I **skills file** *Anhang mit Lern- und Arbeitstechniken* I
°**fill in** [ˌfɪl_'ɪn]
1. einsetzen
2. ausfüllen
film [fɪlm] Film I • **film star** Filmstar I
find [faɪnd], **found, found** finden I **find out (about)** herausfinden (über) I
finder ['faɪndə] Finder I
fine [faɪn]
1. gut, schön; in Ordnung II 2 (28)
2. *(gesundheitlich)* gut II 3 (45)
I'm/He's fine. Es geht mir/ihm gut. II 3 (45/159)
finger ['fɪŋgə] Finger I
finish ['fɪnɪʃ] beenden, zu Ende machen; enden I
fire ['faɪə] Feuer, Brand II 3 (49)
fireman/-woman ['faɪəmən, 'faɪəˌwʊmən] Feuerwehrmann/-frau II 4 (70)
°**fireworks** *(pl)* ['faɪəwɜːks] Feuerwerk
first [fɜːst]
1. erste(r, s) I
2. zuerst, als Erstes I
be first der/die Erste sein I
fish, *pl* **fish** [fɪʃ] Fisch I
fit (-tt-) [fɪt] passen I
°**flag** [flæg] Flagge, Fahne
°**flash** [flæʃ]: **in a flash** blitzartig, wie der Blitz
flat [flæt] Wohnung I
flew [fluː] *siehe* **fly**
flight [flaɪt] Flug II 1 (12)
°**float** [fl48t] schweben
floor [flɔː]
1. Fußboden I
°2. Stockwerk
°**flow chart** ['fləʊ tʃɑːt] Flussdiagramm
°**flower** ['flaʊə] Blume; Blüte
flown [fləʊn] *siehe* **fly**
fly [flaɪ], **flew, flown** fliegen II Welc (6)
°**fly** [flaɪ] Fliege
fog [fɒg] Nebel II Welc (8/152)
foggy ['fɒgi] neblig II Welc (8)
follow ['fɒləʊ] folgen; verfolgen I
food [fuːd]
1. Essen; Lebensmittel I
2. Futter I
foot [fʊt], *pl* **feet** [fiːt] Fuß I
football ['fʊtbɔːl] Fußball I **football boots** Fußballschuhe, -stiefel I
°**footprint** ['fʊtprɪnt] Fußabdruck
for [fə, fɔː] für I • **for breakfast/lunch/dinner** zum Frühstück/Mittagessen/Abendbrot I • °**for example** zum Beispiel • **for lots of reasons** aus vielen Gründen I **for miles** meilenweit II 1 (12) • **for three days** drei Tage (lang) I • **just for fun** nur zum Spaß I • **What for?** Wofür? II 2 (29) • **What's for homework?** Was haben wir als Hausaufgabe auf? I
foreground ['fɔːgraʊnd] Vordergrund II 1 (10)
forest ['fɒrɪst] Wald II 4 (58)
forget (-tt-) [fə'get], **forgot, forgotten** vergessen I
forgot [fə'gɒt] *siehe* **forget**
forgotten [fə'gɒtn] *siehe* **forget**
form [fɔːm]
1. (Schul-)Klasse I • **form teacher** Klassenlehrer/in I
°2. Form
°**form** [fɔːm] bilden
°**fort** [fɔːt] Fort
°**fortune-teller** ['fɔːtʃuːn telə] Wahrsager/in
°**fought** [fɔːt] *siehe* **fight**
found [faʊnd] *siehe* **find**
fox [fɒks] Fuchs II 3 (42)
free [friː]
1. frei I • **free time** Freizeit, freie Zeit I
2. kostenlos I
°**freeze** [friːz], **froze, frozen** einfrieren, gefrieren; *hier:* stillstehen, erstarren
French [frentʃ] Französisch I
Friday ['fraɪdeɪ, 'fraɪdi] Freitag I
fridge [frɪdʒ] Kühlschrank I
friend [frend] Freund/in I
°**friendly** ['frendli] freundlich
frog [frɒg] Frosch II 3 (43)
from [frəm, frɒm]
1. aus I
2. von I
°**from … to …** von … bis … • **I'm from …** Ich komme aus … / Ich bin aus … I • **Where are you from?** Wo kommst du her? I
front [frʌnt]: **in front of** vor *(räumlich)* I • **front door** [ˌfrʌnt 'dɔː] Wohnungstür, Haustür I
°**froze** [frəʊz] *siehe* **freeze**
°**frozen** ['frəʊzn] *siehe* **freeze**
fruit [fruːt] Obst, Früchte; Frucht I **fruit salad** ['fruːt ˌsæləd] Obstsalat I
full [fʊl] voll I
fun [fʌn] Spaß I • **have fun** Spaß haben, sich amüsieren I • **Have fun!** Viel Spaß! I • **just for fun** nur zum Spaß I • **Riding is fun.** Reiten macht Spaß. I
funny ['fʌni] witzig, komisch I
°**future** ['fjuːtʃə] Zukunft

G

game [geɪm] Spiel I
°**gap** [gæp] Lücke
garage ['gærɑːʒ] Garage II 3 (46)
garden ['gɑːdn] Garten I
gave [geɪv] *siehe* **give**
geography [dʒi'ɒgrəfi] Geografie, Erdkunde I
°**Georgian** ['dʒɔːdʒən] georgianisch *(aus der Zeit der britischen Könige Georg I–IV)*
German ['dʒɜːmən] Deutsch; deutsch; Deutsche(r) I
Germany ['dʒɜːməni] Deutschland I

get (-tt-) [get], **got, got**
1. bekommen, kriegen II 1 (22/154)
2. holen, besorgen II 1 (22)
3. gelangen, (hin)kommen I
4. get angry/hot/... wütend/heiß/ ... werden II 1 (14)
5. get off (the train/bus) (aus dem Zug/Bus) aussteigen I • **get on (the train/bus)** (in den Zug/Bus) einsteigen I
6. get up aufstehen I
get dressed sich anziehen I
get ready (for) sich fertig machen (für), sich vorbereiten (auf) I • **get things ready** Dinge fertig machen, vorbereiten I
► S.154 (to) get

getting by in English [ˌgetɪŋ ˈbaɪ] *etwa:* auf Englisch zurechtkommen I

ghost [gəʊst] Geist, Gespenst II 4 (60)

giraffe [dʒəˈrɑːf] Giraffe II 3 (52/160)

girl [gɜːl] Mädchen I

give [gɪv], **gave, given** geben I

given [ˈgɪvn] *siehe* **give**

glass [glɑːs] Glas I • **a glass of water** ein Glas Wasser I

glasses *(pl)* [ˈglɑːsɪz] (eine) Brille I
► S.156 Plural words

glue [gluː] (auf-, ein)kleben II 4 (60/162)

glue [gluː] Klebstoff I • **glue stick** [ˈgluː stɪk] Klebestift I

go [gəʊ], **went, gone** gehen I; fahren II Welc (7) • **go by car/train/bike/...** mit dem Auto/Zug/Rad/... fahren II Welc (7) • **go for a walk** spazieren gehen, einen Spaziergang machen II Welc (6) • **go home** nach Hause gehen I • **go on** weitermachen I • **Go on.** Mach weiter. / Erzähl weiter. I • **go on a trip** einen Ausflug machen II Welc (7/151)
go on holiday in Urlaub fahren II Welc (7/151) • **go riding** reiten gehen I • **go shopping** einkaufen gehen I • **go surfing** wellenreiten gehen, surfen gehen II 1 (23)
go swimming schwimmen gehen I • **go to bed** ins Bett gehen I
go to the cinema ins Kino gehen II 1 (14) • **go together** zusammenpassen, -gehören II Welc (7) • **Let's go.** Auf geht's! *(wörtlich:* Lass uns gehen.) I • °**go with** passen zu
► S.151 (to) go

°**goat** [gəʊt] Ziege

gone [gɒn] *siehe* **go**

good [gʊd]
1. gut I • **Good afternoon.** Guten Tag. *(nachmittags)* I • **Good luck (with ...)!** Viel Glück (bei/mit ...)! I
Good morning. Guten Morgen. I
2. brav II 3 (55)

Goodbye. [ˌgʊdˈbaɪ] Auf Wiedersehen. I • **say goodbye** sich verabschieden I

got [gɒt] *siehe* **get**

got [gɒt]**: I've got ...** Ich habe ... I
I haven't got a chair. Ich habe keinen Stuhl. I

grammar [ˈgræmə] Grammatik I
grammar file *Grammatikanhang* I

°**grand** [grænd] prachtvoll, großartig

grandchild [ˈgræntʃaɪld], *pl* **grandchildren** [ˈ-tʃɪldrən] Enkel/in I

°**granddaughter** [ˈgrændɔːtə] Enkelin

grandfather [ˈgrænfɑːðə] Großvater I

grandma [ˈgrænmɑː] Oma I

grandmother [ˈgrænmʌðə] Großmutter I

grandpa [ˈgrænpɑː] Opa I

grandparents [ˈgrænpeərənts] Großeltern I

granny [ˈgræni] Oma II 4 (60)

great [greɪt] großartig, toll I
► S.167 big – large – great

green [griːn] grün I

grew [gruː] *siehe* **grow**

grey [greɪ] grau II 3 (43)

group [gruːp] Gruppe I • **group word** Oberbegriff II 2 (27)

grow [grəʊ], **grew, grown** *(Getreide usw.)* anbauen, anpflanzen II 5 (75)

grown [grəʊn] *siehe* **grow**

grumble [ˈgrʌmbl] murren, nörgeln I

°**guess** [ges] raten, erraten

guest [gest] Gast I

°**guide** [gaɪd] Fremdenführer/in, Reiseleiter/in

guinea pig [ˈgɪni pɪg] Meerschweinchen I

guitar [gɪˈtɑː] Gitarre I • **play the guitar** Gitarre spielen I

°**gun** [gʌn] (Schuss-)Waffe

°**gunpowder** [ˈgʌnpaʊdə] Schießpulver

H

had [hæd] *siehe* **have** *und* **have got**

hair *(no pl)* [heə] Haar, Haare I

half [hɑːf]**: half past 11** halb zwölf (11.30 / 23.30) I

hall [hɔːl] Flur, Diele I

hamburger [ˈhæmbɜːgə] Hamburger I

hamster [ˈhæmstə] Hamster I

hand [hænd] Hand I

happen (to) [ˈhæpən] geschehen, passieren (mit) I

happy [ˈhæpi] glücklich, froh I
Happy birthday. Herzlichen Glückwunsch zum Geburtstag. I
happy ending Happyend II 1 (23)

harbour [ˈhɑːbə] Hafen II 5 (79)

hard [hɑːd] hart; schwer, schwierig II 3 (47) • **work hard** hart arbeiten II 3 (47)

hat [hæt] Hut II 2 (38)

hate [heɪt] hassen, gar nicht mögen I

have [həv, hæv], **had, had** haben, besitzen II 2 (28) • **have a baby** ein Baby/Kind bekommen II 3 (47)
have a bath baden, ein Bad nehmen II 6 (92/170) • **have a cold** erkältet sein, eine Erkältung haben II 4 (62/164) • **have a picnic** ein Picknick machen I • **have a sauna** in die Sauna gehen II 6 (92) • **have a shower** (sich) duschen I • **have a sore throat** Halsschmerzen haben II 4 (62) • **have a temperature** Fieber haben II 4 (62) • **have breakfast/dinner** frühstücken/Abendbrot essen I • **have ... for breakfast** ... zum Frühstück essen/trinken I • **have fun** Spaß haben, sich amüsieren I • **have to do** tun müssen I

have got: I've got ... [aɪv ˈgɒt] Ich habe ... I • **I haven't got a chair.** Ich habe keinen Stuhl. I

he [hiː] er I

head [hed] Kopf I • °**heads and tails** [ˌhedz‿ənd ˈteɪlz] *wörtlich:* Köpfe und Schwänze; *hier:* (Satz-) Anfänge und Enden

headache [ˈhedeɪk] Kopfschmerzen II 4 (62)
► S.164 I don't feel well

°**heading** [ˈhedɪŋ] Überschrift, Titel

healthy [ˈhelθi] gesund II 5 (74)

hear [hɪə], **heard, heard** hören I

heard [hɜːd] *siehe* **hear**

heart [hɑːt] Herz II 3 (54/161)

hedgehog [ˈhedʒhɒg] Igel II 3 (43)

held [held] *siehe* **hold**

helicopter [ˈhelɪkɒptə] Hubschrauber, Helikopter II 4 (71)

Hello. [həˈləʊ] Hallo. / Guten Tag. I

help [help] helfen I • **Can I help you?** Kann ich Ihnen helfen? / Was kann ich für Sie tun? *(im Geschäft)* I

help [help] Hilfe I

her [hə, hɜː]
1. ihr, ihre I
2. sie; ihr I

here [hɪə]
1. hier I

2. hierher I
Here you are. Bitte sehr. / Hier bitte. I
hers [hɜːz] ihrer, ihre, ihrs II 2 (28/156)
► S.156 Possessive pronouns
Hi! [haɪ] Hallo! I • **Say hi to Dilip for me.** Grüß Dilip von mir. I
°**hibiscus** [hɪˈbɪskəs] Hibiskus
hid [hɪd] *siehe* **hide**
hidden [ˈhɪdn] *siehe* **hide**
hide [haɪd], **hid, hidden** sich verstecken; *(etwas)* verstecken I
°**high** [haɪ] hoch
°**high school** [ˈhaɪ skuːl] *Gesamtschule in den USA mit den Klassen 7–12 für 13- bis 18-Jährige*
hill [hɪl] Hügel II 4 (58)
him [hɪm] ihn; ihm I
hippo [ˈhɪpəʊ] Flusspferd II 3 (52/160)
his [hɪz]
1. sein, seine I
2. seiner, seine, seins II 2 (28/156)
► S.156 Possessive pronouns
history [ˈhɪstri] Geschichte I
hit (-tt-) [hɪt], **hit, hit** schlagen II 3 (52)
hobby [ˈhɒbi] Hobby I
hockey [ˈhɒki] Hockey I • **hockey shoes** Hockeyschuhe I
°**hog** [hɒg] Schwein
hold [həʊld], **held, held** halten II 4 (71) • °**hold up** hochhalten
°**hole** [həʊl] Loch
holiday(s) [ˈhɒlədeɪ(z)] Ferien I
holiday flat Ferienwohnung II Welc (6) • °**be on holiday** in Urlaub sein; Ferien haben/machen
go on holiday in Urlaub fahren II Welc (7/151)
home [həʊm] Heim, Zuhause I
at home daheim, zu Hause I
come home nach Hause kommen I • **get home** nach Hause kommen I • **go home** nach Hause gehen I
homework *(no pl)* [ˈhəʊmwɜːk] Hausaufgabe(n) I • **do homework** die Hausaufgabe(n) machen I • **What's for homework?** Was haben wir als Hausaufgabe auf? I
Hooray! [huˈreɪ] Hurra! II 6 (104)
°**hop (-pp-)** [hɒp] hüpfen
hope [həʊp] hoffen II 4 (71)
horrible [ˈhɒrəbl] scheußlich, grauenhaft II 3 (46)
horse [hɔːs] Pferd I
hospital [ˈhɒspɪtl] Krankenhaus II 4 (71)
hot [hɒt] heiß I • **hot chocolate** heiße Schokolade I • °**hot-water bottle** Wärmflasche
hotel [həʊˈtel] Hotel II 3 (48)
hotline [ˈhɒtlaɪn] Hotline II 3 (44)
hour [ˈaʊə] Stunde II 1 (18)
house [haʊs] Haus I • **at the Shaws' house** im Haus der Shaws / bei den Shaws zu Hause I
how [haʊ] wie I • **How are you?** Wie geht es dir/Ihnen/euch? II 6 (94)
How do you know ...? Woher weißt/kennst du ...? I • **how many?** wie viele? I • **how much?** wie viel? I • **How much is/are ...?** Was kostet/kosten ...? / Wie viel kostet/kosten ...? I • **How old are you?** Wie alt bist du? I • **How was ...?** Wie war ...? I
hundred [ˈhʌndrəd] hundert I
°**hurricane** [ˈhʌrɪkən] Hurrikan; Orkan
hurry [ˈhʌri] eilen; sich beeilen II 2 (38) • **hurry up** sich beeilen I
hurry [ˈhʌri]**: be in a hurry** in Eile sein, es eilig haben I
hurt [hɜːt], **hurt, hurt** wehtun; verletzen I
hurt [hɜːt] verletzt II 4 (70)
husband [ˈhʌzbənd] Ehemann II 4 (71)
hutch [hʌtʃ] (Kaninchen-)Stall I

I

I [aɪ] ich I • **I'm** [aɪm] ich bin I
I'm from ... Ich komme aus ... / Ich bin aus ... I • **I'm ... years old.** Ich bin ... Jahre alt. I • **I'm sorry.** Entschuldigung. / Tut mir leid. I
ice: ice cream [ˌaɪs ˈkriːm] (Speise-) Eis I • **ice rink** [ˈaɪs rɪŋk] Schlittschuhbahn II 6 (99)
idea [aɪˈdɪə] Idee, Einfall I
if [ɪf]
1. falls, wenn II 3 (45)
2. ob II 6 (105)
ill [ɪl] krank II 3 (45)
°**imagine sth.** [ɪˈmædʒɪn] sich etwas vorstellen
important [ɪmˈpɔːtnt] wichtig II 3 (45)
impossible [ɪmˈpɒsəbl] unmöglich II 5 (78)
in [ɪn] in I • **in ... Street** in der ...straße I • **in English** auf Englisch I • **in front of** vor *(räumlich)* I • **in here** hier drinnen I • °**in one piece** heil, ganz • **in the afternoon** nachmittags, am Nachmittag I • **in the country** auf dem Land II Welc (6/151) • **in the evening** abends, am Abend I • **in the field** auf dem Feld II 4 (58/162)
in the morning am Morgen, morgens I • **in the photo** auf dem Foto I • **in the picture** auf dem Bild I • **in the yard** auf dem Hof II 3 (44/159) • **in time** rechtzeitig II 1 (23) • °**one in five people** jede(r) Fünfte, eine(r) von fünf(en)
°**including** [ɪnˈkluːdɪŋ] einschließlich
°**Independence Day** [ˌɪndɪˈpendəns deɪ] Unabhängigkeitstag
infinitive [ɪnˈfɪnətɪv] Infinitiv *(Grundform des Verbs)* I
information (about/on) *(no pl)* [ˌɪnfəˈmeɪʃn] Information(en) (über) II 5 (80)
°**injure** [ˈɪndʒə] (sich) verletzen
inside [ˌɪnˈsaɪd]
1. innen (drin), drinnen I
2. nach drinnen II 3 (44)
3. inside the car ins Auto (hinein), ins Innere des Autos II 4 (71)
install [ɪnˈstɔːl] installieren, einrichten II 4 (63)
instructions *(pl)* [ɪnˈstrʌkʃnz] (Gebrauchs-)Anweisung(en), Anleitung(en) II 4 (63)
interesting [ˈɪntrəstɪŋ] interessant I
interview [ˈɪntəvjuː] Interview I
interview [ˈɪntəvjuː] interviewen, befragen II 4 (60/162)
into [ˈɪntə, ˈɪntʊ] in ... (hinein) I
invitation (to) [ˌɪnvɪˈteɪʃn] Einladung (zu) I
invite (to) [ɪnˈvaɪt] einladen (zu) I
°**irregular** [ɪˈregjələ] unregelmäßig
is [ɪz] ist I
island [ˈaɪlənd] Insel II Welc (6)
it [ɪt] er/sie/es I • **It's £1.** Er/Sie/Es kostet 1 Pfund. I • **It says here: ...** Hier steht: ... / Es heißt hier: ... II 4 (63)
its [ɪts] sein/seine; ihr/ihre I

J

January [ˈdʒænjuəri] Januar I
jacket [ˈdʒækɪt] Jacke, Jackett II 2 (27)
jeans *(pl)* [dʒiːnz] Jeans I
► S.156 Plural words
°**jiggle** [ˈdʒɪgl] herumhampeln
job [dʒɒb] Aufgabe, Job I
join sb. [dʒɔɪn] sich jm. anschließen; bei jm. mitmachen II 2 (38)
joke [dʒəʊk] Witz I
joke [dʒəʊk] scherzen, Witze machen II 4 (60/162)
judo [ˈdʒuːdəʊ] Judo I • **do judo** Judo machen I
jug [dʒʌg] Krug I • **a jug of milk** ein Krug Milch I
juice [dʒuːs] Saft I
July [dʒuˈlaɪ] Juli I

°**jumble** ['dʒʌmbl] gebrauchte Sachen, Trödel
jumble sale ['dʒʌmbl seɪl] Wohltätigkeitsbasar I
jump [dʒʌmp] springen II 3 (54)
June [dʒu:n] Juni I
junior ['dʒu:niə] Junioren-, Jugend- I
just [dʒʌst]
1. (einfach) nur, bloß I
2. gerade (eben), soeben II 4 (61)
°3. **they just don't fit** sie passen einfach nicht
► S.163 The present perfect: statements

K

kangaroo [ˌkæŋgə'ru:] Känguru II 3 (52/160)
°**kayaking** ['kaɪækɪŋ] Kajak fahren
keep sth. warm/cool/open/... [ki:p], **kept, kept** etwas warm/kühl/offen/... halten II 3 (45) • °**keep a diary** ein Tagebuch führen
kept [kept] *siehe* **keep**
key [ki:] Schlüssel II 5 (86) • **key ring** Schlüsselring II 5 (86) • **key word** Stichwort, Schlüsselwort I
kid [kɪd] Kind, Jugendliche(r) I
kill [kɪl] töten I
°**kilometre (km)** ['kɪləmi:tə, kɪ'lɒmɪtə] Kilometer (km)
king [kɪŋ] König I
kitchen ['kɪtʃɪn] Küche I
kite [kaɪt] Drachen I
kiwi ['ki:wi:] Kiwi II 5 (78)
knee [ni:] Knie I
knew [nju:] *siehe* **know**
know [nəʊ], **knew, known**
1. wissen I
2. kennen I
know about sth. von etwas wissen; über etwas Bescheid wissen II 1 (23) • **How do you know ...?** Woher weißt du ...? / Woher kennst du ...? I • **I don't know.** Ich weiß es nicht. I • **..., you know.** ..., wissen Sie. / ..., weißt du. I • **You know what, Sophie?** Weißt du was, Sophie? I
known [nəʊn] *siehe* **know**

L

°**label** ['leɪbl] beschriften, etikettieren
°**lady** ['leɪdi] Dame
laid [leɪd] *siehe* **lay**
lake [leɪk] (Binnen-)See II Welc (9)
lamp [læmp] Lampe I
land [lænd] landen II 2 (38)
land [lænd] Land, Grund und Boden II 5 (75)
language ['læŋgwɪdʒ] Sprache I
large [lɑ:dʒ] groß II 5 (78)
► S.167 big – large – great
lasagne [lə'zænjə] Lasagne I
last [lɑ:st] letzte(r, s) I • **the last day** der letzte Tag I • **at last** endlich, schließlich I
late [leɪt] spät; zu spät I • **be late** zu spät sein/kommen I • **Sorry, I'm late.** Entschuldigung, dass ich zu spät bin/komme. I
later ['leɪtə] später I
laugh [lɑ:f] lachen I
laughter ['lɑ:ftə] Gelächter II 6 (105)
lay the table [leɪ], **laid, laid** den Tisch decken I
°**lean** [li:n] sich neigen
°**leaning tower** [ˌli:nɪŋ 'taʊə] schiefer Turm
°**leap** [li:p] springen
learn [lɜ:n] lernen I • **learn sth. about sth.** etwas über etwas erfahren, etwas über etwas herausfinden II 5 (74)
least: at least [ət 'li:st] zumindest, wenigstens I
leave [li:v], **left, left**
1. (weg)gehen; abfahren II 3 (54)
2. verlassen II 3 (54/161)
3. zurücklassen II 3 (54/161)
► S.161 (to) leave
left [left] *siehe* **leave**
left [left] linke(r, s) II 1 (10/152) • **look left** nach links schauen II 1 (10/152) **on the left** links, auf der linken Seite II 1 (10/152) • **turn left** (nach) links abbiegen II 6 (95)
► S.152 left – right
leg [leg] Bein I
°**legend** ['ledʒənd] Legende, Sage
leisure centre ['leʒə sentə] Freizeitzentrum, -park II 6 (104)
lemonade [ˌlemə'neɪd] Limonade I
lesson ['lesn] (Unterrichts-)Stunde I
lessons *(pl)* ['lesnz] Unterricht I
let [let], **let, let** lassen II 3 (44/159)
Let's ... Lass uns ... / Lasst uns ... I
Let's go. Auf geht's! (*wörtlich:* Lass uns gehen.) I • **Let's look at the list.** Sehen wir uns die Liste an. / Lasst uns die Liste ansehen. I
letter ['letə]
1. Buchstabe I
2. **letter (to)** Brief (an) II 3 (55)
lettuce ['letɪs] (Kopf-)Salat II 6 (104)
library ['laɪbrəri] Bibliothek, Bücherei I
life [laɪf], *pl* **lives** [laɪvz] Leben I
°**lifeboat** ['laɪfbəʊt] Rettungsboot, -schiff • °**lifeboatmen** *(pl)* ['laɪfbəʊtmən] *die Besatzung eines Rettungsbootes*
lift [lɪft] Fahrstuhl, Aufzug II 1 (12)
like [laɪk] wie I • **What was the weather like?** Wie war das Wetter? II Welc (7) • °**like that / like this** so
like [laɪk] mögen, gernhaben I
°**like sth. best** etwas am liebsten mögen • **like sth. better** etwas lieber mögen II 6 (103) • **I like swimming/dancing.** Ich schwimme/tanze gern. I • **I'd like ... (= I would like ...)** Ich hätte gern ... / Ich möchte gern ... I • **I'd like to talk about ... (= I would like to talk about ...)** Ich möchte/würde gern über ... reden I • **Would you like ...?** Möchtest du ...? / Möchten Sie ...? I • **Would you like some?** Möchtest du etwas/ein paar? / Möchten Sie etwas/ein paar? I
line [laɪn]
1. Zeile II 3 (55)
°2. Linie
link [lɪŋk] verbinden, verknüpfen I
linking word ['lɪŋkɪŋ wɜ:d] Bindewort II 1 (18)
lion ['laɪən] Löwe II 3 (52/160)
list [lɪst] Liste I
list [lɪst] auflisten, aufzählen II 4 (60/162)
listen (to) ['lɪsn] zuhören; sich *etwas* anhören I
listener ['lɪsnə] Zuhörer/in II 3 (53)
little ['lɪtl] klein I
live [lɪv] leben, wohnen I • °**live on** weiterleben
live music [laɪv] Livemusik II 1 (20)
lives [laɪvz] *Plural von „life"* I
living room ['lɪvɪŋ ru:m] Wohnzimmer I
local ['ləʊkl] Orts-, örtlich II 5 (76)
°**log** [lɒg] Holzscheit, Baumstamm
long [lɒŋ] lang I
look [lʊk]
1. schauen, gucken I
2. **look different/great/old** anders/toll/alt aussehen I
look after sth./sb. auf etwas/jn. aufpassen; sich um etwas/jn. kümmern II 5 (87) • **look at** ansehen, anschauen I • **look for** suchen II 5 (87) • **look left/right** nach links/rechts schauen II 1 (10/152)
look round sich umsehen I
look up (from) hochsehen, aufschauen (von) II 2 (29) • °**look up words** Wörter nachschlagen
lose [lu:z], **lost, lost** verlieren II 2 (28)
lost [lɒst] *siehe* **lose**

lot [lɒt]**: a lot (of)** eine Menge, viel, viele II 2 (30) • **Thanks a lot!** Vielen Dank! I • **He likes her a lot.** Er mag sie sehr. I • **lots more** viel mehr I • **lots of ...** eine Menge ..., viele ..., viel ... I
loud [laʊd] laut I
love [lʌv] lieben, sehr mögen II 2 (38)
love [lʌv] Liebe II 2 (38/158) • **Love ...** Liebe Grüße, ... *(Briefschluss)* I
luck [lʌk]**: Good luck (with ...)!** Viel Glück (bei/mit ...)! I
luckily ['lʌkɪli] zum Glück, glücklicherweise II 6 (103)
lunch [lʌntʃ] Mittagessen I
lunch break Mittagspause I

M

mad [mæd] verrückt I
made [meɪd] *siehe* **make**
magazine [ˌmægə'ziːn] Zeitschrift, Magazin I
mail sb. [meɪl] jn. anmailen II 3 (44)
make [meɪk]**, made, made** machen; bauen I • **make a mess** alles durcheinanderbringen, alles in Unordnung bringen I • °**make comparisons** Vergleiche anstellen, vergleichen • °**make notes** sich Notizen machen
make-up ['meɪkʌp] Make-up II 2 (27)
man [mæn]**,** *pl* **men** [men] Mann I
many ['meni] viele I • **how many?** wie viele? I
map [mæp] Landkarte, Stadtplan II 6 (95)
March [mɑːtʃ] März I
mark sth. up [ˌmɑːk_'ʌp] etwas markieren, kennzeichnen II 5 (77)
market ['mɑːkɪt] Markt II 5 (74)
marmalade ['mɑːməleɪd] (Orangen-)Marmelade I
married (to) ['mærɪd] verheiratet (mit) I
match [mætʃ] Spiel, Wettkampf I
°**match** [mætʃ]
1. passen zu
2. zuordnen
°**Match the letters and numbers.** Ordne die Buchstaben den Zahlen zu.
°**mate** [meɪt] Kumpel
°**material** [mə'tɪəriəl] Material
maths [mæθs] Mathematik I
matter ['mætə]**: What's the matter?** Was ist los? / Was ist denn? II 2 (28)
May [meɪ] Mai I
°**may** [meɪ] dürfen
maybe ['meɪbi] vielleicht I
°**mayonnaise** [ˌmeɪə'neɪz] Majonäse
me [miː] mir; mich I • **Me too.** Ich auch. I • **more than me** mehr als ich II 2 (29/156) • **That's me.** Das bin ich. I • **Why me?** Warum ich? I
mean [miːn]**, meant, meant**
1. meinen *(sagen wollen)* II 5 (86)
°**2.** bedeuten
meant [ment] *siehe* **mean**
meat [miːt] Fleisch I
mediation [ˌmiːdi'eɪʃn] Vermittlung, Sprachmittlung, Mediation II (3)
medium ['miːdiəm] mittel(groß) II 5 (78)
meet [miːt]**, met, met**
1. treffen; kennenlernen I
2. sich treffen I
men [men] *Plural von „man"* I
menu ['menjuː] Speisekarte II 5 (78)
°**Merry Christmas.** [ˌmeri 'krɪsməs] Frohe Weihnachten.
mess [mes]**: be a mess** sehr unordentlich sein; fürchterlich aussehen II 4 (67) • **make a mess** alles durcheinanderbringen, alles in Unordnung bringen I
°**message** ['mesɪdʒ] Nachricht, Botschaft • °**message in a bottle** Flaschenpost
met [met] *siehe* **meet**
metre ['miːtə] Meter II 4 (70)
mice [maɪs] *Plural von „mouse"* I
middle (of) ['mɪdl] Mitte I; Mittelteil II 5 (79)
mile [maɪl] Meile *(= ca. 1,6 km)* II 1 (12) • **for miles** meilenweit II 1 (12)
milk [mɪlk] Milch I
°**million** ['mɪljən] Million
mime [maɪm] pantomimisch darstellen, vorspielen II 6 (103)
°**mime** [maɪm] Pantomime
mind map ['maɪnd mæp] Mindmap („Gedankenkarte", „Wissensnetz") I
Mind your own business. [ˌmaɪnd jər_ˌəʊn 'bɪznəs] Das geht dich nichts an! / Kümmere dich um deine eigenen Angelegenheiten! II 1 (13)
mine [maɪn] meiner, meine, meins II 2 (28)
► S. 156 Possessive pronouns
°**minister** ['mɪnɪstə] Minister/in
mints *(pl)* [mɪnts] Pfefferminzbonbons I
minute ['mɪnɪt] Minute I • **Wait a minute.** Warte mal! / Moment mal! II 5 (87)
mirror ['mɪrə] Spiegel II 2 (38)
miss [mɪs]
1. vermissen II 3 (54)
2. Miss a turn. Einmal aussetzen. II 5 (74)
Miss White [mɪs] Frau White *(unverheiratet)* I
missing ['mɪsɪŋ]**: be missing** fehlen II 6 (96) • °**the missing information/words** die fehlenden Informationen/Wörter
mistake [mɪ'steɪk] Fehler I
°**mix up** [ˌmɪks_'ʌp] durcheinanderbringen
°**mobile** ['məʊbaɪl] Mobile
mobile (phone) ['məʊbaɪl] Mobiltelefon, Handy I
model ['mɒdl] Modell*(-flugzeug, -schiff usw.)* I; (Foto-)Modell II 2 (39)
°**modern** ['mɒdn] modern
mole [məʊl] Maulwurf II 3 (43)
Monday ['mʌndeɪ, 'mʌndi] Montag I • **Monday morning** Montagmorgen I
money ['mʌni] Geld I
monkey ['mʌŋki] Affe II 3 (52/160)
monster ['mɒnstə] Ungeheuer, Monster II 5 (76)
month [mʌnθ] Monat I
moon [muːn] Mond II 3 (44)
more [mɔː] mehr I • **lots more** viel mehr I • **more than** mehr als II 2 (29) • **more than me** mehr als ich II 2 (29/156) • **more boring (than)** langweiliger (als) II 2 (31)
no more music keine Musik mehr I
morning ['mɔːnɪŋ] Morgen, Vormittag I • **in the morning** morgens, am Morgen I • **Monday morning** Montagmorgen I • **on Friday morning** freitagmorgens, am Freitagmorgen I
°**mosaic** [məʊ'zeɪɪk] Mosaik
most [məʊst] (der/die/das) meiste ...; am meisten II 2 (135) • **most people** die meisten Leute I
(the) most boring der/die/das langweiligste ...; am langweiligsten II 2 (31)
mother ['mʌðə] Mutter I
mountain ['maʊntən] Berg II Welc (6/150)
mouse [maʊs]**,** *pl* **mice** [maɪs] Maus I
mouth [maʊθ] Mund I
move [muːv]
1. bewegen; sich bewegen II 4 (62)
Move back one space. Geh ein Feld zurück. II 5 (74) • **Move on one space.** Geh ein Feld vor. II 5 (74)
2. move (to) umziehen (nach, in) II 3 (54/161) • **move in** einziehen

II 3 (54/161) • **move out** ausziehen II 3 (54)
movement ['mu:vmənt] Bewegung II 6 (104)
°**movies** *(pl)* ['mu:viz] Kino
MP3 player [ˌempi:'θri: ˌpleɪə] MP3-Spieler I
Mr ... ['mɪstə] Herr ... I
Mrs ... ['mɪsɪz] Frau ... I
Ms ... [mɪz, məz] Frau ... II 1 (18)
much [mʌtʃ] viel I • **how much?** wie viel? I • **How much is/are ...?** Was kostet/kosten ...? / Wie viel kostet/kosten ...? I • **like/love sth. very much** etwas sehr mögen/sehr lieben II 3 (45/159)
multiple choice [ˌmʌltɪpl 'tʃɔɪs] Multiple-Choice II 3 (49)
mum [mʌm] Mama, Mutti; Mutter I
museum [mju'zi:əm] Museum I
music ['mju:zɪk] Musik I
musical ['mju:zɪkl] Musical I
must [mʌst] müssen I
► S.171 must – needn't – mustn't
mustn't do ['mʌsnt] nicht tun dürfen II 6 (96)
► S.171 must – needn't – mustn't
°**mutineer** [ˌmju:tə'nɪə] Meuterer, Meuterin
my [maɪ] mein/e I

N

name [neɪm] Name I • **My name is ...** Ich heiße ... / Mein Name ist ... I • **What's your name?** Wie heißt du? I
name [neɪm] nennen; benennen II 4 (60/162)
°**national** ['næʃnəl] national
°**Natural History Unit** [ˌnætʃrəl 'hɪstri ˌju:nɪt] Naturkundeabteilung *(im Museum)*
near [nɪə] in der Nähe von, nahe (bei) I
neat [ni:t] gepflegt II 3 (54) • **neat and tidy** schön ordentlich II 3 (54)
need [ni:d] brauchen, benötigen I
needn't do ['ni:dnt] nicht tun müssen, nicht zu tun brauchen II 6 (96)
► S.171 must – needn't – mustn't
neighbour ['neɪbə] Nachbar/in I
nervous ['nɜ:vəs] nervös, aufgeregt I
°**network** ['netwɜ:k] (Wörter-)Netz
never ['nevə] nie, niemals I
► S.163 The present perfect: statements
new [nju:] neu I
newspaper ['nju:speɪpə] Zeitung I
next [nekst]: **be next** der/die Nächste sein I • **the next morning/day** am nächsten Morgen/Tag I • **What have we got next?** Was haben wir als Nächstes? I
next to [nekst] neben II 1 (10)
nice [naɪs] schön, nett I
night [naɪt] Nacht, später Abend I
at night nachts, in der Nacht I
on Friday night freitagnachts, Freitagnacht I
no [nəʊ] nein I
no [nəʊ] kein, keine I • **no more music** keine Musik mehr I • °**no one** niemand • **No way!** Auf keinen Fall! / Kommt nicht in Frage! II 1 (14)
nobody ['nəʊbədi] niemand II Welc (9)
nod (-dd-) [nɒd] nicken (mit) II 4 (62)
noise [nɔɪz] Geräusch; Lärm I
noisy ['nɔɪzi] laut, lärmend II 4 (58)
nose [nəʊz] Nase I
not [nɒt] nicht I • **not (...) any** kein, keine I • **not (...) anybody** niemand II 5 (88/169) • **not (...) anything** nichts II 5 (88/169) • **not (...) anywhere** nirgendwo(hin) II 5 (88/169) • **not (...) yet** noch nicht II 4 (61)
note [nəʊt] Mitteilung, Notiz I
°**make notes** sich Notizen machen
take notes sich Notizen machen I
nothing ['nʌθɪŋ] nichts II 1 (14)
°**There's nothing like a mate.** *etwa:* Nichts geht über einen guten Kumpel.
°**notice** ['nəʊtɪs] Notiz, Mitteilung
notice board Anschlagtafel, schwarzes Brett I
November [nəʊ'vembə] November I
now [naʊ] nun, jetzt I
number ['nʌmbə] Zahl, Ziffer, Nummer I

O

o [əʊ] null I
°**observatory** [əb'zɜ:vətri] Observatorium; Aussichtsplattform
o'clock [ə'klɒk]: **eleven o'clock** elf Uhr I
October [ɒk'təʊbə] Oktober I
°**odd** [ɒd]: **What word is the odd one out?** Welches Wort passt nicht dazu / gehört nicht dazu?
of [əv, ɒv] von I
of course [əv 'kɔ:s] natürlich, selbstverständlich I
off [ɒf]: **take sth. off** etwas ausziehen *(Kleidung)* II 4 (70/165)
take 10c off 10 Cent abziehen I
often ['ɒfn] oft, häufig I
Oh dear! [əʊ 'dɪə] Oje! II 3 (55)
Oh well ... [əʊ 'wel] Na ja ... / Na gut ... I
OK [əʊ'keɪ] okay, gut, in Ordnung I
old [əʊld] alt I
on [ɒn]
1. auf I
2. be on eingeschaltet sein, an sein *(Radio, Licht usw.)* II 1 (20)
on 13th June am 13. Juni I • **on Friday** am Freitag I • **on Friday afternoon** freitagnachmittags, am Freitagnachmittag I • **on Friday evening** freitagabends, am Freitagabend I • **on Friday morning** freitagmorgens, am Freitagmorgen I • **on Friday night** freitagnachts, Freitagnacht I • **on the beach** am Strand II Welc (6) • **on the board** an die Tafel I • **on the corner of Green Street and London Road** Green Street, Ecke London Road II 6 (95/171) • **on the left** links, auf der linken Seite II 1 (11/152) • **on the phone** am Telefon I • **on the plane** im Flugzeug II Welc (7/151) • **on the radio** im Radio I • **on the right** rechts, auf der rechten Seite II 1 (11/152) • **on the train** im Zug I • **on TV** im Fernsehen I • **What page are we on?** Auf welcher Seite sind wir? I • **go on holiday** in Urlaub fahren II Welc (7/151)
straight on geradeaus weiter II 6 (95)
°**once** [wʌns] einst; (früher) einmal
one [wʌn] eins, ein, eine I • **one day** eines Tages I • **a new one** ein neuer / eine neue / ein neues II 2 (29/156) • **my old ones** meine alten II 2 (29) • °**one in five people** jede(r) Fünfte, eine(r) von fünf(en)
only ['əʊnli]
1. nur, bloß I
2. the only guest der einzige Gast I
°**onto** ['ɒntə, 'ɒntu] auf (... hinauf)
open ['əʊpən] öffnen, aufmachen I
open ['əʊpən] offen, geöffnet II 2 (38)
°**opening hours** ['əʊpnɪŋ‿aʊəz] Öffnungszeiten
opposite ['ɒpəzɪt] Gegenteil I
or [ɔ:] oder I
orange ['ɒrɪndʒ] orange(farben) I
orange ['ɒrɪndʒ] Orange, Apfelsine I
orange juice ['ɒrɪndʒ dʒu:s] Orangensaft I
°**order** ['ɔ:də]
1. Reihenfolge • **in the right order** in der richtigen Reihenfolge
word order Wortstellung
2. Befehl

°**organization** [ˌɔːɡənaɪˈzeɪʃn] Organisation
other [ˈʌðə] andere(r, s) I • **the others** die anderen I • **the other way round** anders herum II 6 (104)
Ouch! [aʊtʃ] Autsch! I
our [ˈaʊə] unser, unsere I
ours [ˈaʊəz] unserer, unsere, unseres II 2 (28/156)
▶ S.156 Possessive pronouns
out heraus, hinaus; draußen II 1 (22/154) • **out of ...** aus ... (heraus/hinaus) I
▶ S.154 out
outfit [ˈaʊtfɪt] Outfit *(Kleidung; Ausrüstung)* II 2 (38)
outside [ˌaʊtˈsaɪd]
1. draußen I
2. nach draußen II 1 (14)
3. outside his room vor seinem Zimmer; außerhalb seines Zimmers I
over [ˈəʊvə]
1. über, oberhalb von I
2. be over vorbei/zu Ende sein I
over there da drüben, dort drüben I • **over to ...** hinüber zu/nach ... II 2 (38)
°**owl** [aʊl] Eule
own [əʊn]**: our own pool** unser eigenes Schwimmbad II Welc (7)
°**Oxfam** [ˈɒksfæm] *bekannteste Wohltätigkeitsorganisation Großbritanniens mit einer Kette von Gebrauchtwarengeschäften*

P

pack [pæk] packen, einpacken II 3 (54)
packet [ˈpækɪt] Päckchen, Packung, Schachtel I • **a packet of mints** ein Päckchen/eine Packung Pfefferminzbonbons I
page [peɪdʒ] (Buch-, Heft-)Seite I **What page are we on?** Auf welcher Seite sind wir? I
paid [peɪd] *siehe* **pay**
paint [peɪnt] (an)malen I
painter [ˈpeɪntə] Maler/in II 3 (53)
pair [peə]**: a pair (of)** ein Paar II 2 (27)
°**palm tree** [ˈpɑːm triː] Palme
°**pants** *(pl)* [pænts] *(AE)* Hose
paper [ˈpeɪpə]
1. Papier I
2. Zeitung II 2 (29)
°**do a paper round** Zeitungen austragen
°**parade** [pəˈreɪd] Parade, Umzug
paragraph [ˈpærəɡrɑːf] Absatz *(in einem Text)* II 4 (60)
paramedic [ˌpærəˈmedɪk] Sanitäter/in II 4 (62)
parcel [ˈpɑːsl] Paket I
parents [ˈpeərənts] Eltern I
park [pɑːk] Park I
°**parliament** [ˈpɑːləmənt] Parlament
parrot [ˈpærət] Papagei I
part [pɑːt] Teil I
partner [ˈpɑːtnə] Partner/in I
party [ˈpɑːti] Party I
pass [pɑːs] (herüber)reichen, weitergeben I • **pass round** herumgeben I
past [pɑːst] Vergangenheit I
past [pɑːst] vorbei (an), vorüber (an) II 6 (95) • **half past 11** halb zwölf (11.30/23.30) I • **quarter past 11** Viertel nach elf (11.15/23.15) I
path [pɑːθ] Pfad, Weg II 6 (94)
pay (for) [peɪ]**, paid, paid** bezahlen II 6 (104)
PE [ˌpiː‿ˈiː]**, Physical Education** [ˌfɪzɪkəl‿edʒuˈkeɪʃn] Turnen, Sportunterricht I
pen [pen] Kugelschreiber, Füller I
pence (p) *(pl)* [pens] Pence *(Plural von „penny")* I
pencil [ˈpensl] Bleistift I • **pencil case** [ˈpensl keɪs] Federmäppchen I • **pencil sharpener** [ˈpensl ʃɑːpnə] Bleistiftanspitzer I
penny [ˈpeni] *kleinste britische Münze* I
people [ˈpiːpl] Menschen, Leute I
°**perhaps** [pəˈhæps] vielleicht
person [ˈpɜːsn] Person II 1 (20)
pet [pet] Haustier I • **pet shop** Tierhandlung I
phone [fəʊn] Telefon I • **on the phone** am Telefon I • **phone call** Anruf, Telefongespräch I • **phone number** Telefonnummer I
phone [fəʊn] telefonieren, anrufen I
photo [ˈfəʊtəʊ] Foto I • **in the photo** auf dem Foto I • **take photos** Fotos machen, fotografieren I
°**phrase** [freɪz] Ausdruck, (Rede-)Wendung
piano [piˈænəʊ] Klavier, Piano I **play the piano** Klavier spielen I
pick sth. up [ˌpɪk‿ˈʌp] etwas hochheben, aufheben II 3 (45)
picnic [ˈpɪknɪk] Picknick I • **have a picnic** ein Picknick machen I
picture [ˈpɪktʃə] Bild I • **in the picture** auf dem Bild I
pie [paɪ] Obstkuchen; Pastete II 4 (61)
piece [piːs]**: a piece of** ein Stück I **a piece of paper** ein Stück Papier I °**in one piece** heil, ganz
pink [pɪŋk] pink(farben), rosa I
pirate [ˈpaɪrət] Pirat, Piratin I
pizza [ˈpiːtsə] Pizza I
place [pleɪs] Ort, Platz I
°**placemat** [ˈpleɪsmæt] Set, Platzdeckchen
plan [plæn] Plan I
plan (-nn-) [plæn] planen I
plane [pleɪn] Flugzeug II Welc (6) **on the plane** im Flugzeug II Welc (7/151)
planet [ˈplænɪt] Planet II 6 (94)
°**plasticine** [ˈplæstəsiːn] Knetmasse
plate [pleɪt] Teller I • **a plate of chips** ein Teller Pommes frites I
play [pleɪ] spielen I • **play football** Fußball spielen I • **play the guitar** Gitarre spielen I • **play the piano** Klavier spielen I
play [pleɪ] Theaterstück I
player [ˈpleɪə] Spieler/in I
please [pliːz] bitte *(in Fragen und Aufforderungen)* I
pm [ˌpiː‿ˈem]**: 7 pm** 7 Uhr abends/ 19 Uhr I
pocket [ˈpɒkɪt] Tasche *(an Kleidungsstück)* II 2 (26/155) • **pocket money** Taschengeld II 2 (26)
poem [ˈpəʊɪm] Gedicht I
°**pohutukawa tree** [pəˌhuːtəˈkɑːwə] Eisenholzbaum
point [pɔɪnt] Punkt II 2 (35)
point (at/to sth.) [pɔɪnt] zeigen, deuten (auf etwas) II 2 (29)
police *(pl)* [pəˈliːs] Polizei I **police station** Polizeiwache, Polizeirevier II 6 (95) • **policeman** Polizist II 4 (70) • **policewoman** Polizistin II 4 (70)
poltergeist [ˈpəʊltəɡaɪst] Poltergeist I
°**pond** [pɒnd] Teich
poor [pɔː, pʊə] arm I • **poor Sophie** (die) arme Sophie I
popcorn [ˈpɒpkɔːn] Popcorn II 4 (67)
°**popular** [ˈpɒpjələ] beliebt, populär
possible [ˈpɒsəbl] möglich II 5 (78)
post office [ˈpəʊst‿ɒfɪs] Postamt II 6 (95)
postcard [ˈpəʊstkɑːd] Postkarte II Welc (6)
poster [ˈpəʊstə] Poster I
potato [pəˈteɪtəʊ]**,** *pl* **potatoes** Kartoffel I
pound (£) [paʊnd] Pfund *(britische Währung)* I
°**powder** [ˈpaʊdə] Pulver
practice [ˈpræktɪs] *hier:* Übungsteil I

practise ['præktɪs] üben; trainieren I
prepare [prɪ'peə] vorbereiten; sich vorbereiten II 2 (39) • **prepare for** sich vorbereiten auf II 2 (39/158)
present ['preznt]
1. Gegenwart I
2. Geschenk I
°**present sth. (to sb.)** [prɪ'zent] (jm.) etwas präsentieren, vorstellen
presentation [ˌprezn'teɪʃn] Präsentation, Vorstellung I
presenter [prɪ'zentə] Moderator/in II 2 (38)
pretty ['prɪti] hübsch I
pretty healthy/good/... ['prɪti] ziemlich gesund/gut/... II 5 (78)
price [praɪs] (Kauf-)Preis I
°**prisoner** ['prɪznə] Gefangene(r)
prize [praɪz] Preis, Gewinn I
probably ['prɒbəbli] wahrscheinlich II 3 (44)
problem ['prɒbləm] Problem II 2 (29)
programme ['prəʊgræm] Programm I
project (about, on) ['prɒdʒekt] Projekt (über, zu) I • **do a project** ein Projekt machen, durchführen II 1 (16)
promise ['prɒmɪs] versprechen II 3 (54)
°**pronounce** [prə'naʊns] aussprechen
pronunciation [prəˌnʌnsi'eɪʃn] Aussprache I
proof *(no pl)* [pru:f] Beweis(e) II 5 (86)
°**Protestant** ['prɒtɪstənt] protestantisch; Protestant/in
proud (of sb./sth.) [praʊd] stolz (auf jn./etwas) II 5 (77)
pub [pʌb] Kneipe, Lokal II 5 (74)
pull [pʊl] ziehen I
pullover ['pʊləʊvə] Pullover II 2 (27)
purple ['pɜ:pl] violett; lila I
purse [pɜ:s] Geldbörse II 5 (86)
push [pʊʃ] drücken, schieben, stoßen I
put (-tt-) [pʊt], **put, put** legen, stellen, *(etwas wohin)* tun I • **put sth. on** etwas anziehen *(Kleidung)* II 4 (70) • °**put on a show** eine Show aufführen, zeigen • °**Put up your hand.** Heb deine Hand. / Hebt eure Hand.
puzzled ['pʌzld] verwirrt II 2 (39)
pyjamas *(pl)* [pə'dʒɑ:məz] Schlafanzug II 4 (59)

Q

quarter ['kwɔ:tə]: **quarter past 11** Viertel nach 11 (11.15 / 23.15) I
quarter to 12 Viertel vor 12 (11.45 / 23.45) I
question ['kwestʃn] Frage I • **ask questions** Fragen stellen I
°**question word** Fragewort
quick [kwɪk] schnell I
quiet ['kwaɪət] leise, still, ruhig I
quite bad/quick/good ... [kwaɪt] ziemlich schlimm/schnell/gut/... II 4 (70)
quiz [kwɪz], *pl* **quizzes** ['kwɪzɪz] Quiz, Ratespiel I

R

rabbit ['ræbɪt] Kaninchen I
radio ['reɪdiəʊ] Radio I • **on the radio** im Radio I
°**raft** [rɑ:ft] Floß
railway ['reɪlweɪ] Eisenbahn II 4 (60)
rain [reɪn] Regen II Welc (6/150)
rain [reɪn] regnen II Welc (6/150)
rainy ['reɪni] regnerisch II Welc (6/150)
ran [ræn] *siehe* **run**
rang [ræŋ] *siehe* **ring**
rap [ræp] Rap *(rhythmischer Sprechgesang)* I
°**rather** ['rɑ:ðə]: **I'd rather be ...** Ich wäre lieber ...
RE [ˌɑ:r_'i:], **Religious Education** [rɪˌlɪdʒəs_edʒu'keɪʃn] Religion, Religionsunterricht I
read [ri:d], **read, read** lesen I
°**read out** vorlesen • °**Read out loud.** Lies laut vor. • °**Read the poem to a partner.** Lies das Gedicht einem Partner/einer Partnerin vor.
read [red] *siehe* **read**
reader ['ri:də] Leser/in II 2 (26)
ready ['redi] bereit, fertig I • **get ready (for)** sich fertig machen (für), sich vorbereiten (auf) I • **get things ready** Dinge fertig machen, vorbereiten I
real [rɪəl] echt, wirklich I
really ['rɪəli] wirklich I
reason ['ri:zn] Grund, Begründung I
for lots of reasons aus vielen Gründen I
°**record** [rɪ'kɔ:d] aufzeichnen, aufnehmen *(auf Band)*
recycled [ˌri:'saɪkld] wiederverwertet, wiederverwendet, recycelt II 2 (31)
recycling [ˌri:'saɪklɪŋ] Wiederverwertung, Recycling II 2 (31)
red [red] rot I
rehearsal [rɪ'hɜ:sl] Probe *(am Theater)* I
rehearse [rɪ'hɜ:s] proben *(am Theater)* I
relax [rɪ'læks] (sich) entspannen, sich ausruhen II 6 (92)
remember sth. [rɪ'membə]
1. sich erinnern (an etwas) I
2. sich etwas merken I
°**Remember ...** Denk dran, ...
°**rent** [rent] leihen, mieten
report (on) [rɪ'pɔ:t] Bericht, Reportage (über) I
report (to sb.) [rɪ'pɔ:t] (jm.) berichten II 4 (60/162)
°**rescue** ['reskju:] Rettung(saktion)
rescue helicopter ['reskju: ˌhelɪkɒptə] Rettungshubschrauber II 4 (71)
rest [rest] Rest II 5 (88)
restaurant ['restrɒnt] Restaurant II 6 (95)
result [rɪ'zʌlt] Ergebnis, Resultat I
°**retell** [ˌri:'tel], **retold, retold** nacherzählen
°**retold** [ˌri:'təʊld] *siehe* **retell**
return ticket [rɪ'tɜ:n ˌtɪkɪt] Rückfahrkarte II 3 (55)
revision [rɪ'vɪʒn] Wiederholung *(des Lernstoffs)* I
rhino ['raɪnəʊ] Nashorn II 3 (52/160)
°**rhyme** [raɪm] (sich) reimen
rich [rɪtʃ] reich II 5 (75)
ridden ['rɪdn] *siehe* **ride**
ride [raɪd], **rode, ridden** reiten I
go riding ['raɪdɪŋ] reiten gehen I
ride a bike Rad fahren I
ride [raɪd]: **(bike) ride** (Rad-)Fahrt II 6 (94)
right [raɪt] richtig I • **all right** [ɔ:l 'raɪt] gut, in Ordnung II 1 (23) • **be right** Recht haben I • **That's right.** Das ist richtig. / Das stimmt. I • **You need a school bag, right?** Du brauchst eine Schultasche, stimmt's? / nicht wahr? I
right [raɪt] rechte(r, s) II 1 (10/152)
look right nach rechts schauen II 1 (10/152) • **on the right** rechts, auf der rechten Seite II 1 (10/152)
turn right (nach) rechts abbiegen II 6 (95)
► S.152 left – right
right [raɪt]: **right now** jetzt sofort; jetzt gerade I • °**right behind you** direkt/genau hinter dir
ring [rɪŋ] Ring II 5 (86)
ring [rɪŋ], **rang, rung** klingeln, läuten II 4 (70)
river ['rɪvə] Fluss II 4 (58)

road [rəʊd] Straße I • **Park Road** [ˌpɑːk 'rəʊd] Parkstraße I
°**rock** [rɒk] Fels, Felsen
rode [rəʊd] *siehe* **ride**
role play ['rəʊl pleɪ] Rollenspiel II 1 (15)
roll [rəʊl] Brötchen I
Roman ['rəʊmən] römisch; Römer, Römerin II 6 (92)
room [ruːm] Raum, Zimmer I
round [raʊnd] rund II 6 (92)
round [raʊnd] um ... (herum); in ... umher II Welc (6) • **the other way round** anders herum II 6 (104)
°**RSPCA (Royal Society for the Prevention of Cruelty to Animals)** [ˌrɔɪəl sə'saɪəti fə ðə prɪ'venʃn‿əv 'kruːəlti tu‿'ænɪmlz] *britischer Tierschutzverein*
rubber ['rʌbə] Radiergummi I
rubbish ['rʌbɪʃ] (Haus-)Müll, Abfall II 3 (44) • °**rubbish collection** ['rʌbɪʃ kəˌlekʃn] Müllabfuhr
rude [ruːd] unhöflich, unverschämt II 1 (13)
ruler ['ruːlə] Lineal I
run [rʌn] (Wett-)Lauf II 3 (47)
run (-nn-) [rʌn], **ran, run** laufen, rennen I
°**run** [rʌn] (Wett-)Lauf
rung [rʌŋ] *siehe* **ring**
runner ['rʌnə] Läufer/in II 3 (53)

S

sad [sæd] traurig II Welc (9)
safe (from) [seɪf] sicher, in Sicherheit (vor) II 3 (46)
said [sed] *siehe* **say**
°**sail** [seɪl] Segel
sailor ['seɪlə] Seemann, Matrose II 5 (79)
salad ['sæləd] Salat *(als Gericht oder Beilage)* I
same [seɪm]: **the same ...** der-/die-/dasselbe ...; dieselben ... I • **be/look the same** gleich sein/aussehen I
°**sand** [sænd] Sand
sandwich ['sænwɪtʃ] Sandwich, *(zusammengeklapptes)* belegtes Brot I • **sandwich box** Brotdose I
sang [sæŋ] *siehe* **sing**
sat [sæt] *siehe* **sit**
Saturday ['sætədeɪ, 'sætədi] Samstag, Sonnabend I
sauna ['sɔːnə] Sauna II 6 (92)
have a sauna in die Sauna gehen II 6 (92)
sausage ['sɒsɪdʒ] (Brat-, Bock-) Würstchen, Wurst I

save [seɪv]
1. retten II 1 (22)
2. sparen II 2 (26)
°**saved** [seɪvd] gerettet
saw [sɔː] *siehe* **see**
°**Saxon: the Saxons** ['sæksnz] die Sachsen
say [seɪ], **said, said** sagen I • **It says here: ...** Hier steht: .../Es heißt hier: ... II 4 (63) • **say goodbye** sich verabschieden I • **Say hi to Dilip for me.** Grüß Dilip von mir. I
say sorry sich entschuldigen II 5 (88)
► S.164 The text says ...
scan a text (-nn-) [skæn] einen Text schnell nach bestimmten Wörtern/Informationen absuchen II 3 (47)
scared [skeəd] verängstigt II 4 (70)
be scared (of) Angst haben (vor) I
scary ['skeəri] unheimlich; gruselig I
scene [siːn] Szene I
school [skuːl] Schule I • **at school** in der Schule I • **school bag** Schultasche I • **school subject** Schulfach I
science ['saɪəns] Naturwissenschaft I
°**screech owl** ['skriːtʃ‿aʊl] Kreischeule
sea [siː] Meer, *(die)* See I
second ['sekənd] zweite(r, s) I
°**second-hand** gebraucht; aus zweiter Hand
°**second** ['sekənd] Sekunde
see [siː], **saw, seen**
1. sehen I
2. **see sb.** jn. besuchen, jn. aufsuchen II 1 (23)
See? Siehst du? I • **See you.** Tschüs. / Bis bald. I
seen [siːn] *siehe* **see**
sell [sel], **sold, sold** verkaufen II 2 (30)
send (to) [send], **sent, sent** schicken, senden (an) II 3 (44)
sent [sent] *siehe* **send**
sentence ['sentəns] Satz I
September [sep'tembə] September I
series, *pl* **series** ['sɪəriːz] (Sende-)Reihe, Serie II 3 (42)
°**servant** ['sɜːvənt] Diener/in
°**service** ['sɜːvɪs] Dienst, Service
setup ['setʌp] Setup II 4 (63)
share sth. (with sb.) [ʃeə] sich etwas teilen (mit jm.) I
she [ʃiː] sie I
sheep, *pl* **sheep** [ʃiːp] Schaf II 4 (58)
shelf [ʃelf], *pl* **shelves** [ʃelvz] Regal(brett) I

°**shelter (from)** ['ʃeltə] Schutz (vor)
shine [ʃaɪn], **shone, shone** scheinen *(Sonne)* II Welc (6)
ship [ʃɪp] Schiff I
shirt [ʃɜːt] Hemd I
°**shiver** ['ʃɪvə] zittern
shoe [ʃuː] Schuh I
shone [ʃɒn] *siehe* **shine**
shop [ʃɒp] Laden, Geschäft I
shop assistant ['ʃɒp‿əˌsɪstənt] Verkäufer/in I • **shop window** Schaufenster II 4 (67)
shop (-pp-) [ʃɒp] einkaufen (gehen) I
shopping ['ʃɒpɪŋ] (das) Einkaufen I • **go shopping** einkaufen gehen I • **shopping list** Einkaufsliste I
short [ʃɔːt] kurz I
shorts *(pl)* [ʃɔːts] Shorts, kurze Hose I
► S.156 Plural words
shoulder ['ʃəʊldə] Schulter I
shout [ʃaʊt] schreien, rufen I
show [ʃəʊ] Show, Vorstellung I
show [ʃəʊ], **showed, shown** zeigen I
shower ['ʃaʊə] Dusche I • **have a shower** (sich) duschen I
shown [ʃəʊn] *siehe* **show**
shut up [ˌʃʌt‿'ʌp], **shut, shut** den Mund halten II 2 (30)
shy [ʃaɪ] schüchtern, scheu II 3 (55)
side [saɪd] Seite II 4 (70)
sights *(pl)* [saɪts] Sehenswürdigkeiten II 4 (60)
°**signal** ['sɪgnəl] Signal, Zeichen
silent letter [ˌsaɪlənt 'letə] „stummer" Buchstabe *(nicht gesprochener Buchstabe)* II 4 (65)
silly ['sɪli] albern, dumm I
°**silver** ['sɪlvə] Silber
sing [sɪŋ], **sang, sung** singen I
singer ['sɪŋə] Sänger/in II 3 (53)
single ['sɪŋgl] ledig, alleinstehend I
sink [sɪŋk] Spüle, Spülbecken I
sister ['sɪstə] Schwester I
sit (-tt-) [sɪt], **sat, sat** sitzen; sich setzen I • **sit down** sich hinsetzen II 3 (44) • **Sit with me.** Setz dich zu mir. / Setzt euch zu mir. I
size [saɪz] Größe I
skate [skeɪt] Inliner fahren I
skateboard ['skeɪtbɔːd] Skateboard I
skates *(pl)* [skeɪts] Inliner I
sketch [sketʃ] Sketch I
skills file ['skɪlz faɪl] *Anhang mit Lern- und Arbeitstechniken* I
skirt [skɜːt] Rock II 2 (27)
sky [skaɪ] Himmel II Welc (7)
slave [sleɪv] Sklave, Sklavin II 5 (75)

sleep [sliːp], **slept, slept** schlafen I
°**sleep** [sliːp] Schlaf
°**sleeve** [sliːv] Ärmel
slept [slept] *siehe* **sleep**
slow [sləʊ] langsam II 1 (12/153)
°**slug** [slʌg] Nacktschnecke
small [smɔːl] klein I
smart [smɑːt] clever, schlau II 2 (30)
smell [smel] riechen II 4 (60)
smell [smel] Geruch II 4 (60/162)
smile [smaɪl] lächeln I • **smile at sb.** jn. anlächeln II 3 (55)
smile [smaɪl] Lächeln II 4 (60/162)
°**smoothie** ['smuːði] *dickflüssiger Fruchtshake mit Milch, Joghurt oder Eiscreme*
snack [snæk] Snack, Imbiss II 5 (74)
snake [sneɪk] Schlange I
snow [snəʊ] Schnee II Welc (6/150)
so [səʊ]
1. also; deshalb, daher I • **So?** Und? / Na und? II 5 (86)
2. so sweet so süß I
3. Do you really think so? Meinst du wirklich? / Glaubst du das wirklich? II 1 (14)
soap [səʊp] Seife I
sock [sɒk] Socke, Strumpf I
sofa ['səʊfə] Sofa I
software ['sɒftweə] Software II 4 (63)
sold [səʊld] *siehe* **sell**
some [səm, sʌm] einige, ein paar I
some cheese/juice etwas Käse/Saft I
somebody ['sʌmbədi] jemand I
Find/Ask somebody who … Finde/Frage jemanden, der … II 1 (20)
► S.169 somebody – anybody
something ['sʌmθɪŋ] etwas II Welc (7)
► S.169 something – anything
sometimes ['sʌmtaɪmz] manchmal I
somewhere ['sʌmweə] irgendwo(hin) II 5 (88/169)
► S.169 somewhere – anywhere
son [sʌn] Sohn I
song [sɒŋ] Lied, Song I
soon [suːn] bald I
sore [sɔː]: **have a sore throat** Halsschmerzen haben II 4 (62)
► S.164 I don't feel well
sorry ['sɒri]: **(I'm) sorry.** Entschuldigung. / Tut mir leid. I • **Sorry, I'm late.** Entschuldigung, dass ich zu spät bin/komme. I • **Sorry?** Wie bitte? I • **say sorry** sich entschuldigen II 5 (88)
sort [sɔːt] Art, Sorte II 5 (78)
sound [saʊnd] klingen, sich *(gut usw.)* anhören I
sound [saʊnd] Laut; Klang I
soup [suːp] Suppe II 4 (60)
°**southeast (of)** [ˌsaʊθ'iːst] südöstlich (von)
°**souvenir** [ˌsuːvə'nɪə] Andenken, Souvenir
space [speɪs]: **Move back one space.** Geh ein Feld zurück. II 5 (74)
Move on one space. Geh ein Feld vor. II 5 (74)
spaghetti [spə'geti] Spaghetti II 2 (33)
speak (to) [spiːk], **spoke, spoken** sprechen (mit), reden (mit) II Welc (9)
special ['speʃl]: **a special day** ein besonderer Tag I
°**speech bubble** ['spiːtʃ bʌbl] Sprechblase
spell [spel] buchstabieren I
°**spelling** ['spelɪŋ] (Recht-)Schreibung, Schreibweise
spend [spend], **spent, spent: spend money (on)** Geld ausgeben (für) II 2 (26) • **spend time (on)** Zeit verbringen (mit) II 2 (26)
spent [spent] *siehe* **spend**
°**spider** ['spaɪdə] Spinne
°**splash** [splæʃ] Klatschen, Platschen
spoke [spəʊk] *siehe* **speak**
spoken ['spəʊkən] *siehe* **speak**
sport [spɔːt] Sport; Sportart I
do sport Sport treiben I • **sports centre** Sportzentrum I
spring [sprɪŋ] Frühling I
spy [spaɪ] Spion/in I
squirrel ['skwɪrəl] Eichhörnchen II 3 (43)
°**stage** [steɪdʒ]: **on stage** auf der Bühne
stairs *(pl)* [steəz] Treppe; Treppenstufen I
stamp [stæmp] Briefmarke I
stand [stænd], **stood, stood** stehen; sich (hin)stellen II 2 (38)
star [stɑː]
1. Stern II 6 (94)
2. (Film-, Pop-)Star I
start [stɑːt] starten, anfangen, beginnen (mit) I
°**statement** ['steɪtmənt] Aussage
station ['steɪʃn] Bahnhof I • **at the station** am Bahnhof I
statue ['stætʃuː] Statue II 5 (77)
stay [steɪ]
1. bleiben I
2. wohnen, übernachten II Welc (6)
°**stay with** wohnen bei
steal [stiːl], **stole, stolen** stehlen II 5 (86)
step [step]
1. Schritt I
°**2.** Stufe
stereo ['steriəʊ] Stereoanlage I
still [stɪl] (immer) noch I
stole [stəʊl] *siehe* **steal**
stolen ['stəʊlən] *siehe* **steal**
stomach ['stʌmək] Magen II 4 (62/164) • **stomach ache** Magenschmerzen, Bauchweh II 4 (62/164)
► S.164 I don't feel well
stone [stəʊn] Stein II 6 (92)
stood [stʊd] *siehe* **stand**
stop (-pp-) [stɒp]
1. aufhören I
2. anhalten I
Stop that! Hör auf damit! / Lass das! I
storm [stɔːm] Sturm; Gewitter II Welc (6/150)
stormy ['stɔːmi] stürmisch II Welc (6/150)
story ['stɔːri] Geschichte, Erzählung I
straight on [streɪt‿'ɒn] geradeaus weiter II 6 (95)
strawberry ['strɔːbəri] Erdbeere II 5 (78)
street [striːt] Straße I • **at 7 Hamilton Street** in der Hamiltonstraße 7 I
°**stretch** [stretʃ] sich strecken
strong [strɒŋ] stark II 4 (70)
structure ['strʌktʃə] strukturieren, aufbauen II 5 (79)
student ['stjuːdənt] Schüler/in; Student/in I
°**study** ['stʌdi] studieren
study skills *(pl)* ['stʌdi skɪlz] Lern- und Arbeitstechniken I
stuff [stʌf] Zeug, Kram II 2 (38)
stupid ['stjuːpɪd] blöd, dämlich II 2 (28)
subject ['sʌbdʒɪkt] Schulfach I
subway ['sʌbweɪ]: **the subway** *(AE)* die U-Bahn II 1 (12)
suddenly ['sʌdnli] plötzlich, auf einmal I
sugar ['ʃʊgə] Zucker II 5 (75)
suitcase ['suːtkeɪs] Koffer II 3 (54)
summer ['sʌmə] Sommer I
°**summertime** ['sʌmətaɪm] Sommer
sun [sʌn] Sonne II Welc (6/150)
Sunday ['sʌndeɪ, 'sʌndi] Sonntag I
sung [sʌŋ] *siehe* **sing**
sunglasses *(pl)* ['sʌnglɑːsɪz] (eine) Sonnenbrille I
► S.156 Plural words
sunny ['sʌni] sonnig II Welc (6/150)
supermarket ['suːpəmɑːkɪt] Supermarkt II 6 (95)
sure [ʃʊə, ʃɔː]: **be sure** sicher sein II 2 (29)

surfboard ['sɜ:fbɔ:d] Surfbrett II 1 (23/155)
surfing ['sɜ:fɪŋ]: **go surfing** wellenreiten gehen, surfen gehen II 1 (23)
°**surprise** [sə'praɪz] Überraschung
°**surprised** [sə'praɪzd] überrascht
survey (on) ['sɜ:veɪ] Umfrage, Untersuchung (über) II 2 (26)
survive [sə'vaɪv] überleben II 3 (42)
°**swallow** ['swɒləʊ] verschlucken, hinunterschlucken
swam [swæm] *siehe* **swim**
°**swap (-pp-)** [swɒp] tauschen
sweatshirt ['swetʃɜ:t] Sweatshirt I
sweet [swi:t] süß I • **sweets** *(pl)* Süßigkeiten I
sweetheart ['swi:thɑ:t] Liebling, Schatz II 3 (54)
swim (-mm-) [swɪm], **swam, swum** schwimmen I • **go swimming** schwimmen gehen I
swimmer ['swɪmə] Schwimmer/in II 1 (22)
swimming pool ['swɪmɪŋ pu:l] Schwimmbad, Schwimmbecken I
swum [swʌm] *siehe* **swim**
syllable ['sɪləbl] Silbe I

T

table ['teɪbl] Tisch I • **table tennis** ['teɪbl tenɪs] Tischtennis I
°**tail: heads and tails** [ˌhedz_ənd 'teɪlz] *wörtlich:* Köpfe und Schwänze; *hier:* (Satz-)Anfänge und Enden
take [teɪk], **took, taken**
1. nehmen I
2. (weg-, hin)bringen I
°**take control** die Kontrolle/Gewalt übernehmen • **take notes** sich Notizen machen I • **take out** herausnehmen I • **take photos** Fotos machen, fotografieren I
take sth. off etwas ausziehen *(Kleidung)* II 4 (70/165) • **take 10c off** 10 Cent abziehen I • °**Take turns.** Wechselt euch ab. • **We'll take them.** *(beim Einkaufen)* Wir nehmen sie. I
taken ['teɪkən] *siehe* **take**
talk [tɔ:k]: **talk (about)** reden (über), sich unterhalten (über) I • **talk (to)** reden (mit), sich unterhalten (mit) I
°**talk** [tɔ:k] Vortrag, Referat, Rede
°**task** [tɑ:sk] Aufgabe
taught [tɔ:t] *siehe* **teach**
tea [ti:] Tee; *(auch:) leichte Nachmittags- oder Abendmahlzeit* I
teach [ti:tʃ], **taught, taught** unterrichten, lehren I
teacher ['ti:tʃə] Lehrer/in I
team [ti:m] Team, Mannschaft I
teenager ['ti:neɪdʒə] Teenager, Jugendliche(r) II 1 (23)
teeth [ti:θ] *Plural von „tooth"* I
telephone ['telɪfəʊn] Telefon I
telephone number Telefonnummer I • **What's your telephone number?** Was ist deine Telefonnummer? I
°**telescope** ['telɪskəʊp] Teleskop
television (TV) ['telɪvɪʒn] Fernsehen I
tell (about) [tel], **told, told** erzählen (von), berichten (über) I • **Tell me your names.** Sagt mir eure Namen. I • **tell sb. the way** jm. den Weg beschreiben II 6 (95)
temperature ['temprətʃə] Temperatur II 4 (62) • **have a temperature** Fieber haben II 4 (62)
► S.164 I don't feel well
tennis ['tenɪs] Tennis I
°**tent** [tent] Zelt
term [tɜ:m] Trimester II 6 (103)
terrible ['terəbl] schrecklich, furchtbar I
°**territory** ['terətri:] Revier, Gebiet, Territorium
test [test] Test, Prüfung II 4 (64)
°**test** [test] prüfen, testen
text [tekst] Text I
than [ðæn, ðən] als II 2 (29/156)
more than mehr als II 2 (29)
more than me mehr als ich II 2 (29/156)
thank [θæŋk]: **Thank you.** Danke (schön). I • **Thanks.** Danke. I
Thanks a lot! Vielen Dank! I
Thanks very much! Danke sehr! / Vielen Dank! II 3 (45)
that [ðət, ðæt]
1. das (dort) I
2. jene(r, s) I
That's me. Das bin ich. I • **That's right.** Das ist richtig. / Das stimmt. I • **That was close.** Das war knapp. II 4 (71)
that [ðət, ðæt] dass I
the [ðə, ði] der, die, das; die I
theatre ['θɪətə] Theater II Welc (6)
their [ðeə] ihr, ihre *(Plural)* I
theirs [ðeəz] ihrer, ihre, ihrs II 2 (28/156)
► S.156 Possessive pronouns
them [ðəm, ðem] sie; ihnen I
then [ðen] dann, danach I
there [ðeə]
1. da, dort I
2. dahin, dorthin I
down there dort unten II 4 (70)
over there da drüben, dort drüben I • **there are** es sind (vorhanden); es gibt I • **there's** es ist (vorhanden); es gibt I • **there isn't a ...** es ist kein/e ...; es gibt kein/e ... I
thermometer [θə'mɒmɪtə] Thermometer II 4 (62)
these [ði:z] diese, die (hier) I
they [ðeɪ] sie *(Plural)* I
thief [θi:f], *pl* **thieves** [θi:vz] Dieb/in II 5 (86)
thing [θɪŋ] Ding, Sache I • **What was the best thing about ...?** Was war das Beste an ...? II 1 (12)
think [θɪŋk], **thought, thought** glauben, meinen, denken I
think about 1. nachdenken über II 4 (71/165); 2. denken über, halten von II 4 (71/165) • **think of** 1. denken über, halten von II 4 (71/165); 2. denken an; sich ausdenken II 4 (71/165)
► S.165 (to) think
third [θɜ:d] dritte(r, s) I
this [ðɪs]
1. dies (hier) I
2. diese(r, s) I
This is Isabel. Hier spricht Isabel. / Hier ist Isabel. *(am Telefon)* II 6 (96)
this morning/afternoon/evening heute Morgen/Nachmittag/Abend I • **this way** hier entlang, in diese Richtung II 5 (87)
those [ðəʊz] die (da), jene (dort) I
thought [θɔ:t] *siehe* **think**
thousand ['θaʊznd] tausend I
threw [θru:] *siehe* **throw**
throat [θrəʊt] Hals, Kehle II 4 (62)
through [θru:] durch II 1 (22)
throw [θrəʊ], **threw, thrown** werfen I
thrown [θrəʊn] *siehe* **throw**
Thursday ['θɜ:zdeɪ, 'θɜ:zdi] Donnerstag I
°**tick** [tɪk] Häkchen
°**tick** [tɪk] ankreuzen, ein Häkchen machen
ticket ['tɪkɪt]
1. Eintrittskarte I
2. Fahrkarte II 3 (55) • **return ticket** Rückfahrkarte II 3 (55)
°**tickle** ['tɪkl] kitzeln
°**tide** [taɪd] Gezeiten, Ebbe und Flut
tidy ['taɪdi] aufräumen I
tidy ['taɪdi] ordentlich, aufgeräumt II 3 (54)
tiger ['taɪgə] Tiger II 3 (52/160)
°**tight** [taɪt] eng
till [tɪl] bis *(zeitlich)* I
time [taɪm]
1. Zeit; Uhrzeit I

2. time(s) Mal(e); -mal II 1 (12)
What's the time? Wie spät ist es? I
in time rechtzeitig II 1 (23)
timetable ['taɪmteɪbl]
1. Stundenplan I
2. Fahrplan II 4 (61)
tip [tɪp] Tipp II 3 (45)
tired ['taɪəd] müde I
title ['taɪtl] Titel, Überschrift I
to [tə, tu]
1. zu, nach I • **to Jenny's** zu Jenny I • **°from … to …** von … bis …
°to the front nach vorn
2. an e-mail to eine E-Mail an I
write to schreiben an I
3. quarter to 12 Viertel vor 12 (11.45 / 23.45) I
4. try to help/to play/… versuchen, zu helfen/zu spielen/… I
5. um zu II 1 (20)
toast [təʊst] Toast(brot) I
tobacco [tə'bækəʊ] Tabak II 5 (75)
today [tə'deɪ] heute I
toe [təʊ] Zeh I
together [tə'geðə] zusammen I
toilet ['tɔɪlət] Toilette I
told [təʊld] *siehe* **tell**
tomato [tə'mɑːtəʊ], *pl* **tomatoes** Tomate II 6 (104)
tomorrow [tə'mɒrəʊ] morgen I
tomorrow's weather das Wetter von morgen II 3 (42/158)
°tongue-twister ['tʌŋtwɪstə] Zungenbrecher
tonight [tə'naɪt] heute Nacht, heute Abend I • **tonight's programme** das Programm von heute Abend; das heutige Abendprogramm II 3 (42/158)
too [tuː]: **from Bristol too** auch aus Bristol I • **Me too.** Ich auch. I
too much/big/… [tuː] zu viel/groß/… I
took [tʊk] *siehe* **take**
°tool [tuːl] Werkzeug
tooth [tuːθ], *pl* **teeth** [tiːθ] Zahn I
toothache ['tuːθeɪk] Zahnschmerzen II 4 (62/164)
► S.164 I don't feel well
top [tɒp]
1. Spitze, oberes Ende I • **at the top (of)** oben, am oberen Ende, an der Spitze (von) I
2. Top, Oberteil I
topic ['tɒpɪk] Thema, Themenbereich I • **topic sentence** *Satz, der in das Thema eines Absatzes einführt* II 4 (60)
tornado [tɔː'neɪdəʊ] Tornado, Wirbelsturm II 5 (84)
tortoise ['tɔːtəs] Schildkröte I
touch [tʌtʃ] berühren, anfassen II 4 (62)
tour (of the house) [tʊə] Rundgang, Tour (durch das Haus) I
tourist ['tʊərɪst] Tourist/in II 5 (74)
tourist information Fremdenverkehrsamt II 5 (74)
towards sb./sth. [tə'wɔːdz] auf jn./etwas zu II 5 (87)
tower ['taʊə] Turm I
town [taʊn] (Klein-)Stadt I
°tradition [trə'dɪʃn] Tradition
°traditional [trə'dɪʃənl] traditionell
traffic ['træfɪk] Verkehr II 4 (58)
train [treɪn] Zug I • **on the train** im Zug I
trainers *(pl)* ['treɪnəz] Turnschuhe II 2 (27)
°translate (into) [træns'leɪt] übersetzen (in)
travel (-ll-) ['trævl] reisen II Welc (6)
°travelcard ['trævlkɑːd] (Tages-)Fahrkarte
tree [triː] Baum I
trick [trɪk]
1. (Zauber-)Kunststück, Trick I • **do tricks** (Zauber-)Kunststücke machen I
2. Streich II 6 (96)
trip [trɪp] Reise; Ausflug I • **go on a trip** einen Ausflug machen II Welc (7/151)
trouble ['trʌbl] Schwierigkeiten, Ärger II 1 (22) • **be in trouble** in Schwierigkeiten sein; Ärger kriegen II 1 (22)
trousers *(pl)* ['traʊzəz] Hose II 2 (27)
► S.156 Plural words
true [truː] wahr II 6 (105)
try [traɪ]
1. versuchen I
2. probieren, kosten I
try and do sth. / try to do sth. versuchen, etwas zu tun I • **try on** anprobieren *(Kleidung)* I
T-shirt ['tiːʃɜːt] T-Shirt I
Tuesday ['tjuːzdeɪ, 'tjuːzdi] Dienstag I
°tuna (fish) ['tjuːnə] Thunfisch
tunnel ['tʌnl] Tunnel II 5 (77)
turn [tɜːn] sich umdrehen II 3 (55)
turn left/right (nach) links/rechts abbiegen II 6 (95) • **turn to sb.** sich jm. zuwenden; sich an jn. wenden II 6 (95/170)
► S.170 (to) turn
turn [tɜːn]: **It's your turn.** Du bist dran / an der Reihe. I • **Miss a turn.** Einmal aussetzen. II 5 (74)
°Take turns. Wechselt euch ab.
Whose turn is it? Wer ist dran / an der Reihe? II 5 (74)
TV [tiː'viː] Fernsehen I • **on TV** im Fernsehen I • **watch TV** fernsehen I
twin [twɪn]: **twin brother** Zwillingsbruder I • **twins** *(pl)* Zwillinge I

U

uncle ['ʌŋkl] Onkel I
°unconscious [ʌn'kɒnʃəs] bewusstlos
under ['ʌndə] unter I
underground ['ʌndəgraʊnd]: **the underground** die U-Bahn II 1 (12)
°underline [ˌʌndə'laɪn] unterstreichen
understand [ˌʌndə'stænd], **understood, understood** verstehen, begreifen I
understood [ˌʌndə'stʊd] *siehe* **understand**
uniform ['juːnɪfɔːm] Uniform I
unit ['juːnɪt] Lektion, Kapitel I
°university [ˌjuːnɪ'vɜːsəti] Universität, Hochschule
up [ʌp] hinauf, herauf, nach oben I
up the hill den Hügel hinauf II 4 (71)
upstairs [ˌʌp'steəz] oben; nach oben I
us [əs, ʌs] uns I
use [juːz] benutzen, verwenden I
°used [juːzd] gebraucht
°useful ['juːsfəl] nützlich
usually ['juːʒuəli] meistens, gewöhnlich, normalerweise I

V

valley ['væli] Tal II 4 (58)
°veggie burger ['vedʒi ˌbɜːgə] Gemüseburger
°verse [vɜːs] Strophe, Vers
very ['veri] sehr I • **like/love sth. very much** etwas sehr mögen/sehr lieben II 3 (45/159) • **Thanks very much!** Danke sehr! / Vielen Dank! II 3 (45)
view [vjuː] Aussicht, Blick II Welc (6)
village ['vɪlɪdʒ] Dorf I
visit ['vɪzɪt] besuchen II Welc (9)
visit ['vɪzɪt] Besuch II 4 (60/162)
visitor ['vɪzɪtə] Besucher/in, Gast I
vocabulary [və'kæbjələri] Vokabelverzeichnis, Wörterverzeichnis I
volleyball ['vɒlibɔːl] Volleyball I
°volunteer [ˌvɒlən'tɪə] Freiwillige(r)
°vowel sound ['vaʊəl saʊnd] Vokallaut

W

wait (for) ['weɪt fɔ:] warten (auf) I **Wait a minute.** Warte mal! / Moment mal! II 5 (87) • **I can't wait to see ...** ich kann es kaum erwarten, ... zu sehen I
waiter ['weɪtə] Kellner II 5 (78)
waitress ['weɪtrəs] Kellnerin II 5 (78/167)
°**wake up** [ˌweɪk_'ʌp], **woke up, woken up** aufwachen
walk [wɔ:k] (zu Fuß) gehen I
walk [wɔ:k] Spaziergang II Welc (6) **go for a walk** spazieren gehen, einen Spaziergang machen II Welc (6)
wall [wɔ:l] Wand; Mauer II 6 (92)
°**Wallop!** ['wɒləp] Schepper!
want [wɒnt] (haben) wollen I **want to do** tun wollen I
wardrobe ['wɔ:drəʊb] Kleiderschrank I
warm [wɔ:m] warm II Welc (6/150)
was [wəz, wɒz]: **(I/he/she/it) was** *siehe* **be**
wash [wɒʃ] waschen I • **I wash my face.** Ich wasche mir das Gesicht. I
washing machine ['wɒʃɪŋ məˌʃi:n] Waschmaschine I
watch [wɒtʃ] beobachten, sich *etwas* ansehen; zusehen I **watch TV** fernsehen I
watch [wɒtʃ] Armbanduhr I
water ['wɔ:tə] Wasser I
wave [weɪv] winken II 1 (22)
°**wave** [weɪv] Welle
way [weɪ]
1. Weg II 6 (95/170) • **ask sb. the way** jn. nach dem Weg fragen II 6 (95/170) **on the way (to)** auf dem Weg (zu/nach) II 6 (95/170) • **tell sb. the way** jm. den Weg beschreiben II 6 (95)
2. Richtung II 5 (87) • **the other way round** anders herum II 6 (104) **the wrong way** in die falsche Richtung II 5 (87) • **this way** hier entlang, in diese Richtung II 5 (87) **which way?** in welche Richtung? / wohin? II 6 (95/170)
3. by the way übrigens II 4 (63)
4. No way! Auf keinen Fall! / Kommt nicht in Frage! II 1 (14)
► S.170 way
we [wi:] wir I
weak [wi:k] schwach II 4 (70/165)
wear [weə], **wore, worn** tragen, anhaben *(Kleidung)* I
weather ['weðə] Wetter II Welc (6/150)
°**weather forecast** ['weðə fɔ:kɑ:st] Wettervorhersage
website ['websaɪt] Website II 1 (11)
Wednesday ['wenzdeɪ, 'wenzdi] Mittwoch I
week [wi:k] Woche I • **days of the week** Wochentage I
weekend [ˌwi:k'end] Wochenende I **at the weekend** am Wochenende I
welcome ['welkəm]
1. Welcome (to Bristol). Willkommen (in Bristol). I
2. You're welcome. Gern geschehen. / Nichts zu danken. I
welcome sb. (to) ['welkəm] jn. begrüßen, willkommen heißen (in) I **They welcome you to ...** Sie heißen dich in ... willkommen I
well [wel]
1. gut II 3 (47) • **You did well.** Das hast du gut gemacht. II 3 (47) • **Oh well ...** Na ja ... / Na gut ... I **Well, ...** Nun, ... / Also, ... I
2. *(gesundheitlich)* gut; gesund, wohlauf II 4 (61)
► S.164 I don't feel well
Welsh [welʃ] walisisch; Walisisch II 4 (60)
went [went] *siehe* **go**
were [wə, wɜ:]: **(we/you/they) were** *siehe* **be**
°**were-rabbit** ['weə ˌræbɪt] Werwolf-Kaninchen
°**west** [west]: **the West Country** *umgangssprachliche Bezeichnung für den Südwesten Englands*
what [wɒt]
1. was I
2. welche(r, s) I
What about ...? **1.** Was ist mit ...? / Und ...? I; **2.** Wie wär's mit ...? I **What are you talking about?** Wovon redest du? I • **What colour is ...?** Welche Farbe hat ...? I • **What for?** Wofür? II 2 (29) • **What have we got next?** Was haben wir als Nächstes? I • **What page are we on?** Auf welcher Seite sind wir? I **What's for homework?** Was haben wir als Hausaufgabe auf? I **What's the matter?** Was ist los? / Was ist denn? II 2 (28) • **What's the time?** Wie spät ist es? I • **What's your name?** Wie heißt du? I **What's your telephone number?** Was ist deine Telefonnummer? I **What was the weather like?** Wie war das Wetter? II Welc (7)
°**wheatgrass** ['wi:tgrɑ:s] Weizengras
wheelchair ['wi:ltʃeə] Rollstuhl I
when [wen] wann I • **When's your birthday?** Wann hast du Geburtstag? I
when [wen]
1. wenn I
2. als I
where [weə]
1. wo I
2. wohin I
Where are you from? Wo kommst du her? I
which [wɪtʃ]: **Which picture ...?** Welches Bild ...? I • **which way?** in welche Richtung? / wohin? II 6 (95/170)
°**which** [wɪtʃ]: **the planet which Herschel discovered** der Planet, den Herschel entdeckte
whisky ['wɪski] Whisky II 4 (65)
whisper ['wɪspə] flüstern I
whistle ['wɪsl] pfeifen II 5 (86)
white [waɪt] weiß I
who [hu:]
1. wer I
2. wen / wem II 5 (86)
► S.168 who?
who [hu:]: **Find/Ask somebody who ...** Finde/Frage jemanden, der ... II 1 (20) • °**the man who lived in this house** der Mann, der in diesem Haus wohnte
whose? [hu:z] wessen? II 5 (74) **Whose are these?** Wem gehören diese? II 5 (74/166) • **Whose turn is it?** Wer ist dran / an der Reihe? II 5 (74)
why [waɪ] warum I • **Why me?** Warum ich? I
wife [waɪf], *pl* **wives** [waɪvz] Ehefrau II 4 (71)
wild [waɪld] wild II 3 (42)
will [wɪl]: **you'll be cold (= you will be cold)** du wirst frieren; ihr werdet frieren II 3 (44) • **you won't be cold** [wəʊnt] **(= you will not be cold)** du wirst nicht frieren; ihr werdet nicht frieren II 3 (44)
win (-nn-) [wɪn], **won, won** gewinnen I
wind [wɪnd] Wind I
window ['wɪndəʊ] Fenster I
windy ['wɪndi] windig I
winner ['wɪnə] Gewinner/in, Sieger/in II 3 (53)
winter ['wɪntə] Winter I
°**wisdom** ['wɪzdəm] Weisheit
°**wise** [waɪz] weise
with [wɪð]
1. mit I
2. bei I
Sit with me. Setz dich zu mir. / Setzt euch zu mir. I
without [wɪ'ðaʊt] ohne I
wives [waɪvz] *Plural von „wife"* II 4 (71)

°**woke up** [ˌwəʊk‿ˈʌp] *siehe* **wake up**
°**woken up** [ˌwəʊkən‿ˈʌp] *siehe* **wake up**
wolf [wʊlf], *pl* **wolves** [wʊlvz] Wolf II 3 (52/160)
woman [ˈwʊmən], *pl* **women** [ˈwɪmɪn] Frau I
won [wʌn] *siehe* **win**
won't [wəʊnt]: **you won't be cold (= you will not be cold)** du wirst nicht frieren; ihr werdet nicht frieren II 3 (44)
wonder [ˈwʌndə] sich fragen, gern wissen wollen II 6 (104)
°**wood** [wʊd] Wald
woodpecker [ˈwʊdpekə] Specht II 3 (43)
word [wɜːd] Wort I • **word building** Wortbildung II 3 (53) °**word order** Wortstellung
wore [wɔː] *siehe* **wear**
work [wɜːk] arbeiten I • **work hard** hart arbeiten II 3 (47) • **work on sth.** an etwas arbeiten I
work [wɜːk] Arbeit I • **at work** bei der Arbeit / am Arbeitsplatz I
worker [ˈwɜːkə] Arbeiter/in II 3 (53)
worksheet [ˈwɜːkʃiːt] Arbeitsblatt I
world [wɜːld] Welt I
worn [wɔːn] *siehe* **wear**
worry [ˈwʌri] Sorge, Kummer II 6 (105)
worry (about) [ˈwʌri] sich Sorgen machen (wegen, um) I • **Don't worry.** Mach dir keine Sorgen. I
worse [wɜːs] schlechter, schlimmer II 2 (30/157)
worst [wɜːst]: **(the) worst** am schlechtesten, schlimmsten; der/die/das schlechteste, schlimmste II 2 (30/157)
would [wəd, wʊd]: **I'd like ... (= I would like ...)** Ich hätte gern ... / Ich möchte gern ... I • **Would you like ...?** Möchtest du ...? / Möchten Sie ...? I • **Would you like some?** Möchtest du etwas/ein paar? / Möchten Sie etwas/ein paar? I **I'd like to talk about ... (= I would like to talk about ...)** Ich möchte über ... reden / Ich würde gern über ... reden I
°**wreck** [rek] Wrack
°**wriggle** [ˈrɪgl] (herum)zappeln
write [raɪt], **wrote, written** schreiben I • **write down** aufschreiben I • **write to** schreiben an I
writer [ˈraɪtə] Schreiber/in; Schriftsteller/in II 3 (53)
written [ˈrɪtn] *siehe* **write**
wrong [rɒŋ] falsch, verkehrt I **be wrong 1.** falsch sein I; **2.** sich irren, Unrecht haben II 2 (30) **the wrong way** in die falsche Richtung II 5 (87)
wrote [rəʊt] *siehe* **write**

Y

yard [jɑːd] Hof II 3 (44) • **in the yard** auf dem Hof II 3 (44/159)
yawn [jɔːn] gähnen II 6 (104)
year [jɪə]
1. Jahr I
2. Jahrgangsstufe I
yellow [ˈjeləʊ] gelb I
yes [jes] ja I
yesterday [ˈjestədeɪ, ˈjestədi] gestern I • **yesterday morning/ afternoon/evening** gestern Morgen/Nachmittag/Abend I **yesterday's homework** die Hausaufgaben von gestern II 3 (42/158)
yet [jet]: **not (...) yet** noch nicht II 4 (61) • **yet?** schon? II 4 (63/164)
► S.163 The present perfect: statements
► S.164 The present perfect: questions
yoga [ˈjəʊgə] Yoga I
you [juː]
1. du; Sie I
2. ihr I • **you two** ihr zwei I
3. dir; dich; euch I
young [jʌŋ] jung I
your [jɔː]
1. dein/e I
2. Ihr I
3. euer/eure I
yours [jɔːz]
1. deiner, deine, deins II 2 (28/156)
2. Ihrer, Ihre, Ihrs II 2 (28/156)
3. eurer, eure, eures II 2 (28/156)
► S.156 Possessive pronouns
°**yourself** [jəˈself, jɔːˈself]: **about yourself** über dich selbst
°**youth** [juːθ] Jugend, Jugend-
°**yuck** [jʌk] igitt

Z

zebra [ˈzebrə] Zebra II 3 (52/160)
zero [ˈzɪərəʊ] null I

English sounds (Englische Laute)

Die Lautschrift in den eckigen Klammern zeigt dir, wie ein Wort ausgesprochen wird.
In der folgenden Übersicht findest du alle Lautzeichen.

Vokale (Selbstlaute)

[iː]	green	[eɪ]	skate
[i]	happy	[aɪ]	time
[ɪ]	in	[ɔɪ]	boy
[e]	yes	[əʊ]	old
[æ]	black	[aʊ]	now
[ɑː]	park	[ɪə]	here
[ɒ]	song	[eə]	where
[ɔː]	morning	[ʊə]	tour
[uː]	blue		
[ʊ]	book		
[ʌ]	mum		
[ɜː]	T-shirt		
[ə]	a partner		

Konsonanten (Mitlaute)

[b]	box	[f]	full
[p]	play	[v]	very
[d]	dad	[s]	sister
[t]	ten	[z]	please
[g]	good	[ʃ]	shop
[k]	cat	[ʒ]	television
[m]	mum	[tʃ]	teacher
[n]	no	[dʒ]	Germany
[ŋ]	sing	[θ]	thanks
[l]	hello	[ð]	this
[r]	red	[h]	he
[w]	we		
[j]	you		

Das **German – English Dictionary** enthält den **Lernwortschatz** der Bände 1 und 2 von *English G 21*.
Es kann dir eine erste Hilfe sein, wenn du vergessen hast, wie etwas auf Englisch heißt.

Wenn du wissen möchtest, wo das englische Wort zum ersten Mal in *English G 21* vorkommt, dann kannst du im **English – German Dictionary** (S. 173–191) nachschlagen.

Im **German – English Dictionary** werden folgende **Abkürzungen** und **Symbole** verwendet:

jm. = jemandem	sb. = somebody	*pl* = *plural* (Mehrzahl)	*BE* = *British English*
jn. = jemanden	sth. = something	*no pl* = *no plural*	*AE* = *American English*

► Der Pfeil verweist auf Kästchen im Vocabulary (S. 150–172), in denen du weitere Informationen findest.

A

abbiegen: (nach) links/rechts abbiegen turn left/right [tɜːn]
► S.170 (to) turn
Abend evening ['iːvnɪŋ]; *(später Abend)* night [naɪt] • **am Abend, abends** in the evening
Abendbrot, Abendessen dinner
Abendbrot essen have dinner
zum Abendbrot for dinner
aber but [bət, bʌt]
abfahren *(wegfahren)* leave [liːv]
Abfall rubbish ['rʌbɪʃ]
Absatz *(in einem Text)* paragraph ['pærəgrɑːf]
abschreiben *(kopieren)* copy ['kɒpi]
abziehen: 10 Cent abziehen take 10c off [ˌteɪk_'ɒf]
Acker field [fiːld]
addieren (zu) add (to) [æd]
Adresse address [ə'dres]
Affe monkey ['mʌŋki]
Aktivität activity [æk'tɪvəti]
Akzent accent ['æksənt]
albern silly
alle *(die ganze Gruppe)* all [ɔːl]
allein alone [ə'ləʊn]
alleinstehend single ['sɪŋgl]
alles everything ['evriθɪŋ]; all [ɔːl]
Alphabet alphabet ['ælfəbet]
als 1. *(zeitlich)* when [wen]; *(während)* as [əz, æz]
2. größer/teurer als bigger/more expensive than [ðæn, ðən]
also *(daher, deshalb)* so [səʊ]
Also, ... Well, ... [wel]
alt old [əʊld]
am 1. am Bahnhof at the station
am oberen Ende (von) at the top (of) • **am Strand** on the beach
am Telefon on the phone • **am unteren Ende (von)** at the bottom (of) ['bɒtəm]
2. *(nahe bei)* **am Meer** by the sea
3. *(zeitlich)* **am 13. Juni** on 13th June
am Morgen/Nachmittag/Abend in the morning/afternoon/evening
am Ende (von) at the end (of)
am Freitag on Friday • **am Freitagmorgen** on Friday morning
am nächsten Morgen/Tag the next morning/day • **am Wochenende** at the weekend
amüsieren: sich amüsieren have fun [hæv 'fʌn]
an 1. an dem/den Tisch (dort) at that table • **an der Spitze** at the top (of) • **an der/die Tafel** on the board • **an jn. schreiben** write to sb.
2. *(nahe bei)* **an der See** by the sea
3. Was war das Beste an ...? What was the best thing about ...?
4. an sein *(Radio, Licht usw.)* be on
anbauen *(Getreide usw.)* grow [grəʊ]
andere(r, s) other ['ʌðə] • **die anderen** the others
anders (als) different (from) ['dɪfrənt]
anders herum the other way round
Anfang beginning [bɪ'gɪnɪŋ]
anfangen (mit) start [stɑːt]
anfassen touch [tʌtʃ]
anfühlen: sich gut anfühlen feel good [fiːl]
Angst haben (vor) be afraid (of) [ə'freɪd]; be scared (of) [skeəd]
anhaben *(Kleidung)* wear [weə]
anhalten stop [stɒp]
anhören 1. sich etwas anhören listen to sth. ['lɪsn]
2. sich gut anhören sound good [saʊnd]
anklicken: etwas anklicken click on sth. [klɪk]
ankommen arrive [ə'raɪv]
anlächeln: jn. anlächeln smile at sb. [smaɪl]
Anleitung(en) *(Gebrauchsanweisungen)* instructions *(pl)* [ɪn'strʌkʃnz]
anmailen: jn. anmailen mail sb. [meɪl]
anmalen paint [peɪnt]
anpflanzen *(Getreide usw.)* grow [grəʊ]
anprobieren *(Kleidung)* try on [ˌtraɪ_'ɒn]
Anruf call; phone call ['fəʊn kɔːl]
anrufen call [kɔːl]; phone [fəʊn]
anschauen look at [lʊk]
Anschlagtafel notice board ['nəʊtɪs bɔːd]
anschließen: sich jm. anschließen join sb. [dʒɔɪn]
Anschrift address [ə'dres]
ansehen: sich etwas ansehen look at sth. [lʊk]; watch sth. [wɒtʃ]
Antwort (auf) answer (to) ['ɑːnsə]
antworten answer ['ɑːnsə]
Anweisung(en) *(Gebrauchsanweisungen)* instructions *(pl)* [ɪn'strʌkʃnz]
anziehen: etwas anziehen *(Kleidung)* put sth. on [ˌpʊt_'ɒn] • **sich anziehen** get dressed [get 'drest]
Apfel apple ['æpl]
Apfelsine orange ['ɒrɪndʒ]
Apotheke chemist ['kemɪst]
April April ['eɪprəl]
Arbeit work [wɜːk] • **bei der Arbeit/am Arbeitsplatz** at work • **gute Arbeit leisten** do a good job
arbeiten (an) work (on) [wɜːk]
Arbeiter/in worker ['wɜːkə]
Arbeitsblatt worksheet ['wɜːkʃiːt]
Arbeits- und Lerntechniken study skills ['stʌdi skɪlz]
Ärger *(Schwierigkeiten)* trouble ['trʌbl] • **Ärger kriegen** be in trouble
arm poor [pɔː, pʊə]
Arm arm [ɑːm]
Armbanduhr watch [wɒtʃ]
Art *(Sorte)* sort [sɔːt]
Arzt/Ärztin doctor ['dɒktə]
auch: auch aus Bristol from Bristol too [tuː]; also from Bristol ['ɔːlsəʊ]
Ich auch. Me too.
auf on [ɒn] • **auf dem Bild/Foto** in the picture/photo • **auf dem Feld** in the field • **auf dem Hof** in the yard • **auf dem Land** in the country • **auf dem Weg (zu/nach)** on the way (to) • **auf einmal**

suddenly ['sʌdnli] • **auf Englisch** in English • **Auf geht's!** Let's go. **auf jn./etwas zu** towards sb./sth. [tə'wɔ:dz] • **Auf keinen Fall!** No way! • **Auf welcher Seite sind wir?** What page are we on? • **Auf Wiedersehen.** Goodbye. [ˌgʊd'baɪ]
aufführen *(Szene, Dialog)* act [ækt]
Aufgabe *(im Schulbuch)* exercise ['eksəsaɪz]; *(Job)* job [dʒɒb]
aufgeräumt *(ordentlich)* tidy ['taɪdi]
aufgeregt *(nervös)* nervous ['nɜ:vəs]
aufheben: etwas aufheben *(hochheben)* pick sth. up [ˌpɪk_'ʌp]
aufhören stop [stɒp]
auflisten list [lɪst]
aufmachen open ['əʊpən]
aufpassen: auf etwas/jn. aufpassen look after sth./sb. [ˌlʊk_'ɑ:ftə]
aufräumen tidy ['taɪdi]
aufregend exciting [ɪk'saɪtɪŋ]
Aufsatz essay ['eseɪ]
aufschauen (von) look up (from) [ˌlʊk_'ʌp]
aufschreiben write down [ˌraɪt 'daʊn]
aufstehen get up [ˌget_'ʌp]
aufsuchen: jn. aufsuchen see sb. [si:]
aufzählen *(auflisten)* list [lɪst]
Aufzug lift [lɪft] *(BE)*; elevator ['elɪveɪtə] *(AE)*
Auge eye [aɪ]
August August ['ɔ:gəst]
aus: Ich komme/bin aus ... I'm from ... [frəm, frɒm] • **aus ... (heraus/hinaus)** out of ... ['aʊt_əv] • **aus dem Zug/Bus aussteigen** get off the train/bus • **aus vielen Gründen** for lots of reasons
ausdenken: sich etwas ausdenken think of sth. [θɪŋk]
► S.165 (to) think
Ausflug trip [trɪp] • **einen Ausflug machen** go on a trip
ausgeben: Geld ausgeben (für) spend money (on) [spend]
ausruhen: sich ausruhen relax [rɪ'læks]
aussehen: anders/toll/alt aussehen look different/great/old [lʊk] **fürchterlich aussehen** be a mess [mes]
außerhalb seines Zimmers outside his room [ˌaʊt'saɪd]
aussetzen: Einmal aussetzen. Miss a turn. [tɜ:n]
Aussicht *(Blick)* view [vju:]
Aussprache pronunciation [prəˌnʌnsi'eɪʃn]
aussteigen (aus dem Zug/Bus) get off (the train/bus) [ˌget_'ɒf]
aussuchen: (sich) etwas aussuchen choose sth. [tʃu:z]
auswählen choose [tʃu:z]
ausziehen 1. *(aus Wohnung)* move out [ˌmu:v_'aʊt]
2. etwas ausziehen *(Kleidung)* take sth. off [ˌteɪk_'ɒf]
Auto car [kɑ:]
Autsch! Ouch! [aʊtʃ]

B

Baby baby ['beɪbi] • **ein Baby bekommen** have a baby
baden *(ein Bad nehmen)* have a bath [bɑ:θ]
Badewanne bath [bɑ:θ]
Badezimmer bathroom ['bɑ:θru:m]
Badminton badminton ['bædmɪntən]
Bahnhof station ['steɪʃn] • **am Bahnhof** at the station
bald soon [su:n] • **Bis bald.** See you. ['si: ju:]
Ball ball [bɔ:l]
Banane banana [bə'nɑ:nə]
Band *(Musikgruppe)* band [bænd]
Bank *(Sparkasse)* bank [bæŋk]
Bankräuber/in bank robber ['rɒbə]
Bar bar [bɑ:]
Bär bear [beə]
Baseball baseball ['beɪsbɔ:l]
Baseballmütze baseball cap [kæp]
Basketball basketball ['bɑ:skɪtbɔ:l]
Bauchweh stomach ache ['stʌmək_eɪk]
► S.164 I don't feel well
bauen build [bɪld]
Bauernhof farm [fɑ:m]
Baum tree [tri:]
beantworten answer ['ɑ:nsə]
beeilen: sich beeilen hurry ['hʌri]; hurry up [ˌhʌri_'ʌp]
beenden finish ['fɪnɪʃ]
Beginn beginning [bɪ'gɪnɪŋ]
beginnen (mit) start [stɑ:t]
begreifen understand [ˌʌndə'stænd]
Begründung reason ['ri:zn]
bei: bei den Shaws zu Hause at the Shaws' house • **bei der Arbeit** at work • **Englisch bei Mr Kingsley** English with Mr Kingsley
beide both [bəʊθ]
Beifall klatschen cheer [tʃɪə]
Bein leg [leg]
bekommen get [get] • **ein Baby bekommen** have a baby
benennen name [kɔ:l]
benötigen need [ni:d]
benutzen use [ju:z]
beobachten watch [wɒtʃ]
bereit ready ['redi]
bereits already [ɔ:l'redi]
Berg mountain ['maʊntən]
Bericht (über) report (on) [rɪ'pɔ:t]
berichten (über) tell (about) [tel]
(jm.) etwas berichten report sth. (to sb.) [rɪ'pɔ:t]
berichtigen correct [kə'rekt]
beruhigen: sich beruhigen calm down [ˌkɑ:m 'daʊn]
berühmt famous ['feɪməs]
berühren touch [tʌtʃ]
Bescheid: über etwas Bescheid wissen know about sth. [nəʊ]
beschreiben: (jm.) etwas beschreiben describe sth. (to sb.) [dɪ'skraɪb]
jm. den Weg beschreiben tell sb. the way
Beschreibung description [dɪ'skrɪpʃn]
besitzen have [həv, hæv]
besondere(r, s): ein besonderer Tag a special day ['speʃl]
besorgen *(holen)* get [get]
besser better ['betə]
► S.157 good – better – best
beste: am besten (the) best [best]
der/die/das beste ...; die besten ... the best ... • **Was war das Beste an ...?** What was the best thing about ...?
► S.157 good – better – best
Besuch visit ['vɪzɪt]
besuchen: jn. besuchen visit sb. ['vɪzɪt]; see sb. [si:]
Besucher/in visitor ['vɪzɪtə]
Bett bed [bed] • **ins Bett gehen** go to bed
Beutel bag [bæg]
bevor before [bɪ'fɔ:]
bewegen: sich bewegen move [mu:v]
Bewegung movement ['mu:vmənt]
Beweis(e) proof *(no pl)* [pru:f]
bewölkt cloudy ['klaʊdi]
bezahlen: etwas bezahlen pay for sth. [peɪ]
Bibliothek library ['laɪbrəri]
Bild picture ['pɪktʃə] • **auf dem Bild** in the picture
billig cheap [tʃi:p]
Bindewort linking word ['lɪŋkɪŋ wɜ:d]
Biologie biology [baɪ'ɒlədʒi]
bis *(zeitlich)* till [tɪl] • **Bis bald.** See you. ['si: ju:]
bisschen: ein bisschen a bit [bɪt]
bitte 1. *(in Fragen und Aufforderungen)* please [pli:z]
2. Bitte sehr. / Hier bitte. Here you are.
3. Bitte, gern geschehen. You're welcome. ['welkəm]
4. Wie bitte? Sorry? ['sɒri]
blau blue [blu:]
bleiben stay [steɪ]
Bleistift pencil ['pensl]

Bleistiftanspitzer pencil sharpener ['pensl ʃɑːpnə]
Blick *(Aussicht)* view [vjuː]
blöd stupid ['stjuːpɪd]
bloß just [dʒʌst]; only ['əʊnli]
Boot boat [bəʊt]
böse sein (auf jn.) be cross (with sb.) [krɒs] • **böse sein (über etwas/auf jn.)** be angry (about sth./with sb.) ['æŋgri]
Brand fire ['faɪə]
brauchen need [niːd] • **nicht zu tun brauchen** needn't do ['niːdnt]
► S.171 must – needn't – mustn't
braun brown [braʊn]
brav good [gʊd]
Brief (an) letter (to) ['letə]
Briefmarke stamp [stæmp]
Brille: (eine) Brille glasses *(pl)* ['glɑːsɪz]
► S.156 Plural words
bringen: (mit-, her)bringen bring [brɪŋ] • **(weg-, hin)bringen** take [teɪk] • **alles durcheinanderbringen/in Unordnung bringen** make a mess
britisch; Brite, Britin British ['brɪtɪʃ]
Broschüre brochure ['brəʊʃə]
Brot bread *(no pl)* [bred]
Brötchen roll [rəʊl]
Brotdose sandwich box ['sænwɪtʃ bɒks]
Brücke bridge [brɪdʒ]
Bruder brother ['brʌðə]
Buch book [bʊk]
Bücherei library ['laɪbrəri]
Buchstabe letter ['letə]
buchstabieren spell [spel]
Burg castle ['kɑːsl]
Bus bus [bʌs]

C

Café café ['kæfeɪ]
Cartoon cartoon [kɑː'tuːn]
CD CD [ˌsiː'diː] • **CD-Spieler** CD player [ˌsiː'diː ˌpleɪə]
Cent cent (c) [sent]
chatten chat [tʃæt]
Chor choir ['kwaɪə]
clever clever ['klevə]; smart [smɑːt]
Clown/in clown [klaʊn]
Cola cola ['kəʊlə]
Comic-Heft comic ['kɒmɪk]
Computer computer [kəm'pjuːtə]
cool cool [kuːl]
Cornflakes cornflakes ['kɔːnfleɪks]
Cousin, Cousine cousin ['kʌzn]

D

da, dahin *(dort, dorthin)* there [ðeə]
da drüben over there [ˌəʊvə 'ðeə]
daheim at home [ət 'həʊm]
daher so [səʊ]
dämlich stupid ['stjuːpɪd]
danach *(zeitlich)* after that [ˌɑːftə 'ðæt]
Danke. Thank you. ['θæŋk juː]; Thanks.
Danke sehr! Thanks very much!
Vielen Dank! Thanks a lot!
dann then [ðen]
darstellende Kunst drama ['drɑːmə]
das *(Artikel)* the [ðə, ði]
das (dort) *(Singular)* that [ðət, ðæt]; *(Plural)* those [ðəʊz] • **Das bin ich.** That's me.
dass that [ðət, ðæt]
dasselbe the same [seɪm]
Datum date [deɪt]
decken: den Tisch decken lay the table [ˌleɪ ðə 'teɪbl]
dein(e) ... your ... [jɔː]
deiner, deine, deins yours [jɔːz]
► S.156 Possessive pronouns
denken think [θɪŋk] • **denken an** think of • **Was denkst du über ...?** What do you think about/of ...?
► S.165 (to) think
der 1. *(Artikel)* the [ðə, ði]
2. Finde/Frage jemanden, der ... Find/Ask somebody who ...
derselbe the same [seɪm]
deshalb so [səʊ]
Detail detail ['diːteɪl]
Detektiv/in detective [dɪ'tektɪv]
deuten (auf etwas) *(zeigen)* point (at/to sth.) [pɔɪnt]
deutlich clear [klɪə]
Deutsch; deutsch; Deutsche(r) German ['dʒɜːmən]
Deutschland Germany ['dʒɜːməni]
Dezember December [dɪ'sembə]
dich you [juː]
die *(Artikel)* the [ðə, ði]
die (dort) *(Singular)* that [ðət, ðæt]; *(Plural)* those [ðəʊz] • **die (hier)** *(Singular)* this [ðɪs]; *(Plural)* these [ðiːz]
Dieb/in thief [θiːf], *pl* thieves [θiːvz]
Diele hall [hɔːl]
Dienstag Tuesday ['tjuːzdeɪ, 'tjuːzdi] *(siehe auch unter „Freitag")*
dies (hier); diese(r, s) *(Singular)* this [ðɪs]; *(Plural)* these [ðiːz]
dieselbe(n) the same [seɪm]
Ding thing [θɪŋ]
dir you [juː]
Disko disco ['dɪskəʊ]
Diskussion discussion [dɪ'skʌʃn]
Doktor doctor ['dɒktə]
Donnerstag Thursday ['θɜːzdeɪ, 'θɜːzdi] *(siehe auch unter „Freitag")*
doppelt, Doppel- double ['dʌbl]
Dorf village ['vɪlɪdʒ]
dort, dorthin there [ðeə] • **dort drüben** over there [ˌəʊvə 'ðeə]
dort unten down there
Dossier dossier ['dɒsieɪ]
Drachen kite [kaɪt]
dran: Ich bin dran. It's my turn. [tɜːn]
draußen outside [ˌaʊt'saɪd]; out [aʊt]
nach draußen outside
► S.154 out
drinnen inside [ˌɪn'saɪd] • **hier drinnen** in here [ˌɪn 'hɪə] • **nach drinnen** inside
dritte(r, s) third [θɜːd]
Drogerie chemist ['kemɪst]
drüben: da/dort drüben over there [ˌəʊvə 'ðeə]
drücken push [pʊʃ]
du you [juː]
dumm *(albern)* silly ['sɪli]
dunkel dark [dɑːk]
durch through [θruː]
durcheinander: alles durcheinanderbringen make a mess [ˌmeɪk‿ə 'mes]
durchführen: ein Projekt durchführen do a project
dürfen can [kən, kæn] • **nicht dürfen** mustn't ['mʌsnt]
► S.171 must – needn't – mustn't
Dusche shower ['ʃaʊə]
duschen; sich duschen have a shower ['ʃaʊə]
DVD DVD [ˌdiː viː' diː]

E

echt real [rɪəl]
Ecke corner ['kɔːnə] • **Green Street, Ecke London Road** on the corner of Green Street and London Road
Ehefrau wife [waɪf], *pl* wives [waɪvz]
Ehemann husband ['hʌzbənd]
Ei egg [eg]
Eichhörnchen squirrel ['skwɪrəl]
eigene(r, s): unser eigenes Schwimmbad our own pool [əʊn]
Eile: in Eile sein be in a hurry ['hʌri]
eilen *(sich beeilen)* hurry ['hʌri]
eilig: es eilig haben be in a hurry ['hʌri]
ein(e) a, an [ə, ən]; one ['wʌn]
ein(e) andere(r, s) ... another ... [ə'nʌðə] • **eine Menge** a lot (of) [lɒt]; lots (of) [lɒts] • **ein neuer / eine neue / ein neues** a new one [wʌn] • **ein paar** some [səm, sʌm]
eines Tages one day

einfach *(nicht schwierig)* easy ['i:zi]
einfach nur just [dʒʌst]
Einfall *(Idee)* idea [aɪ'dɪə]
eingeschaltet sein *(Licht usw.)* be on
einige some [səm, sʌm]; *(einige wenige)* a few [fju:]
einigen: sich einigen (auf) agree (on) [ə'gri:]
einkaufen shop [ʃɒp] • **einkaufen gehen** go shopping; shop
Einkaufen shopping ['ʃɒpɪŋ]
Einkaufsliste shopping list
einladen (zu) invite (to) [ɪn'vaɪt]
Einladung (zu) invitation (to) [,ɪnvɪ'teɪʃn]
einmal: Einmal aussetzen. Miss a turn. [tɜ:n] • **auf einmal** suddenly ['sʌdnli]
einpacken pack [pæk]
eins, ein, eine one ['wʌn]
einschüchtern bully ['bʊli]
einsteigen (in den Zug/Bus) get on (the train/bus) [,get_'ɒn]
eintreffen *(ankommen)* arrive [ə'raɪv]
Eintrittskarte ticket ['tɪkɪt]
Einzelheit detail ['di:teɪl]
einziehen *(in Wohnung)* move in [,mu:v_'ɪn]
einzig: der einzige Gast the only guest ['əʊnli]
Eis *(Speiseeis)* ice cream [,aɪs 'kri:m]
Eisenbahn railway ['reɪlweɪ]
Elefant elephant ['elɪfənt]
Eltern parents ['peərənts]
E-Mail (an) e-mail (to) ['i:meɪl]
Ende 1. end [end] • **am Ende (von)** at the end (of) • **zu Ende machen** finish ['fɪnɪʃ] • **zu Ende sein** be over ['əʊvə]
2. oberes Ende *(Spitze)* top [tɒp]
am oberen Ende at the top
3. unteres Ende bottom ['bɒtəm]
am unteren Ende (von) at the bottom (of) ['bɒtəm]
enden finish ['fɪnɪʃ]
endlich at last [ət 'lɑ:st]
Engel angel ['eɪndʒl]
Englisch; englisch English ['ɪŋglɪʃ]
Enkel/in grandchild ['græntʃaɪld], *pl* grandchildren ['græntʃɪldrən]
Entdecker/in explorer [ɪk'splɔ:rə]
entlang der Straße / die Straße entlang along the street [ə'lɒŋ]
entschuldigen: sich entschuldigen say sorry ['sɒri]
Entschuldigung 1. *(Tut mir leid)* I'm sorry. ['sɒri] • **Entschuldigung, dass ich zu spät bin/komme.** Sorry, I'm late.
2. Entschuldigung, ... / Entschuldigen Sie, ... *(Darf ich mal stören?)* Excuse me, ... [ɪk'skju:z mi:]

entspannen; sich entspannen relax [rɪ'læks]
entwerfen design [dɪ'zaɪn]
er 1. *(männliche Person)* he [hi:]
2. *(Ding, Tier)* it [ɪt]
Erdbeere strawberry ['strɔ:bəri]
Erdkunde geography [dʒi'ɒgrəfi]
erfahren: etwas über etwas erfahren learn sth. about sth. [lɜ:n]
erforschen explore [ɪk'splɔ:]
ergänzen add (to) [æd]
Ergebnis result [rɪ'zʌlt]
erinnern: sich erinnern (an) remember [rɪ'membə]
erkältet sein have a cold [kəʊld]
► S.164 I don't feel well
Erkältung cold [kəʊld] • **eine Erkältung haben** have a cold
► S.164 I don't feel well
erklären: jm. etwas erklären explain sth. to sb. [ɪk'spleɪn]
Erklärung explanation [,eksplə'neɪʃn]
erkunden explore [ɪk'splɔ:]
erläutern: jm. etwas erläutern explain sth. to sb. [ɪk'spleɪn]
erstaunlich amazing [ə'meɪzɪŋ]
erste(r, s) first [fɜ:st] • **als Erstes** first • **der erste Tag** the first day
der/die Erste sein be first
erwarten: ich kann es kaum erwarten, ... zu sehen I can't wait to see ... [weɪt]
erwischen *(fangen)* catch [kætʃ]
erzählen (von) tell (about) [tel]
Erzählung story ['stɔ:ri]
es it [ɪt] • **es gibt** *(es ist vorhanden)* there's; *(es sind vorhanden)* there are
Essen food [fu:d]
essen eat [i:t] • **Abendbrot essen** have dinner • **Toast zum Frühstück essen** have toast for breakfast
Esszimmer dining room ['daɪnɪŋ ru:m]
Etagenbett bunk (bed) [bʌŋk]
etwas something ['sʌmθɪŋ]; *(irgendetwas)* anything ['eniθɪŋ]; *(ein bisschen)* a bit [bɪt] • **etwas Käse/Saft** some cheese/juice [səm, sʌm]
► S.169 something – anything
euch you [ju:]
euer, eure ... your ... [jɔ:]
eurer, eure, eures yours [jɔ:z]
► S.156 Possessive pronouns
Euro euro ['jʊərəʊ]

F

Fabrik factory ['fæktri]
fahren go [gəʊ]; *(ein Auto/mit dem Auto)* drive [draɪv] • **in Urlaub fahren** go on holiday • **mit dem Auto/Zug/Rad/... fahren** go by car/train/bike/... • **Inliner/Skateboard fahren** skate [skeɪt] • **Rad fahren** cycle ['saɪkl]; ride a bike [,raɪd ə 'baɪk]
Fahrer/in driver ['draɪvə]
Fahrkarte ticket ['tɪkɪt]
Fahrplan timetable ['taɪmteɪbl]
Fahrrad bike [baɪk]
Fahrstuhl lift [lɪft] *(BE)*; elevator ['elɪveɪtə] *(AE)*
Fahrt: (Rad-)Fahrt (bike) ride [raɪd]
fair fair [feə]
Fall *(Kriminalfall)* case [keɪs]
fallen fall [fɔ:l]
fallen lassen drop [drɒp]
falls if [ɪf]
falsch wrong [rɒŋ] • **in die falsche Richtung** the wrong way
Familie family ['fæməli]
Fan fan [fæn]
fangen catch [kætʃ]
fantastisch fantastic [fæn'tæstɪk]
Farbe colour ['kʌlə] • **Welche Farbe hat ...?** What colour is ...?
Farm farm [fɑ:m]
Februar February ['februəri]
Federball badminton ['bædmɪntən]
Federmäppchen pencil case ['pensl keɪs]
fehlen be missing ['mɪsɪŋ]
Fehler mistake [mɪ'steɪk]
Feind/in enemy ['enəmi]
Feld 1. field [fi:ld] • **auf dem Feld** in the field
2. *(bei Brettspielen)* **Geh ein Feld vor.** Move on one space. [speɪs] • **Geh ein Feld zurück.** Move back one space.
Fenster window ['wɪndəʊ]
Ferien holiday(s) ['hɒlədeɪ(z)]
Ferienwohnung holiday flat ['hɒlədeɪ flæt]
Fernsehen television ['telɪvɪʒn]; TV [ti:'vi:] • **im Fernsehen** on TV
fernsehen watch TV [,wɒtʃ ti:'vi:]
fertig *(bereit)* ready ['redi] • **sich fertig machen (für)** *(sich vorbereiten)* get ready (for) • **Dinge fertig machen (für)** *(vorbereiten)* get things ready (for)
Feuer fire ['faɪə]
Feuerwehrfrau firewoman ['faɪə,wʊmən]
Feuerwehrmann fireman ['faɪəmən]
Fieber haben have a temperature ['temprətʃə]
► S.164 I don't feel well
Film film [fɪlm]
Filmstar film star ['fɪlm stɑ:]
Filzstift felt tip ['felt tɪp]
finden *(entdecken)* find [faɪnd]

Finder finder ['faɪndə]
Finger finger ['fɪŋgə]
Fisch fish, *pl* fish [fɪʃ]
Flasche bottle ['bɒtl] • **eine Flasche Milch** a bottle of milk
Fleisch meat [mi:t]
fliegen fly [flaɪ]
Flug flight [flaɪt]
Flugzeug plane [pleɪn] • **im Flugzeug** on the plane
Flur hall [hɔ:l]
Fluss river ['rɪvə]
Flusspferd hippo ['hɪpəʊ]
flüstern whisper ['wɪspə]
folgen follow ['fɒləʊ]
Football American football [əˌmerɪkən 'fʊtbɔ:l]
Forscher/in explorer [ɪk'splɔ:rə]
fort away [ə'weɪ]
Foto photo ['fəʊtəʊ] • **auf dem Foto** in the photo • **Fotos machen** take photos
Fotoapparat camera ['kæmərə]
fotografieren take photos [teɪk 'fəʊtəʊz]
Frage question ['kwestʃn] • **Fragen stellen** ask questions • **Kommt nicht in Frage!** No way!
fragen ask [ɑ:sk] • **nach etwas fragen** ask about sth. • **jn. nach dem Weg fragen** ask sb. the way
sich fragen wonder ['wʌndə]
Französisch French [frentʃ]
Frau woman ['wʊmən], *pl* women ['wɪmɪn] • **Frau Brown** Mrs Brown ['mɪsɪz]; Ms Brown [mɪz, məz] • **Frau White** *(unverheiratet)* Miss White [mɪs]
frei [fri:] free • **freie Zeit** free time
Freitag Friday ['fraɪdeɪ, 'fraɪdi]
freitagabends, am Freitagabend on Friday evening • **freitagnachts, Freitagnacht** on Friday night
Freizeit free time [ˌfri: 'taɪm]
Freizeitzentrum, -park leisure centre ['leʒə sentə]
Fremdenverkehrsamt tourist information ['tʊərɪst_ɪnfəˌmeɪʃn]
Freund/in friend [frend]
frieren be cold [kəʊld]
froh happy ['hæpi]
Frosch frog [frɒg]
Frucht, Früchte fruit [fru:t]
früh early ['ɜ:li]
Frühling spring [sprɪŋ]
Frühstück breakfast ['brekfəst] **zum Frühstück** for breakfast
frühstücken have breakfast
Frühstückspension Bed and Breakfast (B&B) [ˌbed_ən 'brekfəst]
Fuchs fox [fɒks]
fühlen; sich fühlen feel [fi:l]
► S.164 I don't feel well
Füller pen [pen]
für for [fə, fɔ:]
furchtbar terrible ['terəbl]; awful ['ɔ:fl]
fürchterlich aussehen be a mess [mes]
Fuß foot [fʊt], *pl* feet [fi:t]
Fußball football ['fʊtbɔ:l] • **Fußball spielen** play football
Fußballschuhe, -stiefel football boots ['fʊtbɔ:l bu:ts]
Fußboden floor [flɔ:]
Futter food [fu:d]
füttern feed [fi:d]

G

gähnen yawn [jɔ:n]
ganz: den ganzen Tag (lang) all day **die ganze Zeit** all the time • **Das ist ganz falsch.** This is all wrong.
Garage garage ['gærɑ:ʒ]
Garten garden ['gɑ:dn]
Gast guest [gest]; *(Besucher/in)* visitor ['vɪzɪtə]
Gebäude building ['bɪldɪŋ]
geben give [gɪv] • **es gibt** *(es ist vorhanden)* there's; *(es sind vorhanden)* there are
geboren sein/werden be born [bɔ:n]
gebrochen *(Arm, Bein)* broken ['brəʊkən]
Geburtstag birthday ['bɜ:θdeɪ] **Herzlichen Glückwunsch zum Geburtstag.** Happy birthday. **Ich habe im Mai / am 13. Juni Geburtstag.** My birthday is in May / on 13th June. • **Wann hast du Geburtstag?** When's your birthday?
Gedicht poem ['pəʊɪm]
gefährlich dangerous ['deɪndʒərəs]
Gegenteil opposite ['ɒpəzɪt]
Gegenwart present ['preznt]
gehen **1.** go [gəʊ]; *(zu Fuß gehen)* walk [wɔ:k]; *(weggehen)* leave [li:v] **Auf geht's!** Let's go. • **einkaufen gehen** go shopping; shop [ʃɒp] **Geh ein Feld vor.** Move on one space. [speɪs] • **Geh ein Feld zurück.** Move back one space. **in die Sauna gehen** have a sauna **ins Bett gehen** go to bed • **ins Kino gehen** go to the cinema **nach Hause gehen** go home **reiten/schwimmen gehen** go riding/swimming • **spazieren gehen** go for a walk [wɔ:k] **2. Es geht mir/ihm gut.** I'm/He's fine. [faɪn] **3. Es geht um Mr Green.** This is about Mr Green. **4. Das geht dich nichts an!** Mind your own business. [ˌmaɪnd jər_ˌəʊn 'bɪznəs]
Geist *(Gespenst)* ghost [gəʊst]
Gelächter laughter ['lɑ:ftə]
gelangen *(hinkommen)* get [get]
gelb yellow ['jeləʊ]
Geld money ['mʌni] • **Geld ausgeben (für)** spend money (on) [spend]
Geldbörse purse [pɜ:s]
genießen enjoy [ɪn'dʒɔɪ]
genug enough [ɪ'nʌf]
geöffnet open ['əʊpən]
Geografie geography [dʒi'ɒgrəfi]
gepflegt neat [ni:t]
gerade *(soeben)* just [dʒʌst] • **jetzt gerade** *(in diesem Moment)* right now [raɪt 'naʊ]
► S.163 The present perfect: statements
geradeaus weiter straight on [streɪt_'ɒn]
Geräusch noise [nɔɪz]
gerecht fair [feə]
gern: Ich hätte gern … / Ich möchte gern … I'd like … (= I would like …) **Ich schwimme/tanze/… gern.** I like swimming/dancing/… • **Ich würde gern über … reden** I'd like to talk about … • **Gern geschehen.** You're welcome. ['welkəm]
gernhaben like [laɪk]
Geruch smell
Geschäft shop [ʃɒp]
geschehen (mit) happen (to) ['hæpən]
Geschenk present ['preznt]
Geschichte **1.** story ['stɔ:ri] **2.** *(vergangene Zeiten)* history ['hɪstri]
geschieden divorced [dɪ'vɔ:st]
Geschirrspülmaschine dishwasher ['dɪʃwɒʃə]
geschlossen closed [kləʊzd]
Gesicht face [feɪs]
Gespenst *(Geist)* ghost [gəʊst]
gestalten design [dɪ'zaɪn]
gestern yesterday ['jestədeɪ, 'jestədi] **gestern Morgen/Nachmittag/Abend** yesterday morning/afternoon/evening • **die Hausaufgaben von gestern** yesterday's homework
gesund healthy ['helθi]; well [wel]
► S.164 I don't feel well
Getränk drink [drɪŋk]
Gewinn prize [praɪz]
gewinnen win [wɪn]
Gewinner/in winner ['wɪnə]
Gewitter storm [stɔ:m]
gewöhnlich usually ['ju:ʒuəli]
Giraffe giraffe [dʒə'rɑ:f]

Gitarre guitar [gɪ'tɑ:] • **Gitarre spielen** play the guitar
Glas glass [glɑ:s] • **ein Glas Wasser** a glass of water
glauben think [θɪŋk] • **Glaubst du das wirklich?** Do you really think so?
gleich sein/aussehen be/look the same [seɪm]
Glück: Viel Glück (bei/mit ...)! Good luck (with ...)! [gʊd 'lʌk] • **zum Glück** *(glücklicherweise)* luckily ['lʌkɪli]
glücklich happy ['hæpi]
glücklicherweise luckily ['lʌkɪli]
Grad degree [dɪ'gri:]
Grammatik grammar ['græmə]
grau grey [greɪ]
grauenhaft horrible ['hɒrəbl]
groß big [bɪg]; large [lɑ:dʒ]
▸ S.167 big – large – great
großartig great [greɪt]
▸ S.167 big – large – great
Größe *(Schuhgröße usw.)* size [saɪz]
Großeltern grandparents ['grænpeərənts]
Großmutter grandmother ['grænmʌðə]
Großstadt city ['sɪti]
Großvater grandfather ['grænfɑ:ðə]
grün green [gri:n]
Grund reason ['ri:zn] • **aus vielen Gründen** for lots of reasons
Gruppe group [gru:p]; *(Musikgruppe)* band [bænd]
gruselig scary ['skeəri]
Gruß: Liebe Grüße, ... *(Briefschluss)* Love ... [lʌv]
Grüß Dilip von mir. Say hi to Dilip for me.
gucken look [lʊk]
gut good [gʊd]; *(okay)* OK [əʊ'keɪ]; *(in Ordnung)* all right [ɔ:l 'raɪt]; *(gesundheitlich gut, wohlauf)* well [wel]; fine [faɪn] • **Es geht mir/ihm gut.** I'm/He's fine. • **gute Arbeit leisten** do a good job • **Guten Morgen.** Good morning. • **Guten Tag.** Hello.; *(nachmittags)* Good afternoon. • **Das hast du gut gemacht.** You did well.
▸ S.157 good – better – best
▸ S.164 I don't feel well

H

Haar, Haare hair *(no pl)* [heə]
haben have got ['hæv gɒt]; have [həv, hæv] • **Ich habe keinen Stuhl.** I haven't got a chair. • **Ich habe am 13. Juni/im Mai Geburtstag.** My birthday is on 13th June/in May. **Wann hast du Geburtstag?** When's your birthday? • **haben wollen** want [wɒnt] • **Was haben wir als Hausaufgabe auf?** What's for homework?
Hafen harbour ['hɑ:bə]
Hähnchen chicken ['tʃɪkɪn]
halb zwölf half past 11 [hɑ:f]
Hallo! Hi! [haɪ]; Hello. [hə'ləʊ]
Hals throat [θrəʊt]
Halsschmerzen haben have a sore throat [sɔ: 'θrəʊt]
▸ S.164 I don't feel well
halten 1. hold [həʊld]
2. etwas warm/kühl/offen/... halten keep sth. warm/cool/open/... [ki:p]
3. Halt den Mund! Shut up. [ˌʃʌt_'ʌp]
4. Was hältst du von ...? What do you think about/of ...?
▸ S.165 (to) think
Hamburger hamburger ['hæmbɜ:gə]
Hamster hamster ['hæmstə]
Hand hand [hænd]
Handy mobile (phone) ['məʊbaɪl]
Happyend happy ending [ˌhæpi_'endɪŋ]
hart hard [hɑ:d] • **hart arbeiten** work hard
hassen hate [heɪt]
häufig often ['ɒfn]
Haus house [haʊs] • **im Haus der Shaws / bei den Shaws zu Hause** at the Shaws' house • **nach Hause gehen** go home [həʊm] • **nach Hause kommen** come home; get home • **zu Hause** at home
Hausaufgabe(n) homework *(no pl)* ['həʊmwɜ:k] • **die Hausaufgabe(n) machen** do homework • **Was haben wir als Hausaufgabe auf?** What's for homework?
Hausmeister/in caretaker ['keəteɪkə]
Haustier pet [pet]
Haustür front door [ˌfrʌnt 'dɔ:]
Heim home [həʊm]
heiß hot [hɒt]
heißen **1. Ich heiße ...** My name is ... **Wie heißt du?** What's your name?
2. Sie heißen dich in ... willkommen They welcome you to ... ['welkəm]
helfen help [help]
Helikopter helicopter ['helɪkɒptə]
hell *(leuchtend)* bright [braɪt]
Hemd shirt [ʃɜ:t]
herauf up [ʌp]
heraus out [aʊt] • **aus ... heraus** out of ... ['aʊt_əv]
▸ S.154 out
herausfinden find out [ˌfaɪnd_'aʊt] **etwas über etwas herausfinden** learn sth. about sth. [lɜ:n]
herausnehmen take out [ˌteɪk_'aʊt]
herbringen bring [brɪŋ]
Herbst autumn ['ɔ:təm]
Herd cooker ['kʊkə]
hereinkommen come in [ˌkʌm_'ɪn]
Herr Brown Mr Brown ['mɪstə]
herum: anders herum the other way round [raʊnd] • **um ... herum** round
herumgeben pass round [ˌpɑ:s 'raʊnd]
herunter down [daʊn]
herunterfallen (von) fall off [ˌfɔ:l_'ɒf]
Herz heart [hɑ:t]
Herzlichen Glückwunsch zum Geburtstag. Happy birthday. [ˌhæpi 'bɜ:θdeɪ]
heute today [tə'deɪ] • **heute Morgen/Nachmittag/Abend** this morning/afternoon/evening **heute Nacht** tonight [tə'naɪt] **das Programm von heute** today's programme
heutig: das heutige Programm today's programme
hier here [hɪə] • **Hier bitte.** *(Bitte sehr.)* Here you are. • **hier drinnen** in here [ˌɪn 'hɪə] • **hier entlang** this way ['ðɪs weɪ] • **Hier spricht Isabel. / Hier ist Isabel.** *(am Telefon)* This is Isabel. • **Hier steht: ... / Es heißt hier: ...** *(im Text)* It says here: ...
▸ S.164 The text says ...
hierher here [hɪə]
Hilfe help [help]
Himmel sky [skaɪ]
hinauf up [ʌp] • **den Hügel hinauf** up the hill
hinaufklettern (auf) climb [klaɪm]
hinaus out [aʊt] • **aus ... hinaus** out of ... ['aʊt_əv]
▸ S.154 out
hinein: in ... hinein into ... ['ɪntə, 'ɪntʊ]
hinfallen fall [fɔ:l]; fall down
hinkommen *(gelangen)* get [get]
hinsetzen: sich hinsetzen sit down
hinstellen: sich hinstellen stand [stænd]
hinter behind [bɪ'haɪnd]
Hintergrund background ['bækgraʊnd]
Hintertür back door
hinüber zu/nach ... over to ... ['əʊvə]
hinunter down [daʊn]
hinzufügen (zu) add (to) [æd]
Hirsch deer, *pl* deer [dɪə]
Hobby hobby ['hɒbi], *pl* hobbies
hochheben: etwas hochheben pick sth. up [ˌpɪk_'ʌp]

hochsehen (von) look up (from) [ˌlʊk_ˈʌp]
Hockey hockey [ˈhɒki]
Hockeyschuhe hockey shoes [ˈhɒki ʃuːz]
Hof yard [jɑːd] • **auf dem Hof** in the yard
hoffen hope [həʊp]
holen *(besorgen)* get [get]
hören hear [hɪə] • **Na hör mal!** Come on. [ˌkʌm_ˈɒn]
Hose trousers *(pl)* [ˈtraʊzəz]
▸ S.156 Plural words
Hotel hotel [həʊˈtel]
Hotline hotline [ˈhɒtlaɪn]
hübsch pretty [ˈprɪti]
Hubschrauber helicopter [ˈhelɪkɒptə]
Hügel hill [hɪl]
Huhn chicken [ˈtʃɪkɪn]
Hülle cover [ˈkʌvə]
Hund dog [dɒg]
hundert hundred [ˈhʌndrəd]
Hurra! Hooray! [huˈreɪ]
Hut hat [hæt]

I

ich I [aɪ] • **Ich auch.** Me too. [ˌmiː ˈtuː] • **Das bin ich.** That's me. **Warum ich?** Why me?
Idee idea [aɪˈdɪə]
Igel hedgehog [ˈhedʒhɒg]
ihm him; *(bei Dingen, Tieren)* it
ihn him; *(bei Dingen, Tieren)* it
ihnen them [ðəm, ðem]
Ihnen *(höfliche Anrede)* you [juː]
ihr *(Plural von „du")* you [juː] • **ihr zwei** you two [ˌjuː ˈtuː]
ihr: Hilf ihr. Help her. [hə, hɜː]
ihr(e) *(besitzanzeigend)* *(zu „she")* her [hə, hɜː]; *(zu „they")* their [ðeə]
Ihr(e) *(höfliche Anrede)* your [jɔː]
ihrer, ihre, ihrs *(zu „she")* hers [hɜːz]; *(zu „they")* theirs [ðeəz]
▸ S.156 Possessive pronouns
Ihrer, Ihre, Ihrs *(höfliche Anrede)* yours [jɔːz]
▸ S.156 Possessive pronouns
im: im Fernsehen on TV • **im Flugzeug** on the plane • **im Haus der Shaws** at the Shaws' house **im Mai** in May • **im Radio** on the radio • **im Zug** on the train
Imbiss snack [snæk]
Imbissstube café [ˈkæfeɪ]
immer always [ˈɔːlweɪz] • **immer noch** still [stɪl]
in in • **in ... (hinein)** into ... [ˈɪntə, ˈɪntʊ] • **in den Zug/Bus einsteigen** get on the train/bus • **in der ...straße** in ... Street • **in der Hamiltonstraße 7** at 7 Hamilton Street • **in der Nacht** at night **in der Nähe von** near • **in der Pause** *(zwischen Schulstunden)* at break • **in der Schule** at school **in die falsche Richtung** the wrong way • **in die Sauna gehen** have a sauna • **in Eile sein** be in a hurry **ins Bett gehen** go to bed • **ins Kino gehen** go to the cinema • **in Urlaub fahren** go on holiday • **in welche Richtung?** which way?
Information(en) (über) information (about/on) *(no pl)* [ˌɪnfəˈmeɪʃn]
Ingenieur/in engineer [ˌendʒɪˈnɪə]
Inliner skates [skeɪts] • **Inliner fahren** skate
innen (drin) inside [ˌɪnˈsaɪd]
Innenstadt city centre [ˌsɪti ˈsentə]
Insel island [ˈaɪlənd]
installieren install [ɪnˈstɔːl]
interessant interesting [ˈɪntrəstɪŋ]
Interview interview [ˈɪntəvjuː]
interviewen interview [ˈɪntəvjuː]
irgendetwas anything [ˈeniθɪŋ]
▸ S.169 something – anything
irgendjemand anybody [ˈenibɒdi]
▸ S.169 somebody – anybody
irgendwelche any [ˈeni]
irgendwo(hin) somewhere [ˈsʌmweə]; anywhere [ˈeniweə]
▸ S.169 somewhere – anywhere
irren: sich irren be wrong [rɒŋ]

J

ja yes [jes]
Jacke, Jackett jacket [ˈdʒækɪt]
Jahr year [jɪə]
Jahrgangsstufe year [jɪə]
Jahrhundert century [ˈsentʃəri]
Januar January [ˈdʒænjuəri]
je? *(jemals?)* ever? [ˈevə]
▸ S.164 The present perfect: questions
Jeans jeans *(pl)* [dʒiːnz]
▸ S.156 Plural words
jede(r, s) ... *(Begleiter)* **1.** every ... [ˈevri] **2.** *(jeder einzelne)* each ... [iːtʃ]
jeder *(alle)* everybody [ˈevribɒdi]
jemals? ever? [ˈevə]
▸ S.164 The present perfect: questions
jemand somebody [ˈsʌmbədi]; *(irgendjemand)* anybody [ˈenibɒdi]
▸ S.169 somebody – anybody
jene(r, s) *(Singular)* that [ðət, ðæt]; *(Plural)* those [ðəʊz]
jetzt now [naʊ] • **jetzt gerade, jetzt sofort** right now
Job job [dʒɒb]
jubeln cheer [tʃɪə]
Judo judo [ˈdʒuːdəʊ] • **Judo machen** do judo
Jugend- junior [ˈdʒuːniə]
Jugendliche(r) kid [kɪd]; teenager [ˈtiːneɪdʒə]
Juli July [dʒuˈlaɪ]
jung young [jʌŋ]
Junge boy [bɔɪ]
Juni June [dʒuːn]
Junioren- junior [ˈdʒuːniə]

K

Käfig cage [keɪdʒ]
Kalender calendar [ˈkælɪndə]
kalt cold [kəʊld]
Kamel camel [ˈkæml]
Kamera camera [ˈkæmərə]
Känguru kangaroo [ˌkæŋgəˈruː]
Kaninchen rabbit [ˈræbɪt]
Kantine canteen [kænˈtiːn]
Kappe cap [kæp]
kaputt broken [ˈbrəʊkən]
Karotte carrot [ˈkærət]
Karte *(Post-, Spielkarte)* card [kɑːd]
Kartoffel potato [pəˈteɪtəʊ], *pl* -toes
Kartoffelchips crisps *(pl)* [krɪsps]
Käse cheese [tʃiːz]
Kästchen, Kasten box [bɒks]
Katze cat [kæt]
kaufen buy [baɪ]
Kaufhaus department store [dɪˈpɑːtmənt stɔː]
Kehle throat [θrəʊt]
kein(e) no; not a; not (...) any • **Ich habe keinen Stuhl.** I haven't got a chair. • **keine Musik mehr** no more music
Keks biscuit [ˈbɪskɪt]
Kellner waiter [ˈweɪtə]
Kellnerin waitress [ˈweɪtrəs]
kennen know [nəʊ]
kennenlernen meet [miːt]
kennzeichnen mark up [ˌmɑːk_ˈʌp]
Kind child [tʃaɪld], *pl* children [ˈtʃɪldrən]; kid [kɪd] • **ein Kind bekommen** have a child
Kino cinema [ˈsɪnəmə] • **ins Kino gehen** go to the cinema
Kirche church [tʃɜːtʃ]
Kirsche cherry [ˈtʃeri]
Kiste box [bɒks]
Kiwi kiwi [ˈkiːwiː]
Klang sound [saʊnd]
klar clear [klɪə]
Klasse class [klɑːs]; form [fɔːm]
Klassenkamerad/in classmate [ˈklɑːsmeɪt]
Klassenlehrer/in class teacher; form teacher
Klassenzimmer classroom [ˈklɑːsruːm]

klatschen: Beifall klatschen cheer [tʃɪə]
Klavier piano [pi'ænəʊ] • **Klavier spielen** play the piano
kleben: (auf-, ein)kleben glue [glu:]
Klebestift glue stick ['glu: stɪk]
Klebstoff glue [glu:]
Kleid dress [dres]
Kleider *(Kleidungsstücke)* clothes *(pl)* [kləʊðz, kləʊz]
Kleiderschrank wardrobe ['wɔ:drəʊb]
Kleidung(sstücke) clothes *(pl)* [kləʊðz, kləʊz]
klein little ['lɪtl]; small [smɔ:l]
Kleinstadt town [taʊn]
klettern climb [klaɪm] • **Klettere auf einen Baum.** Climb a tree.
klingeln ring [rɪŋ]
klingen sound [saʊnd]
Klinik clinic ['klɪnɪk]
Klub club [klʌb]
klug clever ['klevə]
knapp: Das war knapp. That was close. [kləʊs]
Kneipe pub [pʌb]
Knie knee [ni:]
kochen cook [kʊk]
Koffer suitcase ['su:tkeɪs]
Koje *(Etagenbett)* bunk (bed) [bʌŋk]
komisch funny ['fʌni]
kommen come [kʌm]; *(hinkommen)* get [get] • **Ich komme aus ...** I'm from ... • **Wo kommst du her?** Where are you from? • **nach Hause kommen** come home; get home • **zu spät kommen** be late **Kommt nicht in Frage!** No way! **Ach komm!** Come on. [ˌkʌm‿'ɒn] **Na los, komm.** Come on.
König king [kɪŋ]
können can [kən, kæn] • **ich kann nicht ...** I can't ... [kɑ:nt] • **Kann ich Ihnen helfen? / Was kann ich für Sie tun?** *(im Laden)* Can I help you?
konnte(n): ich/er konnte ... I/he could ... [kəd, kʊd]
kontrollieren *(überprüfen)* check [tʃek]
Kopf head [hed]
Kopfschmerzen headache ['hedeɪk]
► S.164 I don't feel well
Kopie copy ['kɒpi]
kopieren copy ['kɒpi]
Korb basket ['bɑ:skɪt] • **ein Korb Äpfel** a basket of apples
Körper body ['bɒdi]
korrigieren correct [kə'rekt]
kosten *(Essen probieren)* try [traɪ]
kosten: Er/Sie/Es kostet 1 Pfund. It's £1. • **Sie kosten 35 Pence.** They are 35p. • **Wie viel kostet/kosten ...?** How much is/are ...?
kostenlos free [fri:]
köstlich delicious [dɪ'lɪʃəs]
Kram stuff [stʌf]
krank ill [ɪl]
► S.164 I don't feel well
Krankenhaus hospital ['hɒspɪtl]
kriegen get [get]
Krokodil crocodile ['krɒkədaɪl]
Krug jug [dʒʌg] • **ein Krug Orangensaft** a jug of orange juice
Küche kitchen ['kɪtʃɪn]
Kuchen cake [keɪk]
Kugelschreiber pen [pen]
Kuh cow [kaʊ]
kühl cool [ku:l]
Kühlschrank fridge [frɪdʒ]
Kummer worry ['wʌri]
kümmern 1. sich um etwas/jn. kümmern look after sth./sb. [ˌlʊk‿'ɑ:ftə]
2. Kümmere dich um deine eigenen Angelegenheiten! Mind your own business. [ˌmaɪnd jər‿ˌəʊn 'bɪznəs]
Kunde, Kundin customer ['kʌstəmə]
Kunst art [ɑ:t]
kurz short [ʃɔ:t] • **kurze Hose** shorts *(pl)* [ʃɔ:ts]
► S.156 Plural words

L

lächeln smile [smaɪl]
Lächeln smile [smaɪl]
lachen laugh [lɑ:f]
Laden *(Geschäft)* shop [ʃɒp]
Lampe lamp [læmp]
Land *(auch als Gegensatz zur Stadt)* country ['kʌntri]; *(Grund und Boden)* land [lænd] • **auf dem Land** in the country
landen land [lænd]
Landkarte map [mæp]
lang long [lɒŋ] • **drei Tage lang** for three days
langsam slow [sləʊ]
langweilig boring ['bɔ:rɪŋ]
Lärm noise [nɔɪz]
lärmend noisy ['nɔɪzi]
Lasagne lasagne [lə'zænjə]
lassen let [let] • **Lass uns ... / Lasst uns ...** Let's ... • **Lass das!** Stop that!
Lauf run [rʌn]
laufen run [rʌn]
Läufer/in runner ['rʌnə]
laut loud [laʊd]; *(lärmend)* noisy ['nɔɪzi]
Laut sound [saʊnd]
läuten ring [rɪŋ]
leben live [lɪv]
Leben life [laɪf], *pl* lives [laɪvz]
Lebensmittel food [fu:d]
lecker delicious [dɪ'lɪʃəs]
ledig single ['sɪŋgl]
leer empty ['empti]
legen *(hin-, ablegen)* put [pʊt]
lehren teach [ti:tʃ]
Lehrer/in teacher ['ti:tʃə]
leicht *(nicht schwierig)* easy ['i:zi]
leider I'm afraid [ə'freɪd]
leidtun: Tut mir leid. I'm sorry. ['sɒri]
leise quiet ['kwaɪət]
Lektion *(im Schulbuch)* unit ['ju:nɪt]
lernen learn [lɜ:n]
Lern- und Arbeitstechniken study skills ['stʌdi skɪlz]
lesen read [ri:d]
Leser/in reader ['ri:də]
letzte(r, s) last [lɑ:st]
leuchtend bright [braɪt]
Leute people ['pi:pl]
Liebe love [lʌv]
Liebe Grüße, ... *(Briefschluss)* Love ... [lʌv]
lieben love [lʌv]
Lieber Jay, ... Dear Jay ... [dɪə]
lieber: etwas lieber mögen like sth. better
Liebling dear [dɪə]; sweetheart ['swi:thɑ:t]
Lieblings-: meine Lieblingsfarbe my favourite colour ['feɪvərɪt]
Lied song [sɒŋ]
lila purple ['pɜ:pl]
Limonade lemonade [ˌlemə'neɪd]
Lineal ruler ['ru:lə]
linke(r, s) left [left] • **links, auf der linken Seite** on the left • **(nach) links abbiegen** turn left • **nach links schauen** look left
► S.152 left – right
Liste list [lɪst]
Livemusik live music [laɪv]
Lokal *(Kneipe)* pub [pʌb]
Löwe lion ['laɪən]

M

machen do [du:]; make [meɪk] • **die Hausaufgabe(n) machen** do homework • **einen Ausflug machen** go on a trip • **einen Spaziergang machen** go for a walk **eine Übung machen** do an exercise • **ein Picknick machen** have a picnic • **Fotos machen** take photos • **Judo machen** do judo • **sich Notizen machen** take notes • **sich Sorgen machen (um, wegen)** worry (about) ['wʌri] **(Zauber-)Kunststücke machen** do

tricks • **Reiten macht Spaß.** Riding is fun.
Mädchen girl [gɜ:l]
Magazin *(Zeitschrift)* magazine [ˌmægəˈzi:n]
Magen stomach [ˈstʌmək]
Magenschmerzen stomach ache [ˈstʌmək‿eɪk]
► S.164 I don't feel well
Magst du ...? Do you like ...? [laɪk] *(siehe auch unter „mögen")*
Mai May [meɪ]
Make-up make-up [ˈmeɪkʌp]
Mal(e); -mal time(s) [taɪm(z)]
malen paint [peɪnt]
Maler/in painter [ˈpeɪntə]
Mama mum [mʌm]
manchmal sometimes [ˈsʌmtaɪmz]
Mann man [mæn], *pl* men [men]
Mannschaft team [ti:m]
Mappe *(des Sprachenportfolios)* dossier [ˈdɒsieɪ]
markieren mark up [ˌmɑ:k‿ˈʌp]
Markt market [ˈmɑ:kɪt]
Marmelade *(Orangenmarmelade)* marmalade [ˈmɑ:məleɪd]
März March [mɑ:tʃ]
Mathematik maths [mæθs]
Matrose sailor [ˈseɪlə]
Mauer wall [wɔ:l]
Maulwurf mole [məʊl]
Maus mouse [maʊs], *pl* mice [maɪs]
Mediation *(Sprachmittlung)* mediation [ˌmi:diˈeɪʃn]
Meer sea [si:]
Meerschweinchen guinea pig [ˈgɪni pɪg]
mehr more [mɔ:] • **mehr als** more than • **mehr als ich** more than me • **viel mehr** lots more **keine Musik mehr** no more music
Meile *(= ca. 1,6 km)* mile [maɪl]
meilenweit for miles [maɪlz]
mein(e) ... my ... [maɪ] • **meine neuen** my new ones [wʌnz]
meinen think [θɪŋk]; *(sagen wollen)* mean [mi:n] • **Meinst du wirklich?** Do you really think so?
meiner, meine, meins mine [maɪn]
► S.156 Possessive pronouns
meist: (der/die/das) meiste ...; am meisten most [məʊst] • **die meisten Leute** most people
meistens usually [ˈju:ʒuəli]
Meister/in *(Champion)* champion [ˈtʃæmpiən]
Menschen people [ˈpi:pl]
merken: sich etwas merken remember sth. [rɪˈmembə]
Meter metre [ˈmi:tə]
mich me [mi:]
Milch milk [mɪlk]
Mindmap mind map [ˈmaɪnd mæp]
Minute minute [ˈmɪnɪt]
mir me [mi:]
mit with [wɪð] • **mit dem Auto/ Zug/Rad/... fahren** go by car/ train/bike/...
mitbringen bring [brɪŋ]
mitmachen: bei etwas/jm. mitmachen join sth./sb. [dʒɔɪn]
Mitschüler/in classmate [ˈklɑ:smeɪt]
Mittagessen lunch [lʌntʃ] • **zum Mittagessen** for lunch
Mittagspause lunch break [ˈlʌntʃ breɪk]
Mitte centre [ˈsentə]; middle (of) [ˈmɪdl]
Mitteilung *(Notiz)* note [nəʊt]
mittel(groß) medium [ˈmi:diəm]
Mittelteil middle [ˈmɪdl]
Mittwoch Wednesday [ˈwenzdeɪ, ˈwenzdi] *(siehe auch unter „Freitag")*
Mobiltelefon mobile phone [ˌməʊbaɪl ˈfəʊn]; mobile [ˈməʊbaɪl]
möchte: Ich möchte gern ... (haben) I'd like ... (= I would like ...) • **Ich möchte über ... reden** I'd like to talk about ... • **Möchtest du etwas (Saft) / ein paar (Kekse)?** Would you like some (juice/biscuits)?
Mode fashion [ˈfæʃn]
Modell*(-auto, -schiff; Fotomodell)* model [ˈmɒdl]
Moderator/in presenter [prɪˈzentə]
mögen like [laɪk]; *(sehr mögen)* love [lʌv] • **etwas lieber mögen** like sth. better
möglich possible [ˈpɒsəbl]
Möhre carrot [ˈkærət]
Moment mal! Wait a minute. [ˈmɪnɪt]
Monat month [mʌnθ]
Mond moon [mu:n]
Monster monster [ˈmɒnstə]
Montag Monday [ˈmʌndeɪ, ˈmʌndi] *(siehe auch unter „Freitag")*
morgen tomorrow [təˈmɒrəʊ] • **das Wetter von morgen** tomorrow's weather
Morgen morning [ˈmɔ:nɪŋ] • **am Morgen, morgens** in the morning **Guten Morgen.** Good morning. **Montagmorgen** Monday morning
MP3-Spieler MP3 player [ˌempi:ˈθri: ˌpleɪə]
müde tired [ˈtaɪəd]
Müll rubbish [ˈrʌbɪʃ]
Mülltonne bin [bɪn]; dustbin [ˈdʌstbɪn]
Multiple-Choice multiple choice [ˌmʌltɪpl ˈtʃɔɪs]
Mund mouth [maʊθ] • **Halt den Mund!** Shut up. [ˌʃʌt‿ˈʌp]
murren grumble [ˈgrʌmbl]
Museum museum [mjuˈzi:əm]
Musical musical [ˈmju:zɪkl]
Musik music [ˈmju:zɪk]
müssen have to; must [mʌst] **nicht müssen** needn't [ˈni:dnt]
► S.171 must – needn't – mustn't
Mutter mother [ˈmʌðə]
Mutti mum [mʌm]
Mütze cap [kæp]

N

Na ja ... / Na gut ... Oh well ... [əʊ ˈwel]
Na und? So? [səʊ]
nach 1. *(örtlich)* to [tə, tu] • **nach draußen** outside • **nach drinnen** inside • **nach Hause gehen** go home • **nach Hause kommen** come home; get home • **nach oben** up; *(im Haus)* upstairs [ˌʌpˈsteəz] • **nach unten** down; *(im Haus)* downstairs [ˌdaʊnˈsteəz]
2. *(zeitlich)* after [ˈɑ:ftə] • **Viertel nach 11** quarter past 11 [pɑ:st]
3. nach etwas fragen ask about sth. [əˈbaʊt]
Nachbar/in neighbour [ˈneɪbə]
nachdem after [ˈɑ:ftə]
nachdenken über think about
► S.165 (to) think
Nachmittag afternoon [ˌɑ:ftəˈnu:n] **am Nachmittag, nachmittags** in the afternoon
nächste(r, s): am nächsten Tag the next day [nekst] • **der Nächste sein** be next • **Was haben wir als Nächstes?** What have we got next?
Nacht night [naɪt] • **heute Nacht** tonight [təˈnaɪt] • **in der Nacht, nachts** at night
nahe (bei) near [nɪə]
Nähe: in der Nähe von near [nɪə]
Name name [neɪm]
Nase nose [nəʊz] • **die Nase voll haben (von etwas)** be fed up (with sth.) [ˌfed‿ˈʌp]
Nashorn rhino [ˈraɪnəʊ]
natürlich of course [əv ˈkɔ:s]
Naturwissenschaft science [ˈsaɪəns]
Nebel fog [fɒg]
neben next to [ˈnekst tə]
neblig foggy [ˈfɒgi]
nehmen take [teɪk] • **Wir nehmen es.** *(beim Einkaufen)* We'll take it.
nein no [nəʊ]
nennen *(rufen, bezeichnen)* call [kɔ:l]; *(benennen)* name [neɪm]
nervös nervous [ˈnɜ:vəs]
nett nice [naɪs]
neu new [nju:]

nicht not [nɒt] • **Du brauchst eine Schultasche, nicht wahr?** You need a school bag, right? [raɪt] • **Ich weiß es nicht.** I don't know. [ˌdəʊnt 'nəʊ]
noch nicht not (...) yet [jet]
▸ S.163 The present perfect: statements
nichts nothing ['nʌθɪŋ]; not (...) anything ['eniθɪŋ] • **Nichts zu danken.** You're welcome. ['welkəm]
▸ S.169 something – anything
nicken (mit) nod [nɒd]
nie, niemals never ['nevə]
▸ S.163 The present perfect: statements
niemand nobody ['nəʊbədi]; not (...) anybody ['enibɒdi]
▸ S.169 somebody – anybody
nirgendwo(hin) not (...) anywhere ['eniweə]
▸ S.169 somewhere – anywhere
noch: noch ein(e) ... another ... [ə'nʌðə] • **noch 45 Pence** another 45p • **noch einmal** again [ə'gen]
noch nicht not (...) yet [jet]
(immer) noch still [stɪl]
▸ S.163 The present perfect: statements
nörgeln grumble ['grʌmbl]
normalerweise usually ['ju:ʒuəli]
Notiz note [nəʊt] • **sich Notizen machen** take notes
November November [nəʊ'vembə]
null o [əʊ]; zero ['zɪərəʊ]
Nummer number ['nʌmbə]
nun now [naʊ] • **Nun, ...** Well, ... [wel]
nur only ['əʊnli]; just [dʒʌst] • **nur zum Spaß** just for fun

O

ob if [ɪf]
oben *(an der Spitze)* at the top (of) [tɒp]; *(im Haus)* upstairs [ˌʌp'steəz]
nach oben up; *(im Haus)* upstairs
Oberbegriff group word ['gru:p wɜ:d]
oberhalb von over ['əʊvə]
Oberteil top [tɒp]
Obst fruit [fru:t]
Obstkuchen pie [paɪ]
Obstsalat fruit salad ['fru:t ˌsæləd]
oder or [ɔ:] • **Das ist nicht dein Ernst, oder?** You're joking, aren't you?
offen open ['əʊpən]
öffnen open ['əʊpən]
oft often ['ɒfn]
ohne without [wɪ'ðaʊt]
Ohr ear [ɪə]
Ohrenschmerzen earache ['ɪəreɪk]
▸ S.164 I don't feel well
Ohrring earring ['ɪərɪŋ]
Oje! Oh dear! [əʊ 'dɪə]
okay OK [əʊ'keɪ]
Oktober October [ɒk'təʊbə]
Oma grandma ['grænmɑ:]; granny ['græni]
Onkel uncle ['ʌŋkl]
Opa grandpa ['grænpɑ:]
Orange orange ['ɒrɪndʒ]
orange(farben) orange ['ɒrɪndʒ]
Orangenmarmelade marmalade ['mɑ:məleɪd]
Orangensaft orange juice ['ɒrɪndʒ dʒu:s]
ordentlich tidy ['taɪdi]
Ordnung: in Ordnung all right [ɔ:l 'raɪt]; fine [faɪn]
Ort place [pleɪs]
Orts-, örtlich local ['ləʊkl]
Outfit *(Kleidung; Ausrüstung)* outfit ['aʊtfɪt]

P

paar: ein paar some [səm, sʌm]; *(einige wenige)* a few [fju:]
Paar: ein Paar a pair (of) [peə]
Päckchen packet ['pækɪt] • **ein Päckchen Pfefferminzbonbons** a packet of mints
packen pack [pæk]
Packung packet ['pækɪt] • **eine Packung Pfefferminzbonbons** a packet of mints
Paket parcel ['pɑ:sl]
pantomimisch darstellen mime [maɪm]
Papa dad [dæd]
Papagei parrot ['pærət]
Papier paper ['peɪpə]
Park park [pɑ:k]
Partner/in partner ['pɑ:tnə]
Party party ['pɑ:ti]
passen fit [fɪt]
passieren (mit) happen (to) ['hæpən]
Pause break [breɪk] • **in der Pause** *(zwischen Schulstunden)* at break
Pence pence (p) [pens]
Person person ['pɜ:sn]
Pfad path [pɑ:θ]
Pfefferminzbonbons mints [mɪnts]
pfeifen whistle ['wɪsl]
Pferd horse [hɔ:s]
Pfund *(britische Währung)* pound (£) [paʊnd] • **Es kostet 1 Pfund.** It's £1.
Piano piano [pi'ænəʊ]
Picknick picnic ['pɪknɪk] • **ein Picknick machen** have a picnic
piepsen bleep [bli:p]
Piepton bleep [bli:p]
pink(farben) pink [pɪŋk]
Pirat/in pirate ['paɪrət]
Pizza pizza ['pi:tsə]
Plan plan [plæn]
planen plan [plæn]
Planet planet ['plænɪt]
Platz *(Ort, Stelle)* place [pleɪs]
Plätzchen biscuit ['bɪskɪt]
plaudern chat [tʃæt]
plötzlich suddenly ['sʌdnli]
Polizei police *(pl)* [pə'li:s]
Polizeiwache, Polizeirevier police station [pə'li:s steɪʃn]
Polizist/in policeman [pə'li:smən]/ policewoman [pə'li:swʊmən]
Poltergeist poltergeist ['pəʊltəgaɪst]
Pommes frites chips *(pl)* [tʃɪps]
Popcorn popcorn ['pɒpkɔ:n]
Postamt post office ['pəʊst_ɒfɪs]
Poster poster ['pəʊstə]
Postkarte postcard ['pəʊstkɑ:d]
Präsentation presentation [ˌprezn'teɪʃn]
Preis *(Kaufpreis)* price [praɪs]; *(Gewinn)* prize [praɪz]
Probe *(am Theater)* rehearsal [rɪ'hɜ:sl]
proben *(am Theater)* rehearse [rɪ'hɜ:s]
probieren try [traɪ]
Problem problem ['prɒbləm]
Programm programme ['prəʊgræm]
Projekt (über, zu) project (on, about) ['prɒdʒekt] • **ein Projekt machen, durchführen** do a project
Prospekt brochure ['brəʊʃə]
prüfen *(überprüfen)* check [tʃek]
Prüfung test [test]
Publikum audience ['ɔ:dɪəns]
Pullover pullover ['pʊləʊvə]
Punkt *(bei Test, Quiz)* point [pɔɪnt]
putzen clean [kli:n] • **Ich putze mir die Zähne.** I clean my teeth.
Putzfrau, -mann cleaner ['kli:nə]

Q

Quiz quiz [kwɪz], *pl* quizzes ['kwɪzɪz]

R

Rad fahren cycle ['saɪkl]; ride a bike [ˌraɪd ə 'baɪk]
Radfahrt bike ride ['baɪk raɪd]
Radiergummi rubber ['rʌbə]
Radio radio ['reɪdiəʊ] • **im Radio** on the radio
Radweg cycle path ['saɪkl pɑ:θ]
Rap rap [ræp]
Ratespiel quiz [kwɪz], *pl* quizzes ['kwɪzɪz]
Raum room [ru:m, rʊm]
Recht haben be right [raɪt]
rechte(r, s) right [raɪt] • **rechts, auf der rechten Seite** on the right

(nach) rechts abbiegen turn right
nach rechts schauen look right
► S.152 left – right
rechtzeitig in time [ɪn 'taɪm]
recycelt recycled [ˌriː'saɪkld]
Recycling recycling [ˌriː'saɪklɪŋ]
reden (mit, über) talk (to, about) [tɔːk]; speak (to, about) [spiːk]
Wovon redest du? What are you talking about?
Regal(brett) shelf [ʃelf], *pl* shelves [ʃelvz]
Regen rain [reɪn]
regnen rain [reɪn]
regnerisch rainy ['reɪni]
Reh deer, *pl* deer [dɪə]
reich rich [rɪtʃ]
reichen *(weitergeben)* pass [pɑːs]
Reihe **1. Du bist an der Reihe.** It's your turn. [tɜːn]
2. *(Sendereihe, Serie)* series, *pl* series ['sɪəriːz]
Reise trip [trɪp]
reisen travel ['trævl]
reiten ride [raɪd] • **reiten gehen** go riding
Religion *(Religionsunterricht)* RE [ˌɑːr_'iː], Religious Education [rɪˌlɪdʒəs_edʒu'keɪʃn]
rennen run [rʌn]
Reportage (über) report (on) [rɪ'pɔːt]
Rest rest [rest]
Restaurant restaurant ['restrɒnt]; *(Imbissstube, Café)* café ['kæfeɪ]
Resultat result [rɪ'zʌlt]
retten save [seɪv]
Rettungshubschrauber rescue helicopter ['reskjuː ˌhelɪkɒptə]
richtig right [raɪt]
Richtung way [weɪ] • **in diese Richtung** this way • **in die falsche Richtung** the wrong way • **in welche Richtung?** which way?
► S.170 way
riechen smell [smel]
Ring ring [rɪŋ]
Rock skirt [skɜːt]
Rollenspiel role play ['rəʊl pleɪ]
Rollstuhl wheelchair ['wiːltʃeə]
römisch; Römer, Römerin Roman ['rəʊmən]
rosa pink [pɪŋk]
rot red [red]
Rückfahrkarte return ticket [rɪ'tɜːn ˌtɪkɪt]
rufen call [kɔːl]; shout [ʃaʊt] • **die Polizei rufen** call the police
ruhig quiet ['kwaɪət]
rund round [raʊnd]
Rundgang (durch das Haus) tour (of the house) [tʊə]

S

Sache thing [θɪŋ]
Saft juice [dʒuːs]
sagen say [seɪ] • **Sagt mir eure Namen.** Tell me your names. [tel]
Salat **1.** *(Kopfsalat)* lettuce ['letɪs]
2. *(Gericht, Beilage)* salad ['sæləd]
sammeln collect [kə'lekt]
Sammler/in collector [kə'lektə]
Samstag Saturday ['sætədeɪ, 'sætədi]
(siehe auch unter „Freitag")
Sandwich sandwich ['sænwɪtʃ, '-wɪdʒ]
Sänger/in singer ['sɪŋə]
Sanitäter/in paramedic [ˌpærə'medɪk]
Satz sentence ['sentəns]
sauber clean [kliːn] • **sauber machen** clean
sauer sein (auf) be cross (with) [krɒs]
Sauna sauna ['sɔːnə] • **in die Sauna gehen** have a sauna
Schachtel packet ['pækɪt]; box [bɒks]
Schaf sheep, *pl* sheep [ʃiːp]
Schale bowl [bəʊl] • **eine Schale Cornflakes** a bowl of cornflakes
Schatz dear [dɪə]; sweetheart ['swiːthɑːt]
schauen look [lʊk] • **nach links/ rechts schauen** look left/right
Schaufenster shop window [ˌʃɒp 'wɪndəʊ]
Schauspiel drama ['drɑːmə]
Schauspieler/in actor ['æktə]
scheinen *(Sonne)* shine [ʃaɪn]
scherzen joke [dʒəʊk]
scheu shy [ʃaɪ]
scheußlich horrible ['hɒrəbl]
schicken (an) send (to) [send]
schieben push [pʊʃ]
Schiff boat [bəʊt]; ship [ʃɪp]
Schildkröte tortoise ['tɔːtəs]
Schinkenspeck bacon ['beɪkən]
Schlafanzug pyjamas *(pl)* [pə'dʒɑːməz]
schlafen sleep [sliːp]; *(nicht wach sein)* be asleep [ə'sliːp]
Schlafzimmer bedroom ['bedruːm]
schlagen hit [hɪt]
Schlange snake [sneɪk]
schlau clever ['klevə]; smart [smɑːt]
schlecht bad [bæd] • **schlechter** worse [wɜːs] • **am schlechtesten; der/die/das schlechteste** (the) worst [wɜːst]
► S.157 bad – worse – worst
schließen *(zumachen)* close [kləʊz]
schließlich at last [ət 'lɑːst]
schlimm bad [bæd] • **schlimmer** worse [wɜːs] • **am schlimmsten; der/die/das schlimmste** (the) worst [wɜːst]
► S.157 bad – worse – worst

Schlittschuhbahn ice rink ['aɪs rɪŋk]
Schloss castle ['kɑːsl]
Schluss end
Schlüssel key [kiː]
Schlüsselring key ring ['kiː rɪŋ]
Schlüsselwort key word ['kiː wɜːd]
schmutzig dirty ['dɜːti]
Schnee snow [snəʊ]
schnell quick [kwɪk]; fast [fɑːst]
Schokolade chocolate ['tʃɒklət]
schon already [ɔːl'redi] • **schon?** yet? [jet] • **schon mal?** ever? ['evə]
► S.163 The present perfect: statements
► S.164 The present perfect: questions
schön beautiful ['bjuːtɪfl]; *(nett)* nice [naɪs]; *(gut, in Ordnung)* fine [faɪn]
schön ordentlich neat and tidy
Schrank cupboard ['kʌbəd]; *(Kleiderschrank)* wardrobe ['wɔːdrəʊb]
schrecklich terrible ['terəbl]; awful ['ɔːfl]
schreiben (an) write (to) [raɪt]
Schreiber/in writer ['raɪtə]
Schreibtisch desk [desk]
schreien shout [ʃaʊt]
Schriftsteller/in writer ['raɪtə]
Schritt step [step]
schüchtern shy [ʃaɪ]
Schuh shoe [ʃuː]
Schule school [skuːl] • **in der Schule** at school
Schüler/in student ['stjuːdənt]
Schulfach (school) subject ['sʌbdʒɪkt]
Schulheft exercise book ['eksəsaɪz bʊk]
Schulmensa canteen [kæn'tiːn]
Schultasche school bag ['skuːl bæg]
Schulter shoulder ['ʃəʊldə]
Schüssel bowl [bəʊl]
schwach weak [wiːk]
schwarz black [blæk] • **schwarzes Brett** notice board ['nəʊtɪs bɔːd]
schwer *(schwierig)* difficult ['dɪfɪkəlt]; hard [hɑːd]
Schwester sister ['sɪstə]
schwierig difficult ['dɪfɪkəlt]; hard [hɑːd]
Schwierigkeiten trouble ['trʌbl] • **in Schwierigkeiten sein** be in trouble
Schwimmbad, -becken swimming pool ['swɪmɪŋ puːl]
schwimmen swim [swɪm]
schwimmen gehen go swimming
Schwimmer/in swimmer ['swɪmə]
See **1.** *(Binnensee)* lake [leɪk]
2. *(die See, das Meer)* sea [siː]
Seemann sailor ['seɪlə]
sehen see [siː] • **Siehst du?** See?
Sehenswürdigkeiten sights *(pl)* [saɪts]
sehr very ['veri] • **Danke sehr!** Thanks very much! • **Er mag sie sehr.** He likes her a lot. [ə 'lɒt]

etwas sehr mögen/sehr lieben like/love sth. very much
Seife soap [səʊp]
sein *(Verb)* be [bi:]
sein(e) *(besitzanzeigend)* *(zu „he")* his; *(zu „it")* its
seiner, seine, seins his [hɪz]
▸ S.156 Possessive pronouns
Seite 1. side [saɪd] • **auf der linken Seite** on the left • **auf der rechten Seite** on the right
2. *(Buch-, Heftseite)* page [peɪdʒ]
Auf welcher Seite sind wir? What page are we on?
selbstverständlich of course [əv 'kɔ:s]
senden (an) send (to) [send]
Sendereihe series, *pl* series ['sɪəri:z]
September September [sep'tembə]
Serie *(Sendereihe)* series, *pl* series ['sɪəri:z]
Sessel armchair ['ɑ:mtʃeə]
Setup setup ['setʌp]
setzen: sich setzen sit [sɪt] • **Setz dich / Setzt euch zu mir.** Sit with me.
Shorts shorts *(pl)* [ʃɔ:ts]
▸ S.156 Plural words
Show show [ʃəʊ]
sicher 1. *(in Sicherheit)* safe (from) [seɪf]
2. sicher sein *(nicht zweifeln)* be sure [ʃʊə, ʃɔ:]
Sicherheit: in Sicherheit (vor) safe (from) [seɪf]
sie 1. *(weibliche Person)* she [ʃi:]
Frag sie. Ask her. [hə, hɜ:]
2. *(Ding, Tier)* it [ɪt]
3. *(Plural)* they [ðeɪ] • **Frag sie.** Ask them. [ðəm, ðem]
Sie *(höfliche Anrede)* you [ju:]
Sieger/in winner ['wɪnə]
Silbe syllable ['sɪləbl]
singen sing [sɪŋ]
sitzen sit [sɪt]
Skateboard skateboard ['skeɪtbɔ:d]
Skateboard fahren skate [skeɪt]
Sketch sketch [sketʃ]
Sklave, Sklavin slave [sleɪv]
Snack snack [snæk]
so: so süß so sweet [səʊ] • **so alt/groß wie** as old/big as
Socke sock [sɒk]
soeben just [dʒʌst]
▸ S.163 The present perfect: statements
Sofa sofa ['səʊfə]
Software software ['sɒftweə]
sogar even ['i:vn]
Sohn son [sʌn]
Sommer summer ['sʌmə]
Song song [sɒŋ]
Sonnabend Saturday ['sætədeɪ, 'sætədi] *(siehe auch unter „Freitag")*
Sonne sun [sʌn]
Sonnenbrille: (eine) Sonnenbrille sunglasses *(pl)* ['sʌnglɑ:sɪz]
▸ S.156 Plural words
sonnig sunny ['sʌni]
Sonntag Sunday ['sʌndeɪ, 'sʌndi] *(siehe auch unter „Freitag")*
Sorge worry ['wʌri] • **sich Sorgen machen (wegen, um)** worry (about) • **Mach dir keine Sorgen.** Don't worry.
sorgfältig careful ['keəfl]
Sorte sort [sɔ:t]
sowieso anyway ['eniweɪ]
Spaghetti spaghetti [spə'geti]
spannend exciting [ɪk'saɪtɪŋ]
sparen save [seɪv]
Spaß fun [fʌn] • **Spaß haben** have fun • **nur zum Spaß** just for fun
Reiten macht Spaß. Riding is fun.
Viel Spaß! Have fun!
spät late [leɪt] • **Wie spät ist es?** What's the time? • **zu spät sein/kommen** be late
später later ['leɪtə]
spazieren gehen go for a walk [wɔ:k]
Spaziergang walk [wɔ:k] • **einen Spaziergang machen** go for a walk
Specht woodpecker ['wʊdpekə]
Speisekarte menu ['menju:]
Spiegel mirror ['mɪrə]
Spiel game [geɪm]; *(Wettkampf)* match [mætʃ]
spielen play [pleɪ]; *(Szene, Dialog)* act [ækt] • **Fußball spielen** play football • **Gitarre/Klavier spielen** play the guitar/the piano
Spieler/in player ['pleɪə]
Spion/in spy [spaɪ]
Spitze *(oberes Ende)* top [tɒp] • **an der Spitze (von)** at the top (of)
Sport; Sportart sport [spɔ:t] • **Sport treiben** do sport
Sportunterricht PE [,pi:‿'i:], Physical Education [,fɪzɪkəl‿edʒu'keɪʃn]
Sportzentrum sports centre ['spɔ:ts ,sentə]
Sprache language ['læŋgwɪdʒ]
Sprachmittlung *(Mediation)* mediation [,mi:di'eɪʃn]
sprechen (mit) speak (to) [spi:k]
Hier spricht Isabel. *(am Telefon)* This is Isabel.
springen jump [dʒʌmp]
Spülbecken, Spüle sink [sɪŋk]
Stadt *(Großstadt)* city ['sɪti]; *(Kleinstadt)* town [taʊn]
Stadtplan map [mæp]
Stadtzentrum city centre [,sɪti 'sentə]
Stall *(für Kaninchen)* hutch [hʌtʃ]
Stammbaum family tree ['fæməli tri:]
Star *(Film-, Popstar)* star [stɑ:]
stark strong [strɒŋ]
starten start [stɑ:t]
Statue statue ['stætʃu:]
stehen stand [stænd] • **Hier steht: ...** *(im Text)* It says here: ...
▸ S.164 The text says ...
stehlen steal [sti:l]
Steigerung comparison [kəm'pærɪsn]
Stein stone [stəʊn]
stellen *(hin-, abstellen)* put [pʊt]
Fragen stellen ask questions
sich (hin)stellen stand [stænd]
sterben (an) die (of) [daɪ]
Stereoanlage stereo ['steriəʊ]
Stern star [stɑ:]
Stichwort *(Schlüsselwort)* key word ['ki: wɜ:d]
Stiefel boot [bu:t]
still quiet ['kwaɪət]
stimmen: Das stimmt. That's right. [raɪt] • **Du brauchst ein Lineal, stimmt's?** You need a ruler, right?
stolz (auf jn./etwas) proud (of sb./sth.) [praʊd]
stoßen push [pʊʃ]
Strand beach [bi:tʃ] • **am Strand** on the beach
Straße road [rəʊd]; street [stri:t]
Streich trick [trɪk]
streiten; sich streiten argue ['ɑ:gju:]
strukturieren structure ['strʌktʃə]
Strumpf sock [sɒk]
Stück piece [pi:s] • **ein Stück Papier** a piece of paper
Student/in student ['stju:dənt]
Stuhl chair [tʃeə]
stumm: „stummer" Buchstabe *(nicht gesprochener Buchstabe)* silent letter [,saɪlənt 'letə]
Stunde hour ['aʊə]; *(Schulstunde)* lesson ['lesn]
Stundenplan timetable ['taɪmteɪbl]
Sturm storm [stɔ:m]
stürmisch stormy ['stɔ:mi]
stürzen *(hinfallen)* fall [fɔ:l]
suchen look for ['lʊk fɔ:]
Supermarkt supermarket ['su:pəmɑ:kɪt]
Suppe soup [su:p]
Surfbrett surfboard ['sɜ:fbɔ:d]
surfen gehen go surfing ['sɜ:fɪŋ]
süß sweet [swi:t]
Süßigkeiten sweets *(pl)* [swi:ts]
Sweatshirt sweatshirt ['swetʃɜ:t]
Szene scene [si:n]

T

Tabak tobacco [tə'bækəʊ]
Tafel *(Wandtafel)* board [bɔ:d] • **an der/die Tafel** on the board

Tag day [deɪ] • **drei Tage (lang)** for three days • **eines Tages** one day **Guten Tag.** Hello.; *(nachmittags)* Good afternoon. [gʊd‿ɑ:ftə'nu:n]
Tagebuch diary ['daɪəri]
Tal valley ['væli]
Tante aunt [ɑ:nt]; auntie ['ɑ:nti]
Tanz dance [dɑ:ns]
tanzen dance [dɑ:ns]
Tanzen dancing ['dɑ:nsɪŋ]
Tänzer/in dancer ['dɑ:nsə]
Tanzstunden, Tanzunterricht dancing lessons ['dɑ:nsɪŋ ˌlesnz]
Tasche *(Tragetasche, Beutel)* bag [bæg]; *(Hosentasche, Jackentasche)* pocket ['pɒkɪt]
Taschengeld pocket money ['pɒkɪt mʌni]
Tätigkeit activity [æk'tɪvəti]
tausend thousand ['θaʊznd]
Team team [ti:m]
Tee tea [ti:]
Teenager teenager ['ti:neɪdʒə]
Teil part [pɑ:t]
teilen: sich etwas teilen (mit jm.) share sth. (with sb.) [ʃeə]
Telefon (tele)phone ['telɪfəʊn] • **am Telefon** on the phone
telefonieren phone [fəʊn]
Telefonnummer (tele)phone number ['telɪfəʊn ˌnʌmbə]
Teller plate [pleɪt] • **ein Teller Pommes frites** a plate of chips
Temperatur temperature ['temprətʃə]
Tennis tennis ['tenɪs]
Termin appointment [ə'pɔɪntmənt]
Terminkalender diary ['daɪəri]
Test test [test]
teuer expensive [ɪk'spensɪv]
Text text [tekst]
Theater theatre ['θɪətə]
Theaterstück play [pleɪ]
Thema, Themenbereich topic ['tɒpɪk]
Thermometer thermometer [θə'mɒmɪtə]
Tier animal ['ænɪml]; *(Haustier)* pet [pet]
Tierhandlung pet shop ['pet ʃɒp]
Tiger tiger ['taɪgə]
Tipp tip [tɪp]
Tisch table ['teɪbl]
Tischtennis table tennis ['teɪbl tenɪs]
Titel title ['taɪtl]
Toast(brot) toast [təʊst]
Tochter daughter ['dɔ:tə]
Toilette toilet ['tɔɪlət]
toll fantastic [fæn'tæstɪk]; great [greɪt]
Tomate tomato [tə'mɑ:təʊ], *pl* tomatoes
Top *(Oberteil)* top [tɒp]
Tornado tornado [tɔ:'neɪdəʊ]
Torte cake [keɪk]
tot dead [ded]
töten kill [kɪl]
Tour (durch das Haus) tour (of the house) [tʊə]
Tourist/in tourist ['tʊərɪst]
tragen *(Kleidung)* wear [weə]
trainieren practise ['præktɪs]
Traum dream [dri:m]
Traumhaus dream house
traurig sad [sæd]
treffen; sich treffen meet [mi:t]
Treppe(nstufen) stairs *(pl)* [steəz]
Trick *(Zauberkunststück)* trick [trɪk]
Trimester term [tɜ:m]
trinken drink [drɪŋk] • **Milch zum Frühstück trinken** have milk for breakfast
trotzdem anyway ['eniweɪ]
Tschüs. Bye. [baɪ]; See you. ['si: ju:]
T-Shirt T-shirt ['ti:ʃɜ:t]
tun do [du:] • **Tue, was ich tue.** Do what I do. • **tun müssen** have to do • **tun wollen** want to do [wɒnt] **Tut mir leid.** I'm sorry. ['sɒri]
Tunnel tunnel ['tʌnl]
Tür door [dɔ:]
Türklingel doorbell ['dɔ:bel]
Turm tower ['taʊə]
Turnen *(Sportunterricht)* PE [ˌpi:‿'i:], Physical Education [ˌfɪzɪkəl‿edʒu'keɪʃn]
Turnschuhe trainers *(pl)* ['treɪnəz]
Tut mir leid. I'm sorry. ['sɒri]
Tüte bag [bæg]
tyrannisieren bully ['bʊli]

U

U-Bahn: die U-Bahn the underground ['ʌndəgraʊnd] *(BE)*; the subway ['sʌbweɪ] *(AE)*
üben practise ['præktɪs]
über about [ə'baʊt]; *(räumlich)* over ['əʊvə]
übereinstimmen: mit jm./etwas übereinstimmen agree with sb./sth. [ə'gri:]
überleben survive [sə'vaɪv]
übernachten *(über Nacht bleiben)* stay [steɪ]
überprüfen check [tʃek]
überqueren cross [krɒs]
Überschrift title ['taɪtl]
übrigens by the way [ˌbaɪ ðə 'weɪ]
Übung *(im Schulbuch)* exercise ['eksəsaɪz] • **eine Übung machen** do an exercise
Übungsheft exercise book ['eksəsaɪz bʊk]
Uhr 1. *(Armbanduhr)* watch [wɒtʃ]; *(Wand-, Stand-, Turmuhr)* clock [klɒk]
2. elf Uhr eleven o'clock • **7 Uhr morgens/vormittags** 7 am [ˌeɪ‿'em] **7 Uhr nachmittags/abends** 7 pm [ˌpi:‿'em] • **um 8 Uhr 45** at 8.45
Uhrzeit time [taɪm]
um 1. *(örtlich)* **um … (herum)** round [raʊnd]
2. *(zeitlich)* **um 8.45** at 8.45
3. **Es geht um Mr Green.** This is about Mr Green.
umdrehen: sich umdrehen turn [tɜ:n]
▸ S.170 (to) turn
Umfrage (über) survey (on) ['sɜ:veɪ]
umsehen: sich umsehen look round [ˌlʊk 'raʊnd]
umziehen (nach, in) *(die Wohnung wechseln)* move (to) [mu:v]
und and [ənd, ænd] • **Und? / Na und?** So? [səʊ]
Unfall accident ['æksɪdənt]
ungefähr about [ə'baʊt]
Ungeheuer monster ['mɒnstə]
unglaublich amazing [ə'meɪzɪŋ]
unheimlich scary ['skeəri]
unhöflich rude [ru:d]
Uniform uniform ['ju:nɪfɔ:m]
unmöglich impossible [ɪm'pɒsəbl]
unordentlich: sehr unordentlich sein *(Zimmer)* be a mess [mes]
Unordnung: alles in Unordnung bringen make a mess [ˌmeɪk‿ə 'mes]
Unrecht haben be wrong [rɒŋ]
uns us [əs, ʌs]
unser(e) … our … ['aʊə] • **unser eigenes Schwimmbad** our own pool [əʊn]
unserer, unsere, unseres ours ['aʊəz]
▸ S.156 Possessive pronouns
unten *(im Haus)* downstairs [ˌdaʊn'steəz] • **am unteren Ende (von)** at the bottom (of) ['bɒtəm] **dort unten** down there • **nach unten** down [daʊn]; *(im Haus)* downstairs
unter under ['ʌndə]
unterhalten: sich unterhalten (mit, über) talk (to, about) [tɔ:k]
Unterricht lessons *(pl)* ['lesnz]
unterrichten teach [ti:tʃ]
unterschiedlich different ['dɪfrənt]
Untersuchung (über) *(Umfrage)* survey (on) ['sɜ:veɪ]
unverschämt rude [ru:d]
Urlaub holiday ['hɒlədeɪ] • **in Urlaub fahren** go on holiday

V

Vater father ['fɑ:ðə]
Vati dad [dæd]

Verabredung appointment [ə'pɔɪntmənt]
verabschieden: sich verabschieden say goodbye [ˌseɪ gʊd'baɪ]
verängstigt scared [skeəd]
verbinden *(einander zuordnen)* link [lɪŋk]
verbringen: Zeit verbringen (mit) spend time (on) [spend]
Verein club [klʌb]
verfolgen follow ['fɒləʊ]
vergessen forget [fə'get]
Vergleich comparison [kəm'pærɪsn]
verheiratet (mit) married (to) ['mærɪd]
verkaufen sell [sel]
Verkäufer/in *(im Geschäft)* shop assistant ['ʃɒp_əˌsɪstənt]
Verkehr traffic ['træfɪk]
verkehrt *(falsch)* wrong [rɒŋ]
verknüpfen *(einander zuordnen)* link [lɪŋk]
verlassen leave [li:v]
verletzen hurt [hɜ:t]
verletzt hurt [hɜ:t]
verlieren lose [lu:z]
vermissen miss [mɪs]
Vermittlung *(Sprachmittlung, Mediation)* mediation [ˌmi:di'eɪʃn]
verrückt mad [mæd]
verschieden *(anders)* different ['dɪfrənt]
verschwinden disappear [ˌdɪsə'pɪə]
versprechen promise ['prɒmɪs]
verstecken; sich verstecken hide [haɪd]
verstehen understand [ˌʌndə'stænd]
versuchen try [traɪ] • **versuchen zu tun** try and do / try to do
verwenden use [ju:z]
verwirrt puzzled ['pʌzld]
viel a lot (of) [lɒt]; lots (of) [lɒts]; much [mʌtʃ] • **viele** a lot (of) [lɒt]; lots (of) [lɒts]; many ['meni] • **Viel Glück (bei/mit ...)!** Good luck (with ...)! • **viel mehr** lots more • **Viel Spaß!** Have fun! • **wie viel?** how much? • **wie viele?** how many? **Vielen Dank!** Thanks a lot!
vielleicht maybe ['meɪbi]
Viertel: Viertel nach 11 quarter past 11 ['kwɔ:tə] • **Viertel vor 12** quarter to 12
violett purple ['pɜ:pl]
Vogel bird [bɜ:d]
Vokabelverzeichnis vocabulary [və'kæbjələri]
voll full [fʊl] • **die Nase voll haben (von etwas)** be fed up (with sth.) [ˌfed_'ʌp]
Volleyball volleyball ['vɒlibɔ:l]
von of [əv, ɒv]; from [frəm, frɒm] • **ein Aufsatz von ...** an essay by ... [baɪ]
vor 1. *(räumlich)* in front of [ɪn 'frʌnt_əv]
2. *(zeitlich)* **vor dem Abendessen** before dinner [bɪ'fɔ:] • **vor einer Minute** a minute ago [ə'gəʊ]
Viertel vor 12 quarter to 12
vorbei (an) *(vorüber)* past [pɑ:st]
vorbei sein be over ['əʊvə]
vorbereiten prepare [prɪ'peə] • **sich vorbereiten (auf)** prepare (for); get ready (for) ['redi] • **Dinge vorbereiten** get things ready
Vordergrund foreground ['fɔ:graʊnd]
Vormittag morning ['mɔ:nɪŋ]
vorsichtig careful ['keəfl]
vorspielen *(pantomimisch darstellen)* mime [maɪm]
Vorstellung *(Präsentation)* presentation [ˌprezn'teɪʃn]; *(Show)* show [ʃəʊ]
vorüber (an) *(vorbei)* past [pɑ:st]

W

wählen *(auswählen, aussuchen)* choose [tʃu:z]
wahr true [tru:]
während *(als)* as [əz, æz]
wahrscheinlich probably ['prɒbəbli]
Wald forest ['fɒrɪst]
walisisch; Walisisch Welsh [welʃ]
Wand wall [wɔ:l]
wann when [wen]
warm warm [wɔ:m]
warten (auf) wait (for) [weɪt]
Warte mal! Wait a minute. ['mɪnɪt]
warum why [waɪ] • **Warum ich?** Why me?
was what [wɒt] • **Was haben wir als Hausaufgabe auf?** What's for homework? • **Was haben wir als Nächstes?** What have we got next? • **Was ist los? / Was ist denn?** What's the matter? ['mætə]
Was ist mit ...? What about ...?
Was kostet/kosten ...? How much is/are ...? • **Was war das Beste an ...?** What was the best thing about ...?
waschen wash [wɒʃ] • **Ich wasche mir das Gesicht.** I wash my face.
Waschmaschine washing machine ['wɒʃɪŋ məˌʃi:n]
Wasser water ['wɔ:tə]
Website website ['websaɪt]
Wechselgeld change [tʃeɪndʒ]
weg away [ə'weɪ]
Weg way [weɪ]; *(Pfad)* path [pɑ:θ]
auf dem Weg (zu/nach) on the way (to) • **jm. den Weg beschreiben** tell sb. the way • **jn. nach dem Weg fragen** ask sb. the way
► S.170 way
weggehen leave [li:v]
wehtun hurt [hɜ:t]
Weide field [fi:ld]
Weihnachten Christmas ['krɪsməs]
weil because [bɪ'kɒz]
weiß white [waɪt]
weit (entfernt) far [fɑ:]
weiter: geradeaus weiter straight on [streɪt_'ɒn]
weitere(r, s): weitere 45 Pence another 45p [ə'nʌðə]
weitergeben pass [pɑ:s]
weitermachen go on [ˌgəʊ_'ɒn]
welche(r, s) which [wɪtʃ] • **Auf welcher Seite sind wir?** What page are we on? [wɒt] • **Welche Farbe hat ...?** What colour is ...?
wellenreiten gehen go surfing ['sɜ:fɪŋ]
Wellensittich budgie ['bʌdʒi]
Welt world [wɜ:ld]
wem? who? [hu:] • **Wem gehören diese?** Whose are these? [hu:z]
► S.168 who?
wen? who? [hu:]
► S.168 who?
wenden: sich an jn. wenden turn to sb. [tɜ:n]
► S.170 (to) turn
wenigstens at least [ət 'li:st]
wenn 1. *(zeitlich)* when [wen]
2. *(falls)* if [ɪf]
wer? who? [hu:] • **Wer ist dran / an der Reihe?** Whose turn is it? [hu:z]
► S.168 who?
werden become [bɪ'kʌm] • **wütend/heiß/... werden** get angry/hot/... • **du wirst frieren; ihr werdet frieren** you'll be cold (= you will be cold) [wɪl] • **du wirst nicht frieren; ihr werdet nicht frieren** you won't be cold (= you will not be cold) [wəʊnt]
werfen throw [θrəʊ]
wessen? whose? [hu:z]
Wetter weather ['weðə]
Wettkampf match [mætʃ]
Whisky whisky ['wɪski]
wichtig important [ɪm'pɔ:tnt]
wie 1. *(Fragewort)* how [haʊ] • **Wie bitte?** Sorry? ['sɒri] • **Wie geht es dir/Ihnen/euch?** How are you? [ˌhaʊ_'ɑ: jʊ] • **Wie heißt du?** What's your name? • **Wie spät ist es?** What's the time? • **wie viel?** how much? • **wie viele?** how many? • **Wie war ...?** How was ...? **Wie war das Wetter?** What was the weather like? • **Wie wär's mit**

...? What about ...?
2. so alt/groß wie as old/big as
3. wie ein Filmstar like a film star [laɪk]
wieder again [ə'gen]
Wiederholung *(des Lernstoffs)* revision [rɪ'vɪʒn]
Wiedersehen: Auf Wiedersehen. Goodbye. [ˌgʊd'baɪ]
wiederverwendet/-verwertet recycled [ˌriː'saɪkld]
Wiederverwertung recycling [ˌriː'saɪklɪŋ]
wild wild [waɪld]
willkommen: Willkommen (in Bristol). Welcome (to Bristol). ['welkəm] • **Sie heißen dich in ... willkommen** They welcome you to ...
Wind wind [wɪnd]
windig windy ['wɪndi]
winken wave [weɪv]
Winter winter ['wɪntə]
wir we [wiː]
Wirbelsturm tornado [tɔː'neɪdəʊ]
wirklich **1.** *(tatsächlich)* really ['rɪəli] **Meinst du wirklich?/Glaubst du das wirklich?** Do you really think so?
2. *(echt)* real [rɪəl]
wissen know [nəʊ] • **Ich weiß es nicht.** I don't know. • **von etwas wissen; über etwas Bescheid wissen** know about sth. • **..., wissen Sie. / ..., weißt du.** ..., you know. **Weißt du was, Sophie?** You know what, Sophie? • **Woher weißt du ...?** How do you know ...?
wissen wollen wonder ['wʌndə]
Witz joke [dʒəʊk] • **Witze machen** joke
witzig funny ['fʌni]
wo where [weə] • **Wo kommst du her?** Where are you from?
Woche week [wiːk]
Wochenende weekend [ˌwiːk'end] **am Wochenende** at the weekend
Wochentage days of the week
Wofür? What for? [ˌwɒt 'fɔː]
Woher weißt du ...? How do you know ...? [nəʊ]
wohin where [weə]; *(in welche Richtung)* which way
wohlauf *(gesund)* well [wel]
► S.164 I don't feel well
Wohltätigkeitsbasar jumble sale ['dʒʌmbl seɪl]
wohnen live [lɪv]
Wohnung flat [flæt]
Wohnungstür front door [ˌfrʌnt 'dɔː]
Wohnwagen caravan ['kærəvæn]
Wohnzimmer living room ['lɪvɪŋ ruːm]
Wolf wolf, *pl* wolves [wʊlf, wʊlvz]
Wolke cloud [klaʊd]
wollen *(haben wollen)* want [wɒnt] **tun wollen** want to do
Wort word [wɜːd]
Wortbildung word building ['wɜːd ˌbɪldɪŋ]
Wörterbuch dictionary ['dɪkʃənri]
Wörterverzeichnis vocabulary [və'kæbjələri]; *(alphabetisches)* dictionary ['dɪkʃənri]
Wovon redest du? What are you talking about?
Würfel dice, *pl* dice [daɪs]
Wurst, Würstchen sausage ['sɒsɪdʒ]
wütend (über etwas/auf jn.) angry (about sth./with sb.) ['æŋgri]

Y

Yoga yoga ['jəʊgə]

Z

Zahl number ['nʌmbə]
zählen count [kaʊnt]
Zahn tooth [tuːθ], *pl* teeth [tiːθ] • **Ich putze mir die Zähne.** I clean my teeth.
Zahnschmerzen toothache ['tuːθeɪk]
► S.164 I don't feel well
zanken; sich zanken argue ['ɑːgjuː]
Zauberkunststück trick [trɪk] • **Zauberkunststücke machen** do tricks
Zebra zebra ['zebrə]
Zeh toe [təʊ]
zeigen show [ʃəʊ] • **auf etwas zeigen** point at/to sth. [pɔɪnt]
Zeile line [laɪn]
Zeit time [taɪm] • **Zeit verbringen (mit)** spend time (on) [spend]
Zeitschrift magazine [ˌmægə'ziːn]
Zeitung newspaper ['njuːspeɪpə]; paper ['peɪpə]
Zentrum centre ['sentə]
zerbrochen broken ['brəʊkən]
Zeug *(Kram)* stuff [stʌf]
ziehen pull [pʊl]
ziemlich gut pretty good ['prɪti]; quite good [kwaɪt]
Ziffer number ['nʌmbə]
Zimmer room [ruːm, rʊm]
zu **1.** *(örtlich)* to [tə, tu] • **zu Jenny** to Jenny's • **zu Hause** at home **Setz dich zu mir.** Sit with me. **auf jn./etwas zu** towards sb./sth. [tə'wɔːdz]
2. zum Frühstück/Mittagessen/Abendbrot for breakfast/lunch/dinner [fə, fɔː]
3. zu viel too much [tuː] • **zu spät sein/kommen** be late
4. versuchen zu tun try and do / try to do
5. *(geschlossen)* closed [kləʊzd]
zubereiten *(kochen)* cook [kʊk]
Zucker sugar ['ʃʊgə]
zuerst first [fɜːst]
Zug train [treɪn] • **im Zug** on the train
Zuhause home [həʊm]
zuhören listen (to) ['lɪsn]
Zuhörer/in listener ['lɪsnə] • **Zuhörer/innen** *(Publikum)* audience ['ɔːdɪəns]
zumachen close [kləʊz]
zumindest at least [ət 'liːst]
zurück (nach) back (to) [bæk]
zurücklassen leave [liːv]
zusammen together [tə'geðə]
zusammenpassen, -gehören go together
zusätzlich extra ['ekstrə]
Zuschauer/innen *(Publikum)* audience ['ɔːdɪəns]
zusehen watch [wɒtʃ]
zustimmen: jm./etwas zustimmen agree with sb./sth. [ə'griː]
zuwenden: sich jm. zuwenden turn to sb. [tɜːn]
► S.170 (to) turn
zweite(r, s) second ['sekənd]
Zwillinge twins *(pl)* [twɪnz]
Zwillingsbruder twin brother ['twɪn ˌbrʌðə]
zwischen between [bɪ'twiːn]

Classroom English

Was DU im Klassenzimmer sagen kannst	What YOU can say in the classroom
Du brauchst Hilfe	**You need help**
Können Sie mir bitte helfen?	**Can you help me, please?**
Auf welcher Seite sind wir?	**What page are we on, please?**
Was heißt ... auf Englisch/Deutsch?	**What's ... in English/German?**
Wie spricht man das erste Wort in Zeile 2 aus?	**How do you say the first word in line 2?**
Können Sie bitte ... buchstabieren?	**Can you spell ..., please?**
Können Sie es bitte an die Tafel schreiben?	**Can you write it on the board, please?**
Kann ich es auf Deutsch sagen?	**Can I say it in German?**
Können Sie/Kannst du bitte lauter sprechen?	**Can you speak louder, please?**
Können Sie/Kannst du das bitte noch mal sagen?	**Can you say that again, please?**
Beim Zuhören und beim Lesen	**Listening and reading**
Ich kann die CD nicht hören.	**I can't hear the CD.**
Ich finde die Geschichte ...	**I think the story is ...**
schön/interessant/langweilig/schrecklich/....	**nice/interesting/boring/terrible/...**
Es war lustig/gruselig/langweilig/..., als ...	**It was funny/scary/boring/... when ...**
Ich fand es gut/nicht gut, als ...	**I liked it/didn't like it when ...**
Ich finde Tom hat recht/nicht recht, weil ...	**I think Tom is right/wrong because ...**
Ich bin mir nicht sicher. Vielleicht ...	**I'm not sure. Maybe ...**
Hausaufgaben und Übungen	**Homework and exercises**
Tut mir leid, ich habe mein Schulheft nicht dabei, Herr ...	**Sorry, I haven't got my exercise book, Mr ...**
Ich habe meine Hausaufgaben vergessen, Frau ...	**I've forgotten my homework, Mrs/Ms/Miss ...**
Ich verstehe diese Übung nicht.	**I don't understand this exercise.**
Ich kann Nummer 3 nicht lösen.	**I can't do number 3.**
Entschuldigung, ich bin noch nicht fertig.	**Sorry, I haven't finished yet.**
Ich habe ... Ist das auch richtig?	**I've got ... Is that right too?**
Tut mir leid, das weiß ich nicht.	**Sorry, I don't know.**
Was haben wir (als Hausaufgabe) auf?	**What's for homework?**
Bei der Partnerarbeit	**Work with a partner**
Kann ich mit Julian arbeiten?	**Can I work with Julian?**
Kann ich bitte dein Lineal/deinen Filzstift/... haben?	**Can I have your ruler/felt tip/..., please?**
Ich bin Lisas Meinung. / Ich bin anderer Meinung.	**I agree with Lisa. / I don't agree (with Lisa).**
Du bist dran.	**It's your turn.**

What YOUR TEACHER says	Was DEIN/E LEHRER/IN sagt
Open your books at page 24, please.	Schlagt bitte Seite 24 auf.
Look at the picture/line 8/... on page 24.	Seht euch das Bild/Zeile 8/... auf Seite 24 an.
Copy/Complete the chart/network/...	Übertragt/Vervollständigt die Tabelle/das Wörternetz/...
Correct the mistakes.	Verbessert die Fehler.
Fill/Put in the right words.	Setzt die richtigen Wörter ein.
Put the words in the right order.	Bringt die Wörter in die richtige Reihenfolge.
Take notes.	Macht euch Notizen.
Do exercise 3 for homework, please.	Macht bitte Übung 3 als Hausaufgabe.
Bring some photos/... to school.	Bringt ein paar Fotos/... mit in die Schule.
Have you finished?	Seid ihr fertig? / Bist du fertig?
Switch off your mobile phones.	Schaltet eure Handys aus.
Don't send text messages in class.	Verschickt keine SMS während des Unterrichts.
Walk around the class and ask other pupils.	Geht durch die Klasse und fragt andere Schüler/innen.

First names (Vornamen)
Adam ['ædəm]
Alan ['ælən]
Alexander [ˌælɪg'zɑ:ndə]
Ananda [ə'nændə]
Angus ['æŋgəs]
Anna ['ænə]
Barnabas ['bɑ:nəbəs]
Bart [bɑ:t]
Becky ['beki]
Ben [ben]
Benjamin ['bendʒəmɪn]
Beth [beθ]
Binta ['bɪntə]
Bob [bɒb]
Bobby ['bɒbi]
Bryn [brɪn]
Carol ['kærəl]
Caroline ['kærəlaɪn]
Catherine ['kæθrɪn]
Christine ['krɪsti:n]
Cid [sɪd]
Dan [dæn]
Daniel ['dænjəl]
David ['deɪvɪd]
Dilip ['dɪlɪp]
Donald ['dɒnld]
Elaine [ɪ'leɪn]
Emily ['eməli]
Emma ['emə]
Fiona [fi'əʊnə]
Graham ['greɪəm]
Greg [greg]
Griselda [grɪ'zeldə]
Guy [gaɪ]
Gwyneth ['gwɪnəθ]
Hannah ['hænə]
Harry ['hæri]
Henry ['henri]
Ilo ['aɪləʊ]
Isabel ['ɪzəbel]
Isambard ['ɪzəmbɑ:d]
Jack [dʒæk]
Jane [dʒeɪn]
Jay [dʒeɪ]
Jo [dʒəʊ]
Jody ['dʒəʊdi]
Johnny ['dʒɒni]
Jonah ['dʒəʊnə]
Kate [keɪt]
Kevin ['kevɪn]
Lesley ['lezli]
Linda ['lɪndə]
Lucy ['lu:si]
Maggie ['mægi]
Mary ['meəri]
Max [mæks]
Merlin ['mɜ:lɪn]
Micky ['mɪki]
Mike [maɪk]
Milly ['mɪli]
Minnie ['mɪni]
Molly ['mɒli]
Natale ['nætəli]
Nathaniel [nə'θæniəl]
Nick [nɪk]
Nicola ['nɪkələ]
Oliver ['ɒlɪvə]
Pat [pæt]
Paul [pɔ:l]
Peter ['pi:tə]
Philip ['fɪlɪp]
Prunella [pru'nelə]
Queenie ['kwi:ni]
Rachel ['reɪtʃəl]
Ravi ['rɑ:vi]
Richard ['rɪtʃəd]
Robinson ['rɒbɪnsən]
Rosie ['rəʊzi]
Ryan ['raɪən]
Sally ['sæli]
Sam [sæm]
Sandra ['sɑ:ndrə]
Shel [ʃel]
Sophie ['səʊfi]
Steve [sti:v]
Susan ['su:zn]
Thomas ['tɒməs]
Toby ['təʊbi]
Tom [tɒm]
Tracy ['treɪsi]
Trixie ['trɪksi]
Val [væl]
Vinny ['vɪni]
Wallace ['wɒlɪs]
Will [wɪl]
William ['wɪljəm]
Willy ['wɪli]
Zoe ['zəʊi]

Family names (Familiennamen)
Baxter ['bækstə]
Bean [bi:n]
Brooks [brʊks]
Brunel [bru'nel]
Carter-Brown [ˌkɑ:tə 'braʊn]
Crusoe ['kru:səʊ]
Defoe [dɪ'fəʊ]
Depp [dep]
Duck [dʌk]
Edwards ['edwədz]
Esker ['eskə]
Evans ['evnz]
Fawkes [fɔ:ks]
Ghent [gent]
Grumble ['grʌmbl]
Gupta ['gʊptə]
Hanson ['hænsn]
Harper ['hɑ:pə]
Herschel ['hɜ:ʃl]
Kapoor [kə'pɔ:, kə'pʊə]
Kingdom ['kɪŋdəm]
Kingsley ['kɪŋzli]
Orleans ['ɔ:li:nz]
Park [pɑ:k]
Pinney ['pɪni]
Potter ['pɒtə]
Rowling ['raʊlɪŋ]
Selkirk ['selkɜ:k]
Shaw [ʃɔ:]
Silverstein ['sɪlvəstaɪn]
Simpson ['sɪmpsn]
Smith [smɪθ]
Thompson ['tɒmpsən]
Walter ['wɔltə]

Place names (Ortsnamen)
Aardman Studios [ˌɑ:dmən 'stju:diəʊz]
Alfred Street ['ælfrəd stri:t]
Bartlett Street ['bɑ:tlət stri:t]
Bath [bɑ:θ]
Battersea ['bætəsi]
Berlin [bɜ:'lɪn]
The **Brecon Beacons** [ˌbrekən 'bi:kənz]
Bristol ['brɪstl]
Cabot Tower [ˌkæbət 'taʊə]
Caerphilly Castle [keəˌfɪli 'kɑ:sl]
Cardiff ['kɑ:dɪf]
Cardozo High School [kɑ:ˌdəʊzəʊ 'haɪ sku:l]
Charlotte Street ['ʃɑ:lət stri:t]
Cheap Street ['tʃi:p stri:t]
Christchurch ['kraɪsttʃɜ:tʃ]
Clifton ['klɪftən]
Cornwall ['kɔ:nwɔ:l]
Cotham ['kɒtəm]
Crickhowell [krɪk'haʊəl]
Dover ['dəʊvə]
The **Downs** [daʊnz]
Duckpool Beach [ˌdʌkpu:l 'bi:tʃ]
The **Empire State Building** [ˌempaɪə 'steɪt ˌbɪldɪŋ]
Fiordland ['fjɔ:dlænd]
George Street ['dʒɔ:dʒ stri:t]
Georgian House [ˌdʒɔ:dʒən 'haʊs]
Hamilton Street ['hæməltən stri:t]
Hanover ['hænəʊvə]
Hayle Beach [ˌheɪl 'bi:tʃ]
Heidelberg ['haɪdlbɜ:g]
Jupiter ['dʒu:pɪtə]
King Street ['kɪŋ stri:t]
Leeds [li:dz]
Llandoger Trow [hlænˌdɒgə 'trəʊ]
London ['lʌndən]
Longleat Safari Park [ˌlɒŋli:t sə'fɑ:ri pɑ:k]
Majorca [mə'jɔ:kə]
Manchester ['mæntʃɪstə]
Manhattan [mæn'hætn]
Mars [mɑ:z]
Milsom Street ['mɪlsəm stri:t]
Newbridge ['nju:brɪdʒ]
New York [ˌnju: 'jɔ:k]
Oslo ['ɒzləʊ]
Paddington Station [ˌpædɪŋtən 'steɪʃn]
Pisa ['pi:zə]
Portsmouth ['pɔ:tsməθ]
Queens [kwi:nz]
Queenstown ['kwi:nztaʊn]
The **River Avon** [ˌrɪvər‿'eɪvn]
Rome [rəʊm]
Saturn ['sætɜ:n]
St Ives [sənt‿'aɪvz]
St Mary Redcliffe Church [sənt ˌmeəri 'redklɪf tʃɜ:tʃ]
St Nicholas Market [sənt ˌnɪkələs 'mɑ:kɪt]
Stockholm ['stɒkhəʊm]
Sussex ['sʌsɪks]
Temple Meads Station [ˌtempl ˌmi:dz 'steɪʃn]
Theatre Royal [ˌθɪətə 'rɔɪəl]
Tredegar [trɪ'di:gə]
Union Street ['ju:niən stri:t]
Uranus ['jʊərənəs]
Valencia [və'lenʃiə]
Venus ['vi:nəs]
Warmley ['wɔ:mli]
York [jɔ:k]

Other names (Andere Namen)
Anansi [ə'nænsɪ]
Batman ['bætmæn]
Blackbeard ['blækbɪəd]
Cawl mamgu [kaʊl 'mæmgi]
Dogwarts University [ˌdɒgwɔ:ts ju:ni'vɜ:səti]
Fifi ['fi:fi:]
Gromit ['grɒmɪt]
Hogwarts ['hɒgwɔ:ts]
Holi ['həʊli]
Marley ['mɑ:li]
Oscar ['ɒskə]
Polly ['pɒli]
Scruffy ['skrʌfi]
Smokey ['sməʊki]
Travelot ['trævəlɒt]

Country/Continent	Adjective	Person	People
Africa ['æfrɪkə] *Afrika*	African ['æfrɪkən]	an African	the Africans
America [ə'merɪkə] *Amerika*	American [ə'merɪkən]	an American	the Americans
Asia ['eɪʃə, 'eɪʒə] *Asien*	Asian ['eɪʃn, 'eɪʒn]	an Asian	the Asians
Australia [ɒ'streɪliə] *Australien*	Australian [ɒ'streɪliən]	an Australian	the Australians
Austria ['ɒstriə] *Österreich*	Austrian ['ɒstriən]	an Austrian	the Austrians
Belgium ['beldʒəm] *Belgien*	Belgian ['beldʒən]	a Belgian	the Belgians
Brazil [brə'zɪl] *Brasilien*	Brazilian [brə'zɪliən]	a Brazilian	the Brazilians
(Great) Britain ['brɪtn] *Großbritannien*	British ['brɪtɪʃ]	a Briton ['brɪtn]	the British
the Caribbean [ˌkærə'bi:ən] *die Karibik*	Caribbean [ˌkærə'bi:ən]	a Caribbean	the Caribbeans
Chile ['tʃɪli] *Chile*	Chilean ['tʃɪliən]	a Chilean	the Chileans
China ['tʃaɪnə] *China*	Chinese [ˌtʃaɪ'ni:z]	a Chinese	the Chinese
Croatia [krəʊ'eɪʃə] *Kroatien*	Croatian [krəʊ'eɪʃn]	a Croatian	the Croatians
the Czech Republic [ˌtʃek rɪ'pʌblɪk] *Tschechien, die Tschechische Republik*	Czech [tʃek]	a Czech	the Czechs
Denmark ['denmɑ:k] *Dänemark*	Danish ['deɪnɪʃ]	a Dane [deɪn]	the Danes
England ['ɪŋglənd] *England*	English ['ɪŋglɪʃ]	an Englishman/-woman	the English
Europe ['jʊərəp] *Europa*	European [ˌjʊərə'pi:ən]	a European	the Europeans
Finland ['fɪnlənd] *Finnland*	Finnish ['fɪnɪʃ]	a Finn [fɪn]	the Finns
France [frɑ:ns] *Frankreich*	French [frentʃ]	a Frenchman/-woman	the French
Germany ['dʒɜ:məni] *Deutschland*	German ['dʒɜ:mən]	a German	the Germans
Greece [gri:s] *Griechenland*	Greek [gri:k]	a Greek	the Greeks
Hungary ['hʌŋgəri] *Ungarn*	Hungarian [hʌŋ'geəriən]	a Hungarian	the Hungarians
India ['ɪndiə] *Indien*	Indian ['ɪndiən]	an Indian	the Indians
Ireland ['aɪələnd] *Irland*	Irish ['aɪrɪʃ]	an Irishman/-woman	the Irish
Italy ['ɪtəli] *Italien*	Italian [ɪ'tæliən]	an Italian	the Italians
Jamaica [dʒə'meɪkə] *Jamaika*	Jamaican [dʒə'meɪkən]	a Jamaican	the Jamaicans
Japan [dʒə'pæn] *Japan*	Japanese [ˌdʒæpə'ni:z]	a Japanese	the Japanese
the Netherlands ['neðələndz] *die Niederlande, Holland*	Dutch [dʌtʃ]	a Dutchman/-woman	the Dutch
New Zealand [ˌnju: 'zi:lənd] *Neuseeland*	New Zealand [ˌnju: 'zi:lənd]	a New Zealander	the New Zealanders
Norway ['nɔ:weɪ] *Norwegen*	Norwegian [nɔ:'wi:dʒən]	a Norwegian	the Norwegians
Poland ['pəʊlənd] *Polen*	Polish ['pəʊlɪʃ]	a Pole [pəʊl]	the Poles
Portugal ['pɔ:tʃʊgl] *Portugal*	Portuguese [ˌpɔ:tʃu'gi:z]	a Portuguese	the Portuguese
Russia ['rʌʃə] *Russland*	Russian ['rʌʃn]	a Russian	the Russians
Scotland ['skɒtlənd] *Schottland*	Scottish ['skɒtɪʃ]	a Scotsman/-woman, a Scot [skɒt]	the Scots, the Scottish
Slovakia [sləʊ'vɑ:kiə, sləʊ'vækiə] *die Slowakei*	Slovak ['sləʊvæk]	a Slovak	the Slovaks
Slovenia [sləʊ'vi:niə] *Slowenien*	Slovenian [sləʊ'vi:niən], Slovene ['sləʊvi:n]	a Slovene, a Slovenian	the Slovenes, the Slovenians
Spain [speɪn] *Spanien*	Spanish ['spænɪʃ]	a Spaniard ['spænɪəd]	the Spaniards
Sweden ['swi:dn] *Schweden*	Swedish ['swi:dɪʃ]	a Swede [swi:d]	the Swedes
Switzerland ['swɪtsələnd] *die Schweiz*	Swiss [swɪs]	a Swiss	the Swiss
Taiwan [taɪ'wɒn, taɪ'wɑ:n] *Taiwan*	Taiwanese [ˌtaɪwə'ni:z]	a Taiwanese	the Taiwanese
Thailand ['taɪlænd] *Thailand*	Thai [taɪ]	a Thai	the Thais
Turkey ['tɜ:ki] *die Türkei*	Turkish ['tɜ:kɪʃ]	a Turk [tɜ:k]	the Turks
Ukraine [ju:'kreɪn] *die Ukraine*	Ukrainian [ju:'kreɪniən]	a Ukrainian	the Ukrainians
the United Kingdom (the UK) [juˌnaɪtɪd 'kɪŋdəm, ju:'keɪ] *das Vereinigte Königreich (Großbritannien und Nordirland)*	British ['brɪtɪʃ]	a Briton ['brɪtn]	the British
the United States of America (the USA) [juˌnaɪtɪd ˌsteɪts_əv_ə'merɪkə, ju:_es_'eɪ] *die Vereinigten Staaten von Amerika*	American [ə'merɪkən]	an American	the Americans
Wales [weɪlz] *Wales*	Welsh [welʃ]	a Welshman/-woman	the Welsh

Infinitive	Simple past form	Past participle	
(to) **be**	**was/were**	**been**	sein
(to) **become**	**became**	**become**	werden
(to) **bring**	**brought**	**brought**	(mit-, her)bringen
(to) **build**	**built**	**built**	bauen
(to) **buy**	**bought**	**bought**	kaufen
(to) **catch**	**caught**	**caught**	fangen; erwischen
(to) **choose** [uː]	**chose** [əʊ]	**chosen** [əʊ]	(aus)wählen; (sich) aussuchen
(to) **come**	**came**	**come**	kommen
(to) **do**	**did**	**done** [ʌ]	tun, machen
(to) **drink**	**drank**	**drunk**	trinken
(to) **drive** [aɪ]	**drove**	**driven** [ɪ]	*(ein Auto)* fahren
(to) **eat**	**ate** [et, eɪt]	**eaten**	essen
(to) **fall**	**fell**	**fallen**	(hin)fallen, stürzen
(to) **feed**	**fed**	**fed**	füttern
(to) **feel**	**felt**	**felt**	(sich) fühlen; sich anfühlen
(to) **find**	**found**	**found**	finden
(to) **fly**	**flew**	**flown**	fliegen
(to) **forget**	**forgot**	**forgotten**	vergessen
(to) **get**	**got**	**got**	bekommen; holen; werden; (hin)kommen
(to) **give**	**gave**	**given**	geben
(to) **go**	**went**	**gone** [ɒ]	gehen, fahren
(to) **grow**	**grew**	**grown**	wachsen; anbauen, anpflanzen
(to) **have (have got)**	**had**	**had**	haben, besitzen
(to) **hear** [ɪə]	**heard** [ɜː]	**heard** [ɜː]	hören
(to) **hide** [aɪ]	**hid** [ɪ]	**hidden** [ɪ]	(sich) verstecken
(to) **hit**	**hit**	**hit**	schlagen
(to) **hold**	**held**	**held**	halten
(to) **hurt**	**hurt**	**hurt**	wehtun; verletzen
(to) **keep**	**kept**	**kept**	*(warm/offen/...)* halten
(to) **know** [nəʊ]	**knew** [njuː]	**known** [nəʊn]	wissen; kennen
(to) **lay** the table	**laid**	**laid**	den Tisch decken
(to) **leave**	**left**	**left**	(weg)gehen; abfahren; verlassen; zurücklassen
(to) **let**	**let**	**let**	lassen
(to) **lose** [uː]	**lost** [ɒ]	**lost** [ɒ]	verlieren
(to) **make**	**made**	**made**	machen; bauen; bilden
(to) **mean** [iː]	**meant** [e]	**meant** [e]	meinen
(to) **meet**	**met**	**met**	(sich) treffen
(to) **pay**	**paid**	**paid**	bezahlen
(to) **put**	**put**	**put**	legen, stellen, *(wohin)* tun
(to) **read** [iː]	**read** [e]	**read** [e]	lesen

Infinitive	Simple past form	Past participle	
(to) **ride** [aɪ]	**rode**	**ridden** [ɪ]	reiten; *(Rad)* fahren
(to) **ring**	**rang**	**rung**	klingeln, läuten
(to) **run**	**ran**	**run**	rennen, laufen
(to) **say** [eɪ]	**said** [e]	**said** [e]	sagen
(to) **see**	**saw**	**seen**	sehen; besuchen, aufsuchen
(to) **sell**	**sold**	**sold**	verkaufen
(to) **send**	**sent**	**sent**	schicken, senden
(to) **shine**	**shone** [ɒ]	**shone** [ɒ]	scheinen *(Sonne)*
(to) **show**	**showed**	**shown**	zeigen
(to) **shut** up	**shut**	**shut**	den Mund halten
(to) **sing**	**sang**	**sung**	singen
(to) **sit**	**sat**	**sat**	sitzen; sich setzen
(to) **sleep**	**slept**	**slept**	schlafen
(to) **speak**	**spoke**	**spoken**	sprechen
(to) **spend**	**spent**	**spent**	*(Zeit)* verbringen; *(Geld)* ausgeben
(to) **stand**	**stood**	**stood**	stehen; sich (hin)stellen
(to) **steal**	**stole**	**stolen**	stehlen
(to) **swim**	**swam**	**swum**	schwimmen
(to) **take**	**took**	**taken**	nehmen; (weg-, hin)bringen
(to) **teach**	**taught**	**taught**	unterrichten, lehren
(to) **tell**	**told**	**told**	erzählen, berichten
(to) **think**	**thought**	**thought**	denken, glauben, meinen
(to) **throw**	**threw**	**thrown**	werfen
(to) **understand**	**understood**	**understood**	verstehen
(to) **wear** [eə]	**wore** [ɔː]	**worn** [ɔː]	tragen *(Kleidung)*
(to) **win**	**won** [ʌ]	**won** [ʌ]	gewinnen
(to) **write**	**wrote**	**written**	schreiben

Illustrationen

Graham-Cameron Illustration, UK; Fliss Cary, Grafikerin (wenn nicht anders angegeben); **Roland Beier**, Berlin (Vignetten vordere Umschlaginnenseite; S. 14–15; 18; 30–34; 35 unten; 50–51; 56–57; 62; 65 oben; 72 unten; 75 unten; 81 unten; 101 (u. 119); 102 Mitte; 109; 120–121 oben; 122 unten; 124–172); **Carlos Borrell**, Berlin (Karten und Stadtpläne: vordere und hintere Umschlaginnenseite; S. 8; 24; 65; 80; 92 unten li.; 95; 99 (u. 112); 106); **Julie Colthorpe**, Berlin (S. 6; 17 unten; 68 re.; 108; 121 Mitte); **Linda Rogers Associates**, London: Gary Rees (S. 89–91); **Michael Teßmer**, Hamburg (S. 92/93 The Roman Baths); **Katherine Wells**, Hamburg (S. 73; 80); **Korinna Wilkes**, Berlin (S. 58/59 Hintergrund).

Fotos

Rob Cousins, Bristol (wenn im Bildquellenverzeichnis nicht anders angegeben)

Bildquellen

AA Guides Ltd, Glenfield (S. 106 map); **AJ Hackett Bungy**, Queenstown (S. 106/107 unten); **Alamy**, Abingdon (S. 6 Bild A: Paul Broadbent; S. 7 Bild D: David Noton Photography; S. 12 oben: Ambient Images Inc./Peter Bennett (M); S. 26 knee elbow guards: Photolibrary; S. 27 oben: Design Pics, Mitte: BananaStock; S. 43 deer: Vic Pigula; S. 75 unten li.: Rolf Richardson; S. 76 oben: Peter Tarry; S. 79 unten: North Wind Picture Archives); **Alpine Recreation Ltd**, Lake Tekapo/www.alpinerecreation.com (S. 107 oben re.); **Avenue Images**, Hamburg (S. 26 hat: Stockbyte); **Bank of England**, London (S. 26/27 banknotes, reproduced with kind permission); **Camillo Beretta**, Berlin (S. 26 magazine, comic, ticket, book); **Britain on View**, London (S. 69 Mitte: www.britainonview.com); **British Empire and Commonwealth Museum**, Bristol (S. 75 oben); **Celtic Scene**, Cornwall (S. 6 Bild B: Claire Sellick); **Corbis**, Düsseldorf (S. 10/11 colourful balls (M): RF; S. 21 u. 113: RF; S. 24 Bild E: Reuters/Daniel Aguilar; S. 41 unten: Kevin R. Morris; S. 43 hedgehog: Herbert Spichtinger/zefa; S. 83: Bureau L.A. Collection; S. 98: RF); **Corel Library** (S. 6/7 seagulls; S. 12 oben clouds (M); S. 26 coke; S. 36; S. 48 woodland; S. 51 u. 110 cat; S. 52 giraffe, tiger; S. 61 re.); **Cornelsen Verlag**, Berlin (S. 26 Genius); **Cotham School**, Bristol (S. 10/11 Website-Frame, Logo); **Destination Bristol**, Bristol (S. 74/75 map; S. 85: Michaela Norris); **Gareth Evans**, Berlin (S. 8; S. 15; S. 29 game); **Explore-at-Bristol**, Bristol (S. 74 Mitte li. u. S. 84: Martin Chainey); **Explore Franz Josef**/www.explorefanzjosef.com (S. 106 unten li.) **FAN travelstock**, Hamburg (S. 24 Bild C); **Fiordland Wilderness Experiences – Sea Kayak Fiordland**, Te Anau/ www.fiordlandseakayak.co.nz, info@fiordlandseakayak.co.nz (S. 107 Mitte u. unten re.); **Georgian House**, Bristol/Bristol Museums & Art Gallery (S. 75); **Getty Images**, München (S. 49 cover photo: Stuart McClymont; S. 61 li.: Ryan McVay); **Glacier Helicopters Ltd**, Franz Josef Glacier (S. 107 unten Mitte); **Bonnie Glänzer**, Berlin (S. 48 li., S. 53); **Hassle-free Tours**, Christchurch (S. 106/107 Mitte); **The Helicopter Line Ltd**, Mt. Cook (S. 106 oben li.); **Herschel House**, Bristol (S. 97 oben re.; S. 101 Bild B u. C); **Ingram Publishing**, UK (S. 27: gift box); **Keystone**, Hamburg (S. 40 oben: TopFoto/Arena Images/Keith Saunders); **Look**, München (S. 40 unten: Karl Johaentges; S. 97 unten: Photo Researchers); **Marketing for Education**, Nelson (S. 10/11 Bild 2–6); **Mauritius**, Hamburg (S. 10/11 boules (M): Image Source; S. 24 Bild D: Fritz Rauschenbach; S. 26 bottle of water: photolibrary rf; S. 30 re.: Rubberball); **New Line Productions, Inc.**, New York (S. 107 Legolas); **Photolibrary Wales**, Cardiff (S. 59 unten; S. 60 Caerphilly Castle.; S. 65); **Picture Alliance**, Frankfurt/Main (S. 41 oben: dpa; S. 43 woodpecker, mole (u. S. 126): Okapia/Manfred Danegger, frog: Okapia/Markus Essler; S. 52 monkey: Godong; S. 75 Wallace and Gromit: obs; S. 129: dpa Report); **Provincial Pictures**, Bath (S. 7 Bild C: Philip Pierce); **Queenstown Adventure Group**, Queenstown (S. 106 Mitte re.); **Real Journeys**, Queenstown/www.realjourneys.co.nz (S. 107 oben Mitte); **RSPCA Photolibrary**, Horsham (S. 45); **Rosco's Milford Sound Sea Kayaks**, Te Anau Fiordland (S. 107 Mitte re.); **Shutterstock**, New York (S. 29 DVDs: Jostein Hauge; S. 42: Mark Simms; S. 43 grey squirrel: John L. Richbourg; S. 51 u. 110 budgie: Joanne Harris and Daniel Bubnich; S. 126 baby moles: Devin Koob); **Somerfield Stores Ltd.**, Bristol (S. 29 juice); **Stills-Online**, Hamburg (S. 10 Bild 1 blue ball (M); S. 26 sweets in bag, pile of sweets, shirt, top, dress, jumper, jacket, trousers, skirt, trainers, CDs; S. 27 unten: mobile, pens, pencils, lipstick, rouge); **Stockfood**, München (S. 26 bottle and glass of orange juice: Christina Peters, chips: Foodcollection, crisps: Kröger/Gross, chocolate: FoodPhotography Eising; S. 29 popcorn: Gerhard Bumann); **Christine Thomas**, Crickhowell (S. 59 sign); **ullstein bild**, Berlin (S. 9 CARO/Sorge; S. 101 Bild D: KPA/HIP Oxford Science Archive); **Visum**, Hamburg (S. 24 Bild B: Markus Hanke); **Wales Tourist Board**, Cardiff (S. 60 unten re.); **Walker Books Ltd.**, London (S. 49: Cover photo © 2005 by Stuart McClymont/Getty Images from NO SMALL THING by Natale Ghent. Reproduced by permission of Walker Books Ltd, London SE11 5HJ); **Wanaka Sightseeing**, Christchurch (S. 106/107 oben).

Titelbild

Rob Cousins, Bristol; **IFA-Bilderteam**, Ottobrunn (Hintergrund Union Jack: Jon Arnold Images); **Mpixel/Achim Meissner**, Krefeld (Himmel).

Textquellen

S. 31: *Why is it?* by Shel Silverstein from "Falling up 10th Anniversary Edition". © Harper Collins Publishers, New York 2006; S. 57: *The Frog on the Log* by Ilo Orleans from: "Prepositions" by Ann Heinrichs, published by The Child's World, Chanhassen 2004; *The song of a mole* by Richard Edwards from: "The Word Party", published by Lutterworth Press, Cambridge 1986.

Liedquellen

S. 56: *I know an old lady*. K. & T.: Rosemary Bedeau, Alan Mills © Peermusic (Germany) GmbH, Hamburg; S. 105: *Summer Holiday*: K. & T.: Bruce Welch, Brian Bennett © Edition Accord Musikverlag GmbH & Co. KG c/o EMI Music Publishing Germany GmbH & KG.
